Vision and Disenchantment: Blake's *Songs* and Wordsworth's *Lyrical Ballads*

Heather Glen

Cambridge University Press

Cambridge

London   New York   New Rochelle

Melbourne   Sydney

Published by the Press Syndicate of the University of Cambridge
The Pitt Building, Trumpington Street, Cambridge CB2 IRP
32 East 57th Street, New York, NY 10022, USA
296 Beaconsfield Parade, Middle Park, Melbourne 3206, Australia

First published 1983

Printed in Great Britain at the University Press, Cambridge

Library of Congress catalogue card number: 82–9565

British Library cataloguing in publication data
Glen, Heather
Vision and disenchantment
1. English poetry – 18th century – history and criticism
I. Title
821'.6'09   PR551

ISBN 0 521 25084 6 hard covers
ISBN 0 521 27198 3 paperback

CE

To Rosemary, Ian and Bruce

Contents

Acknowledgements

I would like to thank the many friends who helped to make this book possible. I am especially grateful to Lionel Knights, under whose guidance I began to work on Blake and Wordsworth; to Edward Thompson, with and against whom much of what follows was argued out; to Myles Burnyeat, John Dunn, Geoffrey Hawthorn, John McGrath, Kiernan Ryan, Stan Smith, Virginia Spate, David Trotter, Richard Tuck and Margaret Walters, all of whom spared time from their own very different work to read and discuss portions of mine; and to Jane Adamson and Sam Goldberg, for their thoughtful criticisms and constant support.

Note on the texts

For the text of Blake's *Songs*, I have used the reproduction of Blake's Illuminated Book, *Songs of Innocence and of Experience*, edited by Sir Geoffrey Keynes, first published in 1967 by Rupert-Hart Davis Ltd and by the Orion Press, New York, in association with the Trianon Press, Paris (1967), and issued as an Oxford University Press paperback in 1970. Other quotations from Blake are taken from *The Complete Writings of William Blake*, ed. Geoffrey Keynes (Oxford University Press, London, 1972) (referred to as K). Quotations from *Lyrical Ballads*, the 1798 Advertisement and the 1800 Preface, are taken from *William Wordsworth & Samuel Coleridge: Lyrical Ballads*, the text of the 1798 edition with the additional 1800 poems and the Preface, ed. R. L. Brett and A. R. Jones (London, 1968) (referred to as Brett and Jones).

Introduction

Blake's *Songs of Innocence and of Experience* and Wordsworth's *Lyrical Ballads* were written within ten years of each other by poets who, at the time of writing, almost certainly did not know of one another's existence. Yet, as one of Blake's earliest editors pointed out,[1] there are some remarkable similarities between the two collections. Both deal with the same kinds of subject matter – childhood, rural life, the poor and outcast of society. Both consist of apparently simple poems, much 'simpler' than most other serious poetry of their day. But each seems to have been regarded by its author as much more important than its form might at first suggest. Blake reissued the *Songs* in hand-coloured copies until the end of his life, changing their order and moving some poems from *Innocence* to *Experience* and back again. There are surviving drafts for only four of the *Songs of Innocence*, and these are probably fair copies; but the notebook drafts of *Songs of Experience* show how carefully he considered and revised them. Wordsworth made more explicit claims for *Lyrical Ballads*, both in the Advertisement to the 1798 volume and in the Preface to that of 1800; and like Blake he seems to have conceived of each collection not as a group of disparate pieces but as a unified whole. Both clearly saw these poems as significant works of art.

This judgment is one in which twentieth-century critics have concurred. But to their original readers, both collections were rather more puzzling. Contemporary reaction seems, in each case, to have been polarized between glowing admiration and unqualified rejection – between the declaration that these poems are works of original genius and a refusal to see them as other than ludicrous failures. Blake was not widely read, but such criticism of the *Songs* as survives from the early years of the nineteenth century suggests very much this pattern of response. On the one hand, there are the few recorded comments of Crabb Robinson's friends, such as Hazlitt – 'They are beautiful ... & only too deep for the vulgar ...'[2] – and Landor: 'A good deal of rattling on the part of W.S.L.: he maintd. Blake to be the greatest of poets.'[3] On the other, there are the earliest published criticisms, in reviews of Benjamin Heath Malkin's *A Father's Memoirs of His Child* (1806):

1

He is celebrated both as an artist and as a poet; but so little judgment is shown, in our opinion, with regard to the proofs of these talents, that we much doubt whether the encomium will be at all useful to the person praised ... As a poet, he seems chiefly inspired by that,

– Nurse of the didactic muse,
Divine Nonsensia. – [4]

if Watts seldom rose above the level of a mere versifier, in what class must we place Mr. Blake, who is certainly very inferior to Dr. Watts?[5]

The poems of *Lyrical Ballads*, of course, were better known, and received more considered commentary. But their initial reception was equally mixed, ranging from Francis Wrangham's favourable review in the *British Critic* – 'The endeavour of the author is to recall our poetry from the fantastical excess of refinement, to simplicity and nature ... we think that in general the author has succeeded in attaining that judicious degree of simplicity, which accomodates [*sic*] itself with ease even to the sublime'[6] – to Dr Burney's attack in the *Monthly Review*: 'Though we have been extremely entertained with the fancy, the facility, and (in general) the sentiments, of these pieces, we cannot regard them as *poetry*, of a class to be cultivated at the expense of a higher species of versification.'[7] It seems clear that contemporary readers were sharply divided, not merely as to the valuation to be placed on these poems, but as to whether to 'regard them as *poetry*' at all.

This divergence of critical opinion is one of the most interesting points of comparison between the two collections. Their similarities of form and subject-matter are, on one level, less surprising. There was in the late eighteenth century a fashion for 'simple' verse, and for verse on the victims of society and the objects of nature: that fashion, as Hazlitt noted in 1825, was intimately related to the complex social and political developments of the time.[8] Yet to explain both collections thus is to flatten out precisely that which is most challenging about them. It does not begin to account for the differences between them – differences at least as striking as the similarities. And it does not explain why, if readers were beginning to be accustomed to 'simple' poems about 'humble' figures, they should have been so disconcerted by and divided about these.

What did contemporary readers expect? Other 'simple' poems on similar subjects seem to have provoked nothing like the critical dissent that Blake's *Songs* and Wordsworth's *Lyrical Ballads* did. Cowper's poems were received with almost unqualified approval by the reviewers and were immediately and lastingly popular with the

reading public:[9] nearly forty years after their first publication,
Hazlitt was to quote 'an exquisite piece of eloquence and poetry'
from them:

> Yon cottager, who weaves at her own door,
> Pillow and bobbins all her little store;
> Content, though mean; and cheerful, if not gay;
> Shuffling her threads about the live-long day,
> Just earns a scanty pittance; and at night
> Lies down secure, her heart and pocket light:
> She, for her humble sphere by nature fit,
> Has little understanding, and no wit,
> Receives no praise; but though her lot be such,
> (Toilsome and indigent) she renders much;
> Just knows, and knows no more, her Bible true –
> A truth the brilliant Frenchman never knew;
> And in that charter reads, with sparkling eyes,
> Her title to a treasure in the skies.
> Oh, happy peasant! Oh, unhappy bard!
> His the mere tinsel, her's the rich reward;
> He prais'd, perhaps, for ages yet to come;
> She never heard of half a mile from home;
> He, lost in errors his vain heart prefers;
> She, safe in the simplicity of her's.[10]

No poem is simply a barometer of contemporary norms. But this
one *was* readily accepted by late eighteenth-century readers, and it is
illuminating to consider its difference from Blake's and Wordsworth's apparently much more controversial dealings with comparable subject matter.

The differences do not seem to be centrally those of ideological
stance. Cowper is fairly conservative: his 'happy peasant' is, of
course, sentimentalized, and her 'humble' place is seen as ordained
by 'nature'. But he does attempt to portray some actual details of her
life and to suggest the challenge she offers to the values of the polite
world: 'understanding' and 'wit' are being given a serious, if rather
heavy-handed, ironic redefinition. Beside this 'realistic' late
eighteenth-century version of pastoral, Blake's 'The Shepherd'
might well at first seem trivial:

> How sweet is the Shepherds sweet lot,
> From the morn to the evening he strays:
> He shall follow his sheep all the day
> And his tongue shall be filled with praise:

> For he hears the lambs innocent call.
> And he hears the ewes tender reply.
> He is watchful while they are in peace,
> For they know when their Shepherd is nigh.

Cowper's readers would have been in no doubt as to the point he was making: his responses and evaluations – 'Oh, happy peasant!'; 'his vain heart' – are prominent throughout. But here, Blake is notably absent. Beyond the tautological first line, he offers no reflection on his Shepherd's life at all.

A contemporary reader might well have slid over this difficulty, simply by reading the customary moral lesson *into* the poem. Indeed, 'The Shepherd' seems to court such conventionalization. It opens with a pastoral celebration which might have been expected to lead to a catalogue of the virtues of the Shepherd's way of life:

> How sweet is the Shepherds sweet lot,
> From the morn to the evening he strays ...

But this implicit promise is not fulfilled. Instead, the stanza is closed off by the prescriptive future tense of the following lines, whose suggestion is Biblical rather than pastoral:

> He shall follow his sheep all the day
> And his tongue shall be filled with praise.

Against the natural freedom of 'strays' Blake is counterpointing a sense of a more ordered and contained joy: a sense which informs the second stanza. Here, the 'tongue' that is 'filled with praise' is echoed in a world of chiming voices, which 'call' and 'reply'. Yet simple as the stanza seems, it is far from simply conceived. In the first two lines, the Shepherd merely 'hears' the voices of his flock: in the last he plays his own active part. As in the first stanza, suggestions of spontaneity and restraint are intermingled rather than simply juxtaposed. The verse presents a harmonious balance between freedom and acceptance: a balance maintained by the use of an adjectival ('He is watchful') rather than active verb form to describe the Shepherd's employment; and by the way in which, within the Biblical cadence of 'He shall follow his sheep all the day' (suggesting a larger order within which human actions are contained), the Shepherd is portrayed not in his Biblical capacity as guide, but as a follower of his sheep. If 'The Shepherd' offers none of the evaluative pointers that contemporary readers might have expected, it is, in its own way, very carefully structured: far more carefully, indeed, than

INTRODUCTION

Cowper's poem, where the slack couplets and easy rhymes give the
impression that they could be indefinitely prolonged.

Yet it is structured in a way which would have been subtly
disconcerting to the late eighteenth-century reader. It is not simply
that it presents a vision at odds with what he would expect (the
Shepherd *following* his sheep, the traditional pastoral *opposition*
between spontaneity and restraint made to seem irrelevant); it
refuses to engage with him in the expected way. Cowper's moralistic
purpose is clear, but Blake offers a vision that could not without
distortion be assimilated to a moral lesson at all – a vision of a
self-sufficient, reciprocally satisfying way of life in which expressive
freedom and ordered security are held in perfect balance. Where
readers accustomed to poems such as Cowper's would have expected
the poet's controlling voice to direct their attitudes to the material
presented, here there is no obvious controlling voice and no such
direction.

We are perhaps beginning to approach some explanation for the
curiously mixed critical reception of Blake's *Songs*. We are also, I
think, beginning to approach their really significant point of
comparison with *Lyrical Ballads* – though at first sight this poem
from the 1798 volume may seem closer to Cowper than to Blake:

Old Man Travelling;

Animal Tranquillity and Decay,

A Sketch

The little hedge-row birds,
That peck along the road, regard him not.
He travels on, and in his face, his step,
His gait, is one expression; every limb,
His look and bending figure, all bespeak
A man who does not move with pain, but moves
With thought – He is insensibly subdued
To settled quiet: he is one by whom
All effort seems forgotten, one to whom
Long patience has such mild composure given,
That patience now doth seem a thing, of which
He hath no need. He is by nature led
To peace so perfect, that the young behold
With envy, what the old man hardly feels.
– I asked him whither he was bound, and what
The object of his journey; he replied
'Sir! I am going many miles to take

5

'A last leave of my son, a mariner,
'Who from a sea-fight has been brought to Falmouth,
'And there is dying in an hospital.'

Like Cowper, Wordsworth seems, at least in the opening section of his poem, to be trying to draw an edifying lesson from the rustic subject he presents. His contemporary readers certainly tried – with some perplexity – to do so.[11] Yet the poem as a whole (reproduced here in its original 1798 version) is more 'aukward'[12] and more resistant to conventional moral interpretations than might at first appear. The reader is not, as in Cowper's poem, presented with a series of definite judgments. At first, the old man is enigmatically opaque, a 'figure' whose feelings must be inferred rather than assumed:

... every limb
His look and bending figure, all *bespeak*
A man who does not move with pain, but moves
With thought.
[my italics]

But the lines which follow dramatize a meditation which gradually, insidiously, transmutes this intractable other into an image – like that of Cowper's old woman – undisturbingly attractive to the polite observer: an image of a perfect peace beyond the reach of pain. It is a meditation which is abruptly terminated by another voice: that of the old man himself, baldly stating the purpose of his journey. An image of peace, of natural 'animal tranquillity and decay' is suddenly replaced by an account of a life cut violently, unnaturally short.[13] And on this the polite speaker offers no reflection at all.

Readers expecting easy reflections on the virtues and blessings of humble life might well have had reason to be disconcerted by this poem. The scores of late eighteenth-century poets who concerned themselves with 'the poor' tended, like Cowper, to assume without question that they could know and evaluate their subjects' thoughts and feelings, even thoughts and feelings which those subjects might not have been able to articulate to themselves. But here Wordsworth explores that assumption in the process of its development – and offers the direct statement of the old man himself as an ironic comment upon it. And in doing so he suggests something of the shock with which the otherness of even the least articulate can assert itself. This old man is not an edifying object: he is a separate individual, with his own voice and history and point of view. The

INTRODUCTION

'peace' which he has been supposed to represent is simply a product of the mind of the observer: *his* feelings remain mysterious. Far from offering a confident meditation upon him, the poem dramatically questions the whole habit of depicting others as objects of meditation at all.

And it does so not argumentatively, but poetically. Contemporary readers would have understood – though they might have disagreed with – a message: 'it is wrong to try to reduce others to one's own frame of reference'. But Wordsworth offers no such message: he simply presents an experience of unresolved confrontation. And in thus refusing to assume what eighteenth-century readers would most fundamentally have expected – the central controlling viewpoint which would direct their responses and draw general conclusions – his whole poem questions the validity of such a viewpoint. In this it is very much closer to 'The Shepherd' than it is to Cowper's lines.

The similarity is not one of subject-matter, or even of attitude to that subject-matter. It lies, rather, in the kind of challenge that each of these poems seems to have offered to readers implicitly expecting verses like Cowper's – and trying, as much early criticism suggests, to assimilate these to familiar patterns. It is here that one can begin to trace the real originality of *Songs of Innocence and of Experience* and of *Lyrical Ballads.* Neither collection simply gives expression to a new way of feeling. Each actively refuses to confirm some of its readers' most basic expectations, expectations which those readers almost certainly would not have articulated even to themselves. And that refusal constitutes a fundamental poetic questioning of some of the most deep-rooted of polite eighteenth-century assumptions.

For the inarticulate expectations which a reader brings to a poem are not peculiar to a specifically literary context. They are more pervasive than this: indications of his whole mode of being in and making sense of the world, pointers to the way in which he structures all his experience, not merely literary experience. They may well come to be so taken for granted, so unconscious, that no other way of conceiving of or ordering experience seems possible. They can hardly be challenged merely on the level of argument: to change them requires an imaginative revolution. And this seems to have been what Blake and Wordsworth, each in a very different way, were attempting in these collections. The implications of the attempt extend, as we shall see, beyond the merely literary.

7

1   Poetic 'Simplicity': Blake's *Songs* and Eighteenth-Century Children's Verse

> Those who are offended with any thing in this book would be offended with the innocence of a child & for the same reason, because it reproaches him with the errors of acquired folly.
>
> (Blake, annotations to Lavater, K87)

In one sense, neither *Songs of Innocence and of Experience* nor *Lyrical Ballads* are 'experimental' collections at all. In their earlier writings, both Blake and Wordsworth *had* experimented widely with contemporary literary forms – ranging in the one case from the Ossianic prose of some of the *Poetical Sketches* to the sharp satire of *An Island in the Moon*, in the other from the meditative-descriptive verse of *An Evening Walk* to the Gothic melodrama of parts of *The Borderers*. Yet in *Songs of Innocence and of Experience* and *Lyrical Ballads* each turned away from such experiments towards what had hitherto been a minor and not very ambitious genre. In presentation and subject-matter, Blake's Songs are closer to late eighteenth-century children's verse than to anything else in the period,[1] while the poems in *Lyrical Ballads* most closely resemble those which were appearing in popular middle-class magazines. The two genres are very different, but there are some significant similarities between them.

Each was enjoying a boom at the end of the eighteenth century. The readers of the magazines had a seemingly limitless appetite for poetry:[2] children's books were the most rapidly expanding branch of publishing.[3] Each was addressed to a fast-growing polite middle-class reading public. And each bore a clear relation to a much less polite cultural tradition. Indeed, children's books had originally been produced by the Puritans in an attempt to counteract what they saw as the pernicious influence of popular chap-books. Throughout the history of eighteenth-century children's publishing one can trace the pressure of that competition: material from chap-books – especially nursery rhymes and riddles – is often to be found enlivening the more expensively produced little books of the polite publishing firms. In a similar way, popular ballads – usually conventionalized to suit contemporary taste – appear alongside modern imitations in the poetry pages of the magazines. Children's books and magazine verse were not, however, necessarily backward-looking in spirit: in fact, both were increasingly used for the expression of 'progressive' ideas. As J. H. Plumb suggests, the parent who bought books for his children was likely to be liberal in his views:

This gentle and more sensitive approach to children was but part of a wider change in social attitudes; a part of that belief that nature was inherently good, not evil, and what evil there was derived from man and his institutions; an attitude which was also reflected among a growing elite in a greater sensitivity towards women, slaves and animals.[4]

Late eighteenth-century children's books contain poems and stories on such subjects as the distresses of poverty, the evils of the slave trade and the need for kindness to animals: most seek to inculcate a mildly progressive humanitarianism. And magazine verse addressed to adult readers could be much more subversive. Sometimes it traced social evils to their causes in a way which provoked alarmed reaction from the Establishment: if the proportion of such poems was small, the fact that the *Anti-Jacobin* found it necessary to parody them so extensively suggests that it was significant. But despite their sometimes innovatory subject-matter, neither magazine verse nor children's poetry were exciting literary forms. Why did Blake and Wordsworth each choose to turn to them? Did they, in doing so, hope to regain some of the vitality of the popular chap-books and ballads? Or does their choice suggest a rather more sophisticated interest in the expectations of the polite readers to whom such books were addressed?

In 1789–90, when *Songs of Innocence* was engraved, the children's book trade was a flourishing one. John Newbery, the most prolific of eighteenth-century children's publishers, had produced over two hundred titles between 1745 and 1770 – and thereby made a fortune.[5] It was a trade which Blake seems to have known well.[6] Not only do the Songs offer internal evidence of his familiarity with eighteenth-century verse for children: in the period between 1780 and 1791 the radical publisher Joseph Johnson commissioned him three times to engrave illustrations for children's books – books which in these years were beginning to be more and more attractively produced. It seems clear that *Songs of Innocence*, with its colourful designs and its introductory promise that 'Every child may joy to hear', was aimed at a known (and growing) market of parents from the polite classes.

I say parents rather than children, for the formally published
children's books, priced at two shillings and sixpence or more, could
hardly have been bought by children. *Songs of Innocence* itself cost five
shillings.[7] As Plumb points out: 'Children do not buy books, adults
do ... So the new children's literature was designed to attract adults,
to project an image of those virtues which parents wished to
inculcate in their offspring, as well as to beguile the child.'[8] And, as
we know from the reminiscences of such readers as Holcroft and
Coleridge, who were boys in the 1780s, the books children *chose*
were the penny chap-books, with their sensational stories and
doggerel rhymes and riddles, rather than refined collections of verse.
But refined collections there were, in plenty. Some were simply
reading-exercises, teaching spelling and pronunciation in words of
one syllable; sometimes, as in this early (1712) example, by the
careful use of half-rhyme:

> Hear you a lark?
> Tell me what clerk
>   Can match her! He that beats
> The next thorn bush,
> May raise a thrush
>   Would put down all our waits.[9]

Perhaps the childish monosyllables and half-rhymes of Blake's
'Spring' were originally intended to offer similar practice in reading
and pronunciation:

> Little Lamb,
> Here I am;
>   Come and lick
> My white neck;
> Let me pull
> Your soft Wool;
> Let me kiss
> Your soft face:
> Merrily, Merrily, we welcome in the Year.

But a large amount of verse for children was more substantial in
content. The earliest and most attractive of such collections was
Bunyan's *A Book for Boys and Girls*, first published in 1686 and
republished (after 1724 with the title *Divine Emblems*) until well into
the Victorian period: a volume which illustrates very clearly that
ambivalence of aim which was to inform books for children
throughout the eighteenth century. Its effort to compete with the

chap-books is apparent in its crude little wood-cuts; and there is a vivid colloquial life about much of the poetry – an imaginative effort to enter into the child's way of seeing the world – which must have been very attractive to young readers. The childish speaker in 'Of the Child with the Bird on the Bush', tries to tempt a bird into captivity:

> Thou subject art to cold o' nights,
> When darkness is thy covering;
> By day thy danger's great by kites,
> How canst thou then sit there and sing?
> Thy food is scarce and scanty too,
> 'Tis worms and trash which thou dost eat;
> Thy present state I pity do,
> Come, I'll provide thee better meat.
> I'll feed thee with white bread and milk,
> And sugar-plums, if thou them crave;
> I'll cover thee with finest silk,
> That from the cold I may thee save.[10]

But the bird remains hauntingly strange: inassimilable to the little everyday world of the child's promises. The same sense of wonder pervades the description, in another poem, of the mysterious self-absorption of the snail:

> She makes no noise, but still seizeth on
>   The Flow'r or Herb, appointed for her food
> The which she quietly doth feed upon,
>   While others range, and gare, but find no good.[11]

In both cases the imaginative effect is achieved by an exact, fascinated observation – that slight disalignment from conventional ways of seeing that is a characteristic of childish vision. But this is only half the story. For in both these poems – as in all the others in the volume – this strangeness and liveliness is contained by and subordinated to an adult moral frame. 'Of the Child with the Bird on the Bush' ends by comparing the bird to a wicked unbeliever who will not listen to Christ's pleadings: the snail becomes a figure of the seeker after Christ. In poem after poem there are similar, often tortuous analogies; sometimes tagged on at the end as a 'moral', sometimes incorporated into the body of the poem. The child who responded with wondering openness to Bunyan's curious images of familiar things would have found himself called upon to subjugate that wonder to the demands of a rigorous adult logic.

This conflict between the desire to appeal to the child's sensibility (and in some measure to recreate it in verse) and the need to instruct and direct can be traced in most of the poetry written for children in the eighteenth century. At best, such verse has an imaginative vitality not unlike that feeling for the strangeness of the everyday which one finds in the riddle collections of the chap-books:

> When Frosts have whiten'd all the Woods,
> Harden'd the Ground and stop'd the Floods,
> How carelessly do Children slide,
> And o'er the deepest Waters glide!
>
> On broadest Ponds in Ranks they spread,
> Where just before they durst not tread,
> And with smooth Motion softly pass
> Along the new delightful Glass.
>
> (from 'Upon Boys Sliding' in Thomas Foxton,
> *Moral Songs Composed for the Use of Children*, 1728)

> It moves with Ease
> Just where I please,
> How swift it bounds and flies!
> With one small Jerk
> I make it work,
> And watch it with my Eyes.
>
> (from 'Miss Playing with her Ball' in John Marchant,
> *Puerilia, or Amusements for the Young*, 1751)

But this vitality is always pressed into the service of a larger didactic purpose. This is true of Isaac Watts, the most popular and influential of such versifiers, whose *Divine and Moral Songs* were republished throughout the century: it is equally true of later, more educationally 'progressive', writers for children. If children's books can be said to reflect contemporary attitudes towards childhood and child-rearing, one must conclude that, however such attitudes changed and varied amongst the polite classes during the eighteenth century,[12] some basic assumptions remained constant. Finally, there is little to choose between Mary Wollstonecraft's *Original Stories from Real Life* and the much more conservative Mrs Trimmer's *Fabulous Histories*: both aim, uncompromisingly, to instruct. Even Mrs Barbauld, in some ways the most liberal of such writers, paid only lip-service to the child's own imaginative powers. She did suggest that a sense of God should be allowed to grow not by dogmatic teaching, but by an early association with 'all that a child sees, all that affects his mind with wonder and delight'.[13] But in her *Hymns in Prose* the only associations which she permits the child are those she herself points out:

> Behold the Shepherd of the flock, he taketh care for his sheep, he leadeth them among clear brooks, he guideth them to fresh pasture; if the young lambs are weary, he carrieth them in his arms; if they wander, he bringeth them back.
> But who is the shepherd's shepherd? who taketh care for him? who guideth him in the path he should go? and if he wander, who shall bring him back? God is the shepherd's shepherd. He is the Shepherd over all; he taketh care for all; the whole earth is his fold: we are all his flock; and every herb, and every green field, is the pasture which he hath prepared for us.
> ...God is our Shepherd, therefore we will follow him: God is our Father, therefore we will love him: God is our King, therefore we will obey him.
>
> (Hymn III, *Hymns in Prose*, 1794)

One might well find Watts' honest didacticism preferable to this relentless insistence. In 1802 Charles Lamb was to write angrily to Coleridge:

> Mrs. Barbauld's stuff has banished all the old classics of the nursery; and the shopman at Newbery's hardly deigned to reach them off an old exploded corner of a shelf, when Mary asked for them. Mrs. B.'s and Mrs. Trimmer's nonsense lay in piles about. Knowledge insignificant and vapid as Mrs. B.'s books convey, it seems, must come to a child in the *shape* of *knowledge*, and his empty noddle must be turned with conceit of his own powers when he has learnt that a Horse is an animal, and Billy is better than a Horse, and such like; instead of that beautiful interest in wild tales which made the child a man, while all the time he suspected himself to be no bigger than a child. Science has succeeded to Poetry no less in the little walks of children than with men. Is there no possibility of averting this sore evil? Think what you would have been now, if instead of being fed with Tales and old wives' fables in childhood, you had been crammed with geography and natural history?
> Damn them! – I mean the cursed Barbauld Crew, those Blights and Blasts of all that is Human in man and child.[14]

Not many eighteenth-century parents can have felt as Lamb did: the 'Barbauld Crew' were enormously successful. But his remarks point to an aspect of such books that the present-day reader, finding a kind of period charm in them, might be tempted to under-estimate. As modern historians have argued, their mere existence points to a growing imaginative sympathy for childhood amongst the middle and upper classes, a growing effort to cater to the child's particular needs and interests, and even, occasionally, to see the world from his point of view. Yet they were written in conscious opposition to the more popular plebeian chap-books, with their unmoralized jokes and riddles and stories of giants and fairies, and their essential aim was authoritarian. The chap-books were hardly 'folk art': they were the much mediated and debased products of the polite literary culture, written for and not by the kinds of people who read them most eagerly.[15] Yet – as their popularity with children suggests – they were infinitely closer to that continuing childish sub-culture of street-games and rhymes and riddles traced in the work of Iona and Peter Opie[16] than the moral verses of Watts or even of Bunyan. In choosing the child's book as a medium Blake was choosing a genre in which real imaginative life (albeit of an ephemeral, sensationalistic kind) was consistently being subordinated to 'instructive' purposes. And he was addressing himself to readers whose expectations would have been formed by the 'Barbauld Crew' whom Lamb deplored. What would such readers have made of *Songs of Innocence and of Experience*?

At first sight Blake's volume would probably not have seemed surprising, though it would have been hard to find another so attractively produced,[17] or one which contained so many different kinds of verses. But the subject-matter of most would have been quite familiar. Some could be read as children's hymns ('The Lamb', 'The Divine Image', 'The Shepherd'). Some are more like the poems about childish experience such as Foxton and Watts had written, and the Lambs and the Taylors were to write ('A Cradle Song', 'The Ecchoing Green', 'Laughing Song', 'The Schoolboy'). Some, like an increasing number of poems written for children in these years, deal with social problems (the two 'Chimney Sweeper' poems, the two 'Holy Thursday's, 'The Little Black Boy', 'London'):[18] others bear more resemblance to straightforward moral fables ('The Clod & the Pebble', 'A Poison Tree'). There are verses about birds and animals, of which there was a whole sub-genre in the children's books of the late eighteenth century ('The Tyger', 'The Blossom', 'The Fly').[19] And there are others which seem closer to the emblem verse which Bunyan had emulated, and of which Newbery had published a popular collection ('Ah! Sunflower', 'The Sick Rose', 'The Lilly').[20] Varied as the collection was, most of the poems in it would have seemed conventional enough in kind.

But as the reader looked more closely at them, he might well have been puzzled. For several of Blake's Songs seem to bear a clear relation to particular eighteenth-century children's verses:[21] at a time when, although children's publishing was flourishing, the number of such verses was still comparatively small, this must have been much more obvious than it is today. And it is a relation not of confirmatory allusion, but of argument[22] or parody.[23] As John Holloway suggests:

the difference between what is in Blake and what is in his predecessor does not simply happen to be a mere incompleteness of resemblance, but looks like the product of choice – of considered and intended difference on Blake's part . . . he was writing what was a genuine and implicit *retort* to what came before him. His poems need to be seen as taking part in – or rather, as initiating – a debate.[24]

Yet why a 'debate' against such minor writers as Isaac Watts or Mrs Barbauld? Why did Blake choose to engage with *this* particular genre, rather than to experiment with those more sophisticated poetic forms in which, as *Poetical Sketches* show, he was proficient?

We might begin to answer this question by considering three examples. The first is a simple set of reading-exercises from William Ronksley's *The Child's Week's-Work*, published in 1712:

Honey licked on the Thorns
is too dearly bought.

He that is afraid of the Leaves
must not go into the Wood.

Tread on a Worm, and it will Turn.

You can have no more
Of a Cat than her skin.

The second is from Dr J. Trusler's *Proverbs Exemplified and Illustrated by Pictures from Real Life*, published in May 1790. Two extracts must suffice. One is part of a little tale written to illustrate the maxim, 'Tread on a Worm, and it will turn':

It is meant to teach us, that how trifling, how abject, how insignificant soever persons may appear to us, at the moment we tread upon them, a change of fortune, and a poignant recollection of injuries, may render their turning upon us serious indeed.

The other tells of a child who has watched his friend being stung by bees, and

has benefited from the experience of his companion, and has escaped the harm; knowing now that *he cannot gather roses* without thorns, or honey without the risk of being stung.   [Trusler's italics]

The third example is Blake's 'The Lilly', published in *Songs of Innocence and of Experience* in 1793:

> The modest Rose puts forth a thorn:
> The humble Sheep a threatning horn:
> While the Lilly white, shall in Love delight,
> Nor a thorn nor a threat stain her beauty bright.

Three examples hardly offer a complete picture. Yet these three do point towards the way in which children's literature developed as a separate genre in eighteenth-century England, and begin to show how Blake engaged with the logic of that development.

Ronksley's little reading-book was printed before the rise of children's publishing. The exercises he gives are very close to the cryptic proverbs and riddles of the penny chap-books and almanacs, and it is still possible to catch some sense of the haunting suggestiveness they would have had for the child who might have owned no other book. These proverbs are not explained: they retain the puzzling ambiguity of the living situations which they describe. The child reading them (and the similarly enigmatic rhymes and riddles by which they are accompanied) would have been free to wonder about them, to mull them over in his mind. He was not called upon immediately to conventionalize them, to assimilate them to adult moral categories. Ronksley's proverbs are not very profound: it is easy enough for the adult reader to see that most of them have a perfectly clear 'point' of a not very sophisticated kind. But they allow a space for the childish imagination to work which was almost totally closed off in the polite children's books of the next fifty years, where lively open-endedness was steadily subordinated to moralizing purposes.

Trusler's book suggests something of what happened. It is a fairly typical example of late eighteenth-century polite children's literature: typical not so much in its blatant pragmatism (though this is not rare) as in the way in which it seeks to inculcate it. There were many writers for children with far more attractive opinions than Trusler's: by the end of the eighteenth century children's books were increasingly being used to depict and deplore the more shocking of contemporary social abuses, such as slavery and cruelty to animals. But if Trusler's attitudes are more complacent and reactionary than some, his mode of presenting them is representative.[25] His aim is to conventionalize and rationalize more ambiguous modes of awareness, such as could be found in the traditional proverb, into straightforward, easily understandable lessons. It is an aim which shapes all the polite children's literature of this period, from Watts' *Divine and Moral Songs* with their didactic concluding verses to Mrs Barbauld's pseudo-Biblical emphases. Different authors may have had very different views of the child – the latter two certainly did – but their fundamental sense of what was required in writing for him was the same. All saw it as a process of simplification: simplification of moral dilemmas, of theological complexity, of social problems, into a plain, rationally intelligible form. Simplicity was their great claim to popularity. And simplicity of a kind they had – of the domineering kind which imposes its own reductive categories upon the baffling diversity of experience, which closes up teasing, suggestive ambiguity and calls for a passive acceptance by rather than a creative encounter with the reader. They did not rouse the child's capacities for wonder: they told him how to think.

Blake too was praised for his 'simplicity' – though it seems to have resisted the understanding of Dr Trusler, to whom he wrote in 1799:

You say that I want somebody to elucidate my Ideas ... But I am happy to find a Great Majority of Fellow Mortals who can elucidate My Visions, & Particularly they have been Elucidated by Children ... Neither Youth nor Childhood is Folly or Incapacity.[26]

Certainly, 'The Lilly' seems much closer to childish speech than do Trusler's ratiocinations. But to the reader whose expectations had been formed by such books as his it would have presented some baffling difficulties. How was he supposed to read it? Which was 'right' – the Rose and the Sheep, or the Lilly? Did the poem advocate the Lilly's pure, innocent confidence in contrast to the defensiveness of Sheep and Rose: or did it condemn her lack of 'modesty' and 'humility'? Blake does not tell, and the drafts of the poem in his 1793 notebook show how he pondered, and worked to frustrate, the notion that there should be an unequivocal moral point. The 'humble' Sheep was originally a 'coward', the 'modest' Rose 'envious' or 'lustful'. The substitutions suggest a doubt about the stability of any moral judgment, which is fundamentally opposed to Trusler's whole enterprise. And the reader – especially the reader alert to the ironies with which Blake often surrounds 'approving' moral terms – is left uncertain. Could the poem perhaps be an ironic exposure of the conditions for 'modesty' and 'humility' in this world? Or must one see them unironically, as terms of approbation?

In its final version the poem remains enigmatic, offering no clue as to how it might be 'elucidated'.

And thus it conveys something of that sense of wonder, of the inassimilability of life to lessons, that one finds still unconventionalized in Ronksley, and intermittently present even in the moralizing children's books of the eighteenth century. In its very refusal to point a moral it celebrates individuality and difference. The Rose is simply one kind of flower, the Lilly another: the opening couplet with its regular iambic rhythms is succeeded quite naturally by the anapaests of the close. As Blake was elsewhere to remark:

Variety does not necessarily suppose deformity, for a rose & a lilly are various & both beautiful.   (annotations to Lavater, K81)

I do not believe that Rafael taught Mich. Angelo, or that Mich. Angelo taught Rafael, any more than I believe that the Rose teaches the Lilly how to grow, or the Apple tree teaches the Pear tree how to bear Fruit. I do not believe the tales of Anecdote writers when they militate against Individual Character.   (annotations to Reynolds, K453)

But the poem's effect on the reader is more sophisticated than that of these straightforward assertions. Its traditionally 'emblematic' subject matter, its neatly conclusive rhyme-scheme, its very appearance in a book of verse for children, all court the expectations formed by fifty years of moral songs like Watts': that there *will* be an unambiguous moral lesson, that the way to read is not to wonder and ponder, but to grasp the point. And in frustrating those expectations, Blake is thrusting his readers' tendency towards simplistic moral categorizing before them as a problem – to be felt in the very process of reading, as the poem resists assimilation to the familiar mould. 'The Lilly' does not merely celebrate variety: it offers an implicit criticism of the modes of thinking and feeling exemplified by such as Dr Trusler, a criticism the more biting because it is not a rational argument, but a poetic questioning of the usually unformulated preconceptions which underlie such argument. Blake is using the form of the late eighteenth-century child's song not as a vehicle for 'ideas' counter to those which it usually expressed, but in order to expose and subvert that whole mode of making sense of the world which it characteristically embodied.

What is true of 'The Lilly' is true, in different ways, of all the Songs. They do seem in many instances to dissent from views expressed by the 'Barbauld Crew'. *Songs of Innocence* is a collection of

Songs *of*, not *for*, and in most of them there is a reversal of expected hierarchies – that the child should be guided by a wiser adult, that the shepherd should lead his sheep, the mother give her child its name. Many of the Songs of *Experience* seem to parody or to show the dark underside of virtues inculcated in contemporary children's books – restraint of anger in 'A Poison Tree', submissive obedience in 'Infant Sorrow'. But this is merely one aspect of a deeper subversiveness. The contemporary reader might well have been disturbed by the view of life implied by the Songs; but more fundamentally – though perhaps less consciously – disturbing is the fact that there seems to be no obvious argument propounded in them at all. The disconcerting inconclusiveness of 'The Shepherd' and 'The Lilly' can be found in them all; and in the context of the children's books of the late eighteenth century it leaps into sharp relief. Where in such books a clear authorial voice imposes its view of that which is presented and directs the reader how to think, here there is no such voice and no direction. Even where – as in many of the Songs of *Experience* – there are distinct dramatized speakers, the authority of those speakers is, as we shall see, poetically undermined. Such moral conclusions as do appear (as in the Innocent 'Holy Thursday' and 'The Chimney Sweeper') seem to be hedged about with ironies: some of the most distressing of the situations presented ('Ah! Sunflower', 'The Sick Rose') are simply left to speak for themselves. At every point where the Songs seem about to fit the expected pattern, they awkwardly refuse.

And what they offer is not merely a subversion of a familiar mode of seeing the world: it is a subtly articulated alternative vision. This is true of a relatively unproblematic poem such as 'The Shepherd': it is equally true of those which deal with more ambiguous subject-matter, and seem more obviously to court comparison with what had come before. The two 'Nurse's Songs', for instance, show an adult advising the children in her charge: a subject which images and epitomizes the aims of all eighteenth-century children's books. Yet in portraying that subject from two such opposing perspectives, Blake throws those aims into question, and counters them in an unexpected way.

The Song of *Experience* is in some ways the simpler of the two. As the reader would have expected, only one voice is heard: that of the adult, who warns the children of the transience and futility of life. But it is very different from the voice of an Isaac Watts or a Bunyan, not merely because it does not exhort to repentance and good works, but because it does not seem to be offered for the reader's unambiguous acceptance:

NURSES Song

When the voices of children, are heard on the green
And whisprings are in the dale:
The days of my youth rise fresh in my mind,
My face turns green and pale.

Then come home my children, the sun is gone down
And the dews of night arise
Your spring & your day, are wasted in play
And your winter and night in disguise.

The first stanza reveals rather more about the speaker than might at first appear. Despite the fact that she is the children's nurse, she seems scarcely aware of them. Their 'voices' are 'heard' at a distance from and not even necessarily by her: the independent 'whisperings' of the following line are far more actively and insistently present to her. For all her desire to impose her views on others, she seems hardly in control of her own experience: things happen *to* her in a sinister way:

The days of my youth rise fresh in my mind,
My face turns green and pale.

Her message to the children, in one way like the 'message' of so much contemporary verse for them, is thus, when it comes, informed with irony: how can *this* speaker adopt a tone of dogmatic certainty? In satirizing her pretensions to authority, the Song parodies that 'instruction' which was central to the children's books of the time. This Nurse is not unlike the terrible Mrs Mason of Mary Wollstonecraft's *Original Stories from Real Life,* and the hovering figure on the plate is very similar to Blake's (surely mocking) engravings of that character.[27] But the effect of the poem is not merely one of ridicule. For the Nurse is shown to be at the mercy of uncontrollable anxieties, which blot out the reality of those she addresses, and imprison her within a closed circle of egocentric 'disguise'. The children's 'voices', remotely there in the opening line, do not enter the poem: the end is not 'ecchoing' confidence, but a forbidding confession of fear. Perhaps the coercive admonitions of the children's books are the products not of assurance, but of something like this.

If a contemporary reader might have found this Song disturbing, he would have found it even harder to know what to make of its

Innocent counterpart. For here the children put their own point of view, in answer to that of their Nurse; and she ends not by advising, but by acquiescing. Unlike the Song of *Experience*, this has not even a parodied 'message': it seems merely an inconsequential account of a moment of happy play. And its difference from other eighteenth-century children's verse lies – like that of 'The Shepherd' and 'The Lilly' – not simply in its refusal to offer such a 'message', but in the nature of the vision it does articulate:

Nurse's Song

When the voices of children are heard on the green
And laughing is heard on the hill,
My heart is at rest within my breast
And everything else is still

Then come home my children, the sun is gone down
And the dews of night arise
Come come leave off play, and let us away
Till the morning appears in the skies

No no let us play, for it is yet day
And we cannot go to sleep
Besides in the sky, the little birds fly
And the hills are all coverd with sheep

Well well go & play till the light fades away
And then go home to bed
The little ones leaped & shouted & laugh'd
And all the hills ecchoed.

The world depicted by this Nurse is a shared, human world. The definite articles – '*the* green' and '*the* hill' – introduce a known landscape, 'on' which 'voices' and 'laughing' are openly 'heard': there is none of the secrecy hinted at in 'in the dale'. The mysterious 'whisprings' of the other poem had a menacingly independent existence; but here all activity is held within a frame of mutual awareness. This speaker registers far more of the scene before her than the Nurse of *Experience*. Yet the passive verbs and the absence of adjectives suggest that she has in some sense withdrawn from active involvement: the one thing she tells of herself is

My heart is at rest within my breast.

She is aware only of the children: for her – again, in striking contrast to the Nurse of *Experience* – 'everything else is still'.
 The children are utterly different. Their world is not distanced,

21

but immediate and animate. To them, the landscape and the living things within it are parts of a satisfying whole: activity – 'in the sky, the little birds fly' – is balanced by passivity – 'the hills are all coverd with sheep'. Against the Nurse's sense of the passing of time, their voices insist on present spontaneity – 'we *cannot* go to sleep'. Yet the dialogue between them is not one of disagreement: its nature and its consequence are embodied in the final word of the poem. Throughout their interchange, the words of one generation are 'ecchoed' even in difference by those of the other – 'Come come leave off play', 'No no let us play', 'Well well go & play'. 'Ecchoed', which can be used both of a passive and an active function of the subject, includes the vitality of the children and the quiescence of the Nurse in the same harmonious concord. They enter a world of life and movement as she withdraws from it: the poem moves from '*come* home' to '*go* home', from her static subjectivity – 'when ... are' – to the perfect tense of a finished action in which she has no part – a change of tense which has a framing effect, encapsulating the action of the poem in a moment of satisfying completion. If it is the moment at which one generation gives way to another, it contains neither nostalgia nor envy, but serene, all-embracing content.

The design of the plate expresses the same feeling. The Nurse sits on the edge of a group of playing children. Unlike the anxiously intrusive Nurse in the *Experience* plate, she does not watch them: she is absorbed in a book. They, too, are absorbed in their own activity: a game which involves linking hands and passing under a ribbon held by the two at the end of the chain. The first are about to pass under, in a line which will exclude the Nurse as they go toward the setting sun. But at the moment that is illustrated their dance forms an incomplete circle which she closes in the visual scheme of the picture. Like the poem, the plate suggests that she has withdrawn from active living, into the stillness of contemplation, and that the children are moving into a world of which she will soon no longer be part. But at this point she and they compose a harmony: just as the passivity of the Nurse is verbally echoed by the activity of the children, so her seated figure visually balances and completes the circle begun by their dancing ones. And as the last word of the poem suggests both perfected reciprocity and a continuing process (for echoes give rise to other echoes), so the children's formation seems about to make a circle, but is actually a line which will never be joined. Both plate and poem delineate a constellation of feelings – focussed in this moment when the children, with her acquiescence, leave the Nurse's control – which could hardly be reduced to a didactic message: clearly yet economically the reader is given a sense of the acceptance of age and the excitement of youth, of the difference between the withdrawal of the one and the responsiveness of the other, and of how the two might nevertheless 'eccho' one another in a harmonious interplay which at once has the contentment of completion and the vigour of forward-moving life.

Blake's refusal to offer what his readers would have expected is not, then, simply a matter of 'parody by omission';[28] these Songs present an 'organized and minutely articulated' (K576) vision of an unprecedented kind. But the implications of that refusal deserve further examination. And they can perhaps most easily be traced from a Song which must have seemed at first far less surprising than either of the 'Nurse's Song's. To Blake's biographer Gilchrist, 'The Lamb' was a 'sweet hymn of tender infantine sentiment': Allan Cunningham, in his earlier *Life*, praised it for its 'religious tenderness of sentiment'.[29] Certainly, at some points it clearly echoes a well-known eighteenth-century hymn for children, Charles Wesley's 'Gentle Jesus, Meek and Mild':

> . . .
>
> Lamb of God, I look to thee,
> Thou shalt my example be;
> Thou art gentle, meek, and mild,
> Thou wast once a little child.
>
> Fain I would be as thou art,
> Give me thy obedient heart;
> Thou art pitiful and kind,
> Let me have thy loving mind.
>
> . . .
>
> Thou didst live to God alone,
> Thou didst never seek thine own,
> Thou thyself didst never please:
> God was all thy happiness.
>
> Loving Jesus, gentle Lamb,
> In thy gracious hands I am;
> Make me, Saviour, what thou art,
> Live thyself within my heart.
>
> I shall then show forth thy praise,
> Serve thee all my happy days;
> Then the world shall always see
> Christ, the holy Child, in me.[30]

Yet the echoes in Blake's poem seem less those of agreement than of difference. Wesley does achieve something of the simplicity and clarity of childish speech.[31] But quite apart from the ethic of self-repression which he preaches – 'Thou thyself didst never please' – there is something most unchildlike in the hymn's propositional structure. It proceeds by means of an adult logic, and its rhymed couplets emphasize rational distinction – between child and Lamb, between Christ on earth and God in heaven – rather than analogical likeness. And in this it contrasts strikingly with Blake:

> Little Lamb who made thee
> Dost thou know who made thee
> Gave thee life & bid thee feed,
> By the stream & o'er the mead;
> Gave thee clothing of delight,
> Softest clothing wooly bright;
> Gave thee such a tender voice,
> Making all the vales rejoice:
> Little Lamb who made thee
> Dost thou know who made thee
>
> Little Lamb I'll tell thee,
> Little Lamb I'll tell thee:
> He is called by thy name,
> For he calls himself a Lamb:
> He is meek, & he is mild,
> He became a little child:
> I a child & thou a lamb,
> We are called by his name.
> Little Lamb God bless thee,
> Little Lamb God bless thee.

Here, the unselfconscious repetitions and false and half rhymes are used to create an impression of childishness: the structure is that of a simple question and answer, with the same phrases rearranged and repeated. But the feeling is less one of incoherence than of a patterning very different from that of Wesley's linear development. Blake is not merely giving expression to a 'delight' in the world very different from Wesley's restrictiveness ('God was all thy happiness'): he is questioning the preconceptions on which Wesley's whole argument is based.

Wesley demystifies the Incarnation by placing it within a rational moral framework: because Christ was once a child, children can the more easily follow his example. But for Blake's child there is no such framework. He seems to be half recalling the lessons taught by Wesley, with a childish inability to give them a logical structure. Yet his unsophisticated repetitions and transpositions harmonize in a way that Wesley's clipped couplets do not: and through that harmony we may trace an implicit questioning of the authoritative definitions of the other poem. His answer to the lamb is not a series of dogmatic assertions: rather, it innocently emphasizes the extra-neousness of such assertions, their distance from the reality they purport to define. His opening questions – 'Little Lamb who made thee / Dost thou know who made thee' – are not directly answered: rather, he speaks of a 'calling' which comes from elsewhere – 'He is called', 'he calls himself', 'We are called'. Where Wesley's poem claims to discriminate important truths, this articulates a perspective from which the very process of discrimination, or 'calling', seems alien and simplifying. The child's words are inverted ('He is called by thy name', 'We are called by his name') in a way which suggests that they cannot encompass that to which they point: the voice of the lamb, heard in the first stanza, is far more powerfully present. Yet the world that is outlined in this childish 'teaching' is a deeply reassuring one: one of protection and loving responsiveness, in which Wesley's hierarchies are subtly but surely dissolved. By the end of the poem, 'I', 'he' and 'you' are merged into 'we'.

'Infant Joy', too, is concerned with 'calling': both with its difference from immediate existence and its capacity to create a satisfying world of echo and confirmation:

> I have no name
> I am but two days old. –
> What shall I call thee?
> I happy am
> Joy is my name, –
> Sweet joy befall thee!
>
> Pretty joy!
> Sweet joy but two days old.
> Sweet joy I call thee:
> Thou dost smile.
> I sing the while
> Sweet joy befall thee.

Here, as elsewhere in *Songs of Innocence*, repetition with slight variation suggests difference yet harmony between two speakers. The child simply *is*, aware only of present happiness: the adult looks

beyond this moment of trustful security – 'Sweet joy befall thee'. Yet
the poem portrays an experience very far from that progression from
unreflexive 'joy' to sterile classification and fearful anxiety which
Blake was to lament in *Jerusalem* Plate 22:

> 'Why wilt thou number every little fibre of my Soul,
> 'Spreading them out before the Sun like stalks of flax to dry?
> 'The Infant Joy is beautiful, but its anatomy
> 'Horrible, ghast & deadly! nought shalt thou find in it
> 'But dark despire & everlasting brooding melancholy!'
>
> (K 645)

In the Song of *Innocence* there is neither protest nor conflict: the adult
speaker does not attempt to anatomize or control. 'Naming' begins
with the child's own feeling of lack – 'I have no name'; definition is
not imposed by another, for he (or she) names himself (or herself).
And although the 'name' which he articulates and which the adult
repeats and 'calls' him enables an echoing interplay between them,
the poem begins and ends with an image of an otherness which
escapes all 'calling':

> Thou dost smile.
> I sing the while
> Sweet joy befall thee.

The difference between these poems and a hymn such as Wesley's
lies not merely in their absence of rational argument. They seem to
be foregrounding and exploring the problematic nature of that
process whereby men seek to categorize and label experience: a
process which to a Wesley presents no problem at all. If, like 'The
Lilly' and the two 'Nurse's Song's, they offer a challenge to the
reader accustomed to authoritative 'instruction', here the radical
nature of that challenge becomes clear. Blake is not simply attacking the assumption – particularly prominent in eighteenth-century
children's books – that the reader must be the passive recipient
of such 'instruction': he is also questioning the perhaps even
deeper eighteenth-century assumption that all experience is (or
ought to be) susceptible of rational definition and that the rational
mind can arrive at truth by a logic which is not open to voices other
than its own.

The distrust thus articulated in these poems may appear idiosyncratic: the product of a uniquely 'peculiar honesty'.[32] But others
besides Blake – and particularly the London artisans and tradesmen
among whom he spent much of his working life – were, in the late

eighteenth century, also questioning controlling definitions of polite 'common sense'. It was a questioning which took widespread and varying forms. In the wake of the French Revolution it found compelling political expression in the writings of Paine and his followers, with their insistence on the mystificatory function of much official 'wisdom': it was manifested in more bizarre, but perhaps not unconnected ways, in popular prophetic movements such as those centering on Richard Brothers and (later) Joanna Southcott.[33] It can be found in the more theologically sophisticated writings of the antinomian sects (some at least of which had survived from the Civil War period) with whose thinking Blake seems to have been intimate.[34] And it can also be traced in the doctrines of the Swedenborgian Church of the New Jerusalem, whose great system of correspondences was premised upon the inadequacy of conventional perception and definition, and whose first General Conference Blake attended in 1789. 'Names', Swedenborg had declared, 'are to them [angels] like dust, or like scales, which fall down when they enter into Heaven'.[35] To the Swedenborgians, distrustful of all human discourse ('I should wish first to observe, that we are not to expect, either in the writings of Baron Swedenborg or in any other human Writings, the REAL TRUTH ITSELF'),[36] the world perceived by common sense and described in its language was merely a set of symbols pointing to a transcendent and finally indescribable spiritual reality.

Paine was a radical atheist, suspicious of all metaphor and allegory:[37] the millenarian prophets saw 'signs' in everything: the Swedenborgians had codified such vision into a great system. To assimilate all to a common way of thinking is to blur differences that were of very real importance both to them and to Blake. But an indiscriminate attack on both radicals and sectarians, published in 1800 by W. H. Reid, points, in its hostile caricature, to the crucial similarity which made it entirely understandable for their adherents to fluctuate between them and for their opponents to conflate them:

One of the principal obstacles to your instruction, I find to be, that flattering notion of Mr. Paine, 'that every man's mind is his own church.'
  Some of you are ready to deify Mr. Paine for this discovery; but let me tell you, he was not the first that broached this deleterious nostrum; it was in the mouths and writings of almost all the sectarists that distracted this kingdom, between the reigns of Charles the First and Second. It is a principle, virtually acknowledged by the Quakers, and was very pointedly urged and insisted upon, by a person in the last century, known by the appellation of Cobler

How; in a pamphlet entitled, 'The sufficiency of the Spirit's Teaching'; and in plain sense, means very little more, than that every man loves to be led by his own whims and fancies, as soon as ever he becomes a Dissenter from the established order of the church. This explanation, I think, is well warranted by the conduct of those who have, from time to time, adopted the principle of *self-sufficiency*.

In fact, so far from answering the end proposed, either by Infidels or Sectarists, I have generally observed, that when this notion is reduced to practice, instead of being sufficient for the teaching of all, it has been the principal reason why none have been sufficiently taught! In cases of common life, men naturally ask the advice of others, but here, in a concern of the last importance, every man's knowledge is supposed sufficient for himself.[38]

Each of these groups in one way or another rejected the authority of the dominant culture. In the case of Paine (who quite clearly dissociated himself from the 'Sectarists', but whose followers seem to have been less sternly opposed to prophecy)[39] this rejection took the form of an extended demystification of its pretensions: in the case of the Swedenborgians and the popular prophets, an articulation of alternative 'readings' of the world. The fact that Reid's attack on them is part of an attack on the growth of literacy suggests a shrewd grasp of the essential nature of their subversiveness. What he deplores in them is not so much straightforward political sedition as a sometimes articulate but sometimes unselfconscious impulse of ideological resistance, of refusal to accept the 'received' (or, as it might be seen, the imposed) wisdom of the polite, an insistence on the importance of quite other 'voices' than that official one. It was an impulse which received its most rational articulation in the writings of Paine, but a perhaps more imaginatively seductive expression in the visionary alternatives of the popular prophets and of the Swedenborgian Church of the New Jerusalem, whose internal debates and disputes seem to have occupied Blake a great deal at the time when he was engraving *Songs of Innocence*.

To see Blake within this context is to see his apparent detachment from the polite literary culture of his day, his ironic relation even to the limited genre he chose for his *Songs*, not as the product of a peculiar individualism but as the coherent imaginative expression of a far from unparalleled and far from detached response to the society in which he lived. But it is also to see his real originality: the way in which he drew upon and followed through the imaginative logic of modes of thinking and feeling that were being expressed around

him, in order to articulate his own distinctive vision. 'The Lilly', for
instance, bears some relation to the writings both of radicals and
'Sectarists'. Its enigmatic ambiguity is not unlike that of the
millenarian prophecies popular in London in the 1790s – though in
these such ambiguity was often merely a safe vagueness: 'tho' the red
rose will bloom fresh and ruddy, the lilly, pale and desponding, must
soon droop' (*The Prophet of Prophets, or Wonderful Prophecies for 1791*).
The ironic sense of 'modesty' and 'humility' articulated in its first
couplet seems (as a cancelled line in the notebook draft – 'The priest
loves war & the soldier peace' – suggests) to spring from the same
political radicalism as the ironic counter-definitions of those who
followed in the wake of Paine:

Unenvied – the virtues of the king, the morality of the Lords, and the
independence of the Commons; the humanity of the Bishops, the impartiality of the Judges, and the learning of the Clergy; the generosity of the Queen,
the economy of the Prince of Wales, and the courage of the Duke of York!
Honi soit qui mal y pense.[40]

And the poem's implicit questioning of any moralizing is framed in
imagery reminiscent of the writings of Jacob Boehme (or Jacob
Behmen), whose influence pervaded the antinomian sects.
Throughout Boehme's works, the promised time of heaven upon
earth is imaged as 'the time of the Lily'[41] – a time which will succeed
'the time of the Nettle' and 'the time of the Rose', and which will
bring an end to the stultifying rigidity of the Moral Law: 'Therefore
we have Need of the Lily, which grows through the Tables of
Moses, (that were graven through), with its strong Smell, which
reaches into the Paradise of God.'[42] Like Boehme's Lily, which ends
the rule of the Law by breaking through 'the Tables of Moses',
Blake's 'Lilly' breaks through the rigid metrical and conceptual
schema that his first couplet has set up and celebrates a life that
escapes the categories of moral judgment:

> The modest Rose puts forth a thorn:
> The humble Sheep, a threatning horn:
> While the Lilly white, shall in Love delight,
> Nor a thorn nor a threat stain her beauty bright.

Yet the poem's effect is far more sophisticated than that of enigmatic
prophecy or of ironic protest or even of Behmenist teaching. And it
depends very centrally upon the fact that Blake is writing within a
recognizable polite genre for readers with definite, if unarticulated,
expectations: readers who would probably have ridiculed 'Wonder-

ful Prophecies', been alarmed by Paine-ite radicalism, and dismissed Boehme's writings as remote mysticism. 'The Lilly' frustrates those expectations in a way which challenges some of the most deep-rooted of polite assumptions. And it does so by realizing the imaginative implications of modes of thinking very far from those of the polite: realizing them with a tight precision which reveals Blake's interest not so much in the detail of such thinking (trivialized or simplified or schematized as the particular manifestations with which he was familiar might be) as in its essential strategies.

Similarly, one can find a parallel between that concern with 'calling' central to 'Infant Joy' and 'The Lamb' and the Swedenborgian argument that 'names are ... like dust, or scales, which fall down when they enter into heaven'. But where Swedenborg offers doctrine, Blake questions univocal 'naming' by dramatizing the naive child's perspective, different from that of adult definition, and allowing that which had hitherto been inarticulate its own harmoniously chiming voice. And in doing so he presents a vision subtly subversive of that of 'common sense', a vision which Swedenborg, with his rational alternative definitions – 'From these things it may be evident that by "a lamb" is signified the good of innocence ... This is especially evident from the fact that the Lord himself is called "the Lamb" and also that those are called "lambs" who love the Lord' (*Arcana Coelestia*, 10132[11]) – could never realize.[43] It is a vision which, once again, is closer to the writings of Boehme than to those of Blake's radical or sectarian contemporaries:

All whatever is spoken, written, or taught of God, without the Knowledge of the Signature is dumb and void of Understanding, for it proceeds only from an historical conjecture, from the Mouth of another, wherein the Spirit without Knowledge is dumb; but if the Spirit opens to him the *Signature*, then he understands the speech of another...

Nature has given to every Thing its Language according to its essence and Form, for out of the Essence the Language or Sound arises, and the Fiat of that Essence forms the Quality of the Essence in the Voice or Virtue which it sends forth, to the Animals in the Sound, and to the Essentials in Smell, Virtue, and Form.

Every Thing has its Mouth to Manifestation; and this is the language of Nature; whence every Thing speaks out of its Property, and continually manifests, declares, and sets forth itself for what is good or profitable.[44]

In rejecting 'official wisdom', Swedenborg had simply replaced it with a different, equally categorical 'wisdom', as Blake perceived and deplored.[45] But Boehme here points toward the more radical potential of that rejection – a potential unrealized by the sectaries of the 1790s. He does not simply question received definitions: he affirms the integrity of that which is distorted or denied by the impulse to categorize and define, and advocates an openness toward 'the speech of another' which was to find imaginative expression in Blake's *Songs*.

For one after another the Songs of *Innocence* present points of view very different from the customary controlling one of polite adult rationalism. The child in the 'Introduction' tells the piper what to do; the children answer their nurse; the glow-worm, in 'A Dream', testifies to the irrelevance of human 'pity' in the self-sufficing other world of nature. And the unprivileged – the chimney sweeper, the black boy, the charity children – have their own distinctive voices: they are not the objects of sympathetic or protesting comment – of any comment at all. The Songs of *Experience* express a concomitant suspicion of that categorical mode of vision which reduces difference to its own mould. 'The Lilly' implies that absolute moral judgment has no meaning in face of the diversity of life: 'The Human Abstract', far more bitingly, exposes the coercion of otherness in which such judgment has its root. And the most confidently authoritative voices – like those of 'NURSES Song', of 'Holy Thursday', of 'Infant Sorrow' – are shown not merely to be closed to that upon which they would pronounce, but those least able to change that which they deplore.

If Boehme's argument points toward the vision which seems to inform the Songs, their language is not that of his theological and alchemical speculation: they do not versify Behmenist, and still less Swedenborgian, ideas. But a vision such as Blake's is not arrived at in isolation from the social and cultural pressures which shape other men. And his brief connection with the New Church offers a suggestive indication of the way in which that vision might be seen in relation to the experience and the reactions of his contemporaries: not as remote from but as grasping and following through (in a way unparalleled in his time, and perhaps since) the imaginative logic of positions which others around him were articulating in very different ways. The Swedenborgians elaborated their alternative 'vision' in a vast system which embodied the controlling rationalism they sought to reject: the radical impulse of refusal did not go deep enough. But Blake saw the significance of that refusal in terms of the social realities of late eighteenth-century England. In choosing to present his vision in the form of a book for children he was choosing to engage directly with the coercive strategies of its dominant culture – strategies which the child's book, with its rationalistic simplification of ambiguous subject-matter, its assumption that its readers should passively accept 'instruction', very clearly embodied. In writing for those accustomed to such books, he was addressing himself to an audience who had internalized those strategies, as an unquestioned 'mental set' of assumptions and expectations, which was called into play in the very act of reading. And by refusing to confirm those assumptions, by frustrating those expectations, he did not merely seek to bring them to their readers' awareness: he exposed their crippling and destructive implications. For in these *Songs*, far 'simpler' than Swedenborgian or antinomian doctrine, or Paine-ite political theory, he depicts the contradictions within a particular, known society which made a rejection of its 'official wisdom' attractive to so many diverse groups within it. And in *Songs of Innocence*, unlike any of his contemporaries, he offers an 'organized and minutely articulated' (K576) vision of a possibility to which that 'wisdom' was closed: a vision of that familiar world structured not in terms of dominance and control, but by an acknowledgment and creative realization of the very different needs and desires of which it was composed.

2 Poetic 'Simplicity': *Lyrical Ballads* and Magazine Verse

> But alas! the multitude of books and the general diffusion of
> literature have produced other and more lamentable effects in the
> world of letters ... now, partly by the labours of successive poets
> and in part by the more artificial state of society and social
> intercourse, language, mechanized as it were into a barrel-organ,
> supplies at once both instrument and tune. Thus even the deaf may
> play so as to delight the many ... Hence of all trades literature at
> present demands the least talent or information; and of all modes of
> literature, the manufacturing of poems ... Now it is no less
> remarkable than true with how little examination works of polite
> literature are commonly perused, not only by the mass of readers,
> but by men of first rate ability.
>
> (Coleridge, *Biographia Literaria* (1817), ch.2)

Despite the claims which Wordsworth made for the 'experimental'
nature of *Lyrical Ballads*, they, like Blake's *Songs*, would have
appeared to belong to a recognizable contemporary genre. Robert
Mayo has pointed to the superficial similarities between these poems
and those which filled the poetry pages of the magazines popular
amongst the educated classes in late eighteenth-century England.[1]
Such poems were often taken from, or eventually published as,
collections by a single author,[2] but the term 'magazine verse' fairly
indicates their ephemeral nature, and is a useful generic label for the
type of poetry which readers of *Lyrical Ballads* would have expected:
poems on humanitarian subjects, such as bereaved mothers, female
vagrants, madmen, convicts and the indigent poor; poems modelled
on ballads; poems about nature; short meditative fragments; anec-
dotes; topographical pieces; reflective and occasional verses. Most of
these were consciously and explicitly 'simple' in style: few were very
distinguished. As Mayo says:

The distinction between 'original', adapted, and reprinted verses is never
sure. The only certainty is that there is a confused and eddying flood of
popular poetry flowing through the magazines from the middle of one
century to the next – some old, some new, some written by hacks, much

33

more written by amateurs, who endlessly copied the accepted masterpieces of the past and rang changes on the approved models of the day. The vast proportion of this verse literature is hopelessly mediocre and deservedly forgotten.[3]

Yet it is to such popular lyric verse as this that *Lyrical Ballads* can most demonstrably and revealingly be related. Wordsworth – as his letters to William Mathews on the subject of their proposed 'monthly Miscellany' in 1794 show – was very familiar with it.[4] His first published poem had been a sonnet printed in the *European Magazine*; his interest in the ballad form seems to have been stimulated by the publication of translations from Bürger in the *Monthly Magazine* for 1796; and it was for the latter journal that the joint 'Ancient Mariner' planned by himself and Coleridge was first intended.[5] In offering a fairly expensive[6] volume of 'simple' ballads and meditative verse on subjects ranging from the indigent poor to the beauties of landscape he was addressing himself to readers whose expectations of such verse were well known to him, and whose taste for it was already well-established and extensively catered for.

The growing middle-class reading public who supported the magazines must have overlapped considerably with those who bought children's books, but the two genres are obviously very different. Each drew on and conventionalized elements of an older, more popular culture. But where children's books forced the proverbs and riddles and stories of the chap-books into the mould of a rigid didacticism, the ballad imitations of the magazines were rather more varied, ranging from humorous parody to effusions of sensibility or melodrama:[7] a variety suggesting a rather more flexible relationship between author and reader than that proposed by the child's book. If the 'simplicity' of children's literature was that of reductive simplification, that of the magazines at least aimed to serve a different purpose. Writing of Cowper (a favourite in the magazines) in *The Flapper* for 1796, Alexander Knox expressed it clearly:

he takes his materials from the everyday walks of life; he seizes on those little domestic circumstances which perhaps no poet before him ever thought of making use of, and he forms from them pictures which astonish no less than they please. We wonder at the interest now for the first time taken in what we have so often seen without any pleasurable sensation, and we wonder still more that such an effect should be so easily produced; we observe no labour, no search for ornament, but on the contrary, an execution as artless as the conception is vigorous ... The discerning reader will easily perceive that simplicity is a prevailing character in the poetry of Cowper, and that his thoughts appear to retain on paper the very order and shape which they assumed at first in his mind.[8]

'The very order and shape which they assumed at first in his mind': where children's verse instructed, that of the magazines assumed a sympathetic rapport with its readers. The magazine poet characteristically sought to share his thoughts and feelings, the sometimes complex reasons for his attitudes, rather than to offer categorical lessons.

The polite magazines were by no means homogeneous: their politics ranged from the conservatism of the *Gentleman's Magazine* to the Dissenting radicalism of the *Monthly Magazine*. But they did share some fundamental modes of expression and of feeling. Although the opinions set forth in the latter journal might have been antipathetic to readers of the former, the reasoned discussion in its letter columns, its essays on philosophical and literary subjects, the effusions of sensibility on its poetry pages, and its always implicit and sometimes explicit belief that the reader is to be educated rather than indoctrinated would have been quite familiar. Like all such contemporary magazines, both were addressed to a polite adult audience, and both inhabit the same frame of reference, within which – it is confidently felt – all experience can satisfactorily be understood and shared.[9]

The poetry pages of the magazines exhibit this confidence more clearly than any other part of them. Much of the verse they contain deals with the same subjects as are discussed in the letters and essays – moral and philosophical issues, the plight of the poor and unfortunate, the influence of natural scenery: almost without exception such verse smooths into acceptable elegance that which is elsewhere found to be more disturbing. This seems to be true even of that written by men whose ideas were far from elegant or acceptable to the Establishment. The most interesting of these – and those whose thinking was closest to Wordsworth's – were the Dissenting radicals associated with the publisher Joseph Johnson, at least three of whom (George Dyer, John Aikin and Joseph Fawcett) wrote enough verse on 'Wordsworthian' themes to justify its publication in slim volumes as well as in the magazines.[10] All three were serious thinkers, and tried to translate their thought into poetic terms: all were aware that a true radicalism in literature involved more than propagandist argument. Dyer, for instance, in the Preface to his *Life of Robinson* published in 1796, wrote:

My language ... will appear naked and unadorned, and my periods will want the harmony, that accompanies a great name. Among writers I appear, as a native of Botany Bay, of Otaheite, among civilized nations ... France has emancipated mankind from these attempts at false greatness.[11]

Aikin had likewise warned against

the vagueness and indistinctness, and sometimes the inconsistency and absurdity, which the neglect of the study of actual nature had introduced into poetical description ... and the danger of suffering falsehood and error to intrude even in matters of the slightest importance.[12]

And the *Monthly Magazine* of which he was editor had tackled the problem in its first issue:

The term, Magazine-poetry, has usually been considered synonymous with the most trivial and imperfect attempt at writing verse. It has been [the editors'] earnest wish, to establish a very different character of the pages devoted to this pleasing object in the *Monthly Magazine*.[13]

But despite these claims, and despite their very real distinction as social and political thinkers, the poetry produced by this circle is disappointingly limp. Fawcett's versified Godwinian view of the criminal as victim is a typical example:

> Society's deserted child!
> From her neglect thine errors flowed:
> She left thine heart untrain'd and wild,
> Nor paid the mother's care she owed.
>
>   ...
>
> Hither, ye erring rulers, come;
> O'er this bland picture roll your eyes;
> Observe how soft the landscape's bloom!
> The tender azure of these skies!
>
> Instructed in this genial school,
> Mellow your crude, inclement plan:
> Copy mild Nature's gentle rule,
> And learn, like her, to smile on Man.[14]

Such arguments may have seemed dangerously radical in the 1790s. But this poem hardly makes radical demands upon its readers. The problems on which it touches are contained by its easy, undisturbed rhythms: its urbanely reasoned appeal and the sentimental clichés of its conclusion bespeak a fundamental assurance that those problems can be dealt with and resolved within a shared, polite frame of reference. There is nothing in the poem to suggest the imaginative pressure of experience outside of and perhaps threatening to that frame. And in this it is entirely characteristic of the genre to which it belongs.

But the 'magazine poets' – both radical and conservative – seem to have been interested in precisely those subjects which might have been felt to threaten polite certainties. It is difficult, in this period, to find magazine verse which is *not* about the poor, the afflicted, the independent world of nature, or irrational and 'sentimental' experience. In part, this might indicate a real desire amongst those who read such verse to widen their mental horizons. But when one considers its actual nature – fairly enough exemplified in Fawcett's lines – its popularity takes on a rather more ambiguous significance. It seems to point to a pressure to bring subjects which might have been felt to be disturbing to or uncontrollable by the categories of the dominant culture firmly within the imaginative confines of that culture, to tame them by reducing them to its terms.[15]. This does not appear to have been a conscious strategy, like the didacticism of the children's verse: one feels it as much in poems like Fawcett's as in those which are far less 'radical'. But the easy clichés and the untroubled regularity of all the magazine verse do seem, at a deep level, to reassure the reader that even these threatening subjects can be incorporated by the polite rational consciousness, that all reasonable men share the same basic values and point of view.

Thus, like the 'instruction' of the children's books, the poetry pages of the magazines – trivial as their contents mostly are – seem to be part of a larger cultural process: in this case, the process by which the polite culture justified itself to itself, coping with and translating into its own terms that which was potentially most challenging to its assumptions. If its simplifications are less dogmatic than those of the children's verse, they are none the less simplifications. Though these poems may appear quite exploratory (and often explicitly aimed to be so) their authoritative assurance and their intimate ease contain what they present securely within the accepted and acceptable mould.

To the readers of such verse much about *Lyrical Ballads* would have appeared unsurprising. Fifteen different poems from the two volumes were in fact reprinted in the magazines between 1798 and 1802, and the collection as a whole achieved a real, if limited, popularity.[16] Yet the relation between Wordworth's poems and this, the genre to which they seem to belong, is rather more problematic than that suggested by Mayo: 'the more one reads the popular poetry of the last quarter of the eighteenth century the more he is likely to feel that the really surprising feature of these poems ... – apart from sheer literary excellence – is their intense fulfilment of an already stale convention.'[17] For despite his appeals, both within the poems and in the Advertisement and the Preface which preceded the two volumes, to a familiar audience with a known and (to a large extent) shared frame of reference, Wordsworth seems to have expected his readers to be disconcerted by them. On one level, the Advertisement to the 1798 volume is a contribution to an existing debate about the propriety of 'simple' verse and 'low' subject-matter;[18] but the *radical* objections which it envisages ('they will look around for poetry, and will be induced to enquire by what species of courtesy these attempts can be permitted to assume that title') and the nature of its arguments against them, suggest that Wordsworth saw these poems as 'experiments' of a kind different from even their most progressive counterparts. Their readers, he says, will 'perhaps have to struggle with feelings of strangeness and aukwardness', and this not because the subject-matter or language of the poems would be unfamiliar to them, but because these poems seek to challenge 'our own pre-established codes of decision' – the grooves along which both poet and audience have been accustomed to order their experience.[19] In choosing to write within this genre, he saw himself as choosing to awaken and engage with the inarticulate expectations which its readers would have brought to it – expectations of elegant regularity, of neat conclusiveness, and of difficulties securely resolved or at least placed within mutually accepted schemata. And in *Lyrical Ballads* (like Blake, very differently, in his *Songs*) he seems to have set out to frustrate those expectations.

What is the significance of this? The answer, as in Blake's case, is best approached by exploring the ways in which these poems differ from those which they superficially resemble. One might, for example, compare some stanzas from an anonymous – and entirely typical – piece published in the *Town & Country Magazine* for 1794 with Wordsworth's 'Lines written in early spring', from the 1798 volume of *Lyrical Ballads*:

> Hark! catch you not their warbling wild,
> That softly flows the leafs among?
> Now loudly shrill – now sweetly mild,
> The descant of their thrilling song.

The earliest primrose of the year,
Beneath delights its flowers to spread;
The clustering harebell lingers near
The cowslip's dew-bespangled bed.

And while the western gales allay
The fervour of the noontide heat,
They whisper where retir'd from day,
The violet scents her low retreat.

             . . .

But heedless wanderer, come not here,
This feast was not prepared for thee,
Unless thy heart feels nought more dear
Than *Nature* and *Simplicity*.
          (from 'Inscription for a Coppice')[20]

I heard a thousand blended notes,
While in a grove I sate reclined,
In that sweet mood when pleasant thoughts
Bring sad thoughts to the mind.

To her fair works did nature link
The human soul that through me ran;
And much it griev'd my heart to think
What man has made of man.

Through primrose-tufts, in that sweet bower,
The periwinkle trail'd its wreathes;
And 'tis my faith that every flower
Enjoys the air it breathes.

The birds around me hopp'd and play'd:
Their thoughts I cannot measure,
But the least motion which they made,
It seem'd a thrill of pleasure.

The budding twigs spread out their fan,
To catch the breezy air;
And I must think, do all I can,
That there was pleasure there.

If I these thoughts may not prevent,
If such be of my creed the plan,
Have I not reason to lament
What man has made of man?
          ('Lines written in early spring')

Wordsworth's poem is clearly, as Mayo would have it, distinguished by its 'sheer literary excellence'. Beside the sentimental platitudes of the *Town & Country* poem, its clarity and precision stand out very sharply indeed. Yet it is difficult, seeing the two together, to find in Wordsworth's lines merely the 'intense fulfilment of an already stale convention'. For the well-worn clichés of 'Inscription for a Coppice' outline and depend upon a way of feeling which Wordsworth is not expressing more 'intensely', but implicitly questioning. Its muted personifications – the primrose which 'delights its flowers to spread', the harebell which 'lingers' and the winds which 'whisper' – all assume that the world of nature is easily assimilable to human attitudes and feelings. And central to 'Lines written in early spring' is a disturbing doubt as to whether it can ever be so assimilated.

Contemporary readers would have found nothing surprising in the first stanza of Wordsworth's poem: they might confidently have expected it to lead on to the same vague praise of '*Nature* and *Simplicity*' as that with which the *Town & Country* poem concludes. But the more alert of them would quickly have been disconcerted. For Wordsworth's poem has none of the mellifluous ease of 'Inscription for a Coppice': its rhythms are awkward and jerky. And this seems to be related to the repeated intrusion of the speaking 'I'. Where the earlier poet says with musical confidence:

> The earliest primrose of the year
> Beneath delights its flowers to spread;

Wordsworth is pedantically hesitant:

> Through primrose-tufts, in that sweet bower,
> The periwinkle trail'd its wreathes;
> *And 'tis my faith* that every flower
> Enjoys the air it breathes.
>
> [my italics]

He is not merely failing to offer the expected graceful clichés. With awkward, naive-seeming honesty he is exposing the complexity of that which such clichés obscure.

Other serious writers had mocked at the easy personifications of popular nature poetry: most famously, perhaps, Goldsmith, in his essay on pastoral in *The Citizen of the World*:

> How sad the groves and plains appear,
> And sympathetic sheep;

> Even pitying hills would drop a tear!
> *If hills could learn to weep.*
>
> ('On the Death of the Right Honourable *** ')

But Wordsworth's poem is not a parody: it is a careful portrayal of an actual experience. The scene he depicts is one of harmonious concord ('a thousand *blended* notes'), of graceful interconnections and interrelationships:

> Through primrose tufts, in that sweet bower,
> The periwinkle trail'd its wreathes;
>
> The budding twigs spread out their fan,
> To catch the breezy air;

But it is a scene from which his speaker is separate and dislocated. It is true that at some level he feels part of it:

> To her fair works did nature link
> The human soul that through me ran.

Yet this 'link' is made not by him, but by a 'nature' not susceptible of rational control. And with this intuition comes a fresh and humble sense of the utter unassimilability of that nature. He does not confidently assume that he can understand it: his attempts to do so register a new kind of uncertainty:

> The birds around me hopp'd and play'd:
> Their thoughts I cannot measure,
> But the least motion which they made,
> It seem'd a thrill of pleasure.

The pattern of the central four stanzas is one of disjunction: an exact articulation of a newly felt gap between the speaker and the world which he sees. The first two lines of each offer a delicate observation –

> The budding twigs spread out their fan,
> To catch the breezy air;

– and the last two his hesitant response:

> And I must think, do all I can,
> That there was pleasure there.

In one way, the effect is awkwardly naive. But the reader is being offered a much more sophisticated sense of the relationship between the reflecting consciousness and the natural world than that which is implicit in the graceful verse of the *Town & Country* poet. Here, nature is not a place of pleasurable retirement, the passive recipient of human projections: it is unfathomably and actively other. And the human being who confronts it is not assertively in control, even of his own reactions:

> And I must think, do all I can ...
>
> If I these thoughts may not prevent ...

The feeling is one of unease.

In the final stanza, the tense changes to the present, and the uneasiness comes to the foreground:

> If I these thoughts may not prevent,
> If such be of my creed the plan,
> Have I not reason to lament
> What man has made of man?

The rhythm is awkward and irregular: the natural harmony of the preceding stanzas – registered distinctly yet from a distance – has disappeared. With a clumsy fidelity to the inconclusiveness of actual experience Wordsworth leaves unresolved the disconcerting sense of isolation and separation that has been present throughout. Where the earlier poet ended decisively, with an assured appeal to '*Nature* and *Simplicity*', here we are left with a question, and a disquiet which there is no confident generalization to resolve.

The 'aukwardness' of 'Lines written in early spring' may be traced in different ways, in many other of the 1798 *Lyrical Ballads*. The reader who came to these poems with expectations formed by the magazine verse which they superficially resembled would have found those expectations frustrated and questioned, either by the speaker's naive fidelity to fact, or by a second dramatic voice within the poem. One after another, the poems in this collection expose the difficulties and complexities inherent in situations which the magazine verse had simplified into acceptable form. In 'Old Man Travelling', the careful dramatization of the first speaker's attempts to assimilate the baffling figure before him, and the old man's unassimilable reply, question that strategy whereby the poor became objects of edification, representatives of a 'simplicity' pleasing to the polite. In 'The Thorn', the narrator tells his story with a plodding loquaciousness which prevents the reader from fitting it into the expected – and satisfying – pattern of Gothic melodrama:

this poem, too, ends in uncertainty. Where a neat moral might have been expected, none is offered. The story of Simon Lee is not summed up by the usual appeal to pity (or – as in the more radical verse – to anger): instead we have the awkward inconclusiveness of the past continuous tense, pointing towards that which cannot be so neatly resolved:

> I've heard of hearts unkind, kind deeds
> With coldness still returning.
> Alas! the gratitude of men
> Has oft'ner left me mourning.

And instead of the 'anecdote' of the magazines, which leads, characteristically, to an edifying lesson, Wordsworth offers an ironic criticism of such attempts to 'point a moral': in 'Anecdote for Fathers' and 'We are seven', the irritating insistence of the rationalizing adult is met and defeated by the child's intransigent refusal to accept his categories.

Sometimes the departure from habitual patterns is explicitly signalled. Readers familiar with the vogue for poems about madness would have expected 'The Idiot Boy' to be resolved by a sentimental appeal to their sympathies: Wordsworth refuses so to resolve it. Instead (in a way more reminiscent of Shakespeare's direct dramatizations of madness than of more conventional eighteenth-century meditations upon it with which his readers would have been familiar),[21] he gives the voice of the boy himself:

> 'The cock did crow to-whoo, to-whoo,
> 'And the sun did shine so cold!'

Indeed, it seems to have been the idiot's inscrutability that attracted Wordsworth to the subject: 'I have often applied to idiots, in my own mind, that sublime expression of Scripture, that *their life is hidden with God*.'[22] But he does not merely present his polite readers with a glimpse of a consciousness quite different from theirs: he mocks their confident expectation that such a consciousness might be understood within their own categories, as part of a 'delightful tale':

> Oh Reader! now that I might tell
> What Johnny and his Horse are doing
> What they've been doing all this time,
> Oh could I put it into rhyme,
> A most delightful tale pursuing!

. . .

> I to the muses have been bound,
> These fourteen years, by strong indentures;
> Oh gentle muses! let me tell
> But half of what to him befel,
> For sure he met with strange adventures.
>
> Oh gentle muses! is this kind?
> Why will ye thus my suit repel?
> Why of your further aid bereave me?

And in 'Simon Lee' he hints at something worse than the absurdity of such expectations. Once again there is an explicit comment on the poem's deviation from the usual pattern –

> My gentle reader, I perceive
> How patiently you've waited,
> And I'm afraid that you expect
> Some tale to be related,

– but here there is a savage irony in that 'gentle'. For the story told in the poem has exposed the culpable limitations of the 'gentle' frame. Simon has not been presented as a picturesque character for an edifying 'tale', but as a real, struggling human being whose otherness shames and rebukes easy sentimentality.

In these poems of 1798 Wordsworth is clearly playing upon and drawing attention to his readers' simplifying schemata, refusing to present this expected subject-matter in easily digestible form, and demanding that they take a much more active attitude towards it:

> What more I have to say is short,
> I hope you'll kindly take it;
> It is no tale; but should you think,
> Perhaps a tale you'll make it.

Yet the actual achievement is rather more limited than the intention. The way in which these ballads draw attention to their own strategies betrays a poetic unsureness. Many of these pointers are very clumsy – jerks and shoves rather than subtle manipulations: Wordsworth's ironies are crude compared to the constantly shifting and really disconcerting attitude to the reader which one finds in, say, Swift or Sterne. In many of these 1798 ballads the reader *is* shocked into an awareness of the distortions involved in the easy superficiality of the magazine verse, the inadequacy of the ways of thinking and feeling it expressed. But the narrator's obtrusive insistence that he should not fall into sentimental simplifications often dominates the poem, and the shock remains closer to a consciousness of violated decorum than to a new sense of what these familiar situations might mean.

If this seems an ungenerous estimate, it is one which is prompted by Wordsworth's own achievement in many of the poems written for the 1800 volume. Here, the difficulties which the magazine verse glossed over and the earlier collection exposed, are far more fully explored – the disturbing sense of the disjunction between the human consciousness and the natural world which surrounds it, in (for instance) 'Nutting' and 'There was a Boy'; the challenge which the reality of the sufferings of others offers to polite sentimentality, in such poems as 'Point Rash-Judgment' and (very differently) 'Michael'. In these poems, Wordsworth is still addressing himself to readers who would have expected to find their habitual modes of thinking and feeling unobtrusively confirmed, rather than brought to consciousness and questioned. But he is now less concerned to disconcert such readers than to confront, in all their intransigent complexity, the subjects which they were used to having presented to them in acceptably graceful form. And in doing so he offers an entirely new poetic sense of the significance of that which the ease of the magazine verse had smoothed away.

One of the finest examples of this is the unnamed 'Lucy' poem:

> Strange fits of passion I have known,
> And I will dare to tell,
> But in the lover's ear alone,
> What once to me befel.
>
> When she I lov'd, was strong and gay
> And like a rose in June,
> I to her cottage bent my way,
> Beneath the evening moon.
>
> Upon the moon I fix'd my eye,
> All over the wide lea;
> My horse trudg'd on, and we drew nigh
> Those paths so dear to me.
>
> And now we reach'd the orchard plot,
> And, as we climb'd the hill,
> Towards the roof of Lucy's cot
> The moon descended still.

In one of those sweet dreams I slept,
Kind Nature's gentlest boon!
And all the while, my eyes I kept
On the descending moon.

My horse mov'd on; hoof after hoof
He rais'd and never stopp'd:
When down behind the cottage roof
At once the planet dropp'd.

What fond and wayward thoughts will slide
Into a Lover's head –
'O mercy!' to myself I cried,
'If Lucy should be dead!'

To its earliest readers this may have seemed a rather clumsy attempt to express a feeling which was a popular theme amongst the magazine poets: that of the lover's heightened vulnerability. Thomas Parnell, writing at the beginning of the century, but still a favourite in the magazines at its end, offers a charmingly typical example:

My days have been so wond'rous free,
    The little Birds that fly
With careless ease from Tree to Tree,
    Were but as bless'd as I.

Ask gliding Waters, if a Tear
    Of mine encreas'd their Stream?
Or ask the flying Gales, if e'er
    I lent one Sigh to them?

But now my former Days retire,
    And I'm by Beauty caught,
The tender Chains of sweet Desire
    Are fix't upon my Thought.

Ye Nightingales, ye twisting Pines!
    Ye Swains that haunt the Grove!
Ye gentle Echoes, breezy Winds!
    Ye close Retreats of Love!

With all of Nature, all of Art,
    Assist the dear Design;
O teach a young, unpractic'd Heart,
    To make my *Nancy* mine.

> The very Thought of Change I hate,
>   As much as of Despair;
> Nor ever covet to be great,
>   Unless it be for her.
>
> 'Tis true, the Passion in my Mind
>   Is mix'd with soft Distress;
> Yet while the Fair I love is kind,
>   I cannot wish it Less.[23]

Parnell's verses accord far more with late eighteenth-century taste than do Wordsworth's. Where his rhythms are easy, Wordsworth's are plodding. Where he moves lightly from one thought to the next, Wordsworth appears to be limited to the painstaking recording of prosaic detail. Yet with startling immediacy, Wordsworth's poem realizes the critical significance of feelings which in Parnell's are distanced by cliché and trivialized into a passing mood.

On one level, indeed, they are presented as *more* trivial. The self-deprecation of the opening lines –

> Strange fits of passion I have known,
> And I will dare to tell,
> But in the lover's ear alone,
> What once to me befel.

– might well have led the reader to expect a ballad-parody of love's foolishness. It is certainly true that in refusing to conventionalize his lover's feelings into the expected tasteful lyricism, Wordsworth exposes the childish egocentricity implicit in poetic postures such as Parnell's. His speaker recounts a simple incident – how he rode up a hill toward his lover's house and saw the moon suddenly disappear from view – and the fearful thought which it brought to his mind – 'If Lucy should be dead!'. But instead of presenting this as gracefully poetic 'sensibility', Wordsworth spells out its unpoetic mechanics. For the lover, the moon is 'descending', partly because of his own approach to the cottage which will block it from his view. With the natural egocentricity of perception he does not reflect on the way in which his own perspective determines what he sees. And this perceptual egocentricity has its ironic parallel in the egocentricity of his feelings. It is his inability to conceive of anything except as it appears from his own immediate point of view that makes the moon's movement out of his line of vision seem like its final disappearance: similarly, it is his failure to see the world except as a

47

mirror of his own emotions that turns that disappearance into terrifying ill-omen. The lover's fashionable vulnerability is less elegant and more childish than verse such as Parnell's would admit.

Yet Wordsworth does not merely expose his lover's foolishness. The narrative suspense he builds up leads the reader to identify with its irrational potency: the fear with which the poem ends remains disturbingly present, unexorcised by his self-disparagement. Indeed, it is subtly reinforced. For the story begins in the past tense, with a commonplace image of transience: perhaps Lucy *is* now dead:

> When she I lov'd, was strong and gay
> And like a rose in June ...

And the lover who travels toward her cottage is in one sense scarcely an agent at all. The monotonous rhythms which mime the steady movement of his horse suggest also his own trance-like state:

> In one of those sweet dreams I slept,
> Kind Nature's gentlest boon!
> And all the while, my eyes I kept
> On the descending moon.

His journey is presented less as a voluntary act than as 'What once *to me* befel' [my italics]: a passive immersion in a larger world of physical process.

And such an immersion, Wordsworth suggests, is the reverse of the security it seems. For the regular rhythms of the poem are not merely mesmeric: they have something of the relentless insistence of a clock:

> My horse mov'd on; hoof after hoof
> He rais'd and never stopp'd ...

And the repeated references to the 'descending' moon reinforce this sense of inexorable progression. Throughout the journey the lover's eyes have been fixed on that moon as his mind has been fixed on Lucy. At first it shines 'all over the wide lea': then, as it 'sinks' towards 'Lucy's cot', it mimes his undeviating journey towards her. But the trance-like state of beatitude which this unconscious identification of moon and Lucy produces in him depends upon its steady presence – and his own movement through time and space means that it will disappear from his view. The conclusion is inevitable; but it seems shockingly sudden:

> When down behind the cottage roof
> At once the planet dropp'd.

'Planet' rather than 'moon': the change of word emphasizes the shock. For 'planets' do not 'drop': they move, as Wordsworth and his readers would have been well aware, in perfectly ordered systems according to regular laws. Yet the reader, drawn into empathy with the lover's trance-like state, feels with him the shattering abruptness of that 'drop'. Objectively, it is an illusion: subjectively, it is a fact. And the unconscious link between moon and Lucy that the poem has been developing makes it a moment of emotional revolution. The lover's journey toward her house no longer seems a purposeful journey toward fulfilment: it has become a type of the movement of time toward her death.

The wry self-mockery with which the speaker announces his story, the literal exactness with which he records it, do, on one level, ridicule that graceful sentimentality which readers accustomed to lyrics like Parnell's might expect. But this lover's 'strange fit of passion' cannot be merely laughed at and dismissed. For the poem also shows it to be a sharply immediate realization of a truth which 'common sense' usually distances from emotional awareness. The laws of the physical world are indifferent to the individual perspective. It is an inescapable fact that as time passes and the lover approaches the cottage the moon which has been at the centre of his vision must disappear from his sight. And it is an equally inescapable fact that Lucy must one day die.

Just as the *Town & Country* poet (and the many others like him) turned their feelings of moral inadequacy before the self-sufficient harmony of nature into facile poetic postures, so writers such as Parnell had smoothed emotional vulnerability into something gracefully controllable. Like the other 'magazine poets', they treat potentially disturbing subject-matter with superficial ease: like them, they assume that such subjects can be contained within a shared framework of polite 'common sense'. But in the poems I have been discussing Wordsworth shows that such an assumption runs counter to the most ordinary – and the most basic – facts of individual experience. In their awkward fidelity to the actualities of such experience, 'Lines written in early spring' reveal a condition of isolation and separation which the conventions of contemporary 'nature poetry' would deny. The poems about the poor in the 1798 volume draw attention to the intransigent otherness of those who had hitherto been seen through the filter of polite pathos or protest. And 'Strange fits of passion' exposes that real vulnerability which the lightness of the magazine love lyric smoothed away. The infantile 'sweet dream' that the self is central to and in control of the world it inhabits perhaps lies somewhere behind Parnell's personifications: the shock of having to realize that the world is not thus controllable behind his easily expressed uneasiness. But his poem submerges such feelings and simplifies them into the acceptable mould. In 'Strange fits of passion' they are brought to light and their power acknowledged. For 'foolish' as the apprehensions to which they lead may be, this poem suggests that to deny them is to deny some of the most crucial truths about human experience.

Within the context of the magazine verse of the later eighteenth century, the poems of *Lyrical Ballads* seem as disconcerting as do Blake's *Songs* beside contemporary children's verse. Where the magazine verse is elegant and finished, these poems are awkward and inconclusive. Like Blake, Wordsworth appears to be challenging the ways of thinking and feeling which the readers he was addressing would have expected, in such a context, to find confirmed – ways of thinking and feeling of which they were probably barely aware. Yet like Blake's very different challenge to the defining voices of polite 'common sense', the impulse towards understanding experiences outside the polite framework which these poems express was one which some of his closest contemporaries shared. Indeed, in Wordsworth's case, it is one which can be traced – however confusedly and ambivalently – within the very genre in which he chose to write. Hitherto I have been emphasizing the imaginatively conservative, simplifying tendencies of the magazine verse. But some of it did, as we have seen, at least attempt to question polite certainties: indeed, enough such poems were printed in the magazines and in collections during the 1790s to provoke satiric parodies in the *Anti-Jacobin*.[24] In producing what appeared to be a collection of polite 'Jacobin' lyrics, Wordsworth was addressing himself to an established audience of readers who wished to have their sympathies enlarged and their sensibilities extended, and was aligning himself with writers who were exploring new kinds of subject-matter in new and consciously 'simple' ways.

His confidence in the existence of such a context of sympathetic progressive feeling is evident not merely in his hopes for the commercial success of *Lyrical Ballads*, but also in the plans he had made three years before for the founding of a 'monthly Miscellany' in collaboration with his friend William Mathews. In a letter to Mathews in June 1794, he discussed the nature of their potential readership:

As to our readers, you think that we should endeavour to obtain as great a variety as possible. You cannot, however, be ignorant that amongst the partizans of this war, and of the suspension of the *habeas corpus* act, amongst the mighty class of selfish alarmists, we cannot obtain a single friend. We must then look for protection entirely amongst the dispossessed advocates of liberty and discussion. These, whether male or female, we must either amuse or instruct; nor will our end be fully obtained unless we do both. The clergy of the Church of England are a body from which periodical publications derive great patronage: they however will turn from us. At the Universities of Oxford and Cambridge, amongst the young men, we shall not look in vain for encouragement. The dissenters, in general, are not rich; but in every town of any size there are some who would receive a work like ours with pleasure. I entirely approve of what you say on the subject of Ireland, and think it very proper that an agent should be appointed in Dublin to disseminate the impression. It would be well if either of you have any friends there to whom you could write soliciting their recommendation. Indeed it would be very desirable to endeavour to have, in each considerable town of Great Britain and Ireland, a person to introduce the publication into notice. To this purpose, when it is further advanced, I shall exert myself amongst all my friends.[25]

The audience envisaged here – an audience very similar to that to which *Lyrical Ballads* is apparently directed – is one which is disaffected from the political and religious Establishment. 'I solemnly affirm that in no writings of mine will I ever admit of any sentiment which can have the least tendency to induce my readers to suppose that the doctrines which are now enforced by banishment, imprisonment, &c, &c, are other than pregnant with every species of misery,' he wrote in a previous letter.[26] But it is a polite audience, one which can be reached through the recommendation of friends, one which may in some sense be 'dispossessed', but which is certainly educated. Wordsworth's sense that there was such an audience – and that it was sufficiently large to support a 'monthly Miscellany' of a progressive kind – is borne out by the experience of the *Monthly Magazine*, which had commenced in February 1796, and which boasted in July 1798, that it had 'attained within the course of three years, A SALE considerably superior to that of any other work of the same designation, and equal to that of any literary journal in this country'. The aim of the *Monthly Magazine* had been very close to that of Wordsworth and Mathews' projected *Philanthropist* – 'that of lending aid to the propagation of those liberal principles respecting some of the most important concerns of mankind, which have been either deserted or virulently opposed by other periodical miscellanies' (Preface to first issue of *Monthly Magazine*, February 1796) – and during the remainder of the decade, it consistently printed articles and letters protesting about the war and about social injustices, arguing for the freedom of the press, and enquiring into more general literary and moral topics.[27] Its poetry pages included Southey's original explorations of the psychology (and not merely the plight) of the poor; translations of Bürger's ballads; and poems with titles such as 'The Penitent Mother' (Miss Holcroft, October 1797), 'Elegy, occasioned by the present frequent and pernicious custom of monopolizing farms' (December 1796), 'The Negro' (Miss Holcroft, October 1797), 'To a Poor boy' (R. Anderson, September 1798). Clearly, the readers who sympathized with and bought such a magazine might be expected to buy *Lyrical Ballads*: and the success of the *Monthly Magazine* suggests that they existed in large numbers.

What were these readers like? They seem to have been liberal, educated men and women (the magazine displays some interest in the rights of women),[28] who were prepared to read sober, philosophical discussions on moral and aesthetic subjects, and whose letters to the journal display the same tone of rational enquiry. Politically, they could be quite radical, as a letter published in the October 1798 issue[29] (and signed simply 'An Englishman') shows:

government was instituted for the good of the many, not the emolument of the few.

That there at all times exists, in the majority of a political society, a right of making such alterations in their form of government, as upon mature deliberation they shall think conducive to the public welfare:

That privileged bodies derive all title to their privileges from the content and advantage of the whole:

That, therefore, wars and public burdens for the particular interest of those bodies are a public injustice.

That a friend of mankind may wish well to the cause of liberty all over the globe, without waiting for the permission of his own partial or prejudiced countrymen.

Finally, *Republicanism*, the spirit of which is, in fact, the very essence of every thing free in political constitutions, is not *Jacobinism*, but the very reverse.

But in many ways, the cultural background of these readers was very similar to that of those who supported the much more conservative *Gentleman's Magazine*. Some, like Wordsworth, were university educated; others were the products of the Dissenting Academies.

Most would have had some classical education, and some training in philosophy, mathematics and Newtonian physics:[30] all could be trusted – as Wordsworth hoped in his 1798 Advertisement – to be 'conversant with our elder writers, and with those in modern times who have been most successful in painting manners and passions'. They might best be described as those members of the middle and upper middle classes who were interested in social change (but, by 1798, almost certainly not in revolution),[31] who wished to explore questions about morality and society and the interconnections between them, and who were prepared to entertain new and progressive ideas.

Wordsworth, then, was writing for what he might have regarded as a sympathetic audience, and one with which he shared a great deal of common ground. But, as we have seen, *Lyrical Ballads* differs significantly from even the most 'radical' of the poetry to which such readers would have been accustomed – poetry written by men whose explicit attitudes were very close to Wordsworth's. Fawcett and Dyer, Thelwall and the young Southey had all written poems speculating on moral questions and meditating on nature; all had tried to poeticize their sense that the poor were 'in the eye of nature and of God, the real equals of their reputed superiors'.[32] But the contrast between the polished conclusiveness of their verse and the 'strangeness and aukwardness' with which readers of *Lyrical Ballads* were warned they would have to 'struggle' points toward the significance of Wordsworth's achievement. In these poems, like Blake in his *Songs*, Wordsworth is realizing the imaginative implications of the thinking of those contemporaries to whom he was closest – in a way which questions, as they did not, the dominant cultural patternings by which that thinking was still fundamentally structured.

For despite the apparent flexibility of the genre, to write acceptable magazine verse in the late eighteenth century was to be pulled toward exactly those patternings. Like children's verse, that published in the magazines was commercially very successful, and the taste for which it catered was, at basis, a taste for the 'polite' and the 'correct'. For the market at which it was aimed increasingly included not merely the upper but also the rising middle classes, a group whose cultural pretensions were closely linked to their upward social mobility.[33] These readers expected the magazine verse they favoured to be unambiguously 'polite': to have that confident ease which assumes control both of one's own experience and of the

human and non-human worlds around one, that secure generalization and moral conclusiveness which spring from the belief that
one's own 'common sense' is truly representative. Such modes of
thinking and feeling were natural to those whose way of life was
based on the control – or the implicit denial – of other kinds of
experience and other standards: and such were the modes of thinking
and feeling that structured the undemanding verse of the magazines.
One sees them in every feature of the poetry – in the regular rhythms
and neatly completing rhymes of the ballads, in the sentimental
appeals to the sensibility of the polite reader, in the implicit
assumption throughout of a shared, unquestioned polite frame of
reference. Their unexamined potency is most striking in that verse
which is 'radical' by intent, addressed to the kind of audience which
Wordsworth and Mathews envisaged. For there they work, poetically, against an imaginative realization of the implications of really
disturbing subject-matter; their pervasiveness as a mental set that is
neither considered nor questioned becomes apparent. It is this
mental set that *Lyrical Ballads*, like Blake's *Songs*, seeks to challenge.

The challenge may be traced in many ways throughout *Songs of
Innocence and of Experience* and *Lyrical Ballads*. Where 'refined'
sentimentality might have been expected, the reader is offered
clumsy and defensive narrative voices which point toward the
stubborn inscrutability of the suffering they would expound
('Simon Lee', 'The Thorn'), or disconcertingly direct attack ('Pity
would be no more / if we did not make somebody poor'). In both
collections, the customary controlling polite speaker is questioned
by voices other than his or her own: the expected generalizations are
not made. The rhythms are changing, sometimes awkward: there
are clumsy, 'inelegant' repetitions. These poems demand a new kind
of activity of their readers: not the passive acceptance of a finished
literary product, but a creative engagement with that which is
suggestively unresolved. Instead of neat, summatory morals and
messages there is teasing ambiguity ('The Lilly'), open-ended
questioning ('The Tyger'), disturbing inconclusiveness ('Simon
Lee') or broken-off exclamation ('Strange fits of passion'). Again
and again, in very different ways, both *Songs of Innocence and of
Experience* and *Lyrical Ballads* seek to disconcert the polite reader, to
foreground and question that which he unquestioningly assumed, to
suggest that his 'natural' modes of feeling and response are not
'natural' at all.

Many of their early readers seem to have registered this challenge simply by feeling that these poems were awkward or difficult to read, or – more extremely – by rejecting their pretensions to poetic status. Even where they were enthusiastically received, this often meant – as Coleridge noted of *Lyrical Ballads* – that the poems had merely been distorted into an acceptable form:

I am not half so irritated by hearing his enemies abuse him for vulgarity of style, subject and conception; as I am disgusted with the gilded side of the same meaning, as displayed by some affected admirers, with whom he is, forsooth, a *sweet, simple poet!* and *so* natural, that little Master Charles and his younger sister are *so* charmed with them, that they play at 'Goody Blake', or at 'Johnny and Betty Foy'![34]

This conventionalization of the unexpected and the disturbing is, as Gombrich and Ehrenzweig have shown, a basic fact of the psychology of artistic perception.[35] But as *Songs of Innocence and of Experience* and *Lyrical Ballads* sharply remind us, such conventionalization is not merely a private psychological mechanism: it is the internalized process by which a dominant culture maintains its hegemony. And each of the rapidly expanding genres within which these poems were written provides a remarkably clear example of the way in which that hegemony was extended in late eighteenth-century England. Each is addressed to a polite audience: each draws upon another, less polite culture – in the case of children's books, that of chap-book stories and verses and of children's jests and riddles; in the case of magazine verse that of traditional songs and ballads – and shapes it in ways acceptable to that audience. It does not seem to have been the 'simple' vitality of these earlier, more popular forms which drew Blake and Wordsworth towards the genres which thus transmuted them. The sophisticated frustration of the reader's expectations which one finds in their 'simple' poems suggests rather an awareness of and a concern with the ways in which those genres expressed, inculcated and reinforced polite modes of consciousness, didactically or reassuringly simplified those elements in contemporary experience which might have seemed threatening to the dominant culture, and actively assimilated that which was other to its mould. For both children's and magazine verse were, in late eighteenth-century England, part of a much wider social process: a process which may be traced in such diverse phenomena as the establishment of charity schools throughout the century[36] (and in the nature of the instruction they provided);[37] the publication of the Cheap Repository Tracts; the increasing official hostility towards plebeian forms of entertainment and belief (the 'moralizing' of the fairy story[38] and the proverb,[39] the sermons against popular superstitions,[40] the opposition to fairs and to popular sports[41]). It is a process whose implications are manifest in the confident simplicity of the children's and the magazine verse, where the potentially baffling or disturbing is brought firmly within the polite frame, where the speaker assumes control of his readers and implicitly claims to be speaking for all reasonable men. By choosing to write as they did within these genres, both Blake and Wordsworth showed an instinctive understanding of the workings of their culture far surer than that of many of the more explicitly radical thinkers of their day. And in these superficially 'simple' little poems they were engaging with and challenging it, not at an argumentative but at an imaginative level.

3   The Real Language of Men

> What usually is called 'creative individuality' is nothing but the
> expression of a particular basic, firmly grounded, and consistent
> line of social orientation.
>   (V. N. Volosinov, *Marxism and the Philosophy of Language*)[1]

Both *Songs of Innocence and of Experience* and *Lyrical Ballads* sought to
challenge some of the most basic expectations of the readers to
whom they were addressed. Yet there are some striking differences
between the two collections. Although the two volumes of *Lyrical
Ballads* contain poems of diverse kinds, sometimes dramatizing
different personae, one can trace a coherent and developing authorial
viewpoint throughout. But in *Songs of Innocence and of Experience*
conflicting views of the same situation are presented simply as
unresolved 'contraries'. *Lyrical Ballads* appeals to a world of shared
experience and a mutual will to understanding: such a world is not
envisaged in the Songs. The speakers there are unmediated and
unannounced: Blake assumes no intimacy with his readers. Yet his
vision, like Wordsworth's, was shaped by experiences and modes of
response which he shared with other men. And the significance of
the difference between their two collections begins to emerge more
clearly when one considers a crucial difference between two groups
with which each was closely associated.

There were many similarities between the early Swedenborgians
and progressive Dissenters such as those who supported the *Monthly
Magazine*. The moving spirits amongst both were educated men,
though their ideas were attractive to those of much more plebeian
origins. Dissenters and Swedenborgians were in various ways
disaffected from the Establishment,[2] and although the disaffection of
the former expressed itself more consistently in political terms, this
distinction was not noted by their opponents.[3] Yet in one important
respect they differed very greatly. The Dissenters had an unwaver-
ing confidence in the possibility of enlightenment through education: to them, the written word was the medium through which
values could be explored and shared. Their position was clearly
stated by Gilbert Wakefield: 'An intimate connection subsists

between letters and morality, between sensibility and taste, between an informed mind and a virtuous heart.'⁴ Dissenters were among the foremost educational theorists and practitioners of the century, and the mainspring of their educational theory (as also of their considerable achievements in science) was their belief in the moral value of learning and of 'candour' – free rational enquiry.⁵ There was nothing necessarily conservative in this belief of theirs: indeed, at a time when the education of the unprivileged was a controversial subject, it seems in some ways revolutionary.⁶ But it is a belief which distinguishes them sharply from early English followers of Swedenborg. One such, Thomas Hartley, in his Preface to the first English edition of Swedenborg's *Heaven and Hell*, suggests the difference very clearly:

Men had lost the true original language of nature (which expressed things according to their qualities and properties) before the flood, even so much of it as had remained among the posterity of Seth and Enoch for a considerable time; and this ignorance they fell into on their losing the knowledge of nature in its correspondence to divine and heavenly things; for nature in its proper order, as observed before, is the book of God, and exhibits spiritual things in material forms. In room therefore of this was substituted a language by letters and reading in books, to help him in this way for attaining to divine knowledge, as rudiments leading thereto in our present state of ignorance, in which literature is mistaken by most for wisdom itself.⁷

There is no faith in a gradual communal progress through education here. Instead, that 'wisdom' which can be conveyed through the official tradition of learning is seen as at best a poor substitute for a 'knowledge' accessible only to those who have not lost the capacity for spiritual vision.

In 1791 and 1792 this difference became the subject of explicit debate, in pamphlets published as 'letters' to one another by Joseph Priestley, the great radical Dissenter, and Robert Hindmarsh, a founder member and minister of the Church of the New Jerusalem.⁸ Priestley attacked the Swedenborgian system of correspondences because he saw it as a violation of the convention implicit in a shared language:

But in cases in which either reason or the plain sense of scripture fails you, you find abundant resources in secondary and spiritual senses of the sacred writings. The sacred writers, however, are far from saying that they had any other meaning than that which appears on the face of their writings, and which is to be found in the customary sense of their words; and if other senses be once admitted, there is no end of diversity of opinion. Different persons interpret even the literal sense differently. What then will be the case, if, besides this literal sense, there be another concealed one, with respect to which every person will, of course, think himself at liberty to form his own conjectures? ...

For though I have probably given as much attention to the scriptures as you have done, the construction that Mr. Swedenborg puts upon them appears to be extremely unnatural; and, divesting myself as much as I am able of all prejudice, I cannot help thinking that, if there be any use in language to express men's meaning, he has strangely misrepresented them.[9]

Hindmarsh, predictably, replied that the system of correspondences was not, like metaphor, arbitrary and personal, but 'the language of God himself'.[10] But Priestley's attack grasps the essence of the problem. Once one has denied the validity of 'customary' meanings, the whole notion of a shared progress through learning is thrown into question – as Hindmarsh himself makes clear:

the more I reflect on the learned, the laboured and the ingenious explanations given by the most celebrated writers on the subject, who have confined their ideas to natural, historical, and external things, the more I am convinced that *not one of them all*, however eminent or distinguished his name, has had even a faint glimpse of it's [sic] real and genuine meaning. I speak this without any derogation from the talents or acquirements of any writer; for I wish to pay a proper respect to every man of learning, who has in any measure laboured for the improvement and information of the world. But it seems to me impossible, that the most acute natural understanding could ever, by virtue of its own powers, penetrate into the interior recesses of the holy Word, which can only be brought to light by means of a revelation from the same Spirit which dictated it.[11]

Where the Dissenters accept 'the customary sense of words', the inherited wisdom of the official culture, the Swedenborgians – and herein lies their important similarity to the popular prophetic movements and antinomian sects deplored by polite observers – do not.[12] The disagreement is absolute.

Blake (who later in his life included Priestley in an unholy trinity with Bacon and Newton)[13] was probably not a Swedenborgian for more than a couple of years: Wordsworth was never formally a Dissenter. Their poetry does not in any simple sense reflect Swedenborgian or Dissenting beliefs. Yet each was deeply familiar with and responsive to the modes of thought of the group with which he associated. And the curious differences between the superficially similar *Songs of Innocence and of Experience* and *Lyrical Ballads* do seem to bear some relation to the difference here argued

VISION AND DISENCHANTMENT

out between these two groups – the one riven by internal quarrels, but by 1791 officially supporting the political Establishment,[14] the schematic dogmatism of its great system of correspondences effectively containing the fundamental cultural radicalism of that anti-traditional metaphoric apprehension of the world on which it was based: the other, politically radical, its proponents bravely defending (and sometimes, like Wakefield and Frend, suffering for) their beliefs, but thinking still within the framework of the dominant culture and its presuppositions. It is a difference which has far-reaching implications.

Distrust of 'learning' was by no means peculiar to the early Swedenborgians: it is to be found, for instance, amongst the antinomian sects of the Civil War period and beyond. And it was not in origin simply a reflex against the weight of inherited tradition, but part of a coherent claim for quite other modes of understanding and communicating which it was felt that 'learning' would destroy. Ultimately, the notion may be traced back via Boehme to Plato's distrust of the written word:

For these [letters], through the negligence of recollection, will produce oblivion in the soul of the learner; because, through trusting to the external and foreign marks of writing, they will not exercise the internal powers of recollection. So that you have not discovered the medicine of memory, but of admonition. You will likewise deliver to your disciples an opinion of wisdom, and not truth. For, in consequence of having many readers without the instruction of a master, the multitude will appear to be knowing in many things of which they are at the same time ignorant; and will become troublesome associates, in consequence of possessing an opinion of wisdom, instead of wisdom itself ... that which is committed to writing contains something very weighty, and truly similar to a picture. For the offspring of a picture project as if they were alive; but, if you ask them any question, they are silent in a perfectly venerable manner. Just so with respect to written discourse, you would think that they spoke as if they possessed some portion of wisdom. But if, desirous to be instructed, you interrogate them about any thing which they assert, they signify one thing only, and this always the same. And every discourse, when it is once written, is everywhere similarly rolled amongst its auditors, and even among those by whom it ought not to be heard; and is perfectly ignorant, to whom it is proper to address itself and to whom not. But when it is faulty or unjustly reviled, it always requires the assistance of its father. For, as to itself, it can neither resist its adversary, nor defend itself.[15]

The grounds of Plato's criticism are twofold: first, that the fixity of writing and its abstraction from the context of communication mean

60

that it is open to misinterpretation; second, that it encourages a passivity on the part of the reader remote from that true understanding which he describes in his *Seventh Letter*:

Thus much however I shall say respecting all those who either have written, or shall write, affirming that they know those things which are the objects of my study, (whether they have heard them from me or from others, or whether they have discovered them themselves), that they have not heard any thing about these particulars conformable to my opinion: for I never have written, nor ever shall write, about them. For a thing of this kind[16] cannot be expressed by words like other disciplines, but by long familiarity, and living in conjunction with the thing itself, a light as it were leaping from a fire will all on a sudden be enkindled in the soul, and there itself nourisheth itself.[17]

The experience here portrayed is akin to that which Boehme and the sectarists were to call 'vision', an experience in every respect the opposite of the passive reception of a decontextualized and fixed written text.[18] At best, in Plato's view, it might be kindled by the art of dialectic – an active interchange between two known partners, demanding a constant energy of engagement and a perpetual adjustment to and realization of what is being spoken:

SOCRATES: But what, shall we not consider another discourse, which is the genuine brother of this, how legitimate it is, and how much better and more powerful it is born than this? . . . That which, in conjunction with science, is written in the soul of the learner, which is able to defend itself, and which knows to whom it ought to speak, and before whom it ought to be silent.

PHAEDRUS: You speak of the living and animated discourse of one endued with knowledge; of which written discourse may be justly called a certain image.

. . .

SOCRATES: He [the man who possesses the science of things] will not, therefore, with anxious and hasty diligence write them in black water, sowing them by this mean with his pen in conjunction with discourses; since it is thus impossible to assist them through speech, and impossible sufficiently to exhibit the truth . . . But in my opinion, a much more beautiful study will result from discourses, when someone employing the dialectic art, and receiving a soul properly adapted for his purpose, plants and sows it in discourses, in conjunction with science; discourses which are sufficiently able to assist both themselves and their planter, and which are not barren, but abound with seed; from whence others springing up in different manners, are always sufficient to extend this immortal benefit, and to render their possessor blessed in as high a degree as is possible to man.[19]

Plato's suspicion of writing was far from populist: essentially, it was a plea for specialized schools of philosophy. It was this elitism which was taken up and stressed by Thomas Taylor, the late eighteenth-century Neoplatonist in whose translation Blake seems to have read Plato's works.[20] But the arguments against the written word developed in *Phaedrus* and the *Seventh Letter* might, in a semi-literate society, be very far from elitist. For if those who possess 'wisdom itself' are not necessarily the educated, they might be exactly the 'vulgar multitude' from whom Taylor believed the Platonic truth should be obscured. Indeed, the appeal to a vision superior to the knowledge transmitted through traditional learning is not merely egalitarian, but potentially revolutionary: for the unlearned, who do not possess 'an opinion of wisdom, instead of wisdom itself', may actually be seen as *more* open to visionary illumination than the educated. This is the feeling which informed the antinomian sects, and which can be traced in garbled form in the writings of the popular prophets: it is most clearly expressed, perhaps, in Boehme:

Our learned ones turn themselves Doctors and Masters, and yet *none of them* understands his *Mother Tongue*; they understand no more of the *Spirit*, than the Countryman does of his Tool to the Tillage of his Ground; they use only the bare contrived Form of the gross compounded Words, and understand not what the Word is in its sense.[21]

But when the Saints comprised their Doctrine in Writings, that thereby in their Absence it might be understood what they taught, then the World fell upon it, and every one desired to be such a Teacher, and thought the Art, Skill, and Knowledge stuck in the Letter; thither they came running, old and new, who for the most Part only stuck in the old Man, and had no knowledge of God; and so taught according to their own Conceits, from the written Words, and explained them according to their own Meaning.[22]

in *Jupiter*, Christ did make the Babes and Ignorant, of a very weak and mean Capacity, Knowing and Understanding, *viz.* of poor Fishermen, Carpenters, and the like Mechanicks, he made Apostles, and the most understanding Men of all; and also of poor, disrespected, vilified People, as of Women and simple ones, he made faithful, devout, dear, godly Children, who apprehended in themselves the Universal without any Art.[23]

And it is a view which was echoed, late in his life, by Blake. In the annotations he made in 1827 to 'Doctor Thornton's Tory Translation' of the Lord's Prayer he confronted Johnson's claim that 'the Bible is the most difficult book in the world to comprehend, nor can it be understood at all by the unlearned, except through the aid of critical and explanatory notes' with the angry comment: 'Christ & his Apostles were Illiterate Men; Caiphas, Pilate & Herod were Learned ... The Beauty of the Bible is that the most Ignorant and Simple Minds Understand it Best ... It is the learned that Mouth, and not the Vulgar' (K786–7).

For Blake, this was not merely a repetition of Behmenist doctrine. It was the expression of an exact and indignant sense of the way in which, within his own society, the polite culture of traditional learning was used to distort and mystify the experience of the 'Vulgar'. In these years such a sense was by no means peculiar to Blake: indeed, it was beginning to be articulated with a new vigour and confidence – most notably in the writings of Cobbett (especially his *Grammar* of 1819) and in the parodies of the Litany, the Catechism and the Lord's Prayer for which Hone had been prosecuted in 1817.[24] These latter certainly seem to lie behind Blake's parody of 'Doctor Thornton's Tory Translation, Translated out of its disguise in the Classical and Scotch Languages into the vulgar English':[25]

Our Father Augustus Caesar, who art in these thy Substantial Astronomical Telescopic Heavens, Holiness to thy Name or Title, and reverence to thy Shadow. Thy Kingship come upon Earth first & thence in Heaven. Give us day by day our Real Taxed Substantial Money bought Bread; deliver from the Holy Ghost so we call nature whatever cannot be Taxed; for all is debts & Taxes between Caesar & us & one another; lead us not to read the Bible, but let our Bible be Virgil and Shakespeare; & deliver us from Poverty in Jesus, that Evil One. For thine is the Kingship, or Allegoric Godship, and the Power, or War, & the Glory, or Law, Ages after Ages in thy descendants; for God is only an Allegory of Kings & nothing Else. Amen.

(K788–9)

But Blake's annotations display a fuller and more acute consciousness of the issues involved than one finds in any other writer of this time, a consciousness forced upon him by his struggles as a creative artist with 'the stubborn structure of the Language' (K668).

They are for him issues to be fought out *within* that language: it is entirely fitting that his rhetorical outburst on behalf of the 'Kingdom of Jesus' and against the 'Classical Learned' – 'I look upon this as a Most Malignant & Artful attack upon the Kingdom of Jesus By the Classical Learned, thro' the Instrumentality of Dr. Thornton. The Greek & Roman Classics is the Antichrist' (K786) – should end with a defiant reference to his own colloquialism – 'I say Is and not Are as most expressive and correct too.' The spoken language may not obey the rules of grammar. But it is 'most expressive and correct too' because it is grounded in rather than removed from daily life. In Thornton's 'New Translation', the concrete images and natural speech rhythms of the Authorized Version had been turned into portentous, Latinate abstractions: the directness of 'Our Father' becoming 'O Father of Mankind'; the simplicity of 'which art in Heaven', 'who dwellist in the highest of Heavens'; and the plain speech of 'Give us this day our daily bread', 'Grant unto me, and the whole world, day by day, an abundant supply of spiritual and corporeal Food'. Such a 'translation' as Blake saw, was mystificatory: it enabled a masking of the contradiction between expressed belief and actual practice which was only too evident when its abstractions were retranslated: 'Give us the Bread that is our due & Right, by taking away Money, or a Price, or Tax upon what is Common to all in thy Kingdom' (K788).

This politically informed defence of the vernacular against the language of 'learning' is very close to Hone or to Cobbett. Yet to think of either of these figures is to realize Blake's essential difference, and the importance of his Behmenist inheritance, with its valuing of 'vision'. For the views developed in his annotations to Thornton were not to him new ideas formed by the emerging 'radical culture' of the 1820s.[26] They were integral to that sense of his society and of the place of artistic creation within it which shaped his whole life's work. These annotations were written at the end of his life, jotted in the margin of a book which angered him. But it is significant that in thinking there about the way in which the spoken language evades rules of 'correctness' the example he chose should be from the 'Introduction' to his early *Songs of Innocence*:

> In a book where all may Read, &
> In a book which all may Read, & } are equally Right
> In a book that all may Read

(K787)

The choice may have been quite fortuitous: also in this last year of his life he wrote to George Cumberland: 'I am now Printing a Set of the Songs of Innocence & Experience for a Friend at Ten Guineas which I cannot do under Six Months consistent with my other Work' (K878). Perhaps he had been working on it when he read Thornton. Yet there seems to be a deeper logic to the association. For what as an old man Blake expressed as an angry, shorthand plea for the language of daily life is in that 'Introduction' articulated as a coherent artistic vision. The gap between actual experience and cultural definition – seen, in the annotations to Thornton, as the source of mystification and hypocrisy – is the subject of the poem:

Introduction

Piping down the valleys wild
Piping songs of pleasant glee
On a cloud I saw a child,
And he laughing said to me.

Pipe a song about a Lamb:
So I piped with merry chear,
Piper pipe that song again –
So I piped, he wept to hear.

Drop thy pipe thy happy pipe
Sing thy songs of happy chear,
So I sung the same again
While he wept with joy to hear.

Piper sit thee down and write
In a book that all may read –
So he vanish'd from my sight,
And I pluck'd a hollow reed.

And I made a rural pen,
And I stain'd the water clear,
And I wrote my happy songs,
Every child may joy to hear.

The two opening lines, with their unattached present participles, give a sense of undirected, timelessly spontaneous energy. It is not until the third that it begins to become clear whence this repeated 'piping' comes, or whether it is to be seen as past or present activity. It is an energy that is, at first, expressive rather than communicative: but as the poem proceeds it becomes channelled and delimited. The self who pipes is defined not in that original expressiveness, but as it confronts another: 'On a cloud I saw a child.' The exchange which follows is one of happy reciprocity, in which each instantly responds to and satisfies the other:

Pipe a song about a Lamb:
So I piped with merry chear,
Piper pipe that song again –
So I piped, he wept to hear.

But it is also one in which spontaneity steadily disappears. The repetition of 'again', here and in the following stanza, underlines the process. Against the unique and changing immediacy of a living situation, in which response can be direct and flexible, is beginning to be placed another possibility: that of a definition which enables repetition, so that something of the emotion felt in the original experience can be transmitted and reproduced. The 'piping' is abandoned for words:

> Drop thy pipe thy happy pipe
> Sing thy songs of happy chear,
> So I sung the same again . . .

And in the two final stanzas, this process of definition reaches what is in one sense its conclusion. The words of the song materialize as the written words of a book: not easily and effortlessly, but by an emphasized process of labour.[27] The process and product of creation are no longer fused, as in the 'piping', but separated out: experience is further abstracted from the original living moment. And as the piper is bidden to write, the child, seemingly inevitably, disappears. The echoing reciprocity of the preceding stanzas, with its satisfying sense of balance and closure, gives way to a series of 'And's' which stress an insistently linear movement. One thing no longer answers to another: instead, there is a determined unilateral action:

> And I *pluck'd* a hollow reed.

> And I *made* a rural pen,
> And I *stain'd* the water clear,
> And I *wrote* my happy songs . . .
> [my italics]

The water is 'stain'd' to make ink.[28] The ambiguity of the image – an image at once of creation and pollution – focusses what has been suggested throughout the poem, as the 'piping' of the opening becomes a material object. To Blake, the writing of a book seems to be a problematic activity. For it involves a shaping of that which is constantly changing and directly 'heard' into fixed and visible form:[29] a shaping in which first expressive spontaneity, and then the satisfying reciprocity of face-to-face communication are lost. And that which replaces them is a medium at once unchanging in appearance and unpredictable in effect, susceptible of varying interpretations – 'Every child *may* joy to hear' – or of no interpretation at all – 'In a book that all *may* read.' For communication becomes more uncertain as it becomes potentially more general:

the sure, mutually responsive relationship between singer and listener is lost in the rigidified book.

In *The Marriage of Heaven and Hell*, engraved in the years between the two collections of Songs, Blake was to give more direct and ironic expression to that sense of books as the mere repositories of contracted vital energies that is hinted at here:

I was in a Printing house in Hell, & saw the method in which knowledge is transmitted from generation to generation.

In the first chamber was a Dragon-Man, clearing away the rubbish from a cave's mouth; within, a number of Dragons were hollowing the cave.

In the second chamber was a Viper folding round the rock & the cave, and others adorning it with gold, silver and precious stones.

In the third chamber was an Eagle with wings and feathers of air: he caused the inside of the cave to be infinite; around were numbers of Eagle-like men who built palaces in the immense cliffs.

In the fourth chamber were Lions of flaming fire, raging round & melting the metals into living fluids.

In the fifth chamber were Unnam'd forms, which cast the metals into the expanse.

There they were receiv'd by Men who occupied the sixth chamber, and took the forms of books & were arranged in libraries. (K154–5)

This is that progression away from 'the true original language of nature' towards 'our present state of ignorance, in which literature is mistaken by most for wisdom itself' which Thomas Hartley had outlined in his Preface to Swedenborg's *Heaven and Hell*: here, vividly imagined and culminating with devastating anticlimax in 'arranged in libraries'. Here, as in Hartley, there is a questioning of the value of that knowledge that can be 'transmitted from generation to generation' – a questioning which had by 1791 found political expression in Paine's *Rights of Man*:

Every age and generation must be as free to act for itself, *in all cases*, as the ages and generations which preceded it. The vanity and presumption of governing beyond the grave, is the most ridiculous and insolent of all tyrannies. Man has no property in man; neither has any generation a property in the generations which are to follow ... I am contending for the rights of the *living*, and against their being willed away, and controlled and contracted for, by the *manuscript assumed authority* of the dead.[30]

But Blake voices his distrust of 'books' not in a religious tract or a political pamphlet, but in an illuminated book which he clearly saw as an enduring work of art. And in the 'Introduction' to *Songs of Innocence* he explores the paradoxical nature of that enterprise.

For the poem does not simply trace a contraction of energy. Its final line might equally suggest an opening out, a leading on to new experience; and this sense is reinforced by its title. It introduces a book of songs, not for the learned, but for 'every child', a book which is accessible to anyone who can read, a book addressed not merely to present readers, but also to posterity. The 'may' of the final line, which moves the poem from the past tense of narrative into the present tense of actuality, registers both a doubt and an affirmation.

> And I wrote my happy songs,
> Every child may joy to hear.

The progression portrayed has led away from spontaneity, vitality and immediate responsiveness. But it has also moved outwards from one particular encounter, toward a potentially joyful relationship not with one, but with 'every child'.

In the galling obscurity of his later years, Blake's claim for the universality and permanence of his art was to become more defiant:

> Still admir'd by Noble minds,
> Follow'd by Envy on the winds,
> Re-engrav'd Time after Time,
> Ever in their youthful prime,
> My designs unchang'd remain.
> Time may rage but rage in vain.
> For above Time's troubled Fountains
> On the Great Atlantic Mountains,
> In my Golden House on high,
> There they Shine Eternally.
>
> (MS. notebook 1808–11 K558)

But this single-minded assertion seems strident beside the careful balance between uncertainty and assurance that is maintained in 'Introduction'; and it serves to point by contrast to the complexity of the view of art that is presented there – 'Not a Letter ... is Insignificant' (K611): and one of the most haunting features of the poem is the slight unexpectedness of its final word. We 'read' rather than 'hear' what is written: while it might be natural for a child's book to be read aloud, Blake's book, with its brightly coloured illustrations and its tiny visual images (such as those on this plate) is obviously meant to be looked at. On the title-page which precedes this, two children are pictured kneeling at the feet of a woman, not looking up and listening, but with heads bent over the book on her lap. And in the series of verbs which describe the making of the

THE REAL LANGUAGE OF MEN

words on the page, Blake stresses the materiality of his book in a way which is curiously at odds with this final 'hear'. The disjunction is unemphatic, but deliberate For this is not simply a poem about the production of a book: it is a poem about the creation of a work of art. And in this apparently simple closing stanza Blake is presenting a far from simple sense of the kind of continuing life the work of art can have.

It lives, for him, not as a reified object, but in the way in which it *may* continue to 'rouze the faculties to act' (K793): in the potential – though only potential – response of 'every child'. The onward movement of proud affirmation in the notebook lines quoted above does not admit this unsureness: but here it is balanced by a vital open-endedness which those lines do not have. For the lastingness of his art is imaged not as an eternal 'Shining' 'above Time's troubled Fountains', but as an individual ('Every', not 'all') renewal of the original child's delight:

> While he wept with joy to hear.

> Every child may joy to hear.

It is a renewal very different from the passive reception of the 'knowledge' which is 'transmitted from generation to generation'. For the poem is not, like that knowledge, a set of abstractions from the flux of real life, but a realization of living experience through all the expressive resources of language: an 'Image' to be 'entered into by the Imagination' (K611), in an act which is itself a new and living experience. And the syntactic alteration in Blake's repetition of 'joy to hear' quietly affirms that although this poetic response may be less certain than the face-to-face interchange which his poem images, it is potentially just as immediate and as dynamically real.[31]

A curiously double attitude towards the written word is thus being articulated in this poem. On the one hand, Blake is pointing to its abstraction from actual life, its tainted materiality, its ambiguous fixity and permanence: on the other, he is suggesting that poetic creation is the 'seed' by which vision may perpetually be renewed (K605). The effect is not one of paradox or contradiction: both attitudes are part of a coherent poetic vision. And it is a vision whose implications are worked out in the *Songs* which this poem introduces.

It is apparent, for instance, in that disconcerting refusal to allow easy generalization which we have traced in 'The Lilly' and shall trace in the dislocated 'morals' of such Songs of *Innocence* as 'The

Chimney Sweeper' and 'Holy Thursday': a refusal which throws the
reader's habitual passivity before 'books' sharply into question, and
exposes the problematic nature of the 'abstraction' which books
represent. Indeed, 'The Human Abstract', which explores the
distortions of abstraction most directly and extensively, is echoed
again and again in the later prophecies, as Blake images the Urizenic
perpetuation of 'the Tree of Mystery' as a relentless process of
writing and reading:[32]

> Soon shot the painted root
> Of Mystery under his heel;
>
> It grew a thick tree: he wrote
> In silence his book of iron,
> Till the horrid plant bending its boughs
> Grew to roots when it felt the earth,
> And again sprang to many a tree.
>
> (*The Book of Ahania*, III, 61–7, K252)

> For Urizen fix'd in envy sat brooding & cover'd with snow;
> His book of iron on his knees, he trac'd the dreadful letters
> While his snows fell & his storms beat to cool the flames of Orc
> Age after Age, till underneath his heel a deadly root
> Struck thro' the rock, the root of Mystery accursed shooting up
> Branches into the heaven of Los: they, pipe form'd, bending down
> Take root again where ever they touch, again branching forth
> In intricate labyrinths o'erspreading many a grizly deep.
>
> Amaz'd started Urizen when he found himself compass'd round
> And high roofed over with trees; he arose, but the stems
> Stood so thick he with difficulty & great pain brought
> His books out of the dismal shade, all but the book of iron.
> Again he took his seat & rang'd his Books around
> On a rock of iron frowning over the foaming fires of Orc.
>
> (*Vala, or The Four Zoas*, Night the Seventh, 28–41 K321)

Such passages illuminate – but are still more illuminated by – the
Songs. For, as two modern writers on the implications of literacy
have argued:

the written word suggests an ideal of definable truths which have an
inherent autonomy and permanence quite different from the phenomena of
the temporal flux and of contradictory verbal usages. In oral cultures, words
– and especially words like 'God', 'Justice', 'Soul', 'Good' – may hardly be
conceived of as separate entities, divorced from both the rest of the sentence
and its social context. But once given the physical reality of writing, they
take on a life of their own.[33]

Songs of Innocence and of Experience, addressed to readers accustomed to assume 'definable truths which have an inherent autonomy and permanence', display an extraordinary sharp awareness of this. For they set out to awaken those readers to a sense of 'the temporal flux and contradictory verbal usages' which have shaped their language, and to expose the mystifying half-life which it has taken on.[34] The volume opens with an image of a creator working with tainted materials: it goes on to show – not by argument, but by a poetic realization of the contradictions within an actual society – how the 'official' language of that society, to the polite reader transparent and unproblematic, is in fact far from transparent and deeply problematic. And since that society was one in which the dominant culture was literate and many of those on whom it sought to impose were not, the image of the book became for Blake a 'minutely Appropriate' (K596) and tangible symbol of the process of abstraction and mystification and control he sought to condemn.[35]

Yet despite this, and despite the egalitarian implications of 'Every child may joy to hear', the book in which these poems are printed is not a cheap chap-book which might be read aloud to the widest possible audience. Indeed, at a time when publishing was a booming industry it is a striking phenomenon. Blake, whose trade as an engraver would have impressed upon him daily the fact that books are reproducible commodities, addresses his appeal to 'every child' not through the medium of such a book, but through a book whose production he was to keep under his own control throughout his life (and beyond) in a way unparalleled by the practice of any other major English writer. The illuminated copies of the *Songs* were not reprintable texts, but unique works of art – and they have remained so, despite the efforts of the Trianon Press. Their uniqueness is the intimate expression of the complex and far from negative sense of the nature of poetic art which is articulated in the 'Introduction' to *Songs of Innocence*. The two final lines of the poem leave the reader with a lasting sense of disjunction – between the material finality of 'wrote', underlined by the fact that it is the fourth of a series of active verbs of creation and violation (all prefixed by an imprinting succession of 'And I's), and the ambiguous airiness of 'may joy to hear'; between that which is stamped down for the eye, and that which is more instantly, less controllably available to the ear. It is a disjunction which is repeated throughout the *Songs* – most obviously in the ambiguous, sometimes ironic and always dialectical difference between text and illustration, a difference which suggests that any one mode of perception is relative, that neither visual nor verbal forms

VISION AND DISENCHANTMENT

may constitute a final or adequate embodiment of abstractable truth. There is no unilateral message for passive acceptance: instead, each plate 'rouzes the faculties to act'. And it is in this capacity to call forth the imaginative energy of the beholder – 'the seed of contemplative Thought' (K605) – that the art consists: not in what is perceived through the differently filtering senses, the 'narrow chinks of his cavern' (K145).

To deal adequately with the interplay between visual and verbal forms in the *Songs* would be the work of another book than this.[36] But the sense of art to which that interplay points can be traced in some of their most puzzling verbal features: their refusal to 'instruct', to confirm expectations of closure, finality, and unambiguous generalization; the apparently unrelated perspectives from which they address their audience. The reader is not offered an authoritative and static text, but called upon to participate in a dynamic act of creation. It is an act of creation which involves a curiously sceptical attitude towards the language of which the poems are made, but that scepticism is far from merely negative. 'The Lamb' and 'Infant Joy', for instance, critically foreground a process of naming which is conventionally one of imposing definitions. But in presenting an entirely different kind of 'calling', springing out of a different mode of relating to the other, they show how such 'calling' might actually create a pattern of satisfying interchange: one which points forward, as definition does not, into changing future possibility. The Songs of *Experience* expose the mystifying function of the reified word: but also, by revealing its genesis in human *praxis*, they point towards the possibility of its being de-fetishized:

> Pity would be no more
> If we did not make somebody poor.

The vision these poems offer is thus very different from that ironic mockery of controlling definition which Blake was to present in *The Marriage of Heaven and Hell* – 'what the religious *call* Good and Evil'; 'Energy, *call'd* Evil', 'the original Archangel, or possessor of the command of the heavenly host, is *call'd* the Devil or Satan, and his children are *call'd* Sin and Death. But in the Book of Job, Milton's Messiah is *call'd* Satan' (Plates 3–6, K149–50, my italics). Less polemically but more precisely and variously than this, the Songs draw attention to the gap between actual experience and its fixed embodiment in language: to the way in which language may be used to mystify and control. But they also display a paradoxical faith in that liberating and creative potentiality which may be realized, and

72

continue to be realized, by the 'Poetic Genius' even within the tainted language of an exploitative society.

In the 1790s the writings of Paine and his followers were to sharpen and politicize awareness of the gulf between the real experience of large sections of the society and the official view of it which the dominant culture maintained. A whole range of sectarists – Swedenborgians, the followers of the popular prophets, antinomian survivals of the Civil War sects – proposed their own more or less confused alternative 'readings' of the times. Blake was familiar with all these groups, and with the actualities of the society to which they responded. And in *Songs of Innocence and of Experience* he offers a poetic articulation of the crucial bases of their thinking – their suspicion of inherited and imposed 'wisdom', and their sense of the way in which that 'wisdom' blocks other possibilities, variously (and in comparison to Blake, vaguely) seen as 'freedom' or 'vision'. The radical possibilities of this political and religious opposition to the dominant culture were never, by these groups, fully realized: the impulse of resistance, the openness to other kinds of experience, became abstracted into doctrines which all too readily mirrored that which they sought to oppose. But the poems in *Songs of Innocence and of Experience*, more than the work of any other English poet resisting abstraction and reproduction, refusing to offer complete and unilateral messages, demand that the reader actively grasps their meaning, and maintain their subversive, unincorporable potentiality: 'Every child may joy to hear.'

Two of the *Lyrical Ballads* of 1798 also explore the difference between unmediated experience and that which can be passed on in books. Yet 'Expostulation and Reply' and 'The Tables Turned' are most unlike the 'Introduction' to *Songs of Innocence*. They have the same simple ballad form: but their language is abstract and Latinate compared to Blake's childlike repetitions:

> She has a world of ready wealth,
> Our minds and hearts to bless –
> Spontaneous wisdom breathed by health,
> Truth breathed by cheerfulness.

> One impulse from a vernal wood
> May teach you more of man;
> Of moral evil and of good,
> Than all the sages can.
> ('The Tables Turned')

And the encounter they dramatize (explicit in the first, implicit in the second) is very different from that between piper and child. It is a debate between two serious-minded friends, who, despite their light-hearted disagreement as to how moral understanding and improvement might be arrived at, share the same basic assumption that these are desirable goals. The speaker of 'One impulse from a vernal wood' has the final word, rather than he who extols 'the spirit breath'd / From dead men to their kind'. But, as the latter image suggests, traditional learning is given some poetic weight, as a living affirmation of community. There is nothing of Blake's ironic sense of 'the knowledge transmitted from generation to generation', nothing like the unreconciled disjunction at the closing of his 'Introduction'. Instead, the opposition remains a superficial one, and each poem ends in a witty paradox which in a sense reconciles speaker and objector – 'wise passiveness', 'a heart / That watches and receives'.

Yet the problem of living experience versus literary text was one which preoccupied Wordsworth, and one which he considered at length in the Prefaces to the two volumes of *Lyrical Ballads*. These, too, are very different from the 'Introduction' to *Songs of Innocence*, and not merely in that they are written in prose. They are addressed not, with ambiguous universality, to 'Every child' who '*may* joy to hear', but to an adult, educated 'Reader' of whom Wordsworth seems to be sure and with whose expectations he seems familiar. They explicitly mediate between this reader and the poems which are to follow: they do not, like that 'Introduction', present an enigmatic challenge. But in some ways the concerns of these prefaces are similar to those we have been tracing in Blake. The latter presents his book not to the learned or sophisticated, but to 'Every child': similarly, Wordsworth argues that: 'The Poet writes under one restriction only, namely, that of the necessity of giving immediate pleasure to a human Being possessed of that information which may be expected of him, not as a lawyer, a physician, a mariner, an astronomer or a natural philosopher, but as a Man.'[37] Both lay stress less on the finished work of art than on the experience it is capable of evoking: where Blake writes, 'just so the Imaginative Image returns, by the seed of Contemplative Thought...' (K605), Wordsworth claims of poetry that: 'its object is truth, not individual and local, but general, and operative; not standing upon external testimony, but carried alive into the heart by passion.'[38] And both are concerned with the way in which the truth of immediate experience – 'Piping

down the valley wild', 'The eye it cannot chuse but see, / W
bid the ear be still' – is lost in the attempt to give it more perma.
form. In *The Marriage of Heaven and Hell* Blake had traced the
contraction of primal energy into 'the forms of books . . . arranged in
libraries': in the 'Appendix on Poetic Diction' to the 1802 edition of
Lyrical Ballads Wordsworth offers a similar account in more
specifically literary terms:

the first Poets, as I have said, spake a language which, though unusual, was
still the language of men. This circumstance, however, was disregarded by
their successors; they found that they could please by easier means: they
became proud of a language which they themselves had invented, and which
was uttered only by themselves; and, with the spirit of a fraternity, they
arrogated it to themselves as their own. In process of time metre became a
symbol or promise of this unusual language, and whoever took upon him to
write in metre, according as he possessed more or less of true poetic genius,
introduced less or more of this adulterated phraseology into his composi-
tions, and the true and the false became so inseparably interwoven that the
taste of men was gradually perverted and this language was received as a
natural language and at length, by the influence of books upon men, did to a
certain degree really become so.[39]

Where Blake focusses on that process of abstraction which is
exemplified by the written word, Wordsworth's subject is the
clichéd language of poetic diction: a language which distorts and
mystifies that actuality it purports to describe: 'and with the progress
of refinement this diction becomes daily more and more corrupt,
thrusting out of sight the plain humanities of nature by a motley
masquerade of tricks, quaintnesses, hieroglyphics, and enigmas'.[40]
Divorced from the flux of real life, and slavishly copied rather than
continually created, it prevents openness toward 'the plain
humanities of nature' and reduces that which might challenge to that
which is merely accepted.

Wordsworth's concern with this may be traced throughout *Lyrical
Ballads*. Many of those of 1798 explicitly question conventional,
clichéd approaches to the subjects with which they deal.[41] Yet
Wordsworth's essential interest is not as much in a particular kind of
debased poetic convention as in the problem of which it is an
extreme example: the fact that no description can ever embrace the
totality of actual experience, that it will inevitably in some way
distort or falsify: 'However exalted a notion we would wish to
cherish of the character of a Poet it is obvious that, while he describes
and imitates passions, his situation is altogether slavish and mechan-

ical, compared with the freedom and power of real and substantial action and suffering.'[42] And thus, in the poems of 1798, the conventional omniscient narrator becomes problematic. In a deliberately literal-minded way, Wordsworth records only what could actually be seen from a single limited point of view, and refuses (in what amounts to a parody of the reader's expectations) to speculate beyond it. Dramatically, he points toward the stubborn actuality of other, and quite unassimilable, points of view. In their disconcerting absence of mediating interpretation, these poems suggest the disquieting nature of a reality which is not filtered through familiar schemata, but which is momentarily confronted as quite unfathomable.

In the very different poems of the 1800 volume, there is a similar sense of the gap between actual experience (whether of the past self or of others) and description, and a similar uneasiness with confident narrative voice. Poem after poem ends not with conclusive resolution, but with an image of apparently intractable otherness:

> I believe, that near his grave
> A full half-hour together I have stood,
> Mute – for he died when he was ten years old.
>
> ('There was a Boy')

> No motion has she now, no force
> She neither hears nor sees
> Roll'd round in earth's diurnal course
> With rocks and stones and trees!
>
> ('A slumber did my spirit seal')

> Matthew is in his grave, yet now
> Methinks I see him stand,
> As at that moment, with his bough
> Of wilding in his hand.
>
> ('The Two April Mornings')

> and the remains
> Of the unfinished Sheep-fold may be seen
> Beside the boisterous brook of Green-head Gill.
>
> ('Michael')

Even in those poems which offer a final moral judgment, experiences like these are presented: experiences which cannot be contained within the terms of that judgment:

his legs so long and lean
That for my single self I look'd at them,
Forgetful of the body they sustain'd.

('Point Rash-Judgment')

Even then, when from the bower I turn'd away,
Exulting, rich beyond the wealth of kings
I felt a sense of pain when I beheld
The silent trees and the intruding sky.

('Nutting')

Something of the feeling behind such passages is indicated, in the 1800 Preface, in Wordsworth's proud plea for fidelity to the uniqueness of the artist's vision, his insistence that it should not be distorted into the shapes which his society finds acceptable:

I have no doubt that in some instances feelings even of the ludicrous may be given to my Readers by expressions which appeared to me tender and pathetic. Such faulty expressions, were I convinced they were faulty at present, and that they must necessarily continue to be so, I would willingly take all reasonable pains to correct. But it is dangerous to make these alterations on the simple authority of a few individuals, or even of certain classes of men; for where the understanding of an Author is not convinced, or his feelings altered, this cannot be done without great injury to himself: for his own feelings are his stay and support, and if he sets them aside in one instance, he may be induced to repeat this act till his mind loses all confidence in itself and becomes utterly debilitated.[43]

This concern with the way in which the essence of new experience escapes definition, and with how inherited modes of formulation can prevent its realization, may seem reminiscent of Blake. But there is nothing in *Lyrical Ballads* comparable to Blake's exploration of the mystifyingly destructive power of reified language in such poems as 'The Human Abstract': and this absence points toward a significant difference between the two collections. For even in those poems from the 1798 volume which dramatize baffling confrontation with otherness, there is a sense not merely of the inadequacy of language, but also of its capacity to signify and memorialize that which it can never wholly incorporate. The wailing of the woman in 'The Thorn' echoes at the end of the poem and continues to compel the narrator. Simon Lee's lost past lives in the communal memory –

I've heard he once was tall ...
To say the least, four counties round
Had heard of Simon Lee.

– and his 'thanks and praises' haunt and disturb. The 'curse' of
Goody Blake – that most violent of performative utterances – is not,
like the Harlot's blasting curse in Blake's 'London', an unanswerable
damnation but the centre of a 'tale' which is remembered by, and
potentially admonishes, a whole community:

> And all who see him say 'tis plain
> That, live as long as live he may,
> He never will be warm again.
>
> Now think ye farmers all, I pray,
> Of Goody Blake and Harry Gill.

And even within the argument of 'Expostulation and Reply',
'books' are not – as they are in Blake's 'Introduction' to *Innocence* –
the questionable products of an abstracting process, fixed in form
but uncertain in effect: they are imaged simply, as a vital inheritance
which affirms a living relationship with those now dead.

By the 1800 volume, this interest in the memorializing power of
language has become a central – and deeply pondered – preoccupation. The little girl of 'We are Seven', asserting the continuing
presence of her family by refusing to use the past tense, was
presented in 1798 as a particular object of wonder: in 'The Brothers'
a similar reanimation of the dead through speech is seen as the
natural activity – in a sense the defining activity – of a whole
community:

> We have no need of names and epitaphs,
> We talk about the dead by our firesides.

And this interest in the commemorative function of language recurs
again and again throughout the collection. Some poems – the
'inscription' poems[44] and the 'Poems on the Naming of Places' – take
their very form from it: the signification of past experience in a
'name' that will continue to recall it. There are several poems about
epitaphs, prefiguring Wordsworth's later interest in epitaphs as
primary literary forms: here they are both written epitaphs –

> By Ellen's side the Bruce is laid,
> And, for the stone upon his head,
> May no rude hand deface it,
> And its forlorn Hic jacet.
>> ('Ellen Irwin')

> Read o'er these lines; and then review
> This tablet, that thus humbly rears

> In such diversity of hue
> Its history of two hundred years.
>   ('If Nature, for a favourite child ... ')

– and oral ones, the communal memories with which poems such as 'The Brothers' and 'To a Sexton' are concerned. The endings of 'Lucy Gray' and of 'Ruth' stress the way in which past tragedy is framed and given present life by the continuing voices of others:

> Yet some maintain that to this day
> She is a living Child.

> And all the congregation sing
> A Christian psalm for thee.

In 'Hart-Leap Well' and in 'Michael', an otherwise meaningless heap of stones becomes a monument to vanished human experience, as the story behind it is recounted. Even absolute loneliness becomes, in the latter poem, the object of the pity and report of a whole surrounding community – a community which continues, as it does in all these poems, into the narrative present:

>   'Tis not forgotten yet
> The pity which was then in every heart
> For the Old Man – and 'tis believ'd by all
> That many and many a day he thither went,
> And never lifted up a single stone.

And most subtly and pervasively suggestive is the recurrence throughout the volume of the present perfect tense, a tense which expresses the enduring presence of that which is past:[45]

> Poor Susan *has pass'd* by the spot and *has heard* ...

>   ... a gentle shock of mild surprise
> *Has carried* far into his heart ...

>   ... near his grave
> A full half-hour together *I have stood* ...

> Strange fits of passion *I have known* ...

> Him from my childhood *have I known* ...

Throughout, past experience is singled out and shaped in a way which affirms its persisting present significance.

    If much of the 'aukwardness' of *Lyrical Ballads* comes from Wordsworth's desire to escape the distorting and distancing pressures of literary convention and the wider 'pre-established codes of

decision' which it embodies,[46] they are also, then, centrally concerned with the fixing and memorializing powers of language – its
promise to transcend the flux of events and the loneliness of
individual experience, and to affirm enduring human community.
And it is this concern which informs the famous description in the
1800 Preface of the nature of poetic creation and reception:

For all good poetry is the spontaneous overflow of powerful feelings; but
though this be true, Poems to which any value can be attached, were never
produced on any variety of subjects but by a man who being possessed of
more than usual organic sensibility had also thought long and deeply. For
our continued influxes of feeling are modified and directed by our thoughts;
which are indeed the representatives of all our past feelings; and as by
contemplating the relation of these general representatives to each other, we
discover what is really important to men, so by the repetition and
continuance of this act feelings connected with important subjects will be
nourished, till at length, if we be originally possessed of much organic
sensibility, such habits of mind will be produced that by obeying blindly and
mechanically the impulses of these habits we shall describe objects and utter
sentiments of such a nature and in such connection with each other, that the
understanding of the being to whom we address ourselves, if he be in a
healthful state of association, must necessarily be in some degree enlightened, his taste exalted, and his affections ameliorated.[47]

Like the 'Introduction' to *Songs of Innocence*, this passage traces the
transmutation of immediate experience into permanent and more
generally accessible literary form: like Blake, Wordsworth sees that
it is only by a process of abstraction that such preservation and
communication becomes possible. Yet if the subject is similar, the
difference from Blake is extreme: 'and as by contemplating the
relation of these general representatives to each other, we discover
what is really important to men'. 'General Representatives!' we can
imagine Blake scribbling in the margin, 'What can we learn from
General Representatives?' Or, as he was later to pronounce: 'General
Knowledge is Remote Knowledge; it is in Particulars that Wisdom
consists & Happiness too' (K611). Yet it seems that to Wordsworth
the distancing of and generalization from immediate experience
which he describes in this passage is entirely unproblematic. Where
'Introduction' to *Songs of Innocence* depicts poetic creation as in
some sense a violation of nature ('And I pluck'd a hollow reed');
'And I stain'd the water clear'), here the implicit claim is that the
process being described is a natural one. The language is that of
associationist psychology, its closest contemporary analogue a

work such as Erasmus Darwin's *Zoonomia*. Poetic creation is seen as not, in its essence, different from the way in which all men assimilate and communicate their experience. The poet's 'influxes of feeling' are, like those of any man, 'modified and directed by ... thoughts'; he compares those thoughts with one another so that a sense of that which is significant gradually develops, and this sense of significance shapes an utterance which has a definite effect on the listener. Where Blake stresses difficulty and uncertainty, Wordsworth is assured. 'Introduction' to *Songs of Innocence* emphasizes physical labour ('pluck'd', 'made', 'stain'd', 'wrote'): the artist is shown grappling with his materials in a way which prefigures that sense of words as intransigent things which will be developed in the later poems. But Wordsworth's image of poetic creation is that of effortless speech: 'describing', 'uttering', 'addressing'. And he has a corresponding confidence in the certainty of the reader's response. Where Blake registers doubt ('Every child may joy to hear'), Wordsworth is categorical ('The being to whom we address ourselves ... must necessarily be in some degree enlightened, his taste exalted, and his affections ameliorated'). The only proviso is that this 'being' must be 'in a healthful state of association' – and the criteria of psychic health are assumed to be unquestionable. To him, poetry is not a written text sundered from its author, but a much more intimate 'address' from one person to another. Its effect is not unpredictable ('may joy to hear'), but inevitable, and inevitably 'enlightening' and 'ameliorating'. And the assumption, implicit in all this, of a fundamental similarity between men, is manifest in the assured use of the first person plural throughout the passage.

Yet, as we have begun to see, the sense of poetic possibility which *Lyrical Ballads* actually conveys is by no means as unambiguous as that which this passage seeks to offer. It is not merely that many of the poems point towards what Wordsworth was later, in *The Prelude* to call 'the sad incompetence of human speech' (Bk VI, l.593): there are doubts, too, as to whether that fundamental community between men which this passage so unquestioningly sees poetry as confirming and perpetuating can be unproblematically assumed. Several of the 1798 ballads, indeed, confront the unfathomable difference of other men in a way which would seem to present a direct challenge to such an assumption. Such doubts are hardly acknowledged in the Preface. If language is there seen as 'slavish and mechanical' compared to the 'real and substantial action and suffering' it describes, there is little concern with its sociological bases (a concern which, as Coleridge was quick to see, might expose division rather than community):[48] the main stress is on its conservative and ameliorative power. But in 'The Old Cumberland Beggar', begun before the publication of the 1798 volume and finally published in that of 1800, some of the implications of these unresolved ambiguities in Wordsworth's thinking are sharply revealed.[49]

It was from a draft of this poem, indeed, that 'Old Man Travelling', one of the most challenging of the 1798 ballads, was originally taken. But in the longer poem, the old man's independence – dramatized, earlier, by his direct speech – is to a large extent smoothed away. He is still an opaque and enigmatic figure, but he had no jarring voice of his own. Rather, he is seen as a focus for the binding together of a community:

> a record which together binds
> Past deeds and offices of charity
> Else unremember'd, and so keeps alive
> The kindly mood in hearts which lapse of years
> And that half-wisdom half-experience gives
> Make slow to feel, and by sure steps resign
> To selfishness and cold oblivious cares. (ll. 81–7)

And the process whereby Wordsworth describes this as being achieved is suggestively analogous to that which, in the Preface to the volume, is portrayed as transforming 'our continued influxes and feelings' into communicable, permanent and 'ameliorating' form. The instinctive acts with which the villagers respond to the old man correspond to 'our continued influxes of feeling'; their reflections upon those acts to the 'thoughts by which feeling is modified and directed'; the developing shared memory of the community to the contemplation of 'the relation of those general representatives to each other'; and the old man, thus transmuted into

> a record which together binds
> Past deeds and offices of charity
> Else unremember'd ... (ll. 81–3)

to the poetic utterance with its unquestionable moral effect. The steady movement of the verse expresses the same certainty that this will be the outcome as does the confident scientific prose of the Preface. By a seemingly natural series of steps the presence of the old man is transformed into a symbol of social cohesion, as inevitably as 'the spontaneous overflow of powerful feelings' is transformed into poetry by which the 'understanding is enlightened . . . taste exalted, and . . . affections ameliorated'.

Yet the poem registers the tensions involved in this process in a way in which the Preface, with its urbane assurance, does not. For this is a curiously uneven poem. If it opens with an impressive portrayal of the old man's enigmatic human dignity, by the end it has collapsed into seeing him, rhetorically, as an object of edification. He is not, it is true, the conventional pitiable object of so much contemporary verse about the poor: his edifying function is carefully demonstrated in associationist terms. But there is an essential incompatibility between seeing him thus and seeing him as the undecipherable other of the opening: an incompatibility which is reflected in the incongruity between the initial image of his impervious figure and the attempt in the final lines to present his inner life – 'the hope whose vital anxiousness / Gives the last human interest to his heart', between his first 'palsied' appearance and the robust symbol of freedom wandering the mountains at the end. The confusion seems to spring from the double impulse behind the poem. On the one hand, there is that sense of the discordant otherness of those whom even the sympathetic polite would assimilate to their categories, which is the subject of 'Old Man Travelling', and which informs, in a more muted way, the inscrutable portrait of the opening. On the other, there is the desire to trace some way in which, even in a society based on inequality, unconsidered and habitual acts of individual charity might lead without conflict towards positive social feeling on a wider scale. And this second impulse necessitates a withdrawal from that shock of confrontation. The poem ends with a paternalistic distancing not merely of the Beggar, but of all the 'unletter'd Villagers' amongst whom he lives:

> Unblam'd, uninjur'd, let him bear about
> The good which the benignant law of heaven
> Has hung around him, and, while life is his,
> Still let him prompt the unletter'd Villagers
> To tender offices and pensive thoughts.   (ll. 159–63)

The poet is no longer, as at the opening, a member of the community which he contemplates: he is a benevolent, unchallenged observer, exhorting those 'Statesmen' whose language he shares with the ring of polite authority.

But Wordsworth's refusal to fall into conventional clichés, his attempt not merely to assert but to explore what the real, half-instinctive roots of social feeling might be, mean that this poem reflects (in a way probably not consciously intended by him) the crucially equivocal nature of the 'community' that is thus achieved and affirmed. The lines describing the 'Villagers'' response to the Beggar are crucially revealing:

> The easy man
> Who sits at his own door, and like the pear
> Which overhangs his head from the green wall,
> Feeds in the sunshine; the robust and young,
> The prosperous and unthinking, they who live
> Shelter'd, and flourish in a little grove
> Of their own kindred, all behold in him
> A silent monitor, which on their minds
> Must needs impress a transitory thought
> Of self-congratulation, to the heart
> Of each recalling his peculiar boons,
> His charters and exemptions; and perchance,
> Though he to no one give the fortitude
> And circumspection needful to preserve
> His present blessings, and to husband up
> The respite of the season, he, at least,
> And 'tis no vulgar service, makes them felt.   (ll. 108–24)

The image is of a society bound together not by fellow-feeling but by a series of separate, identical processes of 'self-congratulation'; one in which men are not questioned by their contact with others, but confirmed in their isolated selfhood; in which the chief function of charity is to reinforce private satisfaction at the 'peculiar boons', and 'charters' and 'exemptions' which belong to a collection of finally atomized individuals. On the surface, these lines celebrate a common feeling: but the world they depict is one of exclusion and division. In a society where a man like the Beggar is needed to create a sense of community, this is the nature of 'community'. It is only by a distancing such as takes place in the closing sections of the poem that it can be seen as such at all.

And it is only by a similar distancing that the poet can claim to be writing in 'the very language of *men*'.[50] That claim, in a period when the dominant culture could exclude large sections of the population from its definition of 'the people',[51] was in one way an expression of defiant egalitarianism. But Wordsworth's sustained attempt to 'keep

84

my Reader in the company of flesh and blood' led him, again and again, towards insights which radically questioned the fundamental assumption behind that claim.[52] One after another, *Lyrical Ballads* suggest that 'men' are not thus generalizable: that each has his own individuality, his own perspective on and sense of the world. And in a divided society there can be no easy reconciliation of these perspectives into a comfortable general view. The assumption that there might be a single 'real language' which might embrace every man's experience is as contradictory as is the attempt, in 'The Old Cumberland Beggar', to affirm an unproblematic community.

In the 1802 addition to the Preface, Wordsworth was to offer a suggestive account of the poet's position:

the Poet is chiefly distinguished from other men by a greater promptness to think and feel without immediate external excitement, and a greater power in expressing such thoughts and feelings as are produced in him in that manner. But those passions and thoughts and feelings are the general passions and thoughts and feelings of men.[53]

'The general passions of men!' Blake might have exclaimed, 'What are general passions?' Wordsworth is clearly trying to affirm a humanity which all men share. But the contradiction in his phrase ('passion' is immediate and particular; 'general', while meaning 'common', carries connotations of abstraction and indefiniteness) reveals the contradiction implicit in that affirmation. Actual experience, in a society in which men are sundered from one another by privilege and exclusion, in which passions may divide as well as unite, might question rather than confirm such a confident appeal to a common humanity. Living language is not necessarily cohesive: it may be multi-accentual and problematic. It is not surprising, therefore, that Wordsworth's desire to affirm the capacity of language to create and sustain community should lead him away from those immediate confrontations dramatized in poems such as 'Old Man Travelling' towards a concern with its memorializing function. And it is entirely logical that his next extended discussion of 'the general language of humanity' should be a series of *Essays upon Epitaphs*: essays which offer a powerful restatement of a familiar eighteenth-century structure of feeling – the affirmation of a common humanity in death, which is consolatory partly because it blurs disturbing differences:

To be born and to die are the two points in which all men feel themselves to be in absolute coincidence.[54]

Such a position is very far from any which Blake ever arrived at: the contrast we have been tracing between his poetry and Wordsworth's is, it seems, far-reaching in its implications. And nowhere is it more sharply focussed – or its basis more clearly seen – than in the style and manner of their respective comments about art. Not the least interesting aspect of the Preface to *Lyrical Ballads* is the language in which it is written: the characteristic language of the educated liberal of the late eighteenth century, steeped in associationist psychology, interested in exploring possibilities for human 'amelioration' through benign development, and aware – even when most speculative – that he and his readers share a great deal of common ground. The magisterial sweep of these sentences, their long series of definite statements and their confident assumption of the first person plural, contrast very strikingly with the repeated conditionals of Blake's evangelical defence of *his* art:

> If the Spectator could Enter into these Images in his Imagination, approaching them on the Fiery Chariot of his Contemplative Thought, if he could Enter into Noah's Rainbow or into his bosom, or could make a Friend & Companion of one of these Images of wonder, which always interests him to leave mortal things (as he must know), then would he arise from his Grave, then would he meet the Lord in the Air & then he would be happy. General Knowledge is Remote Knowledge; it is in Particulars that Wisdom consists & Happiness too.
>
> (*A Vision of the Last Judgment*, K611)

Wordsworth's appeal, throughout the Preface, is for a poetic language which, while 'looking steadily at its subject'[55] will nevertheless unquestionably enable socially integrative and enriching generalization from one context to another. But Blake (writing here of a painting) sees artistic response as particular, unique, ungeneralizable – and uncertain of achievement. In his own way he is no less confident: but his is a confidence that comes less from an awareness of like-minded others than from an inner conviction that – as the final short categorical statements suggest – is almost defiant in tone. And his language and imagery is not that of reasoned discourse but that of 'enthusiasm'.[56]

Wordsworth's confidence, his appeal to common areas of experience and common values, was an entirely natural one. His position was not without its contradictions. As an educated man with little independent means of livelihood he was, as Ben Ross Schneider has pointed out, 'intellectually of the élite but socially beyond the pale'.[57] He had been cheated out of his patrimony for many years by his father's aristocratic employer Lord Lonsdale: he had been in the inferior position of a sizar at Cambridge.[58] He had himself known subordination and poverty, and he had seen much more extreme poverty at close quarters in rural Somerset and West Cumberland. Yet as a Cambridge-educated man he belonged to the polite culture in a way in which Blake never did. His closest associates in the years preceding the publication of *Lyrical Ballads* were, in various ways, disaffected from the Establishment: but they shared a common polite frame of reference. Such men were his readers: his familiarity with their ways of thinking, and the easy sense of audience which this gave him, is symbolized in his close relationship with Coleridge. Moreover, the 'poor' whom he knew best were the statesmen of West Cumberland, land-owners whose way of life (threatened as it was) in many ways mirrored rather than challenged that of the polite classes.[59] As he was to observe in *The Prelude*, it was his early acquaintance with them (as well as the equally ambiguous experience of Cambridge) which had helped to shape his own proud egalitarianism:

> It was my fortune scarcely to have seen
> Through the whole tenor of my schoolday time
> The face of one, who, whether boy or man,
> Was vested with attention or respect
> Through claims of wealth or blood. Nor was it least
> Of many debts which afterwards I owed
> To Cambridge and an academic life,
> That something there was holden up to view
> Of a republic, where all stood thus far
> Upon equal ground, that they were brothers all
> In honour, as of one community –
> Scholars and gentlemen.
>
> (1805 version, Book ix ll. 222–33)

Yet, as these lines also reveal, his was a life-trajectory which enabled a curious blurring of that division between privileged and unprivileged of which he himself was at times most pressingly aware.

No such blurring was possible to Blake. As an engraver and sometime printshop keeper in London, he was familiar with – and in a sense belonged to – two different worlds: that of the polite society which patronized and supported him; and that of those urban artisans whose attraction towards 'enthusiastic' and millenarian movements was by the early 1790s becoming combined with an increasingly articulate political consciousness – men who were beginning to see themselves as fundamentally opposed to the culture of the polite. The latter, especially on its more Bohemian and artistic fringes, might be sympathetic towards them. But their characteristic modes of thinking and feeling were utterly different – as one sees very quickly if one compares a work of 'polite' radicalism, such as Dyer's *The Complaints of the Poor People of England* with the anonymous letters that were written by the poor during these years.[60] Or the *Monthly Magazine* with the *Arminian Magazine* of the Methodists, in which evangelical exhortation and popular superstition are strangely mixed. Many English poets have occupied some kind of borderline within society. But few can have moved daily between, and had such intimate knowledge of, groups whose presuppositions and life-experience were so radically opposed as did Blake in the London of the 1790s.

The political ferment of these years made the nature of this gulf increasingly apparent. In 1791 Thomas Paine's *Rights of Man* offered an extended – and phenomenally successful – demystification of the rhetoric of the polite culture to those who were most ready to receive it: the newly literate artisan classes whose daily experience contradicted the implicit claims of that rhetoric:

Many things in the English government appear to me the reverse of what they ought to be, and of what they are said to be. The Parliament, imperfectly and capriciously elected as it is, is nevertheless *supposed* to hold the national purse in *trust* for the nation: but in the manner in which the English parliament is constructed, it is like a man both mortgager and mortgagee; and in the case of misapplication of trust, it is the criminal sitting in judgment upon himself. If those who vote the supplies are the same persons who receive the supplies when voted, and are to account for the expenditure of those supplies to those who voted them, it is *themselves accountable to themselves*, and the Comedy of Errors concludes with the Pantomime of HUSH. Neither the ministerial party, nor the opposition, will touch upon this case. The national purse is the common hack which each mounts upon. It is like what the country people call, 'Ride and tie – You ride a little way, and then I' – They order these things better in France.[61]

And this was followed, in the early 1790s, by a wave of cheap radical publications which challenged not merely the institutions, but also the language of the dominant culture. Sometimes the attack on the mystificatory pretensions of the polite was framed as an attack on classical learning:

THE REAL LANGUAGE OF MEN

F. Suppose you were to toss puss into the fire!
S. Why then she would spring out again.
F. I'll tell you the reason; she is a brute beast, and neither understands
    Greek nor Latin, nor the admirable frame of our excellent constitution,
    the best constitution in the world, George!
S. The cat, all cat as she is, understands self-preservation, and though she
    has taken no degree, she has the philosophy of feeling, and knows fire
    will disolve the frame of her own constitution.
F. Learnedly spoken! Now turn it into Latin.
S. I comprehend you, Sir. To shift quarters is to emigrate; and the natives
    of one country never emigrate to another freely till they feel themselves
    hurt.[62]

This is not merely the anger of the excluded: the connection of
'Greek and Latin' with unquestioning passivity is a shrewd one. For
the education of the polite classes, based as it was on the study of dead
languages, reinforced a sense of language – and hence of the whole
socially constructed world – as a stable rather than a mutable thing, a
ready-made artefact handed down from preceding generations
rather than something generated and changed in actual use and
experience.[63] It is perhaps not insignificant that Paine's compelling
challenge to established 'truth' (and to those who had established it)
came from one who had the unusual experience of a grammar school
education which included no classical learning.[64]

   But the attack was not merely upon the 'Classical Learned' (K786),
Much of the radical writing addressed to plebeian audiences in the
1790s is informed, like Paine's, by a new confidence in the liberating
power of the vernacular, and a newly ironic sense of the way in
which language had been used to mystify and control:

A hard, working Man, and a 'Poor Devil' are synonymous terms in the
language of Aristocracy.[65]

In other countries the most virtuous and good are esteemed the most high
and illustrious, but in Bull-Land these titles are often bestowed on the most
vicious and extravagant.[66]

XXVI. The text (Render unto Caesar the things that are Caesar's) makes as much
against kings as for them, for it says plainly, that some things are not
Caesar's. But divines make choice of it, first in flattery, and then because of
the other part adjoined to it (Render unto God the things that are God's), where
they bring in the church.[67]

Language was beginning to be seen, consciously, as the vehicle of
ideology. In 1795 Daniel Eaton published Pigott's Political

Dictionary: a work which was to be reprinted again and again in cheap selections with titles such as *The Rights of Priests, The Rights of Man, The Wrongs of Man* and *A Warning to Tyrants*. Against the definitions of the polite were placed opposing, bitterly ironic definitions:

People. – The commonalty; the vulgar, the *Swinish Multitude*; or whatever the *ennobled race* may, in their *infinite goodness and mercy*, be pleased to term them.

Hell. – a place of torment; where there is neither liberty of speech, nor liberty of thought, nor liberty of action; where men can be imprisoned at the will of a minister, without ever being brought to trial; where the rich exult and riot at the expense of the poor; where vice triumphs, profligacy prevails, and war, taxes, and desolation are the CONSOLATIONS of the people.

Nick-name. – To call the king, sapiens; the judges, probi; and the bishops, literati.

Church. – A patent for hypocrisy; the refuge of sloth, ignorance and superstition, the cornerstone of tyranny.[68]

Another such 'dictionary', *A Political Dictionary for the Guinea-Less Pigs*, observed in its Preface:

Friends and Fellow Citizens,
    The prostitution of Language has lately, been so glaring, and notorious, that in my opinion, it requires a nice discrimination to distinguish, even in our own Language, the true intent, and signification, of many Phrases, now in general use. In order to elucidate this observation, I shall submit the following little Glossary, to the public consideration; leaving it with them, to determine whether the defects, do not in general arise, from the cunning, craft, and subtlety, of time serving Villains.[69]

    In practice, this suspicion of polite rhetoric was tempered by an impulse toward education and a desire to find written precedent and sanction for a newly radical politics. Thus, *Politics for the People* prints apposite quotations from the Bible, from Shakespeare, even from Dryden, on its title-page;[70] thus, the numerous publications of 'Old Hubert' (an apothecary called Parkinson), which collected quotations from all manner of writers (Cato, Locke, Selden, Defoe, even Paley) in order to reveal the radical uses to which 'ancient wisdom' – hitherto the property of the polite – might be put. The struggle to *use*, rather than be mystified by, the language of the dominant culture – to become able to use it while retaining a proper suspicion of it – is evident throughout. But despite this sometimes confusing double aim, these cheap, poorly printed pamphlets offer an unprecedented attack on the pretensions of that language from the perspective of those whose articulacy was being forged in conscious opposition to it. As recent researches have begun to show, the disadvantaged of eighteenth-century England did not all humbly and unquestioningly internalize the polite view of their society: some at least had their own different perspective, their own alternative evaluations.[71] The evidence that remains of this from earlier in the century is sketchy, for many of them were illiterate. But these writings of Paine and his followers, addressed to and indeed creating a fast-growing reading public,[72] with their energetic refusal to accept the given or to be mystified by rolling periods and grand-sounding phrases, insist for the first time sustainedly and in print on the reality and validity of experiences which contradict polite definitions. Sometimes they are brash: sometimes they over-simplify. But throughout them one traces a sophisticated consciousness of their critical distance from the dominant discourse: a distance which is now being sharply and ironically defined.[73]

And, as the Notebook which he kept in the early 1790s shows, it was out of this context that Blake was writing; writing while moving daily between groups for whom the same words bore very different resonances, groups who saw the reverse sides of one another's 'reality'.[74] *An Island in the Moon* reveals his keen feeling for the differing tones and idioms of the speech he heard around him – speech ranging from the fashionable language of 'sensibility' to that of bawdy scurrility, from that of philosophical speculation to that of children's games, from that of the salons of London to that of its streets. More immediately and imaginatively than his Paine-ite contemporaries, he registered what was to them a political perception to be struggled for – the fact that the 'shared' language of late eighteenth-century England was riddled with contradictory implications, the arena for ideological conflict rather than the means whereby such conflict might be smoothed out; not expressive of 'the general passions and thoughts and feelings of men', but capable of bearing such varying 'meanings' that there could be no certainty as to how, abstracted from a particular context of utterance, it might be understood. The confidence of his vision – as one can see most clearly in his questioning of polite moral terminology – obviously owed a great deal to his familiarity with antinomian modes of thought. But these seem to have remained a potent presence for him (as for others at this time) less because of their theological attractiveness than because they so precisely expressed those contradictions which were part of his daily experience: contradictions of which, as a poet extraordinarily sensitive to words and their meanings, he could not fail to be pressingly aware.

Wordsworth too had moved in politically radical circles, and had even projected a radical magazine. The difference between that questioning of the dominant culture which he and his associates attempted and that with which I have been connecting Blake might not, initially, seem very great. Indeed, within the periodical publications of the period the two are mingled. The Paine-ite challenge to polite 'wisdom' is sometimes, as we have seen, complicated by a desire to appropriate it: conversely, the writings of Wordsworth's friend Thelwall sometimes verge on the ironies of the political dictionaries –

What then? If the *many* were not *created* for the *few*, and the few to tyrannize over the *many* – if the majority of the nation are not to be considered as forming no part of that nation – if the *most useful* members of *society* are not to be regarded as unworthy of any *social* consideration – what can be the meaning of these haughty terms? – Wealth! Grandeur! Power!

The *wealth* of a nation, the majority of whose members cannot, with their utmost labour, procure the common comforts of life, and set a joint of meat once a week before their hungry families! – The *grandeur* of a state, three-fourths of whose inhabitants are huddled together in wretched smoky cabins, or shivering through the winter in rags and wretchedness! – The *dignity* of a people, who, to support the splendor of a few oppressors, graze like beasts of the field, upon turnips; and bow to the party coloured livery of servitude, as a happy escape from the drudgery by which they cannot live!!!⁷⁵

– and sometimes uncritically accept the privileged stance of the polite moralizer:

I often shudder to reflect on the cruel and selfish dispositions which nature seemed at one time to have implanted in my bosom. Nor was it 'till frequent opportunities of contemplating, with enamoured eye, the varied beauties of creation, in my eccentric rambles, and indulging the poetical studies to which they conducted, had soothed and meliorated my heart, that the blossoms of sensibility began to unfold themselves, and I awakened to a sympathetic feeling for every sentient tennant [*sic*] of this many-peopled sphere.⁷⁶

Yet the distinction between those who fundamentally accepted and those who consciously rejected the polite frame of reference is a crucial one: and it is one which might be focussed by considering an argument which does seem to have taken place on the subject in these years. One protagonist is again Joseph Priestley. In his *An Answer to Mr. Paine's Age of Reason*, published by Joseph Johnson in 1795, he quotes some of Paine's more explicit remarks on language:

Human language is local and changeable, and is therefore incapable of being used as the means of unchangeable and useful information.

As to translations, every man who knows any thing of languages, knows that it is impossible to translate from one language into another, not only without losing a great part of the original, but frequently mistaking the sense.

and objects that

the truth of revelation does not depend upon niceties of ideas, which it is difficult to express, or upon the niceties of any particular language, which it is difficult to translate into another language. What mistake has ever arisen, or can possibly arise, from the translation of the *ten commandments*, or the *Lord's prayer*, into all the languages in the world? Mr. Paine might as well say, that the great facts in the Roman History, such as the conquest of Carthage and the death of Julius Caesar, could never be credible, because they are recorded in human language, which is local and changeable, and the translation of it uncertain, as that Mosaic or Christian history is incredible on that account.[77]

Priestley's is the voice of urbane reasonableness and good sense. But in these 'irrationally' iconoclastic passages Paine is expressing the same intuition as informs *Rights of Man*: that a language which claims a fixed and reified authority for itself is mystificatory. And what 'Mr. Paine might as well say,' Mr Blake does say, in his notes on Bishop Watson's reply on the same book:

Nothing can be more contemptible than to suppose Public RECORDS to be true. Read them & Judge, if you are not a Fool. Of what consequence is it whether Moses wrote the Pentateuch or not? If Paine trifles in some of his objections it is folly to confute him so seriously in them & leave his more material ones unanswered. Public Records! As if Public Records were true! Impossible: for the facts are such as none but the actor could tell.

(K392)

For Blake, there are no 'facts' worth knowing that can be abstracted from actuality: 'Public Records' which purport to offer such abstracted information are, quite literally, 'incredible'. And the grounds for his suspicion are evident in his commentary on Thornton's translation of the Lord's Prayer.

For Priestley, however, there is nothing in principle problematic about such a translation: his appeal is to a common truth which transcends local distinctions. And in this he is akin to Wordsworth, who in 1817 was to write to Daniel Stuart on the subject of Hone's parodies:

There has been a general outcry among sensible people in this neighbourhood against the remissness of Government in permitting the free circulation of injurious writings. It has been especially felt in regard to the blasphemous parodies upon the Liturgy; no one can comprehend why these things should not be suppressed and the Authors or publishers punished.[78]

Although the political views expressed in this letter are very different from those which he espoused at the turn of the century, Wordsworth's opposition to these parodies – which were of course designed to draw attention to the problem discussed by Paine – has as its basis the same desire for social cohesion, a 'moral cement' which has been created by 'substantial amity and interchanges of hospitality from generation to generation', that informs 'The Old Cumberland Beggar'.[79] His opposition is as entirely the logical consequence of his earlier (and much more apparently radical) position as are Blake's parodies the result of his very differently radical views. The difference is not merely a difference in opinion: it is expressed in the way in which each uses the language which is the most intimate register and vehicle of his society's experience.

For Blake, the generalization which would aim to be a 'common language of men' is a mystifying block to understanding: hence, his deliberate poetic emphasis on the decontextualized ambiguity of its moral judgments:

> The *modest* Rose puts forth a thorn,
> The *humble* Sheep a threatning horn.

Hence, his suspicion of the abstracted, reified word –

> *Pity* would *be* no more
> If we did not make somebody Poor ...

– and his assertion of a very different kind of life for his art –

> Every child may joy to *hear*.   [my italics]

But despite those differences to which some (especially) of the 1798 *Lyrical Ballads* point, Wordsworth assumes a fundamentally 'common language', a potentially rich medium within which experience hitherto not confronted by the polite literary culture can be explored to 'ameliorative' effect. Hence, his creative reanimation of abstract words – words which acquire in his poetry a rich new complexity of suggestion, a revived metaphoric life:

94

> for she can so *inform*
> The mind that is within us, so *impress*
> With quietness and beauty, and so feed
> With lofty thoughts ...
>
> ('Tintern Abbey')
>
> What *fond* and wayward thoughts will slide
> Into a Lover's head ...
>
> ('Strange fits of Passion') [my italics]

The different meanings and resonances which these words can bear here enrich one another: they do not clash. In his letter to Charles James Fox about *Lyrical Ballads*, Wordsworth expressed the assurance which made this creativity possible: he also revealed the assumptions which enabled it:

> The poems are faithful copies from nature; and I hope, whatever effect they may have upon you, you will at least be able to perceive that they may excite *profitable* sympathies in many kind and good hearts, and may in some small degree enlarge our feelings of reverence for our species and our knowledge of human nature, by shewing that our best qualities are possessed by men whom we are too apt to consider, not with reference to the points in which they resemble us, but to those in which they manifestly differ from us.[80]

The concern to show how the poor and the unprivileged might be seen to manifest the 'best qualities' esteemed by the polite culture was, in an age when such men were often thought of as belonging to a different species, a radical one. But it is very different from Blake's sense that 'our best qualities' themselves – mercy and pity, modesty and humility – might be open to fundamental questioning when seen in the light of experiences very different from 'ours': that because it is 'we' who 'make somebody Poor', the very language which 'we' use is a doubtful and displaced medium, one whose meanings have in crucial areas become radically problematic. This difference informs their poetry.

The implications of this difference are sharply apparent in those two poems from their respective collections which seem superficially most similar: 'The Chimney Sweeper' from *Songs of Innocence* and 'Poor Susan' from *Lyrical Ballads* (1800).[81] Both are rather different from their closest contemporary analogues;[82] but there are some striking resemblances between them. In Blake's poem, a little chimney-sweeper describes the dream of another sweep, which has seemed to transform their miserable existence: in Wordsworth's, a

95

ondon hears a thrush which reminds her of
ness that for a moment she seems to be there,
s almost disappear. The 'protest' in each case is
ppeal to the reader's pity. Instead, each poem
orming power of the human imagination in face
omising circumstances. And each makes its own
t on the established 'reality' of the society it
port

'The Chimney Sweeper' engages obviously and directly with the material of contemporary social protest: by 1789 the plight of the sweeps had aroused considerable humanitarian concern. But the bleak recitation of facts in Blake's opening stanza comes not from the conventional perspective of protest: it is the voice of a victim himself. There is no explicit appeal to the reader's sympathy, and no call for amelioration. The sweep tells his story without questioning the logic of its progression, in much the same way as real sweeps in these years were giving evidence to coroners' courts and committees of enquiry:

> When my mother died I was very young,
> And my father sold me while yet my tongue,
> Could scarcely cry weep weep weep weep.
> So your chimneys I sweep & in soot I sleep.

The facts that he recounts are the familiar facts of the late eighteenth-century chimney-sweeper's life.[83] Yet the poetic effect is disconcerting. The child's awkwardly prosaic speaking voice prevents any metrical regularity: his acceptance of this state of affairs is not confirmed by the verse. Moreover, that sentimental 'pity' which informs contemporary protest verse is impossible here, for Blake allows no position from which it might unhypocritically be directed. Even as he follows the child's story to its dismal conclusion, the polite reader is unemphatically but inescapably implicated:

> So *your* chimneys I sweep.

Yet when, in the second stanza, the sweep turns from his description of his own plight to empathize with that of another, the verse suddenly changes:

> There's little Tom Dacre, who cried when his head,
> That curl'd like a lamb's back, was shav'd: so I said
> Hush Tom never mind it, for when your head's bare,
> You know that the soot cannot spoil your white hair.

The logical connections 'There's ...', 'when ...', 'so ...', 'for ...', 'You know ...') which in the first stanza seemed jarring, here fall easily into metrical patterning;[84] the 'official' language of courtroom evidence changes to an excited colloquialism. It is an entirely natural transition – the child abandoning his prosaic summary to focus on that which really concerns him – but in presenting it Blake also evaluates it. This 'childish' mode of experience is felt, in the very movement of the verse, in the liveliness of its realization, to have a potent immediacy which the 'official' mode does not. Yet by the standards of adult rationality, it is 'unrealistic'. The sweep's sympathetic delight in another child's beauty leads naturally to an ingenuous assurance that in *their* sight it cannot be destroyed:

> for when your head's bare,
> You know that the soot cannot spoil your white hair.

The debased pragmatism of the masters has been transformed into an irrational affirmation of transcendence.

And this childish logic is taken up and elaborated in little Tom Dacre's reported dream: a dream whose whole sense of the world is the reverse of that of the opening stanza. The distanced facts of a single child's life are replaced by a dynamic vision of present possibility, in which 'thousands of sweepers' are involved; in which the harsh circumstances of their lives are not ignored or denied, but transfigured. The chimneys which were often literally the sweeps' coffins are here; the sky which they could glimpse beyond them as they worked becomes the natural place of their freedom – 'They rise upon clouds and sport in the wind.' The New River to which 'among the less respectable class of chimney-sweepers the boys were taken ... [for washing] on a Sunday morning, in the summer season'[85] is now like the river of life of the Apocalypse:

> Then down a green plain leaping laughing they run
> And wash in a river and shine in the Sun.

Even their naked 'whiteness' is a dream-realization of the ironic epithet applied to sweeps in the canting slang of the London underworld – 'the lilly-whites'.[86] And their 'leaping laughing' procession has its 'realistic' counterpart in the customary May Day procession of the sweeps, described thirty years later by Southey:

Yesterday, I was amused by a spectacle which you will think better adapted to wild African negroes than to so refined a people as the English. Three or four boys of different ages were dancing in the street; their clothes seemed as if they had been dragged through the chimney, as indeed had been the case, and these sooty habiliments were bedecked with pieces of foil, and with ribbons of all gay colours, flying like streamers in every direction as they whisked round: their sooty faces were reddened with rose-pink, and in the middle of each cheek was a patch of gold leaf, the hair was frizzed out, and as white as powder could make it, and they wore an old hat cocked for the occasion, and in like manner ornamented with ribbons, and foil, and flowers. In this array were they dancing through the streets, clapping a wooden plate, frightening the horses by their noise, and still more by their strange appearance, and soliciting money from all whom they met.

The first days of May are the Saturnalia of these people, – a wretched class of men, who exist in no other country than England, and it is devoutly to be hoped, for the sake of humanity, will not long continue to exist there.[87]

To an observer like Southey, chimney-sweepers are a generalized group of unfortunates – 'a wretched class of men'; to little Tom Dacre, they are known individuals with familiar names, 'Dick, Joe, Ned and Jack', and their dancing is not a grotesquely pathetic spectacle, but a delighted movement in which he empathizes.

This poem is not a pitiful portrait of exploited children: it has a sharper edge than that. It ends with a 'moral': the expected conclusion of the eighteenth-century children's verse:

So if all do their duty, they need not fear harm.

This is the 'official' language of the society: behind the line, one hears the voice of a master telling the sweep that if he works hard he will not be punished – or the more compassionate voice of an observer such as Hanway:

I have now before my eyes a particular object of the misery I have endeavoured to describe ... The object in question, to judge from his discourse, has the full exercise of his reason, and all its glorious faculties; and affections not inferior to the common race of men. He is now twelve years of age, a cripple on crutches, hardly three feet seven inches in stature ... His hair felt like a hog's bristles, and his head like a warm cinder ... He repeats the Lord's prayer, and the belief, seemingly acquired by the force of genius, or an instinctive power: he had also heard of such a thing as the *Commandments*.

This boy, from a certain active spirit and goodness of heart, still performs his duty to his mistress; and though he cannot move on the surface of the earth without the assistance of crutches, and has aid from the parish, he climbs and sweeps a chimney.

... Still it might be said, so long as childhood keeps them from being polluted by sin, 'of such is the kingdom of heaven'.[88]

There is an obvious, pathetic irony in the little sweep's repetition or the precepts of a morality which allows and even justifies suffering such as his.[89] But the shared dream of the sweeps has a potency which makes it hard to see them merely as embodiments of quiescent goodness and unpolluted innocence. Coming after that dream, this 'moral' seems disturbingly abstract and uncertain of reference: far from a summary of that which the poem has presented. And it is also disconcertingly double-edged.

For the chimney-sweeps of late eighteenth-century London were not merely seen as pitiable victims. Until about 1760, M. Dorothy George points out, they 'had been regarded as villains ripening for the gallows rather than as objects of compassion'.[90] The seasonal nature of their work meant that they were often forced to turn to begging or to crime for sustenance, and the fact that they called the streets for trade meant that they had much greater freedom than did most other apprentices. Their popular image was one of lawlessness and disorder, and to some extent remained so: in 1802 mill-owners objecting to Peel's Act for the protection of apprentices in cotton mills argued that such apprentices were 'the children of beggars, chimney-sweepers and others accustomed to live in total idleness and not infrequently addicted to stealing, swearing and other vices'.[91] The sense that they flouted the accepted constraints of society was enhanced by the obvious sexual symbolism of their trade – a sexual symbolism acknowledged in popular folklore well into this century, in the custom of a sweep kissing the bride at a wedding,[92] and taken up by Swedenborg in a passage with which Blake seems to have been familiar: one whose imagery is strikingly similar to that of this poem:

There are also Spirits amongst those from the Earth Jupiter, whom they call Sweepers of Chimnies, because they appear in like Garments, and likewise with sooty faces ... One of these Spirits came to me, and anxiously requested that I would intercede for him to be admitted into heaven; he said, that he was not conscious of having done any Evil, only that he had reprimanded the Inhabitants of his Earth, and that after reprimanding he instructed them ... I was informed that they are such at first, who are afterwards received amongst those who constitute the Province of the *Seminal Vessels* in the Grand Man or Heaven; for in those vessels the Semen is collected, and is encompassed with a covering of suitable Matter, fit to preserve the prolific Principle of the Semen from being dissipated, but which may be put off in the Neck of the Uterus, thus what is reserved within may serve for Conception or the Impregnation of the Ovulum; hence also that the seminal Matter hath a strong Tendency and as it were a burning

Desire to put itself off, and leave the Semen to accomplish it's [sic] end: Somewhat similar appeared likewise in this Spirit: He came again to me, in vile Raiment, and again said, that he had a burning Desire to be admitted into Heaven, and that now he perceived himself to be qualified for that Purpose; it was given me to tell him, that possibly this was a Token that he would shortly be admitted: at that Instant the Angel called to him to cast off his Raiment, which he did immediately with inconceivable Quickness from the Vehemence of his Desire; whereby was represented what is the Nature of their Desires, who are in the Province to which the seminal Vessels correspond. I was informed that such, when they are prepared for Heaven, are stripped of their own Garments, and are cloathed with new shining Raiment, and become Angels. They are likened unto Caterpillars, which having passed through that vile State of their Existence are changed into Nymphs and thus into Butterflies, in which last state they are gifted with new Cloathing, and also with Wings of various Colours, as blue, yellow, silver, or golden; at the same Time they have Liberty to fly in the open Air as in their Heaven, and to celebrate their Marriages, and to lay their Eggs, and thus to provide for the Propagation of their Kind.[93]

The unruly sweeps who called the streets of London can hardly have been seen by many as images of a merely spiritual 'Desire': indeed, in the Wilkes riots of the 1760s and the 1770s they had been favourite symbols of subversion. John Brewer cites a suggestive incident:

on April Fool's day 1771, effigies of the Princess Dowager, Lord Bute, the Speaker of the House of Commons and the two Fox brothers were placed in two carts preceded by a hearse, and taken through the streets of London to the properly constituted execution place of all traitors, Tower Hill, where they were decapitated by a chimney-sweep who also doubled as the officiating minister; they were then ceremoniously burnt.[94]

This chimney-sweep is very different from Blake's innocent child. But the fact that such associations could cluster around such a figure – would inevitably do so for readers for whom the Wilkes riots were a recent memory – points toward another feeling in his poem's closing line. For the 'moral' which the little sweep innocently repeats is not merely a comforting cliché: read in another way, it is a warning: 'So if all do their duty, they need not fear harm.' With its enigmatic conditional, its deliberate uncertainty of target, this has the same threatening quality as the ambiguously veiled political 'prophecies' which circulated among the artisan classes of London in these years. But unlike those prophecies it is not a cryptic utterance deliberately divorced from any context. It is the conclusion of a poem which

THE REAL LANGUAGE OF MEN

offers a concrete realization of the social contradictions that could
charge such prophecies with radical meaning.

For the society which Blake presents in 'The Chimney Sweeper' is
one which patently does not actualize the values to which it seeks to
appeal. It models its religion on the myth of a paternalism which
demands dutiful obedience –

> And the angel told Tom, if he'd be a good boy,
> He'd have God for his father & never want joy.

– but within it the nurturant functions of paternalism have collapsed
in the most fundamental way. For the poem's speaker, the relation
between father and child has been a negative financial transaction:
'And my father sold me ...' And the 'duty' he has been taught and
unquestioningly invokes, as his innocently recounted story shows,
has become radically problematic. For his is a society that is founded
on division. His simple statement – 'So *your* chimneys *I* sweep' –
foregrounds that which in late eighteenth-century 'protest' verse
was usually distanced by sentimentality: the fact that there is no 'we'
which can encompass both this child and the polite reader. The
moralizing confidence which assumes such a 'we' is fundamentally
displaced from the reality to which it purports to relate.

In one way, the little sweep activates new meaning in the platitude
he repeats. He does do his duty, if by 'duty' is meant the spontaneous
and quickwitted and understanding love he shows for another
frightened little boy: in a similar way, little Tom's dream focusses on
the release of *others*. And because of this, they do not 'fear harm',
however harsh their lives. The unselfregarding wonder with which
they respond to others – 'his head / That curl'd like a lamb's back',
'thousands of sweepers Dick, Joe, Ned & Jack' – takes on an
imaginative potency which transcends the domination of 'fact',
creating a world of warmth and happiness and mutual concern that is
more vivid and in poetic terms more real than the world of darkness
and cold and exploitation within which they must live.[95] But in
another sense, this appeal to a 'duty' which is unselfregarding love
rebounds unanswerably on those who allow and even profit from
their plight. The 'all' of the final line is as much an unstressed
indictment as the 'your' of the third: if *all* did their duty, in the sense
in which this child by his practice defines it, then his life would not be
as it is. And thus the conditional structure of this apparently innocent
'moral' takes on a threatening resonance. Where a father can sell his
child, where little children are driven up chimneys for others' profit

101

and comfort, 'they' (and the vagueness of the pronoun suggests the universality of the disaster) must indeed 'fear harm', for exploited and exploiters are debased together.

The effect of this closing line is one of ambiguous dislocation. A summation such as this, pointing to a generally applicable 'moral', would have been exactly what the polite reader of eighteenth-century children's verse would have expected. But here it seems at worst a hypocritical rationalization, at best an empty phrase which can be charged with contradictory meanings. It stands in disconcerting contrast to the unambiguous clarity and imaginative empathy of the child's other-directed vision – a vision which is responsive rather than rationalizing and particular rather than generalizing; one which creates its own actuality rather than holding a pre-established 'reality' at an uneasy distance. In parrotting the precept he has learned, this child is not merely laying the pretensions of his instructors open to question, but also their whole way of conceiving of and ordering experience. And in presenting the disjunction between their morality and his vision Blake is not merely dramatizing the hollowness of any appeal to common values in the society he portrays. He is also showing that abstracting, generalizing schemata of the dominant culture cannot embody that society's most potentially transforming experiences.

For as we have begun to see, in an important sense, the imagery of Tom Dacre's dream is not merely that of private fantasy. Through that dream, Blake seems to be giving poetic articulation to impulses which the established official religion and morality of late eighteenth-century England sought to contain; impulses which by this time were beginning to find partial expression in such diverse phenomena as the Wilkes riots and in Swedenborgian theories of spiritual fulfilment through 'conjugial love'. From the point of view of the dominant culture such impulses could, as the final line of this poem suggests, appear threatening: they *were* a threat to established modes of social organization. But as realized in the vivid particularities of the child's dream – 'innocent' of polite cultural constraint – they can be seen as disclosing a human potential for an unjudging wholeness of vision, for unselfseeking, loving relationship, that is manifestly not actualized by the official structures of the society in which he lives, and which its morality cannot encompass.

The alert eighteenth-century reader would have found much to disconcert him in this poem. Wordsworth's 'Poor Susan' would have appeared less recalcitrant, and partly for the reason suggested by its title. Unlike the chimney-sweeper, 'Susan' is described by a sympathetic observer. Where Blake's poem asserts division ('So *your* chimneys *I* sweep') Wordsworth's appeals to a 'common humanity'; the homesickness and regret Susan feels are emotions such as the polite reader – however different his plight – might be expected to enter into and understand. And the metrical ease and conclusiveness of its final stanza – very different from the enigmatic ambiguity of Blake's – is reassuring rather than disturbing:

> Poor Outcast! return – to receive thee once more
> The house of thy Father will open its door,
> And thou once again, in thy plain russet gown,
> May'st hear the thrush sing from a tree of its own.

Yet 'Poor Susan' is not simply an exercise in sentimental humanitarianism. Like 'The Chimney Sweeper' – though very differently – it explores a mode of vision which challenges the dominance of established 'common sense', and to some extent affirms its transforming power.

The poem begins not with an unmediated voice and an awkward recitation of facts, but from a much more conventional narrative standpoint:

> At the corner of Wood-Street, when day-light appears,
> There's a Thrush that sings loud, it has sung for three years:
> Poor Susan has pass'd by the spot and has heard
> In the silence of morning the song of the bird.

The opening definite article and the recurrent present perfect tense ('has sung', 'has pass'd', 'has heard') suggest a close and familiar relation to these facts that is quite different from the alienated and finally accusing distance implied by the little sweep's account of his life. The world described here is a de-naturalized one, in which dawn, unlike the dawn of the countryside, is a time of unwonted silence and the song of a bird an isolated phenomenon. '*Poor* Susan', out before others are awake, is clearly a victim of this environment, but her present situation is only obliquely registered.[96] Wordsworth does not explore the reasons for her predicament: he shows none of Blake's interest in the exploitative dynamics of the society. Yet he does not present her (as readers of magazine verse would have expected) simply as a figure of pathos. She is seen as a person, with a personal history in which the speaker is sympathetically interested, and a fantasy-life which he finds imaginatively compelling.

Nevertheless, the difference between his viewpoint and the chimney-sweep's warm identification with little Tom Dacre is extreme:

> 'Tis a note of enchantment; what ails her? She sees
> A mountain ascending, a vision of trees ...

''Tis a note of enchantment'; the polite observer's conventional rhapsody lightly acknowledges that he, too, is moved. But to him, Susan's more profound emotional response – a genuine and quite unconventional surrender to 'enchantment' – is an 'ailment'. She has been afflicted by 'reverie': in his 1815 collection of *Poems*, Wordsworth retitled this 'The Reverie of Poor Susan', thus underlining and confirming his polite speaker's judgment. For in the 1790s 'reverie' was seen as a form of mental illness:

When we are employed with great sensations of pleasure, or with great efforts of volition, in the pursuit of some interesting train of ideas, we cease to be conscious of our existence, are inattentive to time and place, and do not distinguish this train of sensitive and voluntary ideas from the irritative ones excited by the presence of external objects, though our organs of sense are surrounded with their accustomed stimuli, till at length this interesting train of ideas becomes exhausted, or the appulses of external objects are applied with unusual violence, and we return with surprise, or with regret, into the common track of life. This is termed reverie, or studium.

(Erasmus Darwin, *Zoonomia, or the Laws of Organic Life*,
London, 1794)[97]

Like the subjects described by Darwin, Susan is suffering from an aberration which the observer regards with sympathetic interest. This poem is, of course, very different from Darwin's case-histories. Susan's 'reverie' is, to some extent, seen from her point of view: as an irresistible force whose present potency is compellingly realized:

> A mountain *ascending*, a vision of trees;
> Bright *volumes* of vapour through Lothbury glide,
> And a river *flows on* through the vale of Cheapside.
>
> [my italics]

But the perspective of polite rationality remains, counterpointing the evocation of her vision, and registering it as hallucinatory even at its most powerful. Always implicit in the description is the speaker's sense of another, more ' accepted' reality than that which she sees. Her 'trees' are an illusory 'vision': her river flows not through the expansive 'green plain' of an immortal landscape but through the prosaically named 'vale of Cheapside'. Where in the little sweep's dream the world of common sense appeared only in emotionally distorted form, here it remains intransigent, not transmuted by but opposed to the ecstatic vision. And in presenting that vision as observed by the eye of sympathetic rationality, and not as shared in wondering empathy, Wordsworth offers a very different sense of its transforming potential from Blake's.

Susan's 'reverie' is not, like Tom Dacre's dream, a world which she enters, but a sight she beholds: 'she sees', 'she views', 'she looks' as from a distance. And it is the focussing and fading of her 'vision' in this sense that the poem traces. By the third stanza, the powerfully forming landscape of the second is laid out before her eyes. But it is already static and conventional:

> Green pastures she views in the midst of the dale,
> Down which she so often has tripp'd with her pail,
> And a single small cottage, a nest like a dove's,
> The only one dwelling on earth that she loves.

There is little imaginative pressure behind these generalized pastoral images or these tripping rhythms. This is a remembered landscape – not, like that of the little sweep, a place of present activity – and it is a landscape already simplified into cliché.[98] Vision has been drawn into the conventionalizing pattern of nostalgia:[99] the first involuntary, unfocussed but emotionally powerful impact of Susan's 'reverie' dissolves even as she begins consciously to remember and project herself into the scene. The stream and the hill which took shape before her 'fade' as she wills them to remain:

> The stream will not flow and the hill will not rise,
> And the colours have all pass'd away from her eyes.

And the loss is presented as inevitable. The rhythms remain regular and confirmatory: there is nothing like the disruptive awkwardness of Blake's first stanza – a 'reverie' such as this, Wordsworth suggests, cannot be sustained in the face of established reality.

Yet if there is acceptance, there is also loss. The 'realistic' muted hope that is offered to Susan in the final stanza is hypothetical and distanced: it has none of the energy of the transcendent landscape that began to form itself in her original, irrational 'reverie'. In the view of polite common sense, that 'reverie' may indeed be an 'ailment', but it remains the most potent force in the poem, and the most vital dimension of her experience. The final effect of the poem is one of diminuendo: of a human reassurance, a return to community, which involves both loss and retreat – 'Poor Outcast! return ...'. It is a closing off very different from that disconcerting opening out into a world of present and contradictory possibilities with which Blake's poem concludes:

> Tho' the morning was cold, Tom was happy and warm,
> So if all do their duty they need not fear harm.

And Susan's submission to the pressure of 'reality' within and without is very different from the little sweep's unshakeable assertion of the sustained and sustaining reality of the logic of dream.

'Poor Susan', with its easy rhythm and its almost-slide into sentimentality, is not like 'The Chimney Sweeper', one of the finest examples of its author's work. But as surely as Wordsworth's greater poems, it bears the stamp of his distinctive vision, and its superficial similarity with Blake's Song makes the comparison between them a suggestive one. Each of these poems is concerned with the human capacity to transcend the 'common sense' framework of an unsatisfactory reality and create an alternative world. But there the similarity ends. Blake's poem registers the particular details of an actual society – partly directly, partly ironically, and partly in dream-distorted form. It contains echoes of many different contemporary 'languages' – the stilted language of the committees of enquiry, the colloquial liveliness of childish speech, the literal-minded transcendentalism of Swedenborg's visions, the enigmatic vagueness of veiled political prophecy, the Gradgrindian pragmatism of the masters, the neat conclusiveness of moral precept. Sometimes, as we have seen, these languages overlap: the closing line, for instance, can be read as an example of any of the last three. Sometimes they are disconcertingly juxtaposed, as in the disjunction between the first and second stanzas. The effect on the reader is disorientating: he literally does not know how to read the poem, for the meanings implied by these 'languages' contradict each other. There are, it seems, divisions within this society which make easy unanimity – a 'common language of men' – impossible: divisions in which the reader is inescapably implicated.

'Poor Susan', on the other hand, tells little about the world in which Susan must live, except that it is the opposite of pastoral. She is seen alone, and the polite narrator is a sympathetic observer, not bound to her by the social ties which bind sweep and reader. Wordsworth's language has a 'simplicity' of a kind very different from Blake's, a 'simplicity' that does not seem to echo any particular contemporary mode of speech – unless the literary-egalitarianism of the *Monthly Magazine* poets. There are no unsettling shifts of register or conflicting possibilities of meaning. Susan is seen from the single perspective of a liberal humanitarianism that is responsive to and takes seriously modes of experience other than its own, but finds its own categories unquestioned by them. Where Blake's sweep speaks directly to the reader – 'So your chimneys I sweep' – she remains the object of the speaker's observation and is finally herself apostrophized by him – 'Poor Outcast! return ...'. Blake offers a bald statement of fact which is also a statement of division, of the impossibility of community: Wordsworth assumes a social community from which Susan is an 'Outcast' and to which she may potentially 'return'. Yet that community is, significantly, a distanced one – and distanced not merely in that to be part of it involves a retreat to the country and the past. Where Blake's poem, albeit accusingly, includes the reader, Wordsworth's, in its rhetorical address to Susan, excludes him. She and the narrator form a circle which cuts him out: they become objects of his contemplation. One is reminded of the distancing of the Beggar and the villagers at the end of 'The Old Cumberland Beggar'.

And this difference is reflected in the way in which each poem sees and values 'vision'. The sweep's dream is a dynamically realized transformation of the facts of his own experience: in it he connects with the real world much more intimately than do those who speak the language of 'common sense'. And in doing so he projects and articulates a possibility which remains to contradict that which they accept as immutable fact: which challenges both established 'reality' and those who have established it. Susan's 'reverie', on the other hand, is not a reshaping of but a withdrawal from the world that surrounds her; an escape to the country and the past rather than an engagement with present actuality. While Tom's dream maintains all its imaginative life in the account of the other little sweep, hers, though sympathetically observed, is peculiarly her own – a unique autobiographical memory: 'And a *single* small cottage, a nest like a dove's, / The *only one* dwelling on earth that *she* loves.' The weight implicitly given to each is thus very different. The chimney-sweeper's dream, transmuting the familiar details of shared experience, is less a dream than a 'vision', in the sense defined by Morris in the final sentence of *News from Nowhere*: 'And if others can see it as I have seen it, then it may be called a vision rather than a dream.' But Susan's 'reverie', however compelling, is essentially private: antithetical to rather than operative within a society composed of different interacting subjectivities. And hence it must inevitably fade.

Each of these two apparently similar little poems reveals a very different orientation towards the world it depicts: each offers a very different sense of the possibilities for human fulfilment within it. In one way, 'Poor Susan' might seem to be more optimistic than 'The Chimney Sweeper'. It envisages some way out of the girl's predicament, whereas the sweeps continue inexorably to 'rise to work'. Yet the satisfaction proposed for Susan is a satisfaction for her alone, not for 'all': and it is much less immediate and potent than that proposed by her imagination. In dramatizing the dynamics of her vision – its first moment of transforming energy, and its gradual fading into regressive nostalgia – Wordsworth is tracing the outline of a feeling which in *The Prelude* and *Ode on the Intimations of Immortality* was to be much more fully explored: the sense that the most vital human aspirations cannot be fulfilled within any society, that their 'eagerness' must be contained and muted within the 'common' framework of an accepted reality.[100] And the unproblematic 'simplicity' of the poem – the assumed 'common language' of a polite liberal culture – reflects this belief as intimately as the radical ambiguities of 'The Chimney Sweeper' reflect Blake's quite different sense of the way in which the possibilities revealed in 'vision' might relate to social fact. Tom's dream is not an escape into a private world of individual subjectivity: it springs from and is informed by an impulse of imaginative empathy, a dramatized relationship between two little boys that is the reverse of the exploitative hierarchy outlined in the first stanza:

> Hush Tom never mind it, for when your head's bare,
> You know that the soot cannot spoil your white hair.

And this relationship – this kernel of alternative feeling within a society that is organized in terms of self-interest – leads naturally into a shared realization of how 'all' might be, a vision which provides not a fantasy escape from the world in which they live, but an unanswerable comment on what that society establishes and accepts as 'reality'. 'Vision' for Wordsworth is a private faculty, which may bring joy to the individual, but which must ultimately 'fade into the light of common day'.[101] But for Blake – drawing upon and transforming the subversive traditions of antinomianism and popular protest, registering the unruly comradeship between the dancing sweeps – it is that which articulates actual, creative potentialities which the dominant culture would incorporate or deny; and constitutes an ever-present, irrepressible challenge to the strategies of that culture and to the reader who shares them. Because he has been taught to do so, the little sweep attempts to summarize his experience in the expected 'common language' of abstract moral precept. But the clashing ambiguities of his closing line demonstrate Blake's outraged conviction that there can be no such 'common language' in this society. And this rejection of that which Wordsworth's poetry so centrally sought to affirm informs his whole revolutionary vision of human possibility.

> Expectantly the gaze of philosopher and man of the world alike is
> fixed on the political scene, where now, so it is believed, the very
> fate of mankind is being debated. Does it not betray a culpable
> indifference to the common weal not to take part in this general
> debate? . . . I hope to convince you that the theme I have chosen is
> far less alien to the needs of our age than to its taste. More than this:
> if man is ever to solve that problem of politics in practice he will
> have to approach it through the problem of the aesthetic, because it
> is only through Beauty that man makes his way to Freedom.
>
> (Friedrich Schiller, *On the Aesthetic Education of Man*, 1795,
> Second Letter)

Songs of Innocence and of Experience stands at a curiously oblique angle
to the official morality of its time. As we have seen, where the late
eighteenth-century reader of a child's book of songs might have
expected neat conclusiveness and straightforward instruction, Blake
offers inconclusiveness and ambiguity: these poems seem deliberately designed to disconcert such a reader's impulses toward secure
moral generalization. Yet the Songs of *Innocence*, at least, do not
merely expose the pretensions of polite morality. Even 'The
Chimney Sweeper', possibly the most double-edged of all the Songs
in this collection, is more centrally concerned with presenting an
alternative vision than with pointing to the hypocrisy of comfortable appeals to 'duty'. And at least one other of these Songs offers a
far more positive sense of moral values than would seem to be
consistent with that suspicion of moral generalization manifested in
others:

> To Mercy Pity Peace and Love,
> All pray in their distress:
> And to these virtues of delight
> Return their thankfulness.

What are we to make of this apparently limpid praise of 'moral
virtues' from one who was later in his life to assert 'Moral Virtues do
not Exist; they are Allegories & dissimulations' (K614); who
elsewhere in this volume displays a rather more ambiguous attitude

towards the accepted values of his society than would seem to be offered here?

One way of answering this question has been to say that Blake is here portraying merely one possible 'state of human soul', a limited perspective which is the 'contrary' of the limited perspective portrayed in *Songs of Experience*. Yet this, it seems to me, underestimates the real achievement of *Songs of Innocence*. These Songs do not dramatize a naively blinkered or partial point of view. The 'Divine Vision' of human *potentia* which they present is coherent and self-sufficient. And it is a vision that depends not on the denial of social realities which Blake was elsewhere to confront, but on a careful poetic exploration of the interpenetration between ideal values and human experience within an actual society: an exploration which engages directly with the fact that the values by which that society sought to express and direct its aspiration and judge its achievement were often questioned by its practice. These Songs offer a powerful affirmation of the way in which a sense of possibility beyond the status quo may be threatened by but *may also be formed and shaped within* an exploitative and alienating society, not as an utopian dream, but as a radical challenge to that society.

This is the sense of *Songs of Innocence* which begins to emerge if we look back to its (apparent) origin in *An Island in the Moon*, Blake's most extended portrayal of the polite drawing-room society for which the volume seems to have been intended. There is no rarefied naivety here. Instead, the novel (or the fragment of it which remains) offers a sharply particular satire of the intellectual fashions and egocentric foibles of an actual social group: a group presented with such intimacy that critic after critic has felt impelled to search for specific contemporary prototypes for the different characters.[1] The manuscript which survives is clearly a draft, bearing all the marks of haste and excitement, and with little more than an episodic shape. Yet it does seem to have more imaginative coherence than the particularity of its humour might lead one to expect. The world it presents is one in which intellectual positions and conversational gambits are the vehicles for egocentric display, and in which any real sense of – and certainly any positive feeling for – others is almost unknown. Its tone is on the whole light-hearted, sometimes hilarious. But its dramatization of a collection of unresponsive, isolated and entrapped individuals suggestively prefigures that of *Songs of Experience*.

From the opening, the emphasis is on the emptiness of human

intercourse within this society: these 'tongues' going 'in question & answer' cannot communicate with one another – or, indeed, express anything very meaningful at all:

In comes Etruscan Column the Antiquarian, & after an abundance of Enquiries to no purpose, sat himself down & described something that nobody listen'd to. So they were employed when Mrs Gimblet came in. The corners of her mouth seem'd – I don't know how, but very odd, as if she hoped you had not an ill opinion of her, – to be sure, we are all poor creatures! Well, she seated herself & seem'd to listen with great attention while the Antiquarian seem'd to be talking of virtuous cats. But it was not so; she was thinking of the shape of her eyes & mouth, & he was thinking of his eternal fame. The three Philosophers at this time were each endeavour- ing to conceal his laughter (not at them but) at his own imagination. This was the situation of this improving company when, in a great hurry, Inflammable Gass and Wind-finder enter'd. They seem'd to rise & salute each other. Etruscan Column & Inflammable Gass fix'd their eyes on each other; their tongues went in question & answer, but their thoughts were otherwise employ'd.

(K44)

As the novel proceeds, 'Phebus', 'Pharoh', Chatterton, Locke and other random figures became pawns in an extended conversational game, ironically indicating the kind of 'eternal fame' any of these characters may hope for in this world. Discussion darts indis- criminately from garbled scraps of 'learning' to pieces of gossip: one after another the characters seek to display their importance and to cover their ignorance. Usually the attempt is a humorous failure. 'Hang names!' says Sipsop the Pythagorean, 'What's Pharoh better than Phebus, or Phebus than Pharoh?' But on a more serious level, *An Island in the Moon* portrays a world in which social intercourse has become so meaningless that 'Hang names!' is the most reasonable response. Sometimes, indeed, language breaks down entirely: 'So all the people in the book enter'd the room, & they could not talk any more to the present purpose' (K49).

The tone is ironic. But Blake's own position is not one of easy superiority. There is self-mockery in the way in which he draws attention to his own novel's limits at the same moment as his characters' – 'all the people in the book'; and this refusal to stand safely aloof from the objects of his satire makes the piece something more than a comedy of manners. 'To be sure we are all poor creatures!' he remarks in the midst of his description of Mrs Gimblet: and this sense that the characters are not just absurd, but also suffering, informs the whole. It is there in the descriptions of surgery, and in the real desolation that breaks through Steelyard the Lawgiver's comically melancholy meditations:

Steelyard the Lawgiver, sitting at his table, taking extracts from Hervey's Meditations among the tombs & Young's Night thoughts. 'He is not able to hurt me', said he, 'more than making me Constable or taking away the parish business. Hah!
        "My crop of corn is but a field of tares",
says Jerome. Happiness is not for us, poor crawling reptiles of the earth. Talk of happiness & happiness! It's no such thing. Every person has a some-thing.'
                                                                          (K 52)

It is sharpest in those moments of isolated self-exposure when the panic which lies beneath the surface of polite social life is glimpsed and quickly thrust away:

'Ah', said Sipsop, 'you think we are rascals – & we think you are rascals. I do as I chuse. What is it to any body what I do? I am always unhappy too. When I think of Surgery – I don't know. I do it because I like it. My father does what he likes & so do I. I think, somehow, I'll leave it off. There was a woman having her cancer cut, & she shriek'd so that I was quite sick.'
                                                                          (K 51)

'I do as I chuse. What is it to any body what I do? I am always unhappy too': this could be the voice of any of the characters, momentarily dropping the mask of self-importance and showing a vulnerable underside of isolation and fear. And it is a sense which is directly expressed in the third of the drafts of the later Songs of *Innocence* which appear in the manuscript: one which was apparently inserted as an afterthought, and (significantly) attributed to three different characters in turn. Here, 'My father does what he likes & so do I' has become:

> 'O father, father, where are you going?
>   'Oh do not walk so fast;
> 'Oh, speak, father, speak to your little boy,
>   'Or else I shall be lost.
>
> 'The night it was dark & no father was there,
>   'And the child was wet with dew.
> 'The mire was deep, & the child did weep,
>   'And away the vapour flew'   (K 60)

The characters depicted in *An Island in the Moon* are not, then, merely egocentric and self-aggrandizing. They are also victims of that lovelessness which they display toward one another; desperately in need of that which they cannot give. Ten years later, Blake was to encapsulate a similar complexity of feeling toward an alienating society by 'marking' not only 'weakness' but also 'woe' in the faces on the London streets: here, it gives the piece not merely a manic, but also an exploratory edge. For in the three songs on public charity which culminate in 'Holy Thursday', the first of the later *Songs of Innocence*, one can trace a developing concern with the implicit question posed by the satire as a whole. How, in a society such as this, might an alternative conception of community – one based in mutuality rather than separating self-interest, one which would answer to that experience of abandonment imaged in the song of the lost little boy – be achieved?

These three songs are part of the succession of songs and song-fragments into which the characters of *An Island in the Moon* repeatedly burst – songs which both reflect and caricature the drawing-room taste of the period. They come not from a perspective of unimplicated purity, but from the mouths of these egocentric, insecure characters. And their subject is a significant one. For if the polite classes of late eighteenth-century England had been accused of lack of social feeling, they would have been likely to point in reply to the many philanthropic institutions which they supported and applauded. Priscilla Wakefield, in a children's guide to London, presents a typical view:

One of the most amiable distinctions of London is the vast number of charitable institutions, many incorporated by royal authority, and many the fruit of private benevolence. There is hardly a species of distress within the limits of human assistance, for which relief is not provided. Education for the young; retreats for the aged; hospitals for the sick; asylums for the penitent; a refuge for the destitute; and reform for the profligate. Not a quarter of the town without places of relief for blind, sick, lame, or unfortunate. It seems as if every means of preventing or alleviating distress, that humanity can suggest, has been contrived by the philanthropic ingenuity of the Londoners; yet you cannot walk the length of a street without meeting some wretched object, that either cannot obtain the benefit of them, or who prefers idle independence to the wholesome restrictions of these institutions.[2]

The modern reader is likely to receive this with a certain irony. Yet it is offered seriously. And if there is irony in Blake's handling of philanthropy in these songs, there is also a good deal more. In dramatizing three very different conceptions of that 'charity' which was the nearest approximation to a feeling for community that the polite classes of his time were able to boast, he is not merely exposing its ambiguities and its limitations. He is also exploring its possibilities, as the matrix wherein a more positive vision of society might be formed.

The first song offers little indication of this. It is a celebration of Sutton, one of the most famous private benefactors of the preceding century: at once a hilarious parody of totally rationalistic 'philanthropy', and a dismal exposure of the imaginative bankruptcy of a world in which self-interest is the only motive. 'To be, or not to be', it begins grandly, sung in a pose that is a caricature of Hamlet-like self-absorption: 'Then Quid call'd upon Obtuse Angle for a Song, & he, wiping his face & looking on a corner of the ceiling, sang ... ' (K57). But with every line the first stanza descends further and further into banality:

> 'To be, or not to be
> 'Of great capacity,
> > 'Like Sir Isaac Newton,
> 'Or Locke, or Doctor South,
> 'Or Sherlock upon death?
> > 'I'd rather be Sutton.

What follows is a devastating portrayal of a 'charity' which barely relates to its object at all: the new kind of impersonal, monetary philanthropy (sometimes financed by joint-stock companies) which had steadily been replacing older, more face-to-face forms of social obligation:[3]

> 'For he did build a house
> 'For aged men & youth
> > 'With walls of brick & stone.
> 'He furnish'd it within
> 'With whatever he could win
> > 'And all his own.
>
> 'He drew out of the Stocks
> 'His money in a box,
> > 'And sent his servant
> 'To Green the Bricklayer
> 'And to the Carpenter:
> > 'He was so fervent.
>
> 'The chimneys were three score,
> 'The windows many more,
> > 'And for convenience

'He sinks & gutters made,
'And all the way he pav'd
'To hinder pestilence.

'Was this not a good man,
'Whose life was but a span,
'Whose name was Sutton, –
'As Locke, or Doctor South,
'Or Sherlock upon Death,
'Or Sir Isaac Newton?'

The objects of Sutton's benevolence are mentioned only in the generalized language of official report: his charity involves no compassion for or even familiarity with its objects. It is simply a building programme; and even this is displaced from him:

'He drew out of the Stocks
'His money in a box,
'And sent his servant
'To Green the Bricklayer ...

Every step is prosaically spelt out: every step is a material transaction rather than a human relationship. From the very opening the verse has emphasized diminishment of possibility – 'To be or not to be' leading not into meditative pentameters, but into a series of short jerky lines, tightly and often ludicrously rhyming. The images, similarly, are all of prosaic constriction (and also, suggestively, of possession): 'all his own', 'in a box', 'but a span'. Philanthropy here is not – as it is in Pope's portrait of the Man of Ross – a magic which transforms the world. The singer who describes it admires it not because it has alleviated suffering or brought happiness, but simply as an individual achievement – a way of ensuring that 'eternal fame' whose nature is suggested by the random catalogue of names with which the song begins and ends. It is not until the final stanza that any other value is invoked; and then it is as an uncertain question: 'Was this not a good man?'

Yet the adjective is taken up in the repeated refrain of the song which follows: 'Good English hospitality, O then it did not fail!' Like the Sutton anthem, this is a celebration of polite philanthropy, though of a different kind. Certainly – perhaps in implicit answer to the previous song – it attempts to depict a more vital sense of community. The rhythms are easy and rollicking, not stilted and constricted: the poor are not distanced, quasi-statistical objects, but enter to eat at a common table:

'This city & this country has brought forth many mayors,
'To sit in state & give forth laws out of their old oak chairs,
'With face as brown as any nut with drinking of strong ale;
'Good English hospitality, O then it did not fail!

'With scarlet gown & broad gold lace would make a yeoman
    sweat,
'With stockings roll'd above their knees & shoes as black as jet,
'With eating beef & drinking beer, O they were stout & hale!
'Good English hospitality, O then it did not fail!

'Thus sitting at the table wide, the Mayor & Aldermen
'Were fit to give law to the city; each eat as much as ten.
'The hungry poor enter'd the hall, to eat good beef & ale.
'Good English hospitality, O then it did not fail!'

But the response of the listeners is telling: 'Here they gave a shout, &
the company broke up' (K58).

The appeal is to a much older tradition of charity than the
mercantile philanthropy of Sutton: to the paternalist ideal of an
agrarian society which had found its characteristic expression in the
communal feast of the big country house.[4] And the use of the word
'hospitality' to describe it would have signalled a familiar set of
associations to Blake's contemporaries. It is a word which had
recurred, since the time of James I, in complaints about the departure
of the English country gentry to the metropolis: a word which was
used to invoke an idealized image of an old paternalist social order
which was (it was claimed) thereby being broken up.[5] Sometimes, in
the eighteenth century, it was specifically distinguished from
conspicuous consumption:

Among all the Vices, Follies, and Extravagancies of the Age, I am surprized
at the present luxurious and fantastical manner of Eating, which many of our
People of Quality and false Taste are fallen into. Magnificence and
Hospitality are certainly highly commendable in Persons of large Fortunes,
but can any Folly be greater than that of laying out as much upon a single
Plate to please the affected Palate of one of these foppish Gluttons, as would
in days of ancient Hospitality, have half feasted a Parish. That is, when the
old Nobility and Gentry of *England* thought it a greater Honour to have the
Praises of their Tenants and the Prayers of the Poor, than the Credit of being
able to devour at one selfish Meal what would support a moderate family a
twelvemonth.

(Anon., *Hell upon Earth: Or, the Town in an Uproar*, 1729)

When a few noblemen in a county, like a few of their own stately oaks
(paternal oaks! which were not often set upon a card), extended their

sheltering branches to shield all the underwood of the forest – when there existed a kind of passive charity, a negative sort of benevolence, which did good of itself; and without effort, exertion, or expence, performed the best functions of bounty, though it did not aspire to the dignity of its name – it was simply this: – great people staid at home; and the sober pomp and orderly magnificence of a noble family, residing at their own castle great part of the year, contributed in the most natural way to the maintenance of the poor; and in a good degree prevented that distress, which it must however thankfully be confessed it is the laudable object of modern bounty to relieve. A man of fortune might not then, it is true, so often dine in public, for the benefit of the poor; but the poor were more regularly and comfortably fed with the abundant crumbs which then fell from the rich man's table. Whereas it cannot be denied that the prevailing mode of living has pared real hospitality to the very quick.

(Hannah More, *An Estimate of the Religion of the Fashionable World*, 1791)

There is an obvious irony, then, in Steelyard the Lawgiver's attempt to discover the virtues of an older, rural order in the gluttonous feasting of the London mayor and aldermen. Possibly there is also an ironic reference to the extravagant eating and drinking at public expense which had been a matter of recurrent scandal throughout the century:[6] ten years later *Pigott's Political Dictionary* was to define *Alderman* thus: ' – stupidity, gluttony, servility, avarice; perfectly represented in the persons of Mess. C-t-s, And-s-n, Le Mes-r-r and S-nd-s-n; turtle feasting, &c. &c.'. With its reference to beef and beer and its recurring nationalistic refrain, this song belongs to the familiar genre of the 'patriotic' drinking song such as Leveridge's 'Roast Beef of Old England', a genre which reflected the degeneration of what had been in some sense a serious concern about the decay of felt social responsibilities into a sentimental nostalgia for 'merrie England'.[7]

But it is a degeneration which may be attributed less to the disappearance of an old social order than to contradictions implicit in the notion of 'hospitality' itself,[8] contradictions upon which in the eighteenth century there was beginning to be ironic comment:

There was once upon a time Hospitality in the Land; an *English* Gentleman at the opening of the great Day [Christmas], had all his Tenants and Neighbours enter'd his Hall by Day-break, the Strong-Beer was broach'd, and the Black-Jack went plentifully about with Toast, Sugar, Nutmeg, and good Cheshire Cheese ... the News-Papers however inform us, that the Spirit of Hospitality has not quite forsaken us; for three or four of them tell us, that several of the Genry are gone down to their respective Seats in the

Country, in order to keep their *Christmas* in the Old Way, and entertain their Tenants and Trades-folks as their Ancestors used to do and I wish them a merry Christmas accordingly ... A merry Gentleman of my Acquaintance desires I will insert, that the old Folks in Days of yore kept open House at *Christmas* out of Interest; for then, says he, they receive the greatest Part of their Rent in Kind; such as Wheat, Barley or Malt, Oxen, Calves, Sheep, Swine, Turkeys, Capons, Geese, and such like; and they not having Room enough to preserve their Grain, or Fodder enough to sustain their Cattle or Poultry, nor Markets to sell off the Overplus, they were obliged to use them in their own Houses; and by treating the People of the Country, gained Credit amongst them, and riveted the Minds and Goodwill of their Neighbours so firmly in them, that no one durst venture to oppose them. The 'Squire's will was done whatever came on it; for if he happened to ask a Neighbour what it was a Clock, they returned with a low Scrape, It is what your Worship pleases.[9]

In no real sense can 'hospitality' be an adequate symbol of community, for implicit in the concept is a division between those who dispense and those who receive, a division which the image of the common table seeks to blur. Like the gluttony of the aldermen, the mystificatory function of the feast was to be savagely attacked in *Pigott's Political Dictionary*:

Festival – ... a Prince of Wales, or Duke of York's birth-day! when *oxen are roasted entire*; and, as if the people were not already sufficiently stupified, they are to be further lethargized by dint of beef and porter, of gluttony and drunkenness. Then they are taught to shout, 'God *save the King*', and to believe human virtue and morality contained in that senseless sound. The *only* Genius which displays itself in these our *English Festivals* is the Genius of Brutality, the Genius of Delusion, or the Genius of Confusion, – the whole system of right and wrong confounded, order perverted, vice and folly exalted to the skies, virtue and talents sunk in the dust.[10]

And something of this outrage is to be found, more obliquely, in Blake's song. For all its images are of blatant consumption and display: 'scarlet gown & broad gold lace would make a yeoman sweat', 'Thus sitting at the table wide ... each eat as much as ten'. The 'mayors' are simply tremendous eaters and drinkers;[11] their social function merely 'to sit in state' and – in a deflating physical image – 'give forth laws'. The colourful, aggressive physical presence of the law-givers almost obscures the shadowy figures of 'the hungry poor', who enter the hall as if by afterthought only in the penultimate line. They appear as outsiders, whose presence is permitted by gracious consent – not as equals with a right to the common table. We are reminded that the meaning of the word 'hospitality' is 'the practice of entertaining *strangers*' [my italics]. The reminder takes us, with a shock, to the closing line of the following song. For the idea of 'entertaining strangers', implicit in this debased 'hospitality' which distances 'the hungry poor' to exactly that status, seems to have been in Blake's mind as he composed this sequence: and the injunction with which 'Holy Thursday' ends echoes – with a significant difference – the Biblical injunction of Hebrews 13: 2: 'Be not forgetful to entertain strangers: for thereby some have entertained angels unawares.' It is a curious relation: the jolly drinking song with its sentimental nostalgia for a past whose mythical nature is exposed by the rhythms and imagery in which it is portrayed, and which even as imaged is riddled with ironies, and the Biblical command pointing to a supernatural reality immanent within the facts of daily life. Yet for Blake it seems to have been of crucial interest.

For these three songs in *An Island in the Moon* do not simply succeed one another as a random series of attempts to image charity. If the first two seem to satirize familiar structures of feeling, the satire has an exploratory edge. They are sung by characters who are portrayed not merely as ridiculous, but also as suffering, characters whose real needs are unanswered, and scarcely even expressed. In these songs, however confusedly and inadequately, we see them reaching for images of a way of relating to others which would be different from that alienating egocentricity which is the dominant mode of their society. There is a real, wavering question of Obtuse Angle's 'Was this not a good man?': a tacit admission of the need for some image of 'goodness' more adequate than that offered in his terrible song. And it is a question which is taken up by Steelyard the Lawgiver, and which in his song comes a step closer to an answer. For whatever its limitations, 'Good English hospitality', a real song like drinking songs that were still being sung in London, has a vigour and liveliness that is missing from Obtuse Angle's dirge-like catalogue. Its 'hungry poor' do enter the hall, and their hunger is admitted: they are a little more present than the statistical 'aged men & youth' of the previous song. However ambiguous 'hospitality' may be as an ideal, it is, Blake seems to be suggesting, less reductive towards its objects than the rationalized monetary charity of Sutton: it does involve *some* kind of recognition of their real, unabstracted existence. But this very fact emphasizes its ambiguity. It offers no real answer to the positive aspiration which is dimly there even amongst the utilitarian absurdities of 'To be or not to be'. For if there is a more direct admission of present failure in the second song than in the first (the insistent past tense, the repeated emphasis of 'O *then* it did not fail!') that admission is safely contained by the regular rhythms and rhyme scheme. And the failure of this vision of conspicuous jollity to prompt any sense of present community is indicated by the way in which it causes its listeners to disperse. Like the preceding song, it is still mainly ironic in its effect, sung by a ridiculous figure whose vision of charity is tainted by his own leading characteristics of self-glorification and display. Although its 'poor' are present, their presence is insubstantial beside that of the 'Mayor & Aldermen': they appear only at the end, and as 'strangers'. It is not until the third song, the 'Holy Thursday' which eventually became one of *Songs of Innocence*, that they are there from the beginning, the subject of the verse.

It is as if we see them coming into clear, sharp focus: in the first song, the distanced objects of professionalized charity; in the second, almost forgotten by their celebrating benefactors; in the third, unannounced and abruptly present:

> 'Upon a holy Thursday, their innocent faces clean,
> 'The children walking two & two in grey & blue & green.

Suddenly they are *there* – not merely in the visual details, their clean faces and their coloured clothes, the specificity of 'Upon a holy Thursday' – but in the rhythm of the verse, marching hobbledehoy through the streets of London. The suddenness and immediacy is there in the syntax: the unrelated present participle, the shifts of tense between past and present exactly recreate the position of an observer who has begun to offer his impression of the procession *in media res*. The beadles have already passed when he begins to speak, the children 'walking two & two' are in the forefront, and they 'flow' 'into the high dome of Paul's' beyond. It is there, too, in the fact that this is not a description of past philanthropy. For unlike either of the two preceding songs, this offers a lively picture of a specific occasion, and a famous and familiar one. Any eighteenth-century Londoner would have known of (and very probably have seen) the charity-children's annual procession to St Paul's for a service of thanksgiving: Mrs Trimmer's, in the *Family Magazine* for June 1788, is one of numerous contemporary accounts:

There is no species of charity which does greater honour to the metropolis and its vicinity, than the numerous institutions for the education of the children of the poor ...

At half past ten o'clock yesterday morning the doors were opened and before eleven the church was crowded with as respectable an audience as St. Paul's ever witnessed ...

The children, to the amount of ten thousand, were seated on a circular scaffolding erected from the organ round the dome of the church. The service commenced a quarter after twelve o'clock, and the children rising and singing the hundredth psalm, with great judgment, had a most solemn effect.

The service was listened to with much more attention than could be expected from so numerous an audience; the singing and chaunting parts being most delightfully warbled by the gentlemen of the choir, the children joining in the Gloria Patri and the Hallelujah.

The sermon, which was excellent, and very apposite, was preached by the Bishop of Norwich.

All these details are faithfully registered in Blake's song, so faithfully that over twenty years later it was used, in a children's guide to London, as an accurate description of the occasion.[12]

Yet the feeling which informs it is very different from that of such accounts as Mrs Trimmer's. Despite its reference to 'the rev'rend men, the guardians of the poor' (in the engraved version, 'aged men, wise guardians of the poor'), there is no complacency in Blake's song – certainly none in its closing line:

Then cherish pity; lest you drive an angel from your door.

If the benevolent observer of the charity-children's procession might have expected to be prompted into further benevolence, he would scarcely have expected a *warning*, not merely against the omission of good works, but against an act of overt hostility. This line has an urgency which resists assimilation to the conventional moralising that might have been expected to conclude such a song: its two active verbs pose a stark alternative that admits of no comfortable resolution. It allows no space for that passive virtue preached by Hannah More in the passage quoted above – 'a kind of passive charity, a negative sort of benevolence, which did good of itself; and without effort, exertion, or expence, performed the best functions of bounty'. Here, either you 'cherish pity', or you 'drive an angel from your door'. When, later, he engraved the song, Blake inserted one of his rare punctuation marks – a semi-colon – between, to mark the division between the two alternatives, a division as absolute as that of the day of judgment. And what it means to 'cherish pity' is suddenly and disquietingly unclear.

Why should Blake warn his readers thus? One answer might be

found simply by recalling what happened to other poor children in London in these years:

The Act of Settlements of 1662 ... provided a useful expedient. For, under its terms, any person not apprenticed in a parish or not occupying a £10 tenement within it might, if he looked like becoming 'chargeable to the Parish' as a pauper, be removed by the justices within forty days and returned to the parish of his origin. So the justices of Westminster and the London out-parishes, prompted by the parish officers, became engaged, as they were in other parts of the country, in a constant game of shunting unwanted paupers across their boundaries: it was a barbarous sport in which the most frequent sufferers were poor working mothers and their children, abandoned by a husband or a father ... In fact, the most notorious feature of the system was its treatment of the infant and adolescent poor. Poor infants were sent out to be nursed by pauper women or left, with their mothers, to the tender mercies of the workhouse. Those who survived these ordeals were apprenticed to a trade ... the Settlement laws being as they were, the parish officers – particularly those of the crowded London parishes – were too often tempted to bind out the children, in return for a modest premium, to masters in other parishes: thus, once the 'forty days' were over, the sponsoring parish would be rid of all further responsibilities, leaving the child to find a 'settlement' in the parish of his trade.[13]

It is hardly possible that Blake, who lived, until 1790 very close to a workhouse, did not know of these practices (just as he knew of the extravagant Mansion House dinners and the joint-stock charity satirized in the two preceding songs).[14] The final line of his song might thus be seen as an outraged admonition to a society which could congratulate itself on the charity-children's procession, while at the same time countenancing the fact that other of its children were being defined as 'strangers' and literally driven from its doors. But if this is part of the feeling it is by no means all: we are very far from the single-minded anger of the second 'Holy Thursday'. Within the context of the poem the line has a richer and more disconcerting meaning.

After the objects of philanthropy in the Sutton song and the passive consumers of 'good English hospitality', the children of 'Holy Thursday' have an extraordinary power and life. And it increases as the poem proceeds. If in the first stanza they are schoolchildren 'walking two & two' with clean faces and coloured uniforms, by the last they are an overwhelming presence. The poem moves from images of sight to those of sound: a movement which (reversing that of the 'Introduction' to the volume) tends towards a greater and greater immediacy. There is nothing unrealistic about this: a *Monthly Magazine* correspondent of 1807 was to note the extraordinary volume of the charity-children's singing, 'Contrasted to the immense force of which the choir seemed as if it were annihilated.' But there is a suggestiveness in it that goes beyond realism, and echoes Revelation 4: 14: 'And I heard as it were the voice of a great multitude, and as the voice of many waters, and as the voice of mighty thunderings, saying Allelulia: for the Lord God omnipotent reigneth.' And this resonance is startlingly different from the usual contemporary view of such children as humble recipients of charity, taught to pray: 'Make me dutiful and obedient to my benefactors ... Make me temperate and chaste, meek and patient, true in all my dealings and industrious in my station.'[15] Blake's children do not learn meekness and patience: they have the force of mighty angels.

In one sense, it is a force which is 'all their own'. Their coloured clothes *do* make a flower-like display in the streets of London, they *are* 'multitudes' moving in an immense procession, they *do* sit above their guardians and sing in unison. In another sense, as Blake carefully shows, the speaker himself invests them with the significance which by the end they bear. For the eight central lines develop a series of metaphors unparalleled in either *Songs of Innocence* or *Songs of Experience*:

> 'Grey headed beadles walk'd before with *wands as white as snow*,
> 'Till into the high dome of Paul's they *like thames' waters flow*.

> 'O what a multitude they seem'd, *these flowers of London town*!
> 'Seated in companies, they sit *with radiance all their own*.

> 'The hum of multitudes were there, but *multitudes of lambs*,
> 'Thousands of little girls & boys raising their innocent hands.

> 'Then *like a mighty wind* they raise to heav'n the voice of song,
> 'Or *like harmonious thunderings the seats of heav'n among*.

> [my italics]

Gradually, the quotidian scene registered in the rhythms and the particular details is transformed into a vision quite unlike that of a Mrs Trimmer. The transformation gathers assurance as it proceeds: the uncertain pause on the caesura before the qualifying clauses in the central stanza has by the end become a swelling confidence. And the transformation is in an important way not merely a private vision.

For the occasion which this song celebrates was not merely an occasion for polite self-congratulation. It was also one of the great theatrical displays of eighteenth-century London. Indeed, the spectacular use of the charity children was not confined to Holy Thursday:

> On great national occasions, such as the celebrations of the Peace of Utrecht, stands were erected in the Strand where the children occupied a conspicuous position, not only that they might see the great but that the great might see them, a spectacle which gave much satisfaction to the spectators. A hundred years later, at the end of another great war, the charity children were exhibited to the distinguished peacemakers, the King of Prussia and Marshall Blücher and Tzar Alexander, who was moved to tears 'by the singing of the Old Hundreth Psalm by the children in full chorus'.[16]

If the aim was partly to win support for the schools, the effect (very consciously intended) was of aesthetic satisfaction:

> The S.P.C.K. and its allies showed no little skill in *dramatizing their work* and thus commending it to the support of the charitable. The special charity service, to which the school children would 'march two and two, in good order all whole and right in the same clothes', had a tremendous appeal and would very likely pack the church.[17]

And it is to this aesthetic dimension of the scene that the speaker of 'Holy Thursday' responds. What he sees is a ceremony in which life seems to take the shape of art and the passing parade of the streets becomes expressive and symbolic and symmetrically formed; in which remembered past and exhorted future benevolence intersect in a 'vision of the Eternal Now' (K77).[18] This is emphasized by the archetypal story-book beginning ('Upon a holy Thursday' in the first version; "twas on . . . ' in the second) and by the way in which the tenses modulate between past and present throughout, giving an effect not merely of immediacy, but also of timelessness. The import of his vision is very different from that customarily ascribed to the charity-children's procession. But it is a vision made possible by a carefully created, shared ceremony, familiar to all in late eighteenth-century London.

The 'glorious sight'[19] of the charity-children's procession and service survived in one form or another for over a hundred years.[20] One might, like the protester of the companion poem in *Songs of Experience*, interpret this fact quite cynically, and see it as designed simply to mystify far from 'glorious' social realities. But the polite classes themselves did not see it thus: to them it was an occasion for fostering feelings of compassion. And it seems to have aroused emotion far in excess even of this, emotion which is recorded again and again in contemporary descriptions and sermons, in the language of eighteenth-century 'sensibility': 'a most solemn effect',[21] 'such an affecting and delightful scene',[22] 'the solemn and affecting Celebration',[23] 'the scene was the most pleasant to be conceived',[24] 'virtue rendered visible'.[25] It was, quite simply, very beautiful: a ceremony which seems to have answered to some deep-seated need for an experience in which social relationships, however fraught with ambiguities in the 'real' world, would take on a symmetry which was profoundly satisfying to all concerned. It was a ceremony in which the children could be *seen*, not merely as the recipients of charity ('aged men & youth', 'the hungry poor') but as real, appealing children with clean faces and upraised 'innocent hands'; in which by their very numbers they appeared powerful, yet by their order, unthreatening; in which their singing drowned out that of their benefactors, yet with harmonious and 'solemn effect'. And it is to this aspect of the scene – hinted at in contemporary accounts, but undeveloped because always subsumed by moralizing – that Blake's Song gives expression.

The vision presented in this poem is not a naive (or naively-satirical) antithesis to the alienating society depicted in *An Island in the Moon*: it grows centrally out of Blake's empathy with his characters' need for an image of an alternative 'good', and their confused struggles to formulate such an image in the two preceding songs.[26] In choosing to present the charity-children's procession in this way, he is giving coherent imaginative articulation to that aspiration toward wholeness and harmony which (in however small a way and however ambiguously) was part of the reason for its existence, an aspiration occasionally glimpsed in some of the charity sermons that were preached at these services: 'It is the intention of our creator. . . that all men should concur in procuring that happiness which every man wishes for, and which every man has an equal capacity to acquire and an equal right to expect.'[27] Implicitly – and in a way disconcerting both to those for whom this procession confirmed feelings of 'benevolent' self-satisfaction and to those like the speaker in the *Experience* 'Holy Thursday' who found in it occasion for protest – he suggests that its beauty offers a concept of potentiality, of what could be, that bespeaks a real kernel of alternative feeling within the society that has produced it.

The children are seen as angels.[28] Blake, with his acute feeling for words, must have been aware of the derivation of this one, from the

Greek *angelos*, a messenger. And these children *are* messengers, signalling the immanence of a quite other possibility within the apparently immutable facts of an unequal society: that of a *communitas* in which traditional hierarchies might be reversed and the powerful potential of those who had hitherto been 'reduc'd to misery' might harmoniously be realized.[29] It is a vision quite unlike that licentious overturning of the conventions which had been a feature of plebeian protest in the eighteenth century,[30] for its formal beauty is carefully stressed:

> The hum of multitudes were there, *but multitudes of lambs*
> Now like a mighty wind they raise to heav'n the voice of *song*
> Or like *harmonious* thunderings the seats of heaven among
> [my italics]

And the significance of this difference emerges strikingly when one compares it with its protesting counterpart in *Songs of Experience*. In that poem, the lines are half the length, and the speaker provides categorical answers to all his own questions about the scene. Here, the longer line serves not merely to convey the rhythm of the children's marching feet: it reflects the speaker's effort to push beyond platitudes (either radical or conservative) and realize, through metaphor, the potentiality that is actualized, however momentarily, before him. And the result is a vision the opposite of that of the second poem; one which is excited rather than 'appalled', in which conventional stratifications are reversed instead of despairingly confirmed, in which children are not seen 'reduc'd to misery' but as 'these flowers of London town', singing not with a 'trembling cry', but with the force of thunder. It is a vision which does not 'protest', for by the very power with which it is realized it breaks through the categories which 'protest' implicitly accepts.

Yet, as the reaction of the listeners in *An Island in the Moon* suggests, it is not a vision which can easily be assimilated to the polite complacencies of the eighteenth-century drawing-room: 'After this they all sat silent for a quarter of an hour' (K 59.) And its relation to those complacencies is indicated by the poem's urgently direct, yet curiously dislocated final line. Like the little sweep's appeal to 'duty', this has the superficial appearance of a conventional moral tag. Yet in its implicit reference to the workings of the contemporary Poor Law, it hints, like that 'moral', at the actual failure of the morality that is being appealed to within this society. And like that 'moral', with its tacit estrangement of polite conceptions of 'duty', this thrusts 'pity' before the reader as a problem. It is no longer a gift which the polite classes graciously bestow upon the humble and powerless but a virtue which they must 'cherish' at their peril: it has ceased to be self-congratulatory and becomes mysterious. In the Sutton song the poor were strangers, not noticed at all except as objects of philanthropy ('aged men & youth'); in 'Good English hospitality' – with its picture of a benevolence that almost forgets to acknowledge their presence – they were even more ironically so. But in this poem – through the rhythms in which the children march, in which they are insistently present, and ever more powerfully – there is a curious sense in which the stranger is 'pity', a 'pity' whose meaning, in the light of what has been presented, has become unfamiliar. For the older meaning of 'cherish' – 'to entertain kindly'[31] – is at play in the line, and reinforces its echo of the Biblical command 'to entertain strangers'. And that which must be 'entertained' is Pity: the polite virtue which has come to seem strange precisely as its objects have ceased to be distanced 'strangers'.

For, like that image of a world of dynamic possibility which grows out of the little sweep's feeling for Tom Dacre's vulnerable beauty, this vision of the children as angels springs not from an abstract idea of what should be (such as seems to have produced the unreal images of 'Good English hospitality') but from a wondering, open responsiveness of what *is*. This speaker does not merely register the details of the scene he confronts: his vision of it, as we see it developing in the series of metaphors which are central to the poem, is an active process. Here, as in 'The Chimney Sweeper', it is a process of imagination: the shaping of images of harmony and wholeness, which breaks free from the determining pressures of conventional ways of seeing and articulates an alternative 'reality' to that which they define. Yet there is no sense here that this imaginative creation is an individual struggle – as it is, for instance, in 'The Tyger', and for Blake's later character, Los. It is portrayed simply as the grasping of a *potentia* immanent within the quotidian: as a vision inspired by a shared ceremony which is itself an imaginative transformation of the everyday world. And it is this imaginative transformation, this 'Poetic Genius', that the poem implicitly defines as that 'pity' which must be cherished.[32]

Blake is very far, then, from merely caricaturing the 'benevolent' aspirations of the polite classes of his day in these three songs from *An Island in the Moon*. Rather, he is exploring a possibility latent even within those ambiguous aspirations: a creative possibility which questions what is and challenges to action. We move from an uncertain questioning of accepted morality – 'Was this not a good man?' – to an urgent revaluing of it: from a sense of the poor as passive recipients of philanthropy, to one of them 'entering' as strangers to be entertained, to a vision of mighty angels. It is not a logical but a poetic development: the resonances of the words and images in one poem are taken up and explored in the next. In these unfolding implicit themes – of the stranger, of hospitality, of entertainment (which by the end has taken on its full metaphoric force – the 'entertainment' of possibility), of the instability of moral values in this society – Blake is not arguing, but playing with language, playing upon its associations, its submerged meanings, its metaphoric core, in a way analogous to that 'play' with everyday life which is manifested in the charity-children's procession and service. And the result is a movement both towards a sharper sense of actuality and also – paradoxically – toward a richer sense of how it might be imaginatively transformed.[33]

It is a 'play' with language which, while it depends on an acute awareness of the different possible resonances of words, and of the different contexts within which meaning is defined, is very different from that ironic sense of its double-edgedness to be found in such contemporary publications as *Piggot's Political Dictionary*. And the difference points to the striking nature of the difference between the demystificatory radical protest of the 1790s and the vision presented in *Songs of Innocence*. Both question the moral authority of the dominant culture: but the Songs question it in an open-ended way. They are not merely ironic about its pretensions: they realize an area of creative possibility ignored by or moralized away by it, but within it. They are Blake's fullest imaginative expression of the 'Divine Vision' of human *potentia* which always informed his sense of the deformations of that 'time of trouble'.

'Holy Thursday' depicts one of the most spectacular occasions of late eighteenth-century London life. But in one sense, all of the *Songs of Innocence* seem to be about analogous moments: moments at which, in different ways, life takes on something of the shape and symmetry of art. Some of them are about actual play: more present a distinctive mode of experience which might, in a wider sense, be described as 'play'.[34] It is a mode of experience which is free and spontaneous, yet also harmoniously patterned – like the mother's baby-talk in 'A Cradle Song', like the straying shepherd and his instinctively following sheep in 'A Shepherd', like the 'sports' of

'The Ecchoing Green': a mode of experience which finds expression in such poetic features as repetition, alternation and half-rhyme. It is satisfying and complete in itself, aiming at nothing beyond itself: this one feels most acutely in the absence of conventional moral directives, and in the circular, 'ecchoing' rather than linear, structure of the‖poems. It is not static, but it does have a curiously timeless quality; a quality epitomized in the archetypal serpent with its tail in its mouth that the dancing children form on the plate for 'Nurse's Song'. It is often exciting, in that within it tensions and even distress and destructiveness are entertained; yet they are safely contained and resolved (as in 'A Dream'; 'The Little Boy lost' and 'The Little Boy found'; and 'Night'). The charity-children's procession, the chimney-sweeper's dream, the moment celebrated in 'Laughing Song' – with its repeated 'when' emphasizing separation – all seem in one way removed from quotidian life. For all these experiences are framed,[35] and the framing makes a space within which *potentia* can creatively be realized. The double frame of 'A Dream' – the woven 'shade' of the dream and the 'angel-guarded bed' of the dreamer – surrounds a world in which dependence and need are freely expressed and immediately answered. The framing presence of the Nurse echoes – and thereby patterns rather than thwarts – the children's play in 'Nurse's Song'. Within this framed space images appear, images different from those apparent to 'common sense' – an image not of submissive recipients of charity, but of mighty angels; an image not of a guiding shepherd and following sheep, but of spontaneity and restraint in harmonious interplay; an image not of a child to be taught, but a 'holy image' of its maker.[36]

Of all these poems, 'Infant Joy' is in one way one of the simplest: the 'image' that is formed is simply a name. Yet the experience of creative 'play' which it articulates is intrinsic to all these Songs. And here, in exploring how that experience manifests itself in and is made possible by a recurring verbal image Blake points to the intimate relationship between such 'play' and the 'Poetic Genius'. The sense of the child that is presented – its self-expressiveness, its essential independence of adult categorizings – is very different from that characteristic of late eighteenth-century children's verse: it seems to owe something to Blake's Behmenist inheritance:

Nature has given to every Thing its Language according to its Essence and Form, for out of the Essence the Language or Sound arises ... Everything has its Mouth to Manifestation; and this is the language of Nature; whence every Thing speaks out of its Property, and continually manifests, declares, and sets forth itself for what is good or profitable.[37]

Yet instead of a child alone, speaking 'the language of Nature', 'Infant Joy' presents two voices which chime with one another. It offers not merely an implicit criticism of that authority which may be assumed over the other in 'naming', but a dramatized alternative – a more creative mode of relationship which expresses itself through a shared language.[38] To set the poem beside this passage from Boehme is to see how Blake has developed and extended Boehme's insight. Reverence for and recognition of the other has become a poetically articulated sense of a positive *potentia* – that creativity which is the 'Poetic Genius' – not within the individual human being but in human relationships. And he traces it not in the esoteric experience of artist or mystic but in the most basic of all human relationships – that from which our original images of wholeness, hope and creative possibility come[39] – the relationship between mother and child.[40]

The title is suggestive. For the active verb 'joy' of the 'Intro-duction' – that exact description of poetic response – has here become a noun, and the subject of the poem. It is a poem about the 'naming' of that which has hitherto been inarticulate (*infans* – unable to speak), a naming seen not as an act of appropriation but as a mutual response to a mutually felt absence ('I have no name'; 'What shall I call thee?'); a reciprocal process in which a shared image that both expresses and communicates individuality is created. The child begins its self-realization in response to the mother's question, first by a simple description of its state – 'I happy am' – and then by the imaging of that state in a 'name' which the mother is able to take up and use, a name which makes possible the patterning interplay with language that structures the world of the poem. This is of course 'unrealistic': a child of two days old cannot speak – or, indeed, smile.[41] But it is a poetic rendering of quite real experience:

A baby's first responses can be seen as part of an actuality consisting of many details of mutual arousal and response. While the baby initially smiles at a mere configuration resembling the human face, the adult cannot help smiling back, filled with expectations of a 'recognition' which he needs to secure from the new being as surely as it needs him. The fact is that the mutuality of adult and baby is the original source of hope, the basic ingredient of all effective as well as ethical human action.[42]

Here, in 'Infant Joy', Blake shows how the child's sense of autonomous selfhood appears within a relationship of mutual 'joy'. That 'name' with which it answers the mother's question is confirmed by her – 'Sweet joy I call thee' – not once, but throughout a whole stanza: its own self-image is returned to it with tenderness and love:

> Pretty joy!
> Sweet joy but two days old.
> Sweet joy I call thee:
> Thou does smile
> I sing the while
> Sweet joy befall thee.

She acknowledges the baby's otherness even as she echoes its name. The child simply is, in the present moment: the adult, as the final line suggests, has some sense of other possibilities in experience. And the mother recognizes this difference, as she describes their separate but chiming activities – 'Thou does smile. / I sing the while.' – and implicitly assumes, like the Nurse in the Innocent 'Nurse's Song', that the child will eventually go its own separate way – 'Sweet joy befall thee.' But here, as there, it is a happy relinquishment, the expression of hope rather than fear.

This holding of an undominating, non-instrumental image of the other *as* other is what makes the creative world of the poem possible, just as the tender clarity with which particular children are seen leads, in 'Holy Thursday' and 'The Chimney Sweeper', into a transcendent vision. Like those poems, this presents a moment of what I have called 'play'. But perhaps even more clearly (because what is being dramatized here is neither ceremony nor dream, but the simple baby-talk of mother with child) it suggests that the 'play' which *Songs of Innocence* present – however different from that which in late eighteenth-century England was seen as 'common-sense reality' – was not to Blake an utopian fiction, but a real experience basic to any creative sense of being in the world at all. The insight is echoed in the writings of modern psychiatrists – 'on the basis of playing is built the whole of man's experiential existence'[43] – and, in a different way, by Blake's great German contemporary, Schiller: 'man only plays when he is in the fullest sense of the word a human being and he is only fully a human being when he plays'.[44] But nowhere has it been more fully articulated and explored – not merely as a psychiatric or philosophic concept, but as a truth whose implications question much that is still taken for granted in (for instance) social and political theory – than in this little volume of apparently simple poems privately published in 1789.[45]

For 'Infant Joy' does not sentimentalize the mother-child relationship, nor does it idealize what Adrienne Rich has called a dangerous archetype: the Mother, source of angelic love and forgiveness in a world increasingly ruthless and impersonal; the feminine, leavening, emotional element in a society ruled by male logic and male claims to 'objective', 'rational' judgment; the symbol and residue of moral values and tenderness in a world of wars, brutal competition, and contempt for human weakness.[46]

Rather, it delineates a particular *mode* of relationship: a possibility which is shown, in *Songs of Innocence* as a whole, to be by no means confined to the interaction between mother and child. Indeed in 'The Divine Image' Blake urges that its continuance *as* a possibility depends on its *not* being limited to a specialized area of experience. Conversely, such *Songs of Experience* as 'Infant Sorrow' and 'NURSES song' suggest that there is nothing holy about infancy, or the care of infants, as such: that this part of human life is as subject to deformation as any other. 'Infant Joy' simply presents one example of that which is celebrated throughout *Songs of Innocence*: an experience of self-realization which is, simultaneously, an experience of recognition of and by the other. It is an experience very different from that depicted in 'Infant Sorrow', where the child is met by constriction rather than recognition, and is forced into a defensive egocentricity; where the world in which it finds itself is an immutable place towards which it must adopt a self-repressive strategy, rather than, as here, one which it plays its own self-expressive part in making. In 'Infant Joy', identity is not defined in opposition, but emerges in relationship. And in portraying the process whereby this comes about, Blake is exploring a separation which is not one of alienation but of interdependence – one which gives creative space for 'play'.

The child at once answers its mother's question and gives voice to its own selfhood in the word 'joy': both a particular 'name' and a word with a shared meaning. It is a word which is less used than played with ('I call thee') so as to create a poetic world of satisfying echoes and assonances, a world which *is* the loving interaction between mother and child. 'Genius and Inspiration', wrote Blake in an Advertisement for an exhibition in 1809, 'are the great Origin and Bond of Society' (K561). And, as this poem's repeated echo of the 'Introduction' to the volume suggests, the poetic creativity which originates in and enables the mode of relationship presented here is a paradigm of that which is explored in different forms throughout *Songs of Innocence*.

These Songs play with language in a way which displaces it from its familiar referential meanings, sometimes in complex and critical ways ('We are *called* by his name'; 'Then cherish *pity*; lest you drive an angel from your door'). Some play with syntax, so that new formal patterns different from those of discursive reasoning are created, imaging a world which stands at an 'obtuse angle' to that of common sense. The curious, incomplete sentence of 'Laughing Song', with its five-times-repeated 'when', is not resolved by a definite present tense:

> When the green woods laugh with the voice of joy
> And the dimpling stream runs laughing by,
> When the air does laugh with our merry wit,
> And the green hill laughs with the noise of it.
>
> When the meadows laugh with lively green
> And the grasshopper laughs in the merry scene,
> When Mary and Susan and Emily,
> With their sweet round mouths sing Ha, Ha, He.
>
> When the painted birds laugh in the shade
> Where our table with cherries and nuts is spread
> Come live & be merry and join with me,
> To sing the sweet chorus of Ha, Ha, He.

Instead, it concludes with a strangely indefinite (future? present?) invitation to 'come', which emphasizes the hypothetical nature of the vision that has been presented. The opening stanza of 'The Ecchoing Green' begins with a series of apparently unconditional statements:

> The Sun does arise,
> And make happy the skies,
> The merry bells ring,
> To welcome the Spring.
> The sky-lark and thrush,
> The birds of the bush,
> Sing louder around,
> To the bells cheerful sound.

But it ends with a projective couplet upon which all these statements seem to be contingent:

> While our sports shall be seen
> On the Ecchoing Green.

Yet the verbal animation of both these poems suggests not nostalgic or utopian fantasy, but living possibility: a dimension of reality whose curious status is perhaps most apparent in the ambiguous syntax of 'A Cradle Song':

> Sweet dreams form a shade,
> O'er my lovely infants head.
> Sweet dreams of pleasant streams,
> By happy silent moony beams.
>
> . . .
>
> Sweet smiles in the night,
> Hover over my delight.
> Sweet smiles Mothers smiles
> All the livelong night beguiles.

The mother's words are at once expressions of hopes and statements of facts: they create a world in which wishes *are* facts. Blake's song is not 'unrealistic': his mother is far more like a real mother singing to her child than is that of the Watt's 'Cradle Hymn' against which he seems to have been writing:

> Sleep, my babe; thy food and raiment,
>   House and home, thy friends provide;
> All without thy care of payment,
>   All thy wants are well supplied.
>
> . . .
>
> May'st thou live to know and fear Him,
>   Trust and love Him all thy days;
> Then go dwell for ever near Him,
>   See His face, and sing his praise!

But he is not, like Watts, using language to describe a given reality, or the fears and hopes it evokes. Rather – through ambiguities of syntax, verbal echoes and assonances – he portrays the mother's seemingly nonsensical, repetitious language shaping itself into a pattern which constitutes a quite different reality.

The experience he presents is by no means an unusual one:

A child wakes up in the night, perhaps from a bad dream, and finds himself surrounded by darkness, alone, beset by nameless threats. At such a moment the contours of trusted reality are blurred or invisible, and in the terror of incipient chaos the child cries out for his mother. It is hardly an exaggeration to say that, at this moment, the mother is being invoked as a high priestess of protective order. It is she (and, in many cases, she alone) who has the power to banish the chaos and to restore the benign shape of the world... To become a parent is to take on the role of world-builder and world-

protector . . . The role that a parent takes on represents not only the order of
this or that society, but order as such, the underlying order of the universe
that it makes sense to trust. It is this role that may be called the role of high
priestess. It is a role that the mother in this scene plays willy-nilly, regardless
of her own awareness or (more likely) lack of awareness of just what it is she
is representing. '*Everything* is in order, *everything* is all right' – this is the basic
formula of maternal and paternal reassurance. Not just this particular
anxiety, not just this particular pain – but *everything* is all right. The formula
can, without in any way violating it, be translated into a statement of cosmic
scope – 'Have trust in being' . . . And if we are to believe the child
psychologists (which we have good reason to do in this instance), this is an
experience that is absolutely essential to the process of becoming a human
person. Put differently, at the very centre of the process of becoming fully
human, at the core of *humanitas*, we find an experience of trust in the order of
reality.[47]

Yet, as this modern account suggests, it is an experience of
extraordinary significance. And in the seemingly simple stanzas of
'A Cradle Song', written almost two hundred years before, Blake
grasps that significance and shows how it may be implicit within the
most unconsidered, irrational 'baby-talk'. His mother does not, like
the mother in Watts' poem, simply offer a reassuring account of a
threatening world, and point towards a faith which might meet its
threats. Her loving interaction with her child (here silent, but present
and separate in her awareness) is portrayed as *constructing* a world, a
world which makes wider trust possible for both:

> Thou his image ever see.
> Heavenly face that smiles on thee.
>
> Smiles on thee on me on all,
> Who became an infant small,
> Infant smiles are his own smiles,
> Heaven & Earth to peace beguiles.

It is *her* face and her 'Mothers smiles' that bend over the infant, and it
is the patterning interplay of phrases with which she reassures the
child that creates the harmony and order here evoked. And the 'trust
in the order of reality' which she enables for her child is, in this final
stanza, shown equally to be created for herself, as she recognizes in
the baby's smiles a dawning reflection of that same impulse towards
loving recognition of the other as is 'imaged' in her own.

The reality created in 'A Cradle Song' and 'Infant Joy' is quite
contrary to that presented in *An Island in the Moon*, where the
characters find nothing to answer the childish panic and despair

which lies beneath their egocentric self-display. It is contrary, too, to that of *Songs of Experience*, where the dynamics of that alienation exposed in the earlier piece are poetically realized; where isolated individuals seek to use and manipulate rather than to 'play' responsively with that which is other, and find themselves in a 'state' which is destructively self-enclosed rather than creatively echoing and outward-pointing. In *Songs of Innocence* there is no isolated individual: no individual exists except in relationship. Language is used 'playfully' – often in illogical patterns – to create images of order and wholeness, of tension answered by relaxation, spontaneity by carefulness, dependence by nurturing: of mutually realized human *potentia*. Unlike those of *Songs of Experience* the different poems of this volume echoingly interconnect: the green landscape of 'Laughing Song' ('When the green woods laugh with the voice of joy') is like the animated world of 'Nurse's Song' ('And laughing is heard on the hill') and finds its apotheosis in 'The Chimney Sweeper' ('Then down a green plain leaping laughing they run … They rise upon clouds, and sport in the wind') – in imagery which recalls the child upon a cloud of the 'Introduction'. Within the world of these *Songs*, identity is expressed, recognized in its otherness, and answered: there is no attempt to appropriate or control. There is no preconceived purpose, but a pattern that evolves freely, in play.

And in poem after poem the nature of this 'play' is explored, and its implications charted. It is the *mode*, rather than a particular *area* of experience that interests Blake. It is true that actual 'play', in the form of traditional plebeian sports and recreations, was under increasing attack from many directions in late eighteenth-century England.[48] Much of this opposition was explicit, springing from increasing concern for effective labour discipline, and increasing fear of the subversive possibilities of large assemblies of the common people. For different, though not unrelated, reasons, both Methodists and Evangelicals suspected 'play'. And other, less deliberately coercive social changes, such as the growth of cities and the enclosure movement, were no less undermining. A writer in 1824 was to point out: 'owing to the inclosure of open lands and commons, the poor have no place in which they may amuse themselves in summer evenings, when the labour of the day is over, or when a holiday occurs'.[49] Blake's most explicit poem about communal 'play', 'The Ecchoing Green', bears, however, only an oblique relation to such facts. Certainly, like many of the other *Songs of Innocence*, it might be seen as offering an implicit retort to that castigation of 'idleness' which was a prominent feature of eighteenth-century children's books:

> In Works of Labour or of Skill
> I would be busy too:
> For Satan finds some Mischief still
> For idle Hands to do.[50]

Yet it presents 'play' not as a specialized, and threatened, area of experience – the leisure sports and pastimes of the people – but as a mode of interaction which informs and is essential to the creative continuance of a whole community.

The poem begins with a picture of an animated nature, within which Sun and skies, bells and Spring, birds and bells, echo and answer to one another. But it is, as we have seen, a picture which is given a curious syntactic status.[51] By the end of the stanza it is revealed to be contingent upon a human state of affairs: this echoing interplay exists 'While our sports shall be seen / On the Ecchoing Green'. Yet it has become so immediately present that 'shall be' is by now more than a simple future tense: it has taken on the force of a performative utterance.[52] The 'common sense' notion of human activity as taking place within a given world has been replaced by a vision of human beings whose 'play' in some sense creates the world they inhabit. It is a 'play' whose significance lies less in its exuberance than in the fact that it is recognized and confirmed by others – as the child's 'joy' is recognized and confirmed by the mother; as, in the Innocent 'Nurse's Song', 'laughing *is heard* on the hill'. These are not merely 'sports', but sports which 'shall be seen':

> Old John with white hair
> Does laugh away care,
> Sitting under the oak,
> Among the old folk.
> They laugh at our play,
> And soon they all say,
> Such such were the joys,
> When we all girls & boys,
> In our youth time were seen,
> On the Ecchoing Green.

'Such such were the joys': not 'our' joys in 'our' past play, for 'joys' here lie not in individual pleasure but in an 'ecchoing' sense of mutual recognition – a sense which the old, having in their time received ('In our youth time *were seen*') are able, unenviously, to

give; a sense which offers the young a frame of security
difference of each is acknowledged, and all have their place. And i
unresentful recognition of it as an 'ecchoing' place – one which has
been occupied by others before – does not merely bind together past,
present and future in a harmonious whole: it makes a certain kind of
communal hope possible:

> Till the little ones weary
> No more can be merry
> The sun does descend,
> And our sports have an end:
> Round the laps of their mothers,
> Many sisters and brothers,
> Like birds in their nest,
> Are ready for rest:
> And sport no more seen,
> On the darkening Green.

For if the poem develops sequentially, from morning to night, its
very shape articulates an implicit questioning of linear time as the
mode within which all experience must take place. The repeated yet
developing refrain – 'shall be seen', 'were seen', 'no more seen' –
frames all that is presented within actual or potential consciousness,
and indicates its difference from a mere succession of events. This is
not just experience, but experience made manifest and – like the
baby's 'joy', echoed and confirmed by others in a way which
removes it from the world of progression and gives it coherent
form.[53] In one way the poem traces a movement from dawn to dusk,
from expectation to completion, from the excited anapaests of

> While our sports shall be seen
> On the Ecchoing Green.

to the slower monosyllabic feet of the first line of the concluding
couplet:

> And sport no more seen
> On the darkening Green.

But in another, as the second of these couplets 'ecchoes' the first, it
assumes the shape of a circle. It is an effect repeated in the play
between linear and circular forms on the plates to the poem. On the
first, the opening stanza is flanked by two children, one with a bat,
the other with a hoop; and the main illustration shows a group
forming a circle around and beneath a sheltering tree. On the second

which would move straightforwardly from one
⟩ the other were it not interrupted by the two
ions within it (the children in front of 'old John'
vards him, the child at the mother's skirts and the
looking up into her face) and by the two figures in
, who prevent the eye from travelling directly across
suggest that this line might be part of a larger circular
structu. ⟩ne is reminded of Coleridge's observation:

The common end of all *narrative*, nay of *all* Poems, is to convert a *series* into a
Whole: to make those events, which in real or imagined History move on in a
strait Line, assume to our Understandings a *circular* motion – the snake with
it's Tail in its Mouth.[54]

The snake with its tail in its mouth is a symbol of eternity. And as
such it is a peculiarly apt image for this poem. Twenty-five years
later Blake was to argue in *Milton*:

'The generations of men run on in the tide of Time,
'But leave their destin'd lineaments permanent for ever & ever'.
(I, 24–5. K505)

In 'The Ecchoing Green' that sense is not argued but affirmed
poetically, in articulation of the 'Eternal Now' that is apprehended in
'play'.[55] For the quiet ending of the poem does not merely imply an
acceptance of individual and even communal extinction: it also
celebrates a human *potentia* for the creation of shared images which
will survive that extinction: 'And sport no more seen, / On the
darkening Green.' By another ambiguity of syntax, even as the
ending of 'our' sports is acknowledged, the possible continuance of
'sport' 'no more seen' by 'us' is affirmed. There is a blend of
uncertainty and confidence here that is very close to that of a passage
from Blake's notebook of 1808–11: 'Everything which is in harmony
with me I call In harmony – But there may be things which are Not
in harmony with Me & yet are in a More perfect Harmony' (K559).
This is the feeling that informs the 'play' of this poem: that feeling
which, in its recognition of the 'ecchoing' difference of others, trusts
the possibility of a harmony not imposed by a single perspective –
and hence opens the way to a faith such as is hinted at here. It affirms
the possibility of a mutually created 'World of Imagination' which
'is Infinite & Eternal, whereas the world of Generation, or Vegeta-
tion, is Finite & Temporal', a world which contains 'the Permanent
Realities of Every Thing which we see reflected in this Vegetable

Glass of Nature' (K605), a world which could endure beyond the ending of the 'ecchoing' life of this community.

Yet this faith which grows out of 'play' seems directly at odds with the intransigent facts of the 'Finite & Temporal' world: the facts of decay and suffering and death. *Songs of Innocence* does not ignore this most obvious of objections. Rather, many of the Songs engage with those experiences which sociologists have labelled 'marginal' – experiences of 'fundamental anxiety' which threaten the mutual reassurances of the society most.[56] Even where such experience is not central to the poem, its critical significance is registered – obliquely, in 'Infant Joy's 'Sweet joy befall thee'; more directly, in the 'moans' of 'A Cradle Song', in the pivotal 'distress' of 'The Divine Image', and in the darkening of the landscape at the end of 'Nurse's Song' and 'The Ecchoing Green'. It is presented most fully, however, in the curious poem 'Night', where Blake enters the world of darkness which is still being postponed in 'Nurse's Song', and attempts to show how the worst threats to 'Organiz'd Innocence' might be met by that faith which is hinted at at the end of 'The Ecchoing Green'.

In the Swedenborgian doctrine with which he was familiar, 'night' and 'faith' were explicitly linked: 'Faith is called "night", because it receives its light from charity, as the moon does from the sun; and therefore faith is also compared to the moon, and is called "the moon".'[57] But if Blake's poem seems to contain some allusion to this, it is hardly a Swedenborgian allegory. It works at a different level of poetic abstraction: by condensing and recombining that which is more fully presented in other poems of the volume. The animated landscape of 'happy' skies ('Spring') and laughing meadows ('Laughing Song'), of sheep in 'clothing of delight' ('The Lamb') – is relinquished:

> Farewell green fields and happy groves,
> Where flocks have took delight;
> Where lambs have nibbled, silent moves
> The feet of angels bright.

And the angel imagery of other Songs –

> Once a dream did weave a shade,
> O'er my Angel-guarded bed.
>> ('A Dream')

> Sweet sleep Angel mild,
> Hover o'er my happy child.
>> ('A Cradle Song')

> And not sit beside the nest
> Pouring pity in their breast.
>
> ('On Anothers Sorrow')

– imagery which throughout *Songs of Innocence* has been linked with 'pity', becomes prominent and active:

> Unseen they pour blessing,
> And joy without ceasing,
> On each bud and blossom,
> And each sleeping bosom.
>
> They look in every thoughtless nest,
> Where birds are coverd warm;
> They visit caves of every beast,
> To keep them all from harm:
> If they see any weeping,
> That should have been sleeping
> They pour sleep on their head
> And sit down by their bed.

Yet, as the poem proceeds, there is an increasingly direct confrontation of that 'harm' which in others of the volume is more marginally present: innocence is not merely threatened, but violently attacked. The protecting angels seem powerless before this: theirs is a curiously passive role:

> When wolves and tygers howl for prey
> They pitying stand and weep;
> Seeking to drive their thirst away,
> And keep them from the sheep,
> But if they rush dreadful;
> The angels most heedful,
> Receive each mild spirit,
> New worlds to inherit.

Yet their 'pitying' is conveyed by a series of active verbs which more than balance the destructive energy which they outface. And the feeling of threat being confronted and contained is reinforced by the stanza form, which changes disconcertingly and re-forms into a new metrical and rhyming pattern at each fifth line. This is a world in which every energy, no matter how terrible, is part of an ordered whole: in which the worst possibilities are not denied, but faced with a steady composure which is an active answering.

It is an answering which in the two final stanzas becomes a projective ('shall flow') image of an order that transcends chaos,

SONGS OF INNOCENCE

an iconic embodiment of that nurture in distress which has been the subject of the poem. The reassuring, antiphonal structuring whereby the disturbing subject-matter has been contained portrays an active 'pitying' which is also a changeless state:

> And there the lions ruddy eyes,
> Shall flow with tears of gold:
> And pitying the tender cries,
> And walking round the fold:
> Saying: wrath by his meekness
> And by his health, sickness,
> Is driven away,
> From our immortal day.

And it leads in the last stanza to a 'vision of the Eternal Now' (K77), which echoes and condenses elements of other Songs of *Innocence*: the lamb who is called by 'his name', the sweeps who 'wash in a river and shine in the Sun':

> And now beside thee bleating lamb,
> I can lie down and sleep;
> Or think on him who bore thy name,
> Grase after thee and weep.
> For wash'd in lifes river,
> My bright mane for ever,
> Shall shine like the gold,
> As I guard o'er the fold.

As in the preceding stanzas, the modulation of rhythm in the last four lines is integral to the meaning. From the pastoral simplicity of the first quatrain the key changes to one of choric grandeur: a movement from innocent acceptance to powerful vision which is perhaps *the* characteristic movement of Songs of *Innocence*. And the image of the lion – an image of destructive energy held and purified, of permanence ('gold') in the midst of contingency ('guard') – encapsulates something of that which has been delineated in the dramatized 'play' of the volume as a whole.[58]

But only something. The sustained, contained tension of this poem seems artificial and static when it is contrasted with the Experienced recoil before that 'rush dreadful', the Experienced view of the death and destruction implicit in the 'world of Generation':

> O Rose thou art sick.
> The invisible worm,
> That flies in the night
> In the howling storm:

Has found out thy bed
Of crimson joy:
And his dark secret love
Does thy life destroy.

Here there are no answering angels, no pity to meet the invading worm, but a unilateral process which ends on 'destroy'. Yet there is a terse energy and complexity of feeling here that is in the end more compelling than the visionary balance of 'Night'. For 'Night' is a more abstract poem than 'The Sick Rose': it has nothing like the gloating emphasis that falls upon the colloquial 'found out' of that poem (the first main verb after the apostrophe, postponed through-out the first quatrain). Instead, as we have seen, it is carefully constructed out of the elements of other Songs of *Innocence*, and the satisfaction it gives is that of formal resolution. Although it depicts visionary transformation, it lacks that tension between quotidian reality and transcendent vision which informs such Songs of *Innocence* as 'Holy Thursday' and 'The Chimney Sweeper': and it likewise, and significantly, lacks their disconcerting immediacy. If with its drama of angels and wolves and tygers, its weeping heraldic lion, it offers a fictional realization of the implications of that which is more naturalistically explored in other Songs of *Innocence*, it is to the other poems of the volume that we must turn to understand the real radicalism of Blake's achievement there.

For not merely 'Night', but one after another all of the poems in *Songs of Innocence* attempt to show how that 'marginal experience' which inspires panic in *An Island in the Moon* might be met and transcended. It is an attempt unparelleled in our literature to articulate what a modern psychoanalyst has called 'the vital illusions by which we live' – the 'illusions' that we are not at the blind mercy of fate, that we can actually construct the world which we inhabit, that desire may be undestructively fulfilled, that a non-instrumental mode of relating to one another is possible, that order can survive chaos and love, aggression.[59] These are the 'illusions' which are necessary for any hopeful or creative sense of life, both for the individual and for society. And they are actualized and imaged in that mode of experience that I have called 'play'. Five years later, Blake's German contemporary Schiller was to write:

In the midst of the fearful kingdom of forces, and in the midst of the sacred kingdom of laws, the aesthetic impulse to form is at work, unnoticed, on the building of a third joyous kingdom of play and of semblance, in which man is relieved of the shackles of circumstance, and released from all that might be called constraint, alike in the physical and in the moral sphere.[60]

In *Songs of Innocence*, Blake portrays this 'third joyous kingdom', not as an ideal but as immanent within the familiar world of late eighteenth-century England. Just as amidst the satire of *An Island in the Moon* he found and imaged in the actual charity-children's procession a 'pity' of a kind radically different from that of polite definitions, a 'pity' analogous to the 'Poetic Genius', so in this later volume he portrayed more extensively those possibilities for secure and joyous creativity which he saw in the alienating society around him, portrayed them not ironically, but as blueprints of human possibility. As he was later to write in his annotations to Watson's *Apology for the Bible*: 'Look over the events of your own life & if you do not find that you have both done such miracles & lived by such you do not see as I do' (K391).

Songs of Innocence do not suggest that man is 'Good by Nature':[61] indeed, they seem to spring from the same impatience with debates about an abstract and hypothetical 'human nature' as one finds in the annotations Blake made to Lavater in 1788:

Man is the ark of God ... knaveries are not human nature; knaveries are knaveries. (K82)

Man is a twofold being, one part capable of evil & the other capable of good; that which is capable of good is not also capable of evil, but that which is capable of evil is also capable of good. (K80)

'Good' exists only as it is actualized in experiences of human relationship: 'as we cannot experience pleasure but by means of others, who experience either pleasure or pain thro' us, and as all of us on earth are united in thought, for it is impossible to think without images of somewhat on earth' (K88). 'It is impossible to think without images of somewhat on earth': but in exploring the nature of this 'third joyous kingdom of play' Blake was not merely seeking appropriate images for an ideal which might be more abstractly conceived. He was charting the real experiences within an actual world which are necessary for the conception of any ideal: experiences of a kind of relationship which does not involve repression or control, exploitation or appropriation – experiences which he found even within the society he had portrayed in *An Island in the Moon*, and which embodied a powerful alternative to its dominant modes of organization.

Yet where Blake engages with the material of contemporary social protest, he seems to be doing so in a curiously indirect way. *Songs of Innocence* are very far from idealizing a plebeian – as opposed to a polite – culture. If on the one hand they portray the subversive dancing of the sweeps, on the other they celebrate the official ceremony of the charity-children's service. 'The Ecchoing Green' does not condemn the contemporary enclosure of village greens, or the suppression of the plebeian sports that took place on them.[62] Where the defence of the greens took the form of an appeal to precedent, Blake's 'Such, such were the joys …' is not a protesting address to the reader, but the answer of the old to the young, the affirmation of an 'ecchoing' circle of experience which escapes the world of linear time. Conversely, 'Nurse's Song' may well, as Stanley Gardner has suggested, have been inspired by a new form of charity being enacted within Blake's own parish: the practice of sending pauper children not to the workhouse but out to nurse in the countryside of Wimbledon.[63] Yet it could hardly be described as a commendation of this practice. As in 'The Ecchoing Green', the focus is on a mode of relationship – free yet secure, spontaneous yet ordered – rather than a particular event, a mode of relationship which is not located in time, but framed out of time by the past tense of the concluding couplet. Other of the Songs take their imagery from less specific, though no less real, experiences – the relationship between mother and child ('Infant Joy', 'A Cradle Song'); the confidence of believing prayer ('The Divine Image'); the world of security imaged in contemporary pastoral and hymn ('The Lamb', 'The Shepherd', 'Night'). Blake's eclecticism in this respect is quite striking.

Yet the diverse subject-matter of the individual Songs is informed by an extraordinarily coherent sense of its significance: a sense quite different from that of other contemporary writers on such themes. In each of these familiar areas of experience Blake traced the possibility of that 'third joyous kingdom of play', within which imagination might work and positive human potentialities might be actualized. The elements of the 'Divine Vision' were there in late eighteenth-century English society. In *Songs of Innocence* the negative aspects of that society – the repressiveness of its institutionalized religion, the authoritarianism of paternalist social control, the exploitation of the weak and the powerless, the complacency of polite 'charity' – are deliberately not stressed, so that this potential is revealed. It is an extraordinary achievement, the reverse of utopianism because so rooted in contemporary actuality. In these Songs, Blake by-passes 'protest' and offers something much more radical: a refusal to accept the terms of the dominant culture, either by agreement or opposition, and a concentration upon that within the society which might implicitly challenge its hegemony by providing not merely a possible image but an actual experience of a wholly different mode of being.

Yet if it does not offer protest, neither does *Songs of Innocence* simply idealize contemporary reality. The relation of this 'innocent' vision to that of 'realistic' common sense is in poem after poem carefully articulated. Partly, we have seen, this is implicit in the very form of the book: in the challenge it offers to readers expecting the straightforward 'instruction' of contemporary children's verse. Partly, it can be seen in the 'minutely articulated' shape of the poems themselves.[64] They are not simply effusions of innocent joy: they precisely delineate the essential configuration of that 'joy' and the conditions for its existence. 'Unorganiz'd Innocence, an Impossibility', Blake was later to write (K380), and he marked Lavater's aphorism, 'Sin and destruction of order are the same', 'a golden sentence' (K65). But the ordering principle of these poems. – a balancing and counterbalancing, a free but harmonious play of difference – is quite different from the definitive order of 'common sense'. It is a difference that is reflected on within the poems themselves: in those which explore the actual process whereby, within 'play', transforming images are produced ('Infant Joy', 'Holy Thursday'), images which are not static artefacts, but part of a potentially continuing vital interplay ('And I wrote my happy songs / Every child may joy to hear'); in those which construct the 'Divine Vision' out of negative 'facts' ('The Chimney Sweeper', 'Holy Thursday', 'Night'); above all in those which use the moral terminology of the polite culture in a way which exposes its problematic character.

For if these Songs offer a vision of what Blake actually saw around him in late eighteenth-century England, there is a much more intimate sense in which they are made of the material of its daily life. They are made of its language. And if they find a quite unconventional significance within the experiences they present, they also use language in a way rather different from what might conventionally have been expected. In many poems, it becomes the material of 'play', a way of entertaining creative possibilities: the meaning of a central word becomes less important than the fact that it can be 'played' with by each of two chiming voices, enabling the construction of a mutually satisfying, harmonious poetic world: thus, the 'joy' of 'Infant Joy', the echoing of children and nurse in

'Nurse's Song', the repetitions and assonances of 'A Cradle Song.'[65] In other poems, however, there is much more reflection on the meaning of key words. And significantly, this questioning centres on the language of morality – that language which emanates from the opposite impulse to that of the 'play' which allows his own harmonizing difference to each; that which generalizes from one person's experience to that of another and all too often seeks to prescribe and control.

We have begun to see the many-sidedness of this questioning in considering the 'duty' of 'The Chimney Sweeper' and the 'pity' of 'Holy Thursday'. For if the former exposes the problems inherent in any appeal to common values in the society the poem presents, the latter – first pondered several years before the collection as a whole was engraved – is altogether more ambiguous: a word at once made strange and charged with new meaning by the 'play' with one conventional occasion for it which the poem presents. 'Pity', indeed, recurs again and again in *Songs of Innocence*:

> To Mercy Pity Peace and Love,
> All pray in their distress

> When wolves and tygers howl for prey
> They pitying stand and weep

> And not sit beside the nest
> Pouring pity in their breast

> Pitying I drop'd a tear

> Then cherish pity, lest you drive an angel from your door.

Such lines are puzzling when placed beside the later Song of *Experience*:

> Pity would be no more,
> If we did not make somebody Poor.

For 'pity' in its unmystifying sense seems to be a pivotal conception in *Innocence*: implicitly defined in 'Holy Thursday' as that 'Poetic Genius' which makes possible and is made possible by the state of 'play'. If it represents a morality, it is a morality very different from the 'instruction' of contemporary children's books. It is not a rule of conduct to be learned: it emerges in those experiences in which men respect and respond to otherness, and hence are able to enter into creative interplay with it. In *Songs of Innocence* 'pity' is always operative within the world – either as a verb ('pitying'); or as something to be given ('pouring pity in their breast') or cherished ('Then cherish pity') or related to ('To Mercy Pity Peace and Love'). It is not, as in 'The Human Abstract', a reified abstraction, apparently displaced from human agency. Its object is another seen with more than usual vividness and clarity – little Tom Dacre, the emmet, the charity children: not a generalized 'somebody' whose only attribute is poverty. And in giving it the name of one of the most central of polite moral virtues – a virtue whose underside he was later to expose – Blake is confronting his reader with an inescapable question. What is the relationship between the mode of experience presented in these poems and the official moral language of the society they depict?

It is a question which is explored most directly in 'The Divine Image':

> To Mercy Pity Peace and Love,
> All pray in their distress:
> And to these virtues of delight
> Return their thankfulness.
>
> For Mercy Pity Peace and Love,
> Is God our father dear:
> And Mercy Pity Peace and Love,
> Is Man his child and care.
>
> For Mercy has a human heart
> Pity, a human face:
> And Love, the human form divine,
> And Peace, the human dress.
>
> Then every man of every clime,
> That prays in his distress,
> Prays to the human form divine
> Love Mercy Pity Peace.
>
> And all must love the human form,
> In heathen, turk or jew.
> Where Mercy, Love & Pity dwell
> There God is dwelling too.

Despite the apparent lucidity which has made it a favourite children's hymn, this is a far from simple poem. Its real complexity emerges in comparison with the popular early eighteenth-century poem which it at points echoes and against which it seems to have been written, Pope's 'The Universal Prayer':[66]

Father of All! in every Age,
   In every Clime ador'd,
By Saint, by Savage, and by Sage,
   Jehovah, Jove, or Lord!

Thou Great First Cause, least Understood!
   Who all my Sense confin'd
To know but this, – that Thou art Good,
   And that my self am blind:

Yet gave me, in this dark Estate,
   To see the Good from Ill;
And binding Nature fast in Fate,
   Left free the Human Will.

         . . .

Teach me to feel another's Woe;
   To hide the Fault I see;
That Mercy I to others show,
   That Mercy show to me.

Mean tho' I am, not wholly so
   Since quicken'd by thy Breath,
O lead me wheresoe'er I go,
   Thro' this day's Life, or Death:

This day, be Bread and Peace my Lot;
   All else beneath the Sun,
Thou know'st if best bestow'd, or not;
   And let Thy Will be done.

To thee, whose Temple is all Space,
   Whose Altar, Earth, Sea, Skies;
One Chorus let all Being raise!
   All Nature's Incence rise!

Pope's poem is long, a rational argument underlined by regular rhythms and a neat rhyme-scheme: Blake's is short, and patterned on many levels other than that of argument. Pope's is an address to God: Blake's is not a prayer, but an exploration of the dynamics of prayer. In 1788 he had written in 'The Voice of one crying in the Wilderness': 'As the true method of knowledge is experiment, the true faculty of knowing must be the faculty which experiences. This faculty I treat of' (*All Religions are One*, K98). In a similar implicit parodying of scientific 'experiment', 'The Divine Image' is constructed like the proof of a theorem, with three stanzas of 'argument' and two of resolution, the former marked off from the latter by the design of the plate. And, with a similar seriousness to that of *All*

Religions are One, it 'treats of' 'the faculty which experiences'. Unlike
Pope's poem, it does not assume a God, or absolute moral standards:
it proceeds not from assumptions, but from a straightforward
account of what human beings feel and do:

> To Mercy Pity Peace and Love,
> All pray in their distress:
> And to these virtues of delight
> Return their thankfulness.

The first line contains four moral abstractions, but, unlike the first
line of 'The Human Abstract', it does not claim a reified existence for
any of them. Instead, Blake describes human experience. Those in
'distress' image and 'pray' to something beyond themselves which
they feel will answer to their need, and if and when that need is
answered, it is to that same image that they 'return their thankfulness'. 'Mercy Pity Peace and Love' are not here unyielding moral
absolutes: they are the objects of one of the most instinctive human
acts, that of praying 'in distress'. Yet if they are imaged in
dependence, they are confirmed only as need is answered: it is in the
'delight' of succour that they are felt to be 'virtues', or powers. They
are not given, but created by human actions: the confession of need
that is also, in its imaging of that which will answer to it, an
instinctive trust: and the answering of need which vindicates and
reinforces that trust. Unobtrusively but exactly, Blake is showing
how the conception of goodness grows out of the experience
common to all human beings, even the most deprived, of dependence being acknowledged and answered: of a 'distress' that ends,
with the naturalness of rhyme, in 'thankfulness'.[67] It is an experience
in which all human beings are equal: there is no division here into
'we' and 'somebody Poor' – '*All* pray in their distress'. And the
implicit claim is that these 'virtues of delight' are not the property of
a particular group (like the 'Pity' of 'The Human Abstract') but
images of possibility common to all men: the core of a common
humanitas.

It is out of this experience of 'Mercy Pity Peace and Love', Blake
suggests, that the human conception of God is formed: 'For Mercy
Pity Peace and Love, / Is God our father dear'. This is the reverse of
the God of natural religion, the remote First Cause of Pope's poem:

> Thou Great First Cause, least Understood,
>   Who all my Sense confin'd
> To know but this, – that Thou art Good,
>   And that my self am blind.

For Blake's God is not apprehended by the isolated individual reason, but created in relationship: the embodiment of a universally shared experience of 'Mercy Pity Peace and Love' which does not separate man from man, but reveals their kinship – '*our* father dear'. And the stanza continues with an implicit retort to Pope's egocentric humility: 'And Mercy Pity Peace and Love, / Is Man his child and care.' God is the father, man is the child: but the stanza, musically affirming that both are 'Mercy Pity Peace and Love', dissolves the hierarchical effect. God is no longer – as for Pope – a teacher and rewarder: nor is morality a legalistic bargaining with Him:

> Teach me to feel another's Woe;
>   To hide the fault I see;
> That Mercy I to others show,
>   That Mercy show to me.

Yet Blake is not sentimentally celebrating a necessary goodness in which man can weakly trust. In another of the *Songs of Innocence* he seems to be commenting directly upon these lines of Pope, in a way which illuminates his exact and radical meaning in this poem:

> Can I see anothers woe,
> And not be in sorrow too.
> Can I see anothers grief,
> And not seek for kind relief.

The 'good' is here located not in a code learned in self-abasement and fear, but in an acceptance and nourishing of a basic human impulse towards 'pity'. The echoing rhymes and half-rhymes (oscillating from possibility to certainty) affirm its naturalness: the active verbs 'be' and 'seek', and the area of contingency opened out by the question form insist that such an impulse must be actualized before it can be trusted. The feeling is akin to that of an annotation which Blake made in his copy of Swedenborg's *Divine Love*, in the year in which this poem was engraved: 'Who does not or *may not* know of love & wisdom in himself?' (K92 my italics). And although this impulse is shown, in *Songs of Innocence*, to be reinforced by the experience of answered need, it is also shown not to be dependent on that experience. Rather, it is active in creating it. In the annotations he made in 1788 to Lavater's *Aphorisms* Blake, pondering this question, had marked against Lavater's 'The unloved cannot love' – 'Doubtful' (K76). In 'The Chimney Sweeper' a child sold by his father maintains the image of an ideal fatherhood – 'He'd have God for his father and never want joy' – and responds to another child with the love which he himself has not been given, creating the joyous security which the 'real' world failed to offer him. And here, in 'The Divine Image', 'Mercy Pity Peace and Love' are imaged before they are experienced: prayer comes before thankfulness. These are not abstract values, but the products of that 'Poetic Genius' which Blake, in these 1789 annotations to Swedenborg, had begun to identify with 'Love' (K90) – that in man which refuses to accept suffering, loneliness, fear and exploitation as the inevitable human lot; which approaches the world not with fear, but with trusting openness; which images that which will answer to need; and which in imaging it, creates it.

Yet 'Mercy Pity Peace and Love' are not made by individual desire. Their creation is a communal process in which 'all' share, and it is a process which is confirmed and completed in experience. For if it is the 'Poetic Genius' which images 'Mercy Pity Peace and Love', it is also the 'Poetic Genius' which creates the human relationships which change them from abstractions to 'virtues of delight'. They are conceived in deed, but their power is felt in 'thankfulness'. And the transformation from the one to the other takes place, as one after another the *Songs of Innocence* show, in those human interactions in which dependence is felt and met, and the claims made by trust are answered:

> For Mercy has a human heart
> Pity, a human face:
> And Love, the human form divine,
> And Peace, the human dress.

'It is impossible to think', Blake had written in the annotations to Lavater, 'without images of somewhat on earth' (K88): here he extends that insight, poetically, into an exploration of the inter-relationship between specific experience and the shared values to which men seek to appeal.

The indefinite article of the first two lines – 'a human heart', 'a human face' – indicates that which is particular, not generally known. But the experience these lines describe is not a private one. If 'a human heart' suggests an impulse felt within the self ('My heart is at rest within my breast', 'Can I see anothers woe / And not be in sorrow too'), 'a human face' is that which is seen as other, like the mother's face bending over the child ('Heavenly face that smiles on thee'). Both the impulse and the otherness which answers to it are part of the value-forming process. By the second half of the stanza the indefinite article has been replaced by the definite, and the imagery is less that of intimate experience than of external appearance ('the human *form* divine', 'the human *dress*'). The sense created in the progression of the stanza is of the intimate impulses of the heart gradually, in being answered, taking on objective and communicable form. We move from the 'heart', the essence of the human being, to the 'face' in which individuality is expressed (in 1789 Blake engraved three plates for Lavater's *Essays on Physiognomy*), to the 'form', which is at once vaguer and less essential, and finally to the outward 'dress'. It is a movement toward embodiment which is also a movement away from the immediacy of particular experience.

The paradox toward which this central stanza points is articulated throughout the poem: in the recurring half-rhymes, which echo rather than snap shut, and in the verbal and metrical and syntactic almost-parallelisms, which at once chime together and deviate from one another. The effect is that of a frame which does not quite fit. 'Mercy Pity Peace and Love', the names which men give to that to which they 'pray' and 'return their thankfulness', cannot encompass its essence, because its only manifestation is in particulars, not in the movement towards generalization that 'naming' involves. Their Innocent existence is a 'virtual' one – 'that is so, in essence or effect, though not formally, admitting of being called by the name so far as the effect or result is concerned' (*OED*). Yet in an imperfect way they point towards that which 'all' know and experience. And their virtual existence enables the confirmatory echoing of the poem: they are not only made possible by but are active in maintaining a world of mutual trust.

For it is to a shared image of a possible 'goodness' that prayer is addressed: to an image which is necessarily an abstraction. Men do not pray to their mothers or their 'Nurses':

> Then every man of every clime,
> That prays in his distress,
> Prays to the human form divine
> Love Mercy Pity Peace.

The specific virtues – separated out in the central stanza to evoke the different particularities of human relating in which they are manifested (the stirring of the heart in mercy, the delighted transformation of the body in love) – are re-merged in one composite image: 'the human form divine'. It is an image that is in one way vague, as the 'good' presents itself to those in 'distress'. But, as Blake was later to affirm, 'General Forms have their vitality in Particulars' (K738). And here, 'the human form divine' is less an ideal which is 'transmitted from generation to generation' (K154) than an image that is kept alive within and recreated by particular experiences. The 'all' of the opening stanza has become an individual man, who 'prays in his distress' to the shared values of *humanitas*.

In one sense the poem seems rounded off here: there is a reaffirmation of the 'virtues of delight' projected in the opening line, and a repeated, though significantly different, image of praying 'in distress'. But the stanza is not, like the first, a rounded one: there is no balancing image of need answered and thankfulness returned. And the poem continues in a way that is suggestively open-ended:

> And all must love the human form,
> In heathen, turk or jew.
> Where Mercy, Love & Pity dwell,
> There God is dwelling too.

At first this seems an innocuous 'moral':[68] a 'moral' which completes the poem's dissolution of Pope's hierarchy with its remote 'First Cause' whom fallen human beings 'adore' and whose laws they try to obey, into a sense of 'God' as potentially immanent within and created by human relationships. But in fact, this stanza subtly transforms the poem from a framed and finished account of how human conceptions of value are formed into something much more disturbing. One of the virtues has become an active verb, replacing 'prays'. That which was presented in the first stanza as an instinctive, universal, seemingly inevitable process of mutual value-formation is suddenly revealed as radically dependent on human actions. 'The human form divine' is simply 'the human form' → and the human form in the shapes least appealing to, least likely to be seen as 'divine' by, the polite eighteenth-century reader. And the last two lines, which in one way affirm the immanence of God, also – in that crucial 'where' – unobtrusively suggest that that immanence is contingent on its realization. The 'virtues' on which it depends are not necessary features of human nature, but activities in which 'all' must share if the 'Mercy, Love & Pity' to which they appeal are to be actualized at all. Once again, the stanza plays upon a significant ambiguity: does 'God' dwell in 'the human form' which is loved, or in him who loves? And the poetic suggestion is that in the activity of love he is created in both. What might have been a quiescent celebration of the human *potentia* for good has become a much more exigent recognition that the *potentia* exists only as it is realized, and that in the actual world its manifestations may be terribly tenuous.

For here 'Peace', hitherto echoing in every stanza, has disappeared. Its disappearance has been augured poetically by its failure to rhyme in the preceding stanza: a failure which suggests that in a world where there is 'distress' it cannot provide that adequate relief which would produce the completion of 'thankfulness'. And its absence gives this ending an edge of threat rather like that of the chimney-sweeper's 'moral'. The feeling is less obtrusive here than there, but it becomes more sharply apparent when one contrasts the penultimate stanza of Pope's poem:

> This day, be Bread and Peace my Lot;
> All else beneath the Sun,
> Thou know'st if best bestow'd, or not;
> And let Thy will be done.

For the juxtaposition of 'Bread and Peace' points to that division in eighteenth-century English society which was to make 'Peace' for Blake such a problematic and superficial virtue. It was a division which Pope himself was later to portray, in lines which display something of Blake's sense of language as the focus of ideological conflict:

> What Nature wants, commodious Gold bestows,
> 'Tis thus we eat the bread another sows:
> But how unequal it bestows, observe,
> 'Tis thus we riot, while who sow it, starve.[69]

Pope's ironic play upon the double meaning of 'riot' – at once the extravagant dissipation of the polite, and that plebeian disorder of which they complained – draws attention to one of the chief threats to domestic 'peace' in eighteenth-century England: the food riot, an unpeaceful demonstration in which those in 'distress' attempted to recall those in positions of social and economic power to their basic responsibilities toward the needy. Such riots posed a constant challenge to the official myth of a peaceful society in which the paternalism of the polite was answered by the deference of those beneath them.[70] In London itself, food riots were unknown until the 1790s, but other riots, equally indicative of fundamental divisions within the society, occurred throughout the century:[71] Blake's familiarity with their symbolism is demonstrated in 'The Chimney Sweeper'. And it is from that poem that we might pursue a particular strand of poetic thinking which connects, significantly, with the disappearance of 'Peace' from 'The Divine Image'.

The pivotal moment of 'The Chimney Sweeper' is a moment of imaginative sympathy between two exploited little boys, in which little Tom Dacre is tenderly seen and comforted:

> Theres little Tom Dacre, who cried when his head
> That curl'd like a lambs back, was shav'd, so I said,
> Hush Tom never mind it, for when your head's bare,
> You know that the soot cannot spoil your white hair.

It is a moment which is recollected, sardonically, in his notebook epigram of the early 1790s:

> 'Why of the sheep do you not learn peace?'
> 'Because I don't want you to shear my fleece'.   (K181)

Later, in 1794 and 1795, this ironic sense of the 'peace' that is preached to the exploited was to be more extensively articulated:

> Do we toil while others reap?
>   Do we starve while others feast?
> Are we sold and shorn, like sheep,
>   By the Despot and the Priest?[72]

There are those who profess to lay down their lives for their flocks; but, alas! we find the sheep utterly forsaken by them, and left to hirelings, who care not a farthing about them, only with respect to the fleece of which they rob them ... They preach charity, yet by their example inspire hatred; They pray to God for unity, peace and concord, while they themselves are using every art and machination to set the People at variance, and sow civil contentions among them, in order that they may the more easily fleece them.[73]

Seen in the light of these later writings, the child's unironic use of the same image in 'The Chimney Sweeper' is extraordinarily suggestive. For far from expressing the quietistic acceptance out of which they seek to jolt their readers, it creates its own reality, different from that of the status quo: it is not pathetic, but powerful. Indeed, by the final line of the poem, the subversive resonances animated by the child's vision have made it impossible to see him merely as a meekly shorn lamb: in his appeal to a 'duty' which 'all' must obey, he is a figure bearing not peace, but a sword.

Similarly, in 'The Divine Image', 'Peace' is imaged as the least essential and the most ambiguous of the values to which men appeal: 'the human dress' might equally be an ornament or a disguise.[74] And its quiet disappearance from the litany of virtues at the end of the poem is an implicit retort to Pope's individualistic prayer – 'This day be Bread and Peace my lot'. For in eighteenth-century England, where many who prayed for bread – who appealed to that 'Mercy, Love & Pity' which might answer to distress – were simply seen as disturbing public order, to invoke 'the Divine Image' could hardly be an act of peace. Blake's sense of this is registered not merely here and in 'The Chimney Sweeper', but also in the final line of 'Holy Thursday', where the refusal to allow a space for passive virtue exposes the violence already implicit within accepted practices. And as that line, with its warning urge to 'Pity', suggests, it is not merely 'Peace' that is problematic for Blake. Within the society he depicts, any attempt to invoke moral values is deeply contradictory. For if those in 'distress' may appeal to such values in order to question the status quo, they are also part of the official-rhetoric which seeks to justify it. And the 'Mercy, Love & Pity' with which 'The Divine Image' closes were in late eighteenth-century England a remarkably two-edged set of 'virtues'.

It is perhaps worth considering their negative aspects a little more closely. 'Mercy' is defined in the *Oxford English Dictionary* as 'Forbearance and compassion shown by one person to another who is in his power and who has no claim to receive kindness'. In other words, it is a virtue dependent on inequality: other than in a religious, it is most frequently invoked in a legal context. The eighteenth-century legal system might not at first seem remarkable for this virtue: between 1688 and 1820 the number of capital offences on the statute books increased by one hundred and ninety.[75] But in 1757 John Brown (by no means alone in defence of that system) was able to write:

The Lenity of our Laws in capital Cases; our Compassion for convicted Criminals, even the general Humanity of our Highwaymen and Robbers, compared with those of other Countries; these are concurrent Proofs, that the Spirit of Humanity is Natural to our Nation.[76]

And in an illuminating study of the law in eighteenth-century England Douglas Hay has pointed to the importance of the concept of 'Mercy' in maintaining this official view:

The prerogative of mercy ran throughout the administration of the criminal law, from the lowest to the highest level . . . The pardon is important because it often put the principal instrument of legal terror – the gallows – directly in the hands of those who held power. In this it was simply the clearest example of the prevailing custom of all levels of criminal justice. Here was the peculiar genius of the law. It allowed the rulers of England to make the courts a selective instrument of class justice, yet simultaneously to proclaim the law's incorruptible impartiality, and absolute determinacy. Their political and social power was reinforced daily by bonds of obligation on one side and condescension on the other, as prosecutors, gentlemen and peers decided to invoke the law or agreed to show mercy. Discretion allowed a prosecutor to terrorize a petty thief and then command his gratitude, or at least the approval of his neighbour as a man of compassion. It allowed the class that passed one of the bloodiest penal codes in England to congratulate itself on its humanity.[77]

Yet Blake, with his actute awareness of the oppressive and mystificatory potentialities of any 'law', could not have failed to see this contemporary 'mercy' as a very exact image of that divine 'mercy' to which the church appealed: that of a God who saves from a wrath which is his own. He was certainly unlikely to have been one of those who saw it unequivocally as a sign of 'humanity'.

'Pity' was even more centrally problematic. It was perhaps the most admired of the polite virtues, and that which was most constantly invoked, in sentimental verses and novels, in tracts, in charity sermons, and in the children's books of the period. But it was a virtue which – as Blake was later, savagely, to point out – might be seen in such contexts to depend on the existence of the misery it sought to soften. In the children's books its less attractive aspects appear perhaps most nakedly: its self-congratulation, its belittling distancing of its objects, and its complacent acceptance of the 'misfortune' of others:

'How comes it, Mamma', [asks little Frederick] 'that altho' I was truly sorry for poor Jacob's misfortune, and tho' I feel both for him and his mother, yet, on the whole, I am more *pleased* than *grieved*?' 'Child', said the lady, 'you have had the opportunity of doing well, and you have made use of it; and believe me throughout life, you will find, that the consciousness of having done a benevolent action will be the most effectual cordial for every painful sensation.'[78]

> As I came by the prison door,
>   I gave a penny to the poor,
> Papa did this good deed approve,
>   And dear Mama cried out for love.
>
> Whene'er the poor come to my gate,
>   Relief I will communicate,
> And show my Sire that I can be
>   As charitably great as he.[79]

This is a 'Pity' very different from that of the closing line of 'Holy Thursday'.

'Pity' and 'Mercy', then, depended, in polite usage, upon the assumption of an inferior other. But such an assumption is by no means implicit in the meaning of 'Love', a 'virtue' called forth by qualities in the other which may be seen as superior to those of the self: it is perhaps because of this that it remains in Blake's poem as the active virtue, becoming a verb in the final stanza. Yet, as he was to lament in 1792, even 'Love' was not without its contemporary deformations:

> I went to the garden of love,
> And I saw what I never had seen:
> A chapel was built in the midst,
> Where I used to play on the green.
>
> And the gates of the chapel were shut,
> And 'thou shalt not' writ over the door.   (K162)

The picture is of a love that allowed 'play' being subsumed by 'instruction', freedom to actualize 'joys and desires' by prescription. We can only guess at the particular crisis which may have prompted these lines:[80] but even in 1788, it seems, Blake had been to 'the garden of love' and found ' "thou shalt not" writ over the door':

There is a strong objection to Lavater's principles (as I understand them) & that is He makes every thing originate in its accident; he makes the vicious propensity not only a leading feature of the man, but the stamina on which all his virtues grow. But as I understand Vice it is a Negative. It does not signify what the laws of Kings & Priests have call'd Vice; we who are philosophers ought not to call the Staminal Virtues of Humanity by the same name that we call the omissions of intellect springing from poverty.

Accident is the omission of act in self & the hindering of act in another; This is Vice, but all Act is Virtue. To hinder another is not an act; it is the contrary; it is a restraint on action both in ourselves & in the person hinder'd, for he who hinders another omits his own duty at the same time...whatever is Negative is Vice. But the origin of this mistake in Lavater & his cotemporaries is, They suppose that Woman's Love is Sin; in consequence all the Loves & Graces with them are Sin.   (K88)

The passionless mildness which 'Lavater & his contemporaries' see as love is the very reverse of that active virtue which might question 'Peace'. And at its root is that fear of the free expression of impulse, that refusal to delight in 'the human form divine', which is manifested in sexual prudery: 'in consequence all the Loves & Graces with them are sin'.

The 'Mercy Pity Peace and Love' preached in late eighteenth-century England might, then, be seen as very ambiguous virtues. In *Songs of Experience* Blake was to point this out with a sharpness of psychological insight and a grasp of the social dynamics of moralizing that is unequalled in any other writings of the 1790s. Yet despite the implicit challenge in its final stanza, 'The Divine Image' does not seek to demystify: simply and apparently unironically it describes the operation of exactly those 'virtues' whose negative undersides the later poems were to expose. And it is unambiguous in its affirmation that the beneficent, active power of 'Mercy Pity Peace and Love' is quite different from the obfuscatory, 'hindering' function which they have acquired in the usage of polite moralizers. The harmonious interplay which they enable in this poem is not that which is preached by those in control, but that which is imaged by those in 'distress'. The present indicative tense of the first four stanzas points not to an utopian dream-world, but to an actually existing reality: a reality which Blake depicted again and again in *Songs of Innocence*. Against the mystificatory, sometimes self-deluding, sometimes hypocritical use of these words in the late eighteenth century, we might place another kind of usage:

[To the Gentlemen of This Parish Greeting]

Know ye not that the Lord of Life Liveth and that he will come again at the Last Day to judge the world in Righteousness to Give unto every man according as his work shall be some to Life Eternal and some to Everlasting punishment would ye not therefore Joyfully receive Mercy and forgiveness for your manifold sins and wickedness at the hand of our most Graceous Lord and Saviour at that Great trybunual Day. Should ye not Likewise therefore have Mercy Upon your poor Destresst Brethren who are Drove into the Greatest Destress of Poverty and to Extreem want at the highest Degree alarming under which Great Oppression and heavy Burden can no Longer be born...the thing that we Do ask is no more than Nature Doth Crave and not so much as things are advanced upon us which is for Every man to have one shilling and sixpence per Day or to be Settled according to the price of wheat Every man to have the value of one Peck of wheat per day supposing from 11 shills to 9 shills and Bushel hours to Labour and Lyquour as used at which time this Great assembly will upon the Period of Death Gain or perish at the atempt to the End that our Little ones for want perish not – all such Gentlemen who are of a Remorse Conscience as have an Eye of pity upon the Destressed which is an object truly Deserving Compassion would be Desired to Meet us there are the Place above mentioned to settle with us in amity Peace an Concord which we shall Gratefully receive but the refusal of such will Return your Recompence Upon your own head and your Reward be given you which may soon Unhappily come Upon you.[81]

Blake did not merely see 'marks of weakness, marks of woe'. He saw a society in which men did invoke and appeal to principles which its official practices often denied: in which an alternative to the status quo might be imaged in terms of exactly those principles.[82] This anonymous letter, pinned to the church door in Crediton in 1795, and one of many written throughout the century, might be compared point by point with 'The Divine Image': in its reminder that no man, not even a 'Gentleman', is above the need for Mercy' and 'Love', that *all* 'pray in their distress'; its insistence that those values be activated in real social relationships; its hope for a possible but by no means certain 'amity Peace an Concord'; its warning – here quite explicit – that those who fail to actualize the values which they profess will not be answered in *their* distress. 'The Divine Image' celebrates a *potentia* that could be found in the actual world of late eighteenth-century England: that which imaged and appealed to and thereby often realized a 'Mercy Pity Peace and Love' all too obviously lacking in the dominant structures of that society. It is a *potentia* which Blake traces throughout *Songs of Innocence*: in the nurturing which is claimed by the trusting innocence of the child;[83] in the non-instrumental sense of others which enables creative interplay, and which is actualized in 'play'; and in the impulse, growing out of both of these, towards creating images of a hitherto unknown symmetry – that which lies behind phenomena as diverse as the charity-children's procession and the little sweep's dream, and also behind the attempt to embody such experiences in a shared language of human values.

The manifestations of this *potentia* might be tenuous: they might, as *Songs of Experience* shows, be distorted and suppressed. The experiences which the poems in *Songs of Innocence* present are peripheral to the official organization of the society they depict: the play of a mother with her child, a moment of sympathetic comradeship, a particular way of seeing a ceremonial procession. The surroundings are the 'dark' and the 'cold'. Yet they are portrayed not as utopian dreams, but as real experiences of fundamental importance, essential to any continuing sense of human community. For it is, Blake suggests, only through the realization of such experiences that the values to which 'all' appeal can have any power. The endings of 'The Chimney Sweeper' and 'Holy Thurs-

day' warn of the consequences of failing to actualize a morality that
has been professed with a double-edged directness reminiscent of the
anonymous letters of the period: 'So if all do their duty, they need
not fear harm', 'Then cherish pity; lest you drive an angel from your
door.' And the final stanza of 'The Divine Image' is in one way a
quiet but unequivocal warning: 'all' must love, for the 'virtues'
which they invoke can have no other existence.

But if it is a warning, it is also a poetic reassurance: 'all must love
the human form' is at once a command and a statement of a universal
instinct. These virtues and the experiences which animate them do
actually exist, and compel human actions. And this second sense, of a
humanly constructed reality from which harmonious possibilities
can spring, is affirmed by the echoing, patterning presence of 'Mercy
Pity Peace and Love'. They wind through the poem like a dance,
continuing and recurring and being embodied in different ways. The
separate virtues have no mystifying rigidity here. They can be
rearranged, separated, recombined: they are not locked into a
particular logical system. They are that to which 'all' men pray: there
is no division here between a 'we' and 'somebody Poor' such as
polite usage assumed. And they are not a set of given absolutes in
which men must be instructed, of which they are the passive
recipients: they are made by men in an active process of maintaining
a continuing *humanitas*, in real living relationships.

'The Divine Image' shows how that world of mutuality and
creative possibility built by the mother's interaction with her child
might be created even in the ambiguous language of a divided
society, in a process of communal value-formation. The 'simplicity'
of this poem, like that of the other *Songs of Innocence*, is deceptive,
for its poetic analysis of the interrelation between a particular mode
of experience and continuing shared ideals – between 'vision' and
the morality of a society – is rigorously thought through and carefully articulated. It engages directly with the moral terminology
whose mystifying uses Blake was later to explore; and it does so
in a way analogous to that creative openness to the *potentia* within
an ambiguous situation that we have seen in 'Holy Thursday'.
Here there is no ironic demystification, such as there is in 'The
Human Abstract' – where 'Pity' and 'Mercy' are seen as the rigid,
reified results of coercive human relationships, where 'Peace'
'breeds' from a negative mutuality of 'fears', and the only 'Love' is
'selfish'. In 'The Divine Image' Blake focusses on and returns to
those words, 'Mercy Pity Peace and Love', 'playing' with them

in the poetry by imaging them singly and together, as they are glimpsed and imaged in particular human experiences. And the result is a double sense: at once of their necessary crudity (they are mere 'names' given to that which is manifested only in particulars), and of their efficacy as embodiments (however imprecise) of an otherwise incommunicable *humanitas*, the means whereby creative possibility may be entertained and shared.

For Blake is here concerned with that which may positively be 'transmitted from generation to generation' and with the mode of its transmission. That concern may be traced in 'Infant Joy' and 'Nurse's Song' and, in a different way, in 'The Ecchoing Green'. But here, in this poem about the moral and religious frame in which the affirmations of society are embodied, he explores it most fully and directly. The creative *potentia* of society is seen not as a fixed body of knowledge or doctrine, but as a process in which new experience has its part. The world of human values is not given, but must be collectively created: by all, not merely by one group or class. It grows out of 'Innocence', that wondering trust which is manifested in 'play'; a trust which is not sentimentally divorced from reality, precisely because it requires nurturing. In the 'obtuse angle' it bears to conventional eighteenth-century pieties, *Songs of Innocence* unobtrusively but powerfully suggests that the claim which 'Innocence' makes upon the world is more radical than that of that 'protest' which does not see beyond what is. For trust is oriented towards the future, and asks that there be a world which will answer to it, that there be a 'Mercy Pity Peace and Love' beyond 'distress'. And in that asking which is also an imaging it calls it forth and creates it. That is why these are *Songs of*, and not for, *Innocence*.

5 The Morality of Experience:
Songs of Experience

> the last hundred years have demonstrated empirically that if an organism or aggregate of organisms sets to work with a focus on its own survival and thinks that that is the way to select its adaptive moves, its 'progress' ends up with a destroyed environment. If the organism ends up destroying its environment, it has in fact destroyed itself.
>
> (Gregory Bateson, 'Form, Substance and Difference', in *Steps to an Ecology of Mind*)

To turn from *Songs of Innocence* to *Songs of Experience* is to enter a different world. The characteristic poetic shape is not one of echoing harmony, the end of the poem confirming yet pointing outward from the beginning, but one of linear progression toward a final disillusion which echoes nothing and leads nowhere. Poem after poem terminates in an image of blight, often a single word: 'despite', 'appall', 'misery', 'disguise', 'destroy'. Instead of the disinterested creativity of *Innocence*, these Songs dramatize explicit attitudes towards the experiences they present – outrage in 'Holy Thursday', complaint in 'The Chimney Sweeper', gloating or 'gladness' in 'A Poison Tree'. Indeed, several seem to be straightforward retorts to their Innocent counterparts: demystifications of that which in the earlier volume had opened out into transcendent possibility:

> Is this a holy thing to see,
> In a rich and fruitful land,
> Babes reducd to misery,
> Fed with cold and usurous hand?
>
> ('Holy Thursday')

> Pity would be no more,
> If we did not make somebody Poor:
> And Mercy no more could be,
> If all were as happy as we.
>
> ('The Human Abstract')

And in this they appear closer to the direct protest, the unambiguous attack on the pretensions of the polite, beginning to be articulated in the writings of Paine and his followers, than they do to any of Blake's own earlier work.

Certainly, such a view is borne out by an examination of that part of his notebook in which many of the Songs of *Experience* were first drafted.[1] For the writing here is very different from that which seems to have led towards the conception of *Songs of Innocence*. Instead of the amorphous, episodic satire of *An Island in the Moon*, these pages contain a series of short spare lyrics, mostly consisting of rhyming quatrains: lyrics charged with an enigmatic irony quite different from the darting ridicule of particular targets to be found in the earlier work. The interest is less in specific satiric observation than in a sophisticated exploration of the imaginative possibilities of paradox, riddle and aphorism:

> The ~~rose puts envious~~
>   ~~lustful~~ modest rose puts forth a thorn
> The ~~coward~~ humble sheep a threat'ning horn,
> While the lilly white shall in love delight,
> ~~And the lion increase freedom & peace.~~
> ~~The priest loves war & the soldier peace.~~
> Nor a thorn, nor a threat, stain her beauty bright.   (K171)

> An ancient Proverb
>
> Remove away that black'ning church:
> Remove away that marriage hearse:
> Remove away that ~~place~~ man of blood:
> ~~'Twill~~ You'll quite remove the ancient curse.   (K176)

There is no lack of confidence in the writing. Indeed, this new cryptic compression suggests a facilitating awareness of a whole context of ironic usages, which enables Blake to play upon multiple possibilities of meaning within a very small compass.

It is a context to which he himself points, on the first page of these notebook drafts:

> I saw a chapel all of gold
> That none did dare to enter in,
> And many weeping stood without,
> Weeping, mourning, worshipping.

> I saw a serpent rise between
> The white pillars of the door,
> And he forc'd & forc'd & forc'd,
> ~~Till he broke the pearly door~~
> Down the golden hinges tore.

And along the pavement sweet,
Set with pearls & rubies bright,
All his slimy length he drew,
Till upon the altar white

Vomiting his poison out
On the bread & on the wine.
So I turn'd into a sty
And laid me down among the swine.   (K163)

The breaking open of the excluding chapel is an image which the Swedenborgians used of their New (as opposed to the old) Church:

Abstracted from the spiritual sense, this sacrament [Holy Communion] is like a house that is shut up, but full of cabinets and caskets of valuable treasures, which is passed by like any other house in the street; and yet, as it was built by the clergy with walls of marble, and its roof is covered with plates of gold, it attracts the eye of all the passengers, and attracts their delight and commendation. The case however is altered when this house is opened, and every one is permitted to enter, and the keeper of the treasures freely distributes them.[2]

Here, however, that breaking open is portrayed not as a liberation but as a violation: if the old is forbidding, the New is disgusting. Clearly – though its extraordinary sexually-charged imagery has a force which goes beyond this – the poem expresses Blake's disenchantment with the New Church: perhaps it was occasioned by an actual dispute amongst the Swedenborgians.[3] But it also, in its final couplet, declares a quite specific change of direction. For in the 1790s, to proclaim solidarity with the 'swine' was, very exactly, to ally oneself with that 'swinish multitude' of newly articulate plebeian radicals, who saw Burke's notorious phrase (all that many of them ever knew of his *Reflections on the Revolution in France*) as encapsulating the attitude of the polite classes towards them, and who challenged polite definitions in pamphlets whose ironic titles bore witness to that fact: *An Address to Burke from the Swinish Multitude. By Old Hubert; Burke's Address to the Swinish Multitude; Pearls cast before Swine, By Edmund Burke, Scraped together by Old Hubert; Hog's Wash; Pig's Meat: or Lessons for the Swinish Multitude* (1793–5).[4] It is in such publications as these that we find similar preoccupations, a similar scorn for established pieties, a similar vocabulary of imagery, and a similar subversive energy to that of Blake's notebook:

if men would analyze governments, they would discover that they are
excessively weak, and are upheld only by those chains of prejudices and
circumstances, by which they hold mankind in awe.

> (*These are the Times that Try Men's Souls*: A letter to John Frost.
> A prisoner in Newgate. (1793), p. 23)

> In every voice, in every ban
> The ~~german~~ mind forg'd ~~links I hear~~ manacles I hear.

> ('London', K170)

Church (Established) – a patent for hypocrisy; the refuge of sloth, ignorance,
and superstition; the corner-stone of tyranny.

> (*The Rights of Priests*, from *Pigott's Political Dictionary* (1795))

> 'Where are thy father & mother, say?
> 'They are both gone up to Church to pray.
>
> . . .
>
> 'And because I am happy & dance & sing,
> 'They think they have done me no injury,
> 'And are gone to praise God & his Priest & King,
> '~~Who wrap themselves up in our misery~~.
> 'Who make up a heaven of our misery.'

> ('The Chimney Sweeper', K180)

Please to observe, my good countrymen, that every tyranny is founded in
wickedness; that it has in itself the seeds of its own destruction, and the curse
of heaven hanging over it; and that it wants only a shock from the heavy
hands of the people to bring it down in ruins on the heads of its supporters.

> (*Meat and Acorns collected by Old Hubert* (Daniel Eaton, n.d.), p. 7)

> But most ~~from every~~ thro' wintry streets I hear
> How the midnight harlot's curse
> Blasts the new born infant's tear,
> And ~~hange~~ smites with plagues the marriage hearse.

> ('London', K170)

hell is the fountain, the grand centre where all the lines of monarchy meet –
are concentrated and blended together, in one general point. The devil is the
body, and tyrants and their abettors are the branches and leaves: its fruit is of
various complexions and of various sizes, but whoever tasteth thereof shall
surely die. I shall enumerate a few of those fruits which are generally visible,
such as avarice, covetousness, luxury, lust, debauchery, incest and adultery;
pride, ambition, vain glory, thirst for filthy lucre, ribbons, garters, and other
play-things; titles, dignities and honours, with others of a darker complex-

ion – as cruelty, revenge, murder, and war, with all the evils attending it.
> (*The Rights of the Devil; or, Consolation for the Democrats* (1st edn
> Sheffield, reprinted Citizen Lee, London, n.d.), p. 16)

> And it bears the fruit of deceit,
> Ruddy & sweet to eat;
> And the raven his nest has made
> In its thickest shade.
>
> ('The human Image', K174)

> In the morning Glad I see
> My foe outstretch'd beneath the tree.
>
> ('Christian Forbearance', K165)

All those men . . . in whom the devil has right and property, and over whom he extends his influence, are, like wolves, easily distinguished from the sheep, to whom he lays no claim, because there is a particular mark whereby you may know these ravenous beasts. Their iron hearts are dead to the feelings of humanity: they regard not the cries of the fatherless; neither doth the cause of the widow come near them.
> (*The Rights of the Devil*, p. 18)

> And ~~see~~ mark in every face I meet
> Marks of weakness, marks of woe.
>
> In every cry of every man
> In ~~every voice of every child~~
>   every infant's cry of fear
> In every voice, in every ban
> The ~~german~~ mind forg'd ~~links I hear~~
>   manacles I hear.
>
> ('London', K170)

The question is not one of 'influence': many of these pamphlets may have been published after the notebook drafts to which they seem related.[5] But they do suggest something of the ambience within which Blake was framing the questions with which *Songs of Experience* engage. There is still in the notebook some evidence of a preoccupation with Swedenborgian issues. The poems about free love and about the repressive chapel with its serpent–priest seem to have been prompted by controversies within the New Church:[6] the 'Angel's Song' of the first drafts of 'The Human Abstract' (K164) may refer, ironically, to 'The Angel's Song' whose words and music were published in the *New Jerusalem Magazine* for 1790, and to the comment in the 'Life of Swedenborg' in the same issue:

were an angel from heaven to come and dwell incarnate amongst us, may we
not suppose that his conversation, discoveries, and conduct of life would
in many ways be so contrary to the errors and prejudices, the ways and
fashions of this world, that many would say with one consent, he is beside
himself.[7]

But it is the presence of this new plebeian radicalism, with its ironic
and often sophisticated awareness of the processes of ideological
mystification, that is most apparent in the compression and assurance of these notebook drafts.

And it is that same compression and assurance which distinguishes them most immediately from the publications of 'Old
Hubert' and 'Citizen Lee'. As the deletions in the notebook show,
Blake worked and worked over these tightly structured verses in a
way which prefigures his later declaration: 'Ideas cannot be Given
but in their minutely Appropriate Words' (K596). Within a single
brief poem allusions to many popular radical concerns – attacks on
war, on the church, on all kinds of exploitation and mystification –
may be brought into play, in ways which sharply focus the
connections between them. Instead of the straightforward protest of
the pamphleteers, there is a more disconcerting irony: in poem after
poem the speaker's professed feeling seems curiously at odds with
what the poetry reveals. And the radicals' confident questioning of
official values has become a much more complex questioning of the
whole nature and function of morality, a questioning whose
dialectical rigour seems (as 'The Lilly' suggests) to owe something to
antinomian traditions of thought. In these drafts, and the *Songs of
Experience* which issued from them, Blake is not simply giving
succinct and effective expression to the ideas of his Paine-ite
contemporaries: he seems to be thinking beyond them, not discursively, but poetically. These poems are not merely attacks on the
established order and the official pieties of late eighteenth-century
English society. They offer an acute and rigorous poetic exploration
of the implications of that new radicalism: an exploration not
opposed to but made from the perspective articulated in *Songs of
Innocence*.

Nowhere is this more evident than in the most overtly 'protesting' poem of *Songs of Experience*, 'Holy Thursday':

> Is this a holy thing to see,
> In a rich and fruitful land,
> Babes reducd to misery,
> Fed with cold and usurous hand?

Is that trembling cry a song?
Can it be a song of joy?
And so many children poor?
It is a land of poverty!

And their sun does never shine.
And their fields are bleak & bare.
And their ways are fill'd with thorns
It is eternal winter there.

For where-e'er the sun does shine,
And where-e'er the rain does fall:
Babe can never hunger there,
Nor poverty the mind appall.

The angry question with which the poem opens is very close to the angry irony of such as Pigott and Lee. The subject – that most public exhibition of polite 'benevolence', the charity-children's procession – is an obvious target for demystificatory attack. Like the writers for the 'swinish multitude', who sardonically assumed their readers' familiarity with oppression and exploitation, Blake's speaker offers no detailed discussion of the reasons for protest. There is none of that close examination of actual social conditions usually to be found in radical writings addressed to the polite reader – such as Wordsworth's 'Guilt and Sorrow', drafted in the year in which this 'Holy Thursday' was engraved. Instead, the first two lines, with their bitterly ironic invocation of the language of the charity sermons, seem to offer the same straightforward challenge to received definitions as we find in *Pig's Meat* or *Pigott's Political Dictionary*.[8]

Yet to come to this poem – as Blake seems to have intended his readers to come to it – after the Innocent 'Holy Thursday' is to receive a different, and more disturbing impression.[9] Where the imagery and rhythms of the earlier song conveyed an immediate sense of actual marching children, and its longer lines enabled a metaphoric transformation of the scene, these short staccato lines with their uncertain pattern of stresses convey neither a sense of actuality nor of the possibility of transforming it. It has been claimed that this 'Holy Thursday' is a 'point by point' refutation of the 'obtuse, roseate view' of the earlier one:[10] certainty, 'point by point' it is quite opposite. But the purpose of the opposition seems to be less to expose a truth which the Innocent poem denied than to offer a subtly scathing poetic exploration of the implications of a 'protest' uninformed by that sense of potentiality which was the mainspring of the earlier Song. At about the time at which this poem was

VISION AND DISENCHANTMENT

drafted, Blake was writing *A Song of Liberty*: his triumphant conclusion was that 'everything that lives is Holy' (K160). Read in the light of this, the opening line of this poem rebounds against its speaker: is it 'holy' to see 'this'? And as the poem continues, the limitations of his mode of vision are more and more devastatingly exposed.

By the second stanza, initial anger has become a doubting unwillingness to perceive anything that does not answer to that feeling:

> Is that trembling cry a song?
> Can it be a song of joy?
> And so many children poor?

The progression from sight to sound is that of the earlier poem: the effect is ironically inverted. For the Holy Thursday ceremonial, whose presence has from the beginning only been inferred by the reader, is here even further distanced: the hissing intimacy of 'this' has been replaced by 'that'. And this withdrawal from actuality means a denial of any sense of potentiality. The powerful crescendo of the children's singing, known to all who knew the ceremony, is here merely a 'trembling cry'; the thought that it might be 'a song of joy' can barely be admitted. The speaker's incipient response to the theatricality of the scene ('a song of joy', 'so many children') wavers into disbelief, and finally hardens into flat denial: 'It is a land of poverty!' 'It', rather than 'this' or 'here'. That which is before him is now seen as completely other: an objective reality in which he is not implicated and on which he cannot act. And this categorical statement leads to a series of similar statements which elaborate a world of static hopelessness:

> And their sun does never shine.
> And their fields are bleak & bare.
> And their ways are fill'd with thorns
> It is eternal winter there.

The movement of recoil which the poem has been tracing is here complete. This place is 'there', like a picture to be regarded, not here, at 'your door': its inhabitants are 'they', not the disturbingly divided 'you' and 'I' of 'The Chimney Sweeper'. There is no verbal liveliness: the flat copulas simply assert. Quite literally, this is an utopia – not the plenteous Utopia of popular imagination, but a hopeless utopia with none of that potentiality for change which actuality always contains.

Yet the speaker goes on, in an attempt to envisage a world different from that which he confronts. In the final stanza of the poem, the defeating logic of his progression becomes manifest:

> For where-e'er the sun does shine,
> And where-e'er the rain does fall:
> Babe can never hunger there,
> Nor poverty the mind appall.

Like the last line of the companion Song of *Innocence*, this would have awakened echoes of a well-known Biblical passage in its eighteenth-century readers; but here those echoes comment ironically on the speaker's shocked withdrawal:

> They shall hunger no more, neither thirst any more; neither shall the sun light on them, nor any heat.
>
> For the Lamb which is in the midst of the throne shall feed them, and shall lead them unto living fountains of waters: and God shall wipe away all tears from their eyes. (Revelation 7: 16–17)

Revelation images a transcendent state, not bound by the laws of the natural world: he gestures flatly towards the order of nature. Revelation expands into a magnificent vision of active succour: he ends with a limply negative hypothesis, 'appalled' by a poverty which in a crucial sense is his own. In a contemporary passage from *Peace and Union* (1792), later reprinted in *Pig's Meat; or, Lessons for the Swinish Multitude*, William Frend had used 'appal' in a similar transitive sense:

> Oh! that I had the warning voice of an ancient Prophet, that I might penetrate into the inmost recesses of palaces, and appal the harangues of senates. I would use no other language than that of the poor market-women. I would cry aloud in the ear of the first magistrate! We are sconced three-pence in the shilling, the fourth part of our labour, for what? Is there a man who could stand out against this eloquence? Yes. Thousands. Threepence in the shilling for spinning conveys no ideas to them.[11]

The contrast with Blake's poem is illuminating. Frend, wishing for 'the voice of an ancient Prophet', 'would use no other language than that of the poor market-women'. But this 'Holy Thursday' (unlike the Innocent Song, with its evocation of the power of the children's singing) admits no voice but that of protest and recoil. Here there is no clearly observed 'poverty' ('We are sconced threepence in the shilling') and no possibility of meaningful action in the world of 'palaces' and 'senates': 'the mind' is 'appalled' into shocked denial.

The ambiguity of the ending encapsulates that which has been dramatized in the progression of the poem: that 'poverty' of spirit which, cutting itself off in angry disenchantment from that which is before it, is finally reduced to dismayed passivity in face of a world which is seen as unalterably given, a world whose alternative can barely be imagined.

'If you go on so, the result is so' (K392). The 'poverty' this speaker confronts may be real enough: his anger may be justified. But in dramatizing him thus, Blake is carefully charting the limiting implications of a stance with which he was becoming familiar – and with which, as his avowal of solidarity with the 'swine' suggests, he felt considerable sympathy. To see nothing but pretension and hypocrisy in a ceremony such as the charity-children's service, to respond merely to the 'poverty' it seeks to mystify, is the reverse of liberating: it leads to a sterile dead end. The criticism is not made discursively, but poetically; yet it is none the less biting for that. For the difference between this vision and that of the first 'Holy Thursday' is minutely articulated. Where the earlier poem began with 'the children walking two and two' and ended with a vision of powerful angels, this begins with a refusal to see anything 'holy' in the scene, and ends with a weak gesture toward the opposite of what is. Where in the first poem the oscillation between past and present tenses and the recurrence of present participles created a sense of constantly available possibility, here there is merely the relentless, imprisoning present indicative. There is no power in the 'babes' of this poem, nothing to compare with the growing might of the 'multitudes of lambs' in the other Song. Here, from the beginning, they are 'reduc'd to misery' – not real, colourfully clad, marching and singing children, but 'many children poor' – and as the poem progresses they fade out rather than increase in potency. This 'Holy Thursday' ends not with an urgent appeal to action, but with an image of 'poverty' which afflicts as much as it outrages, a 'poverty' which prevents the realization of any potentiality for change in what is.[12]

The diagnosis of impasse this poem presents is a prophetic one. The demystificatory writings of Paine and his followers do not have the obvious sterility of this Song of *Experience*: they are often distinguished by vigour and wit. But despite the biting acuteness with which they challenge both an exploitative social system and the pretensions of its apologists, they are finally limited by a failure to project any compelling alternative, or to imagine – beyond millenarian gestures toward total revolution – how such an alternative might be realized within the society which is the object of their criticisms.[13] They do appeal to human values which they feel are being violated; even where organized religion is attacked, Christianity is often the implicit standard of reference:

Hierarchy – an ecclesiastical establishment, whose principles are *pomp, splendour,* and *revenue.* Jesus Christ, the founder of our religion, on the contrary, preached *poverty, humility, equality.* Christian Bishops delight and revel in wealth and palaces, yet departing so wide from its maxims, they are insolent enough to uphòld the excellence and orthodoxy of the Christian system.[14]

But there is little attempt to explore how such 'virtues' might be maintained and nurtured in a creative rather than a mystifying way; no developed vision (apart from the crudely rationalistic blueprints of Paine and Spence) of what a society within which they were operative might be like; and little indication of where, in the actual present, its seeds might be found.[15]

And it is precisely this failure that this 'Holy Thursday', so carefully contrasted to its Innocent counterpart, diagnoses and dramatizes. The voice of *Experience* is a single, ineffectually protesting one; a voice whose protest blocks out those other powerful voices which resound in 'harmonious thunderings' through the closing stanzas of the earlier poem. There, the developing vision of the children as angels does not merely question official pieties: it points, compellingly, to an immanent alternative. But here there is no such vision. Instead, Blake exposes the inherent fatalism of that 'experience' whose 'method' is judgment and disillusion.[16] And he exposes it not through the voice of an apologist for the status quo, but through the voice of that demystificatory protest which claimed, in the early 1790s, to offer liberation from the 'mind-forg'd manacles' which shackled his society; that 'swinish' opposition whose ironic refusal of polite definitions was in some ways like his own.

The 'Holy Thursday' of *Experience* offers a poetic criticism not of the details but of the logic of that protest: a criticism which can be traced throughout the 1792 notebook, in poems on subjects as apparently diverse as possessive love and repressive religion. In these compressed and much-revised lyrics Blake engages with and questions the thinking of those contemporaries to whom he now felt closest, pushing their preconceptions to their necessary conclusions, testing them always (sometimes implicitly, sometimes – as in 'Holy Thursday' – by explicit contrast) against his own already realized vision of Innocence. Yet these poems are far from variations on a single theme: like the different *Songs of Innocence*, each demands a separate, strenuous activity of the reader at just those points where he might be disposed to assimilate what is offered to a familiar message. Thus 'The Clod & the Pebble', unlike 'Holy Thursday', gives not merely the monologic voice of 'holiness', but also that which would question it:

> Love seeketh not Itself to please,
> Nor for itself hath any care;
> But for another gives its ease,
> And builds a Heaven in Hells despair.

> So sang a little Clod of Clay,
> Trodden with the cattles feet;
> But a Pebble of the brook,
> Warbled out these metres meet.

> Love seeketh only Self to please,
> To bind another to Its delight:
> Joys in anothers loss of ease,
> And builds a Hell in Heavens despite.

And the temptation – even more pressing to readers more used to definitive moral judgment than we – is to decide which of these voices is 'right'.[17] Yet the poem itself undermines that question in a way hardly possible to discursive speech.

Its oddity might best be illuminated by considering the difference between its opposition of 'heavenly' and 'hellish' love, and that of the Swedenborgian argument which must have been familiar to Blake:

In short, the love of self and the love of the world are in direct opposition to the love of the Lord and the love of our neighbour: therefore the love of self and the love of the world, as described above, are infernal loves; they do likewise actually reign in hell, and also constitute hell with man: but love to the Lord and love towards our neighbour are heavenly loves; they likewise actually reign in heaven, and also constitute heaven with man.[18]

Where Swedenborg presents an abstract moral argument, Blake offers two definitions, each emanating from a different concrete situation, and each justifying a particular mode of survival. The first comes from a 'Clod of Clay' which is trodden underfoot, and has no choice but to be malleable; the second from a 'Pebble of the brook' necessarily hardened against the water which flows around it. Each offers its definition of Love as eternal and categorical truth: but the poem as a whole ironically exposes their relativity. Here, once again, we might trace a movement on Blakes's part from Swedenborgian to 'swinish' concerns. For 'The Clod & the Pebble' seems to offer a neat dramatization of that insight at the centre of much contemporary radical thinking: the sense that the same word might bear quite disparate meanings, according to the perspective from which it is uttered. Yet the word this poem chooses is not one at the centre of political debate, such as the 'charter'd' of 'London', or even an ambiguous 'polite' virtue such as 'Pity': it is that most apparently unquestionable of absolutes, 'Love'. And the poetic effect is very different from that of publications such as *Pigott's Political Dictionary*.

For although their surface meanings may be opposite, the counter-definitions offered by Clod and by Pebble are poetically not opposite at all. Blake's only direct judgment within the poem is a trenchant one:

> But a Pebble of the brook,
> Warbled out these metres *meet.*
> [my italics]

'Meet' does not merely mean 'suitable, fit or proper': it can also mean 'equal to, on the same level as' and 'close-fitting, of the same dimensions'.[19] And when we compare the Pebble's words with those of the Clod, this is exactly what we find:

> Love seeketh not Itself to please,
> Nor for itself hath any care;
> But for another gives its ease,
> And builds a Heaven in Hells despair.

> Love seeketh only Self to please,
> To bind another to Its delight:
> Joys in anothers loss of ease,
> And builds a Hell in Heavens despite.

The two stanzas echo one another tellingly. For 'self' is just as insistently present in the first as in the second: its 'pleasure', its 'care', its 'ease', is the underlying subject of these lines – just held under by the negatives. In comparison, 'another' remains a vague and insubstantial presence. For this conscious negation of self, as Blake's neat exploitation of one of the most paradoxical resources of poetry shows, involves a concentration upon exactly that which is negated.[20]

This negative distancing of the essential subject of the first stanza accounts for the curious sense both of logical inevitability and of release of energy which comes in the last. For if in discursive terms that stanza presents the opposite point of view, a counter-definition, poetically it gives direct expression to the implicit meaning of the first. What was there contorted and held in check is here demystified and driven directly forward: just as on the plate the leaping frogs and swimming duck and upward-reaching vine of the bottom half contrast with the static, bending animals and shading tree of the top. Here the verbs of which 'Love' is the subject are all straightforwardly active. 'Seeketh not' becomes 'seeketh only': 'gives' is replaced by the intransitive 'Joys', which forces a gloating trochaic substitution, and seems an ironic echo of *Songs of Innocence*. Equally ironically, 'another' (still vague) is twice as present in the poetry.

Seen thus, the two definitions of the poem do not seem to be given equal weight: the second exposes an unattractive truth which the first would conceal, and thereby generates an energy choked off in the opening stanza. The Pebble is 'of the brook', while the Clod is on its margin: and on the plate, the poem *is* the brook. Yet the vigorous compulsion with which the final stanza echoes the first is the reverse of satisfying. The reader is left with a sense not of liberation, but of contradiction and deadlock – a sense which has become more, not less oppressive as the poem proceeds. And the reason lies not simply in the savage malevolence of the Pebble's words, but in the fact that those words offer no release from the closed circle set up by the Clod's definition. One is reminded of Blake's retort to Swedenborg's distinction between Heaven and Hell: 'Heaven & Hell are born together' (K96). Here, while both speakers define Love from opposite points of view, they do so from within the same universe of discourse – a universe of oppositional relationships. Both assume the primacy and controlling power of the self, the distancing of 'another', and a world in which the pleasure and ease of one lies in denying that of the other. It is a conception of the world familiar in other of *Songs of Experience* – 'Pity would be no more, / If we did not make somebody Poor'; 'Who make up a heaven of our misery'; 'And his dark secret love / Does thy life destroy': its logical conclusion is that killing of the other which is dramatized in 'A Poison Tree'. Here, the sterile equivalence between the two definitions is dramatized by the tight patterning of the poem itself, the venomous sharpness with which the final stanza contradicts, yet fails to move beyond the basic framework of, the second. 'Despite', sound-linked to 'despair', does not rhyme with it: but in its rhyme with 'delight' it snaps the poem tightly, triumphantly, unsatisfyingly shut.

   The poetic effect of this is very different from that of the confirmatory half-rhymes of 'The Divine Image', or the echoing yet distinct voices of 'Infant Joy'. In *Songs of Innocence* there is no contradiction, though the poetry dramatizes different points of view. Instead, there is creative interaction, which leads outward from the poem – 'Come come leave off play'; 'No no let us play'; 'Well well go & play'. But in 'The Clod & the Pebble' each voice claims fixed and universal truth for its definition, and there is no room for interaction between them. There is certainly no outward movement beyond them, for the second, despite its release of malevolent energy, merely confirms the hidden meaning of the first: it does not, like the exchanges between children and nurse, open out into echoing futurity. And when it is read – as Blake intended it to be read – in the wake of *Songs of Innocence*, the reason for the hopeless paradox which these counter-definitions generate becomes clear.[21] For neither that of 'Heaven' nor of 'Hell' envisages the possibility, articulated again and again in the earlier collection, of a love which is a realization both of self *and* other; a love which is not the product of humbly accepted suffering or of conscious self-denial, like the 'Christian' love of the Pebble; a love which is manifested in the mutually expressive spontaneity of 'play'.[22] The 'joy' of 'Infant Joy' is not an abstraction which must be defined: it is, first, a feeling voiced by the child, and then a 'name' which the mother 'calls' it – a name which enables and embodies her hopes for its future. The little sweep's love for Tom Dacre is not a repression of selfish desire, but an immediate impulse of imaginative responsiveness: the unself-conscious excitement of his speech registers both his own delight and the particular and beautiful reality of the other child.

   In 'The Clod & the Pebble', as in 'Holy Thursday', Blake is entering into implicit debate with those of his contemporaries to whom he might seem to be closest. If the energy with which the Pebble unmasks the hidden logic of the Clod's position suggests some imaginative sympathy with their 'hellish' opposition to official values, the trapped mirror-imaging of the one by the other demonstrates forcefully that there is nothing liberating about demystification as such. But the poem does not merely present deadlock: in a quite different way to 'Holy Thursday' it exposes some of the reasons for it. The categorical assertions of both Clod and Pebble merely justify their own responses to their own situations – softening before or hardening against an unalterable environment: their implicit assumption of a freely choosing 'Self' is an illusion. Instead, that 'Self' is an abstracted, alienated, inauthentic individual, hypo-statized in opposition to the other, and seeking to impose its own rationalizations as universal truth. The 'Love' which each seeks to define is thus very different from the mutually created 'Love' of 'The Divine Image'. There, too, Blake offers opposing definitions, but they chime together rather than contradict, in a way which subverts any claim to fixed or final truth:

> For Mercy Pity Peace and Love,
> Is God our father dear:
> And Mercy Pity Peace and Love,
> Is Man his child and care.

And the 'Love' of 'The Divine Image' finally emerges not as a noun but as a verb: an activity in which 'all must' engage. For the 'names' of *Songs of Innocence* ('joy'; 'Mercy Pity Peace and Love') have an operative, not a reified reality: they are the means whereby very different particular experiences – experiences in which difference is recognized and accepted – are focussed, expressed and (paradoxi-cally) enabled. Their meanings are not imposed by a single controlling voice, but manifested within that interpersonal world which they themselves create. In contrast, the Clod and the Pebble begin not from experience ('I happy am'; 'To Mercy Pity Peace and Love / All pray ... ') but from an abstraction, which each separately defines in a way which will not admit the possibility of difference. They are thus pulled apart into opposition even as they are linked together by the same limiting framework. And the word which both use is not a shared creation: it is a static rigidifying point which prevents escape from that dichotomy between self and other around which the poem is constructed.

It is a dichotomy with manifold implications. Epistemologically, it means an abstraction of the self from its environment, so that that which is other is not related to, but distanced and defined. The paradigm thus becomes (as Martin Buber has put it) the I-It rather than the I-Thou relationship, a relationship of linear control rather than of interaction.[23] Ideologically, it presupposes an unequal social system in which self succeeds at the expense of others, or others at the expense of self: a system of competition rather than of inter-dependence, of appropriation and exploitation rather than of mutual recognition. Psychologically, it means inflexible isolation, a refusal or denial of interpersonal (as distinct from oppositional) relationships: the other becomes threatening to the self rather than the locus of creative difference. It is a dichotomy whose sterile logic is exposed in the taut closure of 'The Clod & the Pebble', where self-denial and selfishness contradict and reflect one another in hopeless deadlock. And in the *Songs of Experience* whose drafts follow this in the notebook, these implications are explored in their interrelatedness.

Throughout, *Songs of Innocence* remains a constant, implicit point of reference – the articulated vision of an alternative mode of being which makes the inner logic of this sharply apparent. Thus, underneath 'Infant Sorrow' echoes of the Innocent 'Introduction' and 'Infant Joy' run like a mocking counterpoint:

> My mother groand! my father wept.
> Into the dangerous world I leapt:
> Helpless, naked, piping loud:
> Like a fiend hid in a cloud.
>
> Struggling in my fathers hands:
> Striving against my swadling bands:
> Bound and weary I thought best
> To sulk upon my mothers breast.

The child which was 'piping' 'on a cloud' in the earlier poem is here 'hid in a cloud': instead of disappearing freely he is caught and 'bound'. Despite the 'hands' and 'bands' that await him, he is 'Helpless' and alone: for there is no answering recognition and nurturing of his essential being, no space for play. Here there are no longer two chiming voices, echoing in a poetically created present, but a single voice which speaks in a fixed past tense. And the story it tells is of a wholly illusory freedom.

This child presents himself as autonomous and independent ('I thought best'); but the poem traces a progressive waning of his original 'fiendish' energy. His first vigorous 'leaping' gives way to mere resistance – 'Struggling in my fathers hands', 'striving against my swadling bands' – and then to calculated, quiescent resentment. The world in which he finds himself is 'dangerous' and inflexible – not to be acted upon but reacted against, and finally withdrawn from into closed-off subjectivity. Yet the locus for that withdrawal is the most primary emblem of natural human relationships, the 'mothers breast'. For the 'unnatural' progression which the poem delineates is not presented as a single terrible occurrence, but as a familiar 'Infant Sorrow',[24] a well-known 'State of the Human Soul' – the dawning of that egocentric selfconsciousness which was a central premise of eighteenth-century philosophy and science: *cogito ergo sum*. This self-definition is very different from that self-realization within an interpersonal world which is presented in 'Infant Joy'. Instead of an opening out, the poem depicts diminution: instead of expressing himself in response to another, this child remains *infans* – dumb. His assertion of freedom is the direct converse of that vision of freedom as an activity including both self and other, in the world rather than opposed to it, of *Songs of Innocence*. For far from being an expression of autonomy, it is an internalization of that which cannot be actualized, a splitting of the self ('I thought best / To sulk . . . ') rather than a relationship with another, an attempt to claim some limited area of control within a world which is felt to be unalterable.

The 'independent' egocentric consciousness whose birth is dramatized in 'Infant Sorrow' is the subject, in a very different way of 'The Fly'. Like 'Infant Sorrow' ('I thought best . . . ') and like 'A Poison Tree' ('Glad I see . . . '), this is a poem which ends with a statement of apparent satisfaction:

> Then am I
> A happy fly,
> If I live,
> Or if I die.

Yet, as in the two other poems, the poetic effect is disquieting. The terse jerkiness of this stanza hardly conveys the tone of 'joyful acceptance' that at least one critic has claimed to find in it:[25] and the poem which it concludes raises questions which are unresolved by it. It is a poem very different from any of the other *Songs of Experience*, for its short two-stress lines and its syllogistic structure seem designed less to express feeling than to hold it in abeyance:

> Little Fly
> Thy summers play,
> My thoughtless hand
> Has brush'd away.
>
> Am not I
> A fly like thee?
> Or art not thou
> A man like me?
>
> For I dance
> And drink & sing:
> Till some blind hand
> Shall brush my wing.

> If thought is life
> And strength & breath:
> And the want
> Of thought is death

The argument developed with such seemingly straightforward logic
has two quite opposite implications, each of which is held in check
by the careful neutrality of the propositions. For the metaphoric
likening of man to fly is virtually meaningless unless one knows in
what spirit they are being likened. Is the emphasis on the carefree
'play' of the fly's life – in which case the opening stanza is warmly
sympathetic: or is it on the fly's vulnerability – in which case it
signals horrified remorse? The whole emotional tone of the rest of
the poem depends on which of these two alternative readings one
adopts.[26] The second stanza becomes either a whimsically tender
recognition, or a frighteningly reductive one: the third, either an
expression of gay insouciance or a terrified realization of defence-
lessness. But the poem itself gives no clue: the reader is simply
offered a series of thinly rational propositions and inferences which
remain suspended between these antithetical alternatives.[27] The
hesitant rhythms imposed by the stanza form work oddly against the
linear development of the argument, and drive home the recognition
that its meaning depends on an imaginative identification, in one
direction or another, which is not being made. Are human life and
death to be seen as part of a reassuring order, or as purposeless and
unintelligible?

And the suspense thus built up is not resolved, even in the final
stanza. Indeed, there the jerky, unsettling emphasis created by the
truncated lines is reinforced by three strong rhymes: the reader is
halted on each phrase as by a question. Even in terms of the logic of
the argument, this conclusion remains ambiguous. Optimism seems
to depend on the premise that 'thought is life / And strength &
breath', yet the poem has begun with a 'thoughtless' act of murder. Is
there really reason to be 'happy': or is the equation of man with fly –
an equation which seems almost a parody of that identity between
God and man which is affirmed in 'The Divine Image' – an ironically
bitter one? One does not know, for the poem does not break out of
its closed circuit of logical argument. Its baffled, broken movement,
mimicking the backward and forward movement of a fly within a
small confined space, seems the expression of an absence whose
significance Blake had diagnosed in 1788 in the Conclusion to his
first series of *There is No Natural Religion*: 'If it were not for the Poetic
or Prophetic character the Philosophic & Experimental would soon

be at the ratio of all things & stand still, unable to do other than repeat the same dull round over again' (K97). The self-circling ratio-cinations of the speaker in 'The Fly' are just such a 'dull round': for those ratiocinations manifest exactly that contraction of significant experience to 'experiment' which *There is No Natural Religion* had questioned.[28] Like the rational Deist or the Newtonian observer, who assumes that an 'objective' knowledge of the universe is possible, this speaker is left with a set of propositions whose human import is terrifyingly ambiguous.[29] In the absence of 'the Poetic or Prophetic character' this is all that can be known.

And 'the Poetic or Prophetic character' is the mainspring of a wholly different mode of relating to the world. Beside this poem we might place 'A Dream', from *Songs of Innocence*, with *its* story of insect disaster:

> Once a dream did weave a shade,
> O'er my Angel-guarded bed,
> That an Emmet lost it's way
> Where on grass methought I lay.
>
> Troubled wilderd and folorn
> Dark benighted travel-worn,
> Over many a tangled spray,
> All heart-broke I hear her say.
>
> O my children! do they cry,
> Do they hear their father sigh.
> Now they look abroad to see,
> Now return and weep for me.
>
> Pitying I drop'd a tear:
> But I saw a glow-worm near:
> Who replied, What wailing wight
> Calls the watchman of the night.
>
> I am set to light the ground,
> While the beetle goes his round:
> Follow now the beetles hum,
> Little wanderer hie thee home.

This speaker does not assume a position of separation and control: he does not rationalize about the Emmet's fate, but pities it. Instead of the later poem's suspended judgment, there is ready empathy: 'All heart-broke' might equally refer to his own feelings or to hers. And this pity, which enables him to hear her lamenting voice – lamenting not for herself, but for others – does not, like the protest or calculation of *Experience*, blind him to those possibilities which might answer to need: it animates them. His 'dream' reveals a world in which there is no separation of self from other, but one in which everything feels for another. Everything, unselfregarding, has its own appointed place: the 'pitying' narrator is himself 'guarded' by angels, and 'a dream' frames the whole. After the careful, logical argument of 'The Fly' this world may seem a fanciful creation. But here, no less than in the more 'realistic' *Songs of Innocence*, Blake is tracing the implications of a real, alternative 'state of the human soul'; a 'state' which in its contrast points towards the limitations of that rational isolation which the later poem dramatizes.

Although he addresses the fly, the speaker of that poem cannot listen to it. For at the opening he has already killed it: it has no voice which might question or feed into his monologue. It is simply the starting point for an argument whose central concern is himself. Yet there is no full or coherent sense of self in the poem, simply a thinly defining 'I', who reasons about rather than relates to that which he confronts: a reasoner whose only act is, ironically and devastatingly, a 'thoughtless' act of murder. His control is illusory: he is trapped like a fruitlessly circling fly within a constricted 'dull round' from which there is nothing to rescue him. His is the voice of 'the Reasoning Power in Man ... separated / From Imagination & closing itself as in steel' (*Jerusalem*, ch. 3, K714). In dramatizing that attenuated voice, rationalizing from a position of separated ego-centricity, Blake might well have remembered sardonically that the lord of the flies is Beelzebub.

And the 'Imagination', or 'Poetic or Prophetic character' which might provide release from this speaker's dilemma is not merely subjective fantasy: it can be actualized only in relationship. Blake's sense of this was powerfully apparent in *Songs of Innocence*: it is apparent in a different way in 'Ah! Sun-flower' of *Experience*:

> Ah Sun-flower! weary of time,
> Who countest the steps of the Sun:
> Seeking after that sweet golden clime,
> Where the travellers journey is done.
>
> Where the Youth pined away with desire,
> And the pale Virgin shrouded in snow:
> Arise from their graves and aspire,
> Where my Sun-flower wishes to go.

The world of this poem is not, like that of 'The Fly', one of contracted rationalism: yet it is one which is equally sterile. All the images are of fruitless longing. Rooted in the earth as it is, the Sun-flower can only 'count the steps of' that Sun towards which it forever points, only 'seek *after*' that which it will never reach. The goal of its aspiration is distanced and sentimentalized – 'that sweet golden clime': its hoped-for satisfaction – 'Where the travellers journey is done' – has the ring at once of tautology and impossibility. For the image is not of futurity, but of the end of longing; and if the 'traveller' is the Sun, its journey is never 'done'. The 'where' of this closing line is repeated at the opening of the second stanza: even within this mythological realm of fulfilment, it seems, there is further aspiration – and aspiration which leads merely into a world of 'wishes'. The poem ends where it began, with an image of the Sun-flower's yearning: all remains within the closed circle of subjective desire.

The transcendence all long for here cannot, it seems, be realized. And the reason for this is delineated by the curious syntax of the poem. There are eight verbal forms within as many lines, but no main verb: the effect is of movement which never reaches completion. Some of these verbal forms point back toward an arrested past – 'pined', 'shrouded': those which indicate present activity all describe a longing which never attains its object – 'countest', 'Seeking', 'Arise', 'aspire', 'wishes to go'. And because the sentence of which they should be part is never completed they are immobilized thus, like a bed of sunflowers all facing the same way – a sense which is reinforced by the repetition of clauses beginning 'Where'. It seems that the desire presented here prevents engagement with actuality as surely as do the 'objective' ratiocinations of 'The Fly'. Because all point thus in the same direction, nothing in the poem relates to anything else: even when the Youth and the Virgin who might answer to one another break away from the fixity of their past participles ('pined away', 'shrouded'), they simply 'arise' and 'aspire' in the same fruitless way. Their longing, like that of the earth-bound Sun-flower, is revealed as mere escapist fantasy. To actualize impulse, to engage with another, is to commit oneself to that 'time' of which the Sun-flower is 'weary': and nothing in this poem will do so, even at the level of verbal completion. Yet the only immortality to be gained by this refusal is shown to be one of self-enclosed yearning: a peculiar frozen impotence very different from the creative interplay that is imaged in *Songs of Innocence*. Against the sterile circularity of this poem we might place the very different, echoing circularity of 'The Ecchoing Green'. There, the transitive verbs and linear development dramatize exactly that commitment to time, to completion, which 'Ah! Sun-flower' seeks to escape. In the Innocent poem there is interaction, for the participants turn toward one another, not towards distanced objects of private – though ironically shared – longing. There, life is lived in a way which enables others to live it: instead of the frustrated Virgin and Youth, Blake portrays 'Round the laps of their mothers, / Many sisters and brothers'. Desire finds fulfilment, and the generations succeed one another in joy. And out of this actualization of desire – which implies also an acceptance of that mortality which the Sun-flower wishes to transcend – genuinely new, non-tautologous possibilities emerge. Ideals are not projected out of deprivation, utopian alternatives to unalterable fates. There is no need for conscious aspiration, because a pattern beyond anything intended by any single participant evolves freely, in play.

Each of these three poems – 'Infant Sorrow', 'The Fly' and 'Ah! Sun-flower' – explores, in a different way, that 'omission of act in self & the hindering of act in another' which Blake had defined as 'vice' in his annotations to Lavater (K88). It is an 'omission' and a 'hindering' which is registered in the peculiar failure of energy so precisely (and yet so differently) traced in each of them: in the contraction of passion into calculation of 'Infant Sorrow', in the constricted lines and thinly defining copulas of 'The Fly', in the absence of any main verb at all in 'Ah! Sun-flower'. The ostensible subject of each poem is, compared to those of many of the other Songs of *Experience*, a 'private one': the moment of birth, the contemplation of a fly or a sunflower. Yet just as Songs of *Innocence* articulated the central significance to a whole society of that which was (and is) customarily defined as private experience, so these poems question such distinctions. That which is seen by their speakers as an assertion of personal freedom is shown to be not separate from but grounded in a particular mode of relating to others, a 'State of the Human Soul' whose implications are by no means merely 'private'. And in other of the Songs of *Experience* that 'State' is explored much more fully in its wide-ranging social manifestations.

One of the most multifariously resonant of such poems is 'A Poison Tree', with its tale of anger expressed and suppressed:

I was angry with my friend:
I told my wrath, my wrath did end.
I was angry with my foe:
I told it not, my wrath did grow.

And I waterd it in fears,
Night & morning with my tears:
And I sunned it with smiles,
And with soft deceitful wiles.

And it grew both day and night,
Till it bore an apple bright.
And my foe beheld it shine,
And he knew that it was mine.

And into my garden stole,
When the night had veild the pole:
In the morning glad I see
My foe outstretched beneath the tree.

Like 'The Clod & The Pebble', this seems at one level a sardonic
demystification of the 'Christian' virtues of self-denial and repression: the notebook draft is entitled 'Christian Forbearance'. Yet the
single narrative voice of this poem is very different from the two
contradicting voices of the earlier one. This speaker makes no
attempt to justify his actions. Instead, with a 'peculiar honesty'
unmediated by moral commentary, he tells a story of concealment
and triumph: a story which ends not in deadlock, but in the
'gladness' of resolution. But the heavy trochees and relentless
rhyming couplets suggest less release than entrapment: that which is
conveyed by the poem seems at odds with the feeling he avows. And
the effect – as Blake's change of title registers – is not simply ironic,
but enigmatic and disturbing.

   Here, as in 'The Clod & the Pebble', Blake seems to be pondering a
Swedenborgian theme – the way in which outward 'piety' ('Christian forbearance') might be used to conceal darker, even murderous,
impulses:

Every man from his infancy enters upon life from externals, learning to act
morally and to speak intelligently . . . nevertheless, as evils spring up from
their native fountain, he harbours them in the recesses of his mind, and also
ingeniously veils them over by reasonings drawn from fallacies, until at
length he no longer knows evil to be evil; and after this, his evils being veiled
over and covered as it were with dust, he no longer thinks anything of them,
only keeping on his guard so as to prevent their appearing before the world.
Thus he studies only to lead a moral life in externals, and so becomes a

two-fold or double man, being in externals a sheep, and in internals a wolf: hence he is like a box of gold filled with poison; or like a person of a foul breath, who keeps in his mouth some sweet-smelling substance, to prevent its being perceived by the bystanders; or he is like a perfumed rat's skin. You profess that you have lived moral lives, and have been attentive to the practice of piety; but let me ask, have you ever examined your internal man, and there perceived any lusts prompting you to take vengeance even to death . . . ?[30]

Something of this interest in a duplicity which leads to alienation from the true self does, as we shall see, shape the narrative of 'A Poison Tree'. Yet here, once again, Blake's emphasis is rather different from Swedenborg's. And the difference may be illuminated by considering another echo which Swedenborg's notion of the 'double man' might have awakened in Blake's mind – that of a popular rhyme, familiar in his day as in ours, which in one respect bears a striking resemblance to 'A Poison Tree':

> There was a man of double deed
> Sowed his garden full of seed.
> When the seed began to grow,
> 'Twas like a garden full of snow;
> When the snow began to melt,
> 'Twas like a ship without a belt;
> When the ship began to sail,
> 'Twas like a bird without a tail;
> When the bird began to fly,
> 'Twas like an eagle in the sky;
> When the sky began to roar,
> 'Twas like a lion at the door;
> When the door began to crack,
> 'Twas like a stick across my back;
> When my back began to smart,
> 'Twas like a penknife in my heart;
> When my heart began to bleed,
> 'Twas death and death and death indeed.[31]

For the central structural principle of these lines – the recurring connective device of the couplets – is exactly that transformation which is more subtly but no less compellingly at the centre of 'A Poison Tree'. Here, as there, metaphor mutates into literal reality: and here, as there, that mutation causes an apparently uncontrollable progression towards a landscape of death. In both cases, it is progression which becomes disconcertingly immediate as it nears its end – that which began as a third person narrative in 'There was a man' suddenly changes to the first person singular; that which was distanced by the narrative past tense in 'A Poison Tree' enters the present in the final couplet. And in both cases, it is a progression which seems to be independent both of the 'man of double deed' and of his victim. The structuring logic of the popular rhyme's riddling couplets is more important than the specific analogies on which they turn: these, in its long history, have had many variations. But Blake's poem 'admits not a Letter that is Insignificant' (K611). Its terse enigmatic story is in fact an incisive poetic exploration of that intuition about human experience which informs the older verses and accounts for their continuing fascination.

The opening lines of the poem are, however, very different:

> I was angry with my friend:
> I told my wrath, my wrath did end.

Here, instead of narrative suspense, there is closural completion. The first line tells of an impulse, the second of its proper fulfilment – a fulfilment which is achieved by its embodiment within an inter-personal context. The adjective 'angry' becomes the noun 'wrath' around which the line balances – first as the object, and then the subject of a verb. In thus owning and objectifying it the speaker allows it to enter a shared world: once 'told', of its own accord it 'ends'. But this satisfaction is absent from the story which follows. For the next two lines initiate a unilateral drama:

> I was angry with my foe:
> I told it not, my wrath did grow.

Here, the speaker's feeling is neither expressed nor completed: it becomes an unembodied 'it'. And the 'wrath' which 'grows' – though he claims it as 'mine' – seems therefore independent of his own, negative action.

In the notebook draft this opening stanza has a line drawn underneath it: possible Blake intended to end here. Certainly, the epigrammatic neatness yet disquieting open-endedness of these four lines sketch in an opposition that is central to the poem. But the feeling of uncompleted process implicit in the last word seems to have led Blake to continue – perhaps with the old English proverb, 'Forbearance is no acquittance', ironically in mind. For the subsequent stanzas follow out the logic of that uneasy sense of a 'growth' displaced from the speaker's agency that is indicated by the syntax here. He portrays himself as making a choice and performing a series of voluntary acts. But the poetry does not see him thus: counter-pointing his own view is a much stronger sense – created partly by the heavy trochaic beat of the verse, partly by the image of the tree's independent growth, and partly by relentless repetition ('And ... ', 'And ... ', 'And ... ') – that he has lost his freedom and become caught in a process over which he has little control. By the second stanza, the 'I' ... ', 'I ... ', 'I ... ', with which every line of the opening stanza had begun has given way to the 'And .... ', 'And .... ', 'And .... ' of this process, within which all action is now contained. And 'It' has taken on an ambiguous life of its own:

> And I waterd it in fears,
> Night & morning with my tears:
> And I sunned it with smiles,
> And with soft deceitful wiles.

The confident free agent of the opening has become a servile attendant, cherishing and placating and hypocritically pandering to a fearful something whose nature is as yet obscure. Despite his candour there is an oddly diminishing sense of the speaker here: his 'tears' and 'smiles' and 'soft deceitful wiles' might equally indicate remorse hardening into conscious duplicity, or a gradually lessening terror. For his withdrawal from the self-actualizing expressiveness of the opening couplet has led to the construction of a 'specious' persona, 'destitute of substance and soul', whose energies are all directed away from the shared world, and contracted into syco-phantic subservience.[32]

By the third stanza, even this diminished self has disappeared: 'it' is growing alone:

> And it grew both day & night,
> Till it bore an apple bright.
> And my foe beheld it shine,
> And he knew that it was mine.

In the draft, the third of these lines originally read, 'And I gave it to my foe': Blake's change underlines the logic of the process being portrayed. For the 'foe' is now more present in the poetry than the speaker who watches 'it': it is through *his* eyes that the apple's luminous beauty is seen – 'And my foe beheld it shine' – and it is against *his* imagined desire that possession is asserted – 'And he knew that it was mine.' And the insubstantial yet pivotal status of 'it' is emphasized by the way in which the poetry identifies 'it' with the process out of which it has grown. The recurrence of this

VISION AND DISENCHANTMENT

ambiguously indeterminate pronoun charts the growth of an other which is not understood, which seems to require slavish attention, and which finally replaces direct interaction between speaker and 'foe':

> I told *it* not...
> And I waterd *it* in fears...
> And I sunned *it* with smiles...
>
> And my foe beheld *it* shine,
> And he knew that *it* was mine.

By the penultimate stanza, 'it' has become that which both separates and locks them together, in mutual yet antagonistic desire.[33]

The final stanza is superficially a statement of triumph: the 'foe' is dead and the speaker is 'glad'. Yet after the self-negating, self-abasing and finally self-obliterating process which the poem has traced, this attempt to affirm feeling has a curious hollowness. The change, in the last line of the poem, from trochees to iambs should bring a lightening sense of release: yet that very change emphasizes the final word of the poem in a way that is the reverse of liberating. For the first time in the poem 'it' becomes manifest. That which the speaker has tended in fear and duplicity is a massy, unchangeable 'tree', existing beyond any action he may perform, and shadowing him no less than his 'outstretchd' foe.[34] And now that that 'foe' is dead it is the only continuing other in his world. On the plate, the poem is ensnared by the serpent-like branches of the depicted tree, which wind around and link on to the second letter of the speaker's final 'my': a 'my' which can now be applied only to the dead foe – certainly not to the independent tree. The sense of sterile entrapment, increasing throughout the poem, is completed in this final stanza. It moves from narrative past tense to a statement of present passivity – 'glad I see': this is the end of any development, an eternal *stasis*, in which no new possibilities can present themselves.

On one level, the poem dramatizes a particular psychic dilemma. It explores the logic of that destructive self-suppression – implicit both in 'Christian Forbearance' and in deliberate dissembling – which assumes that feelings aroused by others need not be actualized in relation to them, but belong to and may be controlled by the self. The poetic suggestion is that such feelings acquire a monstrous pseudo-reality, perverting and imprisoning both self and other: this 'freedom' leads to nothing but death. The psychological insight is acute. Yet the poem has resonances which extend beyond this. For its

speaker is more paradigmatic than individualized: and at least as
important as his ironic loss of freedom is the growth of the tree.
The image of a tree bearing poison fruit is a suggestive one. On
another page in his notebook, Blake alludes to the contemporary
story which seems to have been the immediate inspiration for the
title of his Song of *Experience*:

> The Queen of France just touched this Globe,
> And the pestilence darted from her robe;
> ~~But the bloodthirsty people across the water~~
> ~~Will not submit to the gibbet & halter~~
> But our good Queen quite grows to the ground,
> ~~There is just such a tree at Java found.~~
> And a great many suckers grow all around.   (K185)

The reference is to the Upas tree of Java, so poisonous that nothing
could live within a fourteen-mile radius of it; a tree to which, it was
said, convicted criminals were sent as punishment. This mythological tree was a popular subject in late eighteenth-century magazines,
with their vogue for the fantastic and sensational. Accounts of it
appeared in the *London Magazine* for 1783, in Erasmus Darwin's
Loves of the Plants in 1789, in the *Gentleman's Magazine* for May 1794,
and – perhaps most significantly from Blake's point of view – in the
Swedenborgian *New Magazine of Knowledge Concerning Heaven and
Hell* in 1790.[35] For the editors of that journal saw it thus:

the influences of *Hell* are as visible in the vegetable productions of certain
parts of this globe, as in the hateful, cruel dispositions of many wild beasts.
Many plants indeed abound with pernicious and fatal juices, which, taken
into the human body, occasion certain death; but the Poison-Tree of Java is a
phenomenon so singular, and so terrible, that it may with propriety be called
the *Tree of Death*, originating in *Hell*.[36]

Blake's 'Poison Tree', too, seems to be a '*Tree of Death*, originating in
Hell'. Yet it is significantly different from this exotic object of
contemporary speculation. Its poison is not in its juice, but in its
shining, covetable fruit: it does not blight the ground about it, but
grows in a garden. And in this it is disturbingly reminiscent of the
Tree of Knowledge of Good and Evil.[37]

The suggestion is disturbing because it seems to link the speaker of
this poem to the God of Genesis: *his* is the luring apple which causes
death. This 'implicit analogy'[38] has led at least one recent critic to see
the poem as a 'counter-myth' to that of the Old Testament: Blake's
exposure of the 'abstractions, the allegorical fables and the

meaningless idols of Genesis' as merely the products of 'contagious, unmotivated anger writ large'.[39] Certainly, 'A Poison Tree' does evoke the story of the Fall in an extremely odd way. Yet if it demystifies that story, it does so obliquely. For the tree which bears tempting fruit – that ancient, evocative image – is not here planted by a God, either angry or beneficent: it grows out of an intimately familiar world, a world of human choices and actions. And in this Blake's poem is closer to Swedenborgian doctrine than to the straightforward Biblical account:

> Those who speak falses from deceit or on purpose, and utter them in a tone of voice that seems to proceed from spiritual affection, and particularly if they intermix them with truths taken from the Word, which thus become falsified, were by the ancients called enchanters ... they were also called Pythons, and serpents of the tree of knowledge of good and evil. Such false speakers, liars, and deceivers, may be likened to those who converse with their enemies in a courteous and friendly manner, and during their conversation hold a dagger behind them to take away their lives. They may also be likened to those who dip their swords in poison, and in this manner attack their enemies; and to those who mix hemlock with water, and poison with sweetmeats.[40]

> the opinion hitherto received and cherished, that the sin of Adam is the cause of that evil which is innate in a man from his parents, will fall to the ground, and it will be seen that it originates, not from this, but from a different cause. That the tree of life, and the tree of knowledge of good and evil, are in every man, and that their being said to be planted in a particular garden signified the free-will which a man enjoys of turning himself to the Lord, and away from him.[41]

Here, in a way which suggests something of the reason for Blake's attraction to his thinking, Swedenborg reinterprets the story of Genesis.[42] The tree of knowledge of good and evil is located not in the distant Garden of Eden, but in 'every man': it is seen as an image not of original sin, but of 'the free-will which a man enjoys of turning himself to the Lord, and away from him'. It thus focusses on a problem with which Blake at this time was preoccupied, a problem which is a central concern in 'A Poison Tree'.[43] For the story the poem tells is not simply one in which 'contagious, unmotivated anger' is 'writ large': it is a story in which the speaker loses his liberty. In exploring the way in which this comes about, Blake is not merely exploring a particular psychological impasse: he is exploring the much larger question of human freedom, and that which enables or prevents it.

And despite the seemingly ungovernable progression toward fixity which the poem dramatizes, its import is not fatalistic. For that progression begins with the speaker's own deliberate choice. In refusing relationship with his foe he initiates a drama which can end only in the other's death, and hypostatizes an 'it' ('I told it not') to which he himself becomes helplessly subject, before whose immutable reality he is finally reduced to passivity. Yet however inexorable his descent into unfreedom seems, it is his own conscious act which leads to his lonely confrontation with the tree. His ability to choose otherwise is made plain in the opening couplet, with its brief portrayal of an alternative scenario – one in which feelings are actualized and completed within a shared world. And the poem thus offers an implicit retort to the predestinarian doctrines which Blake deplored: salvation or damnation are not determined for the individual, but decided by him.

Yet its relation to the predestinarian debate is a curiously tangential and heretical one. The opposition of the opening stanza is not between different responses to a judging deity, but between different choices in a human world: the anger of the poem is not the wrath of God, but human anger. And the growing, dominating image of the tree which shadows both speaker and 'foe' suggests that Blake is less concerned with how the individual might make his own salvation or damnation than with the ways in which, through their freely chosen modes of relating to one another, men can arrive at a seemingly irresolvable situation of mutual entrapment and destruction. It is true that here, as in other *Songs of Experience*, it is less relationship than isolation that is most immediately apparent – the chilling, confessional isolation of a single speaker, who has already killed the 'foe' of whom he speaks, and seems trapped in private subjectivity. But it is significant that that which compels the poem forward, like that which structures 'There was a man of double deed' – the transformation of a metaphor into literal concreteness – is one of the marks of that failure to connect 'private' and 'public' realities that we call schizophrenia.[44] (Indeed, on one level the whole poem – with its speaker's implicit identification with a God who 'owns' the tempting apple, controls the world and causes his foe's death – could be seen as a dramatization of the genesis of a schizophrenia.) In showing how this deliberately chosen schizoid position leads to the growth of the mysterious 'Poison Tree', Blake is exploring – far more acutely than those of his contemporaries who inveighed against official mystification – the way in which such mystification is rooted in social interchange, and enslaves those who offer no less than those who receive it.

And if this speaker's energy-fixating self-diminishing withdrawal from the human world is akin to that described in modern accounts of schizophrenia, the sense of his compulsive, slavish labour and its alien product – that object of the 'foe''s desire which replaces direct interaction between them – prefigures Marx's account of the alienation of the worker from his own activity, and the substitution of relations between commodities for those between human beings:

This is the relationship of the worker to his own activity as something alien and not belonging to him, activity as suffering (passivity), strength as powerlessness, creation as emasculation, the *personal* physical and mental energy of the worker, his personal life (for what is life but activity?), as an activity which is directed against himself, independent of him and not belonging to him. This is *self-alienation* as against the above-mentioned alienation of the thing.[45]

There is a definite social relation between men, that assumes, in their eyes, the fantastic form of a relation between things. In order, therefore, to find an analogy, we must have recourse to the mist-enveloped regions of the religious world. In that world the productions of the human brain appear as independent beings endowed with life, and entering into relations both with one another and the human race. So it is in the world of commodities with the products of men's hands. This I call the Fetishism which attaches itself to the products of labour.[46]

Here, in 'simple' language close to that of popular rhyme, working with complex precision within a peculiarly succinct art form, Blake is tracing the essential structure of and connection between psychological and political processes of which very different schools of more recent theory have offered their own separate accounts. That refusal of relationship which defines the other as 'foe' is shown to lead to a reification of privatized desire which is an alienation both from self and other, yet binds both destructively together. The apple, so hauntingly reminiscent of the forbidden fruit of the Garden of Eden, is that Thing not valued for its own sake but coveted because it is private property.[47] And the 'Tree poisonous and deadly' which bears it, though it grows out of human choices and actions, takes on a life that is independent of human agency: it ends by dominating a world which both speaker and foe are now powerless to change.

'A Poison Tree' is not, then, merely an exploration of the dynamics of 'Christian Forbearance'. If its imagery evokes religious rather than political speculation, it engages with questions which

Blake's contemporaries were debating passionately in both spheres –
in the disputes about free-will and predestination which occupied
the relatively obscure Swedenborgian Church, and in that heated
argument about the ways in which differing modes of social
organization might enable or prevent human freedom, which
occupied the centre of the political stage. As Blake himself was later
to write 'Are not Religion and Politics the same Thing?' (K 689).
And this poem shows his remarkable ability to draw upon Biblical
resonances in order to convey a more haunting and more exploratory sense of the mystificatory processes he saw at work in the
society around him than is to be found in the single-minded
rationalism of writers such as Paine. For where those who addressed
the 'swinish multitude' expose such mystification with irony and
reversal, this poem, through a single, paradigmatic instance, and in a
much more powerfully disquieting way, delineates the coercive
logic of those intertwined social and psychological strategies
whereby men can imprison and destroy themselves and one another:
delineates it from the perspective provided by *Songs of Innocence*.

For it is suggestive that that creative subversion of an alienating
established 'reality' which *Songs of Innocence* one after another
present, is in many of them shown to come about through a process
exactly the reverse of that which the final fourteen lines of this poem
trace. In 'Holy Thursday' and 'The Chimney Sweeper', 'reality' is
transformed by metaphor: a wondering analogy ('Now like a
mighty wind...'; '...his head / That curl'd like a lamb's back') leads
to a vision of transforming possibility, in which all are included.
The speakers of these poems register that which is before them with
vividness and clarity: each poem is informed by the tension between
the actualities of the children's procession and service, the sweeps'
miserable, comradely and sometimes unruly lives, and the
metaphoric transformation which is made of them. But in 'A Poison
Tree' there is no such pressure of actuality. There is no creative
tension, but a unilateral process in which metaphor takes on a literal
materiality, blocking relationship with the other and closing off
potential for change. Where the Songs of *Innocence*, beginning with
lively portrayals of a familiar world and ending in direct and urgent
appeals to the reader, show how imaginative recognition of the existence of others can lead to a confidence in the possibility of a transforming change within a shared actuality, the thin, monologic con
fession of 'A Poison Tree' acknowledges no connection with anyone,
and ends in passivity before a reified, undynamic set of facts. The

progression it dramatizes cannot be dismissed simply with irony; for Blake's sense of its compulsive force is registered in the poetic imbalance between the opening couplet and the fourteen lines of narrative which follow. In this respect, at least, his poem seems far more pessimistic than the writings of the Paine-ite radicals.

But only in this respect. For the couplet which precedes this story of wrath untold remains as an outline of that 'divine vision' of realized human *potentia*, of men in creative relationship, completely articulated in the *Songs of Innocence* with which the volume opens: a 'divine vision' which none of those radicals, for all their optimistic rhetoric, ever achieved. It is only sketched in here. But it stands as an affirmation of human freedom, an image of an alternative possibility, even here, at the opening of one of the bleakest poems of *Songs of Experience*. Before the linear and pernicious logic of denial and reification is set the satisfying balance of a completed situation, in which the other is recognized, and feeling is actualized, embodied and fulfilled. And its presence gives the poem an entirely different force and meaning.

If an alternative is there, like 'the end of a golden string' (K551), at the beginning of 'A Poison Tree', it is there also, hidden within a negatively expressed hypothesis, in the opening couplet of 'The Human Abstract':

> Pity would be no more,
> If we did not make somebody Poor.

Yet here, as in 'A Poison Tree', it is the pernicious progression traced in the rest of the poem which dominates. The twenty-two lines that follow offer a devastating account of a world which is premised on that denial and exploitation of the other which is explored in Song after Song of *Experience*: a world in which the virtues of 'The Divine Image' become monstrously and destructively displaced from human agency. It is an account which directly articulates that suspicion of moral precept touched on in other of the *Songs of Innocence and of Experience*, and here as elsewhere it is more complex, more subtly thought through, than the succinct logic of the poetry might initially suggest. For the curious ambiguity of its opening couplet leads to an exploration of human strategies and social processes that is far from simply demystificatory.

Its nature comes into focus when one compares the drafts in the notebook with the finally engraved poem. The earliest draft seems to be 'I heard an Angel singing' (K164), a first-person narrative which presents two opposing *dramatis personae*. The first, a conventionally moral Angel, sings over the gathered harvest:

> 'Mercy, Pity, Peace.
> 'Is the world's release.'

The second, a Devil, curses 'Over the heath & the furze':

> 'Mercy could be no more,
> 'If there was nobody poor,
>
> 'And pity no more could be,
> 'If all were as happy as we.'

Thus far, with its two differently situated speakers offering apparently opposing definitions of abstract values, the poem seems not unlike 'The Clod & the Pebble'. But it lacks that poem's tight structuring. And from this paradoxical beginning it moves into an extended satiric exposure of a familiar polite eighteenth-century apologia for the status quo – the doctrine that suffering is an essential part of a general scheme of good, and that poverty and unhappiness were designed by God to call forth the desirable virtues of mercy and pity in those fortunate enough not to experience them.[48] Such 'Mercy & Pity & Peace', the poem suggests, are not so attractive when seen from the worm's-eye view:

> Down pour'd the heavy rain
> Over the new reap'd grain,
> And Mercy & Pity & Peace descended
> The farmers were ruin'd & harvest was ended.

The irony is a simple one, and not very different from that ironic rejection of official definitions to be found in publications such as *Pigott's Political Dictionary*. But the draft goes on, re-working and re-wording the Devil's intuition, as though examining what, in face of it, the virtues celebrated in 'The Divine Image' can mean:

> ~~And Mercy, Pity, Peace~~
> ~~Joy'd at their increase~~
> ~~With Poverty's Increase~~
> ~~Are ...~~
> ~~And by distress increase~~
> ~~Mercy, Pity, Peace,~~
> ~~By Misery to increase~~
> ~~Mercy, Pity, Peace.~~
> And Miseries' increase
> Is Mercy, Pity, Peace.   (K164)

'Mercy could *be* no more ...', the Devil had begun, asserting the alien, reified existence of that which in the Song of *Innocence* had been seen only as projected and operative within and maintained by actual human experience. And in these fragments Blake pushes that insight a stage further. Abstracted from that experience, Mercy, Pity and Peace are portrayed as having an active and independent life of their own –

> And Mercy & Pity *descended*
>
> And Mercy, Pity, Peace
> *Joy'd* at their increase ...
>
> And by distress *increase*
> Mercy, Pity, Peace ...

– a life which hardens, in the unerased closing couplet, into a massy presence:

> And Miseries' increase
> Is Mercy, Pity, Peace.

This interest in the extraneous, substantial reality of an abstracted 'Mercy & Pity & Peace' is very different from simple irony. And it is this interest which is pursued in the second of the notebook drafts, 'The human Image' (K174) which, after a number of deletions, became 'The Human Abstract' of *Songs of Experience*.

This poem began with the Devil's curse of the earlier draft, no longer contained within a distancing narrative framework. Instead of the clearly identified speakers of 'I heard an Angel singing' there was an unannounced general proposition:

> Mercy could be no more,
> If there was nobody poor.

But then Blake made some significant changes. 'Mercy' was deleted, and 'Pity' written in – a logical enough substitution, since the 'poor' in the late eighteenth century were more likely to be the recipients of the latter than of the former. And the second line was replaced by one whose rhythmic awkwardness shatters any lingering echoes of the original 'Angel's song:

> If we did not make somebody poor.

Every change here is significant. And together the changes constitute an incisive re-thinking of the bases of the ironic paradox which in the earlier draft had so fascinated Blake.

The most striking alteration is in the verb. Suddenly, the line portrays an active process, not a static structure: we have moved away from the original implicit assumption of an order of things not causally 'envisaged and hence apparently unchangeable ('if there was') into a disturbingly direct accusation. In 1798 Blake was to respond angrily to the title of a sermon by Bishop Watson, *The Wisdom and Goodness of God, in having made both Rich and Poor*: 'God made man happy & Rich, but the Subtil made the innocent, Poor' (K384). The change in this draft from 'if there was' to 'if we did not make' expresses the same insight: these distinctions are not 'made' by God, but by man. Yet it is far more directly disturbing than the accusation of the later annotation. For here the blame lies not with some separate, definable, exploiting group ('the Subtil') but more intimately to hand. 'We', not 'I' or 'you': the pronoun refuses to allow either paralysing self-reproach or simple condemnation, for the process to which the line points is brought about by polite author and reader. 'We' are implicated; not merely in that 'we' are the beneficiaries of an exploiting social order ('So your chimneys I sweep') but because even in our manifestation of the admired virtue 'Pity' we play an active part in creating and maintaining that order.

How? The third change in the line is unobtrusive, but significant: 'If there was *nobody* poor', becomes 'If we did not make *somebody* poor'. The object of polite 'Pity' is now momentarily there in the poetry: a real individual 'somebody'. Yet this 'somebody' is not a known other, to be loved and responded to, as little Tom Dacre is loved and responded to: his or her separate reality is immediately swallowed up by the definition 'poor'. And this distancing of the other initiates a process which the next couplet – ending as it does on the dominant 'we' – takes a stage further:[49]

> And Mercy no more could be,
> If all were as happy as we.

An individual, 'somebody', with whom relationship might have been possible, has become the more generalized 'all'; and the sense of active implication glimpsed in the first couplet ('make somebody poor') has slid into a static opposition between a happy 'we' and an 'all' whose unhappiness is acknowledged only obliquely. Any sense of the possibility of change is similarly diminished: the conditional 'would', with its strong implicit reference to an alternative state of affairs, is replaced by the weaker 'could', which awakens doubt as to the feasibility of that toward which it points.

The rest of the poem (now, with the exception of a couple of deletions, the same as that published as 'The Human Abstract'),[50] explores the nature of the world in which 'we' are dominant, in which complementary relationship with the other, such as was portrayed in *Songs of Innocence*, is denied. Like that of 'A Poison Tree', this is a world not of reciprocity but of dominance and submission, not of balance but of linear progression: its processes appear as a mysterious unilateral growth. It is a world which has its own kind of energy: in the second stanza, the contorted negative hypothesis of the opening is suddenly replaced by a succession of four active verbs, one in each line:

> And mutual fear brings peace:
> Till the selfish loves increase.
> Then Cruelty knits a snare,
> And spreads his bait with care.

We are thrust into the present tense: things as they are, not as they 'would' or 'could' be. But the sense of active reality thus created is counterpointed by another sense, of dislocation and unreality. For the subject of these verbs is no longer that challengingly intimate and unspecific 'we'. It is a series of abstract nouns – nouns which involve a further displacement from the world of human agency indirectly present in the opening stanza. The other, never the subject of a main clause, has likewise disappeared: the actual division between 'we' and 'somebody' or 'all' has been subsumed into an ironically 'mutual' entity, 'fear'. The dynamic activity imaged here is quite removed from that point of interpersonal conflict (and hence of potential change) identified in the opening couplet. Here it is not 'we' but *things* that act.

At first, these things are feelings – 'mutual fear', 'selfish loves' – feelings which sardonically recall 'Peace' and 'Love', the remaining two virtues of 'The Divine Image'. 'Love', however, is no longer a transitive verb but a plural noun, directed not toward an other but 'increasing' unilaterally. That which in the Song of *Innocence* was an active relation has become a multiplying thing – the first of a series of proliferating entities, each of which seems beyond the control of the last:

> Then Cruelty knits a snare,
> And spreads his baits with care.
>
> He sits down with holy fears,
> And waters the ground with tears:

Then Humility takes its root
Underneath his foot.

Soon spreads the dismal shade
Of Mystery over his head;
And the Catterpiller and Fly
Feed on the Mystery.

And it bears the fruit of Deceit,
Ruddy and sweet to eat:
And the Raven his nest has made
In its thickest shade.

The pattern is one of an ungovernable generation of unpredictable, parasitic and threatening otherness: an escalating process which seems to grow out of the displacement of feelings from their possessor so that they become objective 'facts'. Nothing is acknowledged, answered or completed: the effect is of repeated, violent dead-ends and new beginnings. And the social and psychological drama which the poem unfolds is thus both compulsively onward-thrusting and jerkily discontinuous. Its onward movement is emphasized by the repeated line-openings, 'And ...', 'Then ...', 'Soon ...'. But any confidence as to causal connections is undercut by the awkward disjointedness of the rhythm. In the three penultimate stanzas the last line has fewer syllables than the rest: the sense is of a petering out at odds with the seeming energy of the process being described. In this world of violent linear development, nothing leads anywhere.

It is beginning to be apparent that 'The Human Abstract' is not merely an ironic commentary on 'Moral Virtue': it is a 'minutely Appropriate' (K596) delineation of a world quite opposite to that of 'The Divine Image' – a world which begins in control and exploitation, in which difference becomes opposition ('we...make somebody Poor') and initiates an autarchic process which is not open to otherness and hence to modification, in which one thing simply follows relentlessly on from the next ('And...', 'Then...', 'Soon...'). This substitution of domination for interaction becomes, as the poem proceeds, more and more opaquely unchallengeable, for despite the poem's appearance of logic (it has been described by Donald Davie as having 'a syntax as of the proposition') causal connections are not realized within it.[51] In the first stanza there is a counterfactual attempt to trace reasons and explanations ('If ...' 'would...', 'could...'); but beyond the first line of the second ('And

203

mutual fear brings peace') the attempt is abandoned. The relationships between the presented phenomena are no longer described:
they simply succeed one another. And the result is that disquieting
sense of an irreversible, unstoppable, yet arbitrary progression
which is the most haunting feature of the poem.

This is not to say that there is not a logic in the process which the
poem traces. Indeed, it offers an extraordinarily acute diagnosis of a
form of psychological and social impasse that has preoccupied
subsequent thinkers in many different spheres.[52] The false peace of
stasis achieved by 'mutual fear' lasts only as long as opposing desires
can be kept in check: when 'the selfish loves increase', 'Then',
suddenly, 'Cruelty' appears. Yet this personified 'Cruelty' seems a
new and uncontrollable entity, displaced from the 'we' of the
opening stanza: an entity which, in order to assuage its own (no
longer mutual, and proliferating) 'fears', must claim a privileged and
'holy' status for them. And when this 'holiness' in the tyrant is
answered by the 'Humility' that 'takes its root / Underneath his foot'
the result is a 'Mystery' which shadows both. Oppressor and
oppressed collude in the creation of a self-confirming, self-
perpetuating system ever further removed from a recognition of the
real, exploitative relationships involved: a 'dismal shade' that takes
on its own over-arching reality, and nourishes further manifestations of parasitism and predacity.[53] 'Cruelty', indeed, has ceased to
be perceived: the reality has become 'it', the action that of 'it''s
growth and fruiting, and of the unsavoury creatures who feed on and
nest within it. In the final stanza 'it' finally hardens into a Tree, a
monstrous and impermeable presence; not, like that of 'A Poison
Tree', simply and unchallengeably there, but actively growing, and
fostering parasites. Yet in the last line of the poem there is a curious
twist. This 'reality' which has been steadily filling the centre of the
poem is suddenly seen from a different perspective: 'There grows
one in the Human Brain.' The essential paradox is revealed. This
which seems so ponderous and given is in another way curiously
insubstantial. It cannot be discovered in 'Nature', for it exists only in
the isolated, yet ironically common, subjectivity of 'the Human
Brain'. Although its growth seems independent, it could not exist
without the denial of reciprocal relationship and consequent abstraction of the other which was identified in the first couplet – 'If we did
not make somebody Poor'.

In the notebook drafts there are two additional fragments. The
first, a couplet –

> They said this mystery never shall cease;
> The priest promotes war & the soldier peace.

– takes up the notion of 'Mystery', and illustrates it with a line which had first appeared in the draft of 'The Lilly'. The result is a slogan whose epigrammatic neatness is more akin to the straightforward ironies of contemporary plebeian protest than to the complex exploration of the preceding poem. But the second, a quatrain, is more interesting:

> There souls of men are bought & sold,
> And ~~cradled~~ milk fed infancy ~~is sold~~ for gold;
> And youths to slaughter houses led,
> And ~~maidens~~ beauty for a bit of bread.

Blake's charting of the growth of this unreal 'Tree' seems to have led him to a confrontation of its devastatingly real consequences. For this is not 'the Human Brain', but the actual world of late eighteenth-century London, where children like the little chimney-sweeper were literally sold; where prostitution was the most frequent fate of poor servant girls from the country,[54] in which young men were being pressed into service in the war with France, and wages were 'trailing wretchedly behind prices'.[55] Blake's lines might be paralleled particularly by the anti-war protest of the period:

when HUMAN BEINGS are thus brought to market, and disposed of as BEASTS, it most certainly verifies Mr. Edmund Burke's memorable observation, applied to the lower orders of people; – according to his immortal phrase, – 'the swinish multitude'. It cannot therefore, agreeably with sound logical reasoning, be denied, that if the PEOPLE are SWINE, he who sells them, who receives so much money for the slaughter of each, is, to all intents and purposes, a SWINE, or HOG-BUTCHER.
  (*The Case of Charles Pigott: contained in the Defence he had prepared, and which would have been delivered by him on his trial, if the Grand Jury had not thrown out the Bill preferred against him,* D. Eaton, 1793)

Yet their difference from such direct protest as this is significant. The quatrain which ends 'The human Image' describes what occurs 'There' – in an enigmatically unspecified, though apparently familiar place. It consists of four unconnected present indicative statements. In its prophetic generality of reference it evokes Ezekiel 13: 19 –

And will ye pollute me among my people for handfuls of barley and for pieces of bread, to slay the souls that should not die, and to save the souls alive that should not live, by your lying to my people that hear your lies?

– and the evocation points backward, to the preceding poem's concern with 'lying', or 'Mystery'. Blake's only verbs are passive: even these are omitted in the second and fourth lines. The realities portrayed are such that the reader seeks, like Piggot, for some focus for blame. None is presented. For this is a state of affairs in which crime is manifest but its authors are obscured: the logical conclusion of that mystificatory abstraction from real acts of exploitation and oppression that has been traced in the rest of the poem. We are left, as in 'A Poison Tree', confronting a world in which there is no sense of human agency, and hence no feeling of potential change: one in which the weak quite simply *are* 'Poor'.

This static picture of an unchallengeable reality is quite different from the urgent appeal which ends 'The Divine Image'. Here, the operative reality of those 'virtues of delight' which is musically affirmed in the earlier song seems utterly undermined. For the mode of relationship which this poem presents – one of exploitation, mystification and control – is quite opposed to that of Innocence. In many ways, it might seem a mode of relationship far more typical of late eighteenth-century English society as Blake knew it. Yet he makes no poetic claim for the greater truth of what is presented here: rather, the claim is the other way. 'The Divine Image' does not, like 'The Human Abstract', begin with a counterfactual conditional, but in the simple present indicative tense – with a pointer to what is, not to what is not. The contrast between the two poems is not one of contradiction: nor do they simply present two different, partial views. Each offers a different order of message. 'The Divine Image' is an account of the real world, of what men do: 'The Human Abstract' is a rational argument. And if, in a rationalistic society, the latter might seem to have a universal, propositional validity, the rhythmically awkward hypothesis with which it opens conveys a very different sense. As Blake was to assert in his annotations to Berkeley nearly thirty years later, 'Knowledge is not by deduction, but Immediate by Perception or Sense at once' (K774). Here, in 'The Human Abstract', there is none of the straightforward assurance of the earlier poem's 'All pray in their distress'. Instead, there is a negative conjecture whose subject is an oddly uncertain third person plural – not the confident collective 'we' of a known social group, but an unspecified and unlocated 'we', which defines itself in opposition to an indefinite other, and with which the reader is forced into uneasy identification. Where 'The Divine Image' begins with a description of actual experience, in which 'virtues' are projected and confirmed, 'The Human Abstract' begins with an abstraction already displaced from – and masking – the real action which has produced it. The propositional form of the poem is an exact expression of that mode of relationship which it explores: that which seeks to dominate and control, reducing otherness to its own categories, and blocking off any possibility of creative interplay. 'Pity' is, from the very first word, and its existence implies that 'we' *do* 'make somebody Poor'. To begin from consequences, even in a demystificatory way, suggests an imaginative acceptance of those consequences, a distancing of the area of choice into the hypothetical. And the logic that begins thus cannot lead towards an engagement with actuality ('And all must love the human form . . . ') but merely back upon itself, into 'the Human Brain'. The final stanza of the poem, with its image of the reified Tree – massively real, yet growing only within the 'Human Brain' – points back to the similarly reified yet dependent 'Pity' of the opening: both are marks of a rigidified status quo whose potential for difference is only negatively seen.

Yet it *is*, in the opening couplet, seen. For that couplet's counterfactual conditional, though it begins with an implicit acceptance of what is, points also, contortedly, towards an almost unimaginable situation in which the other-belittling mystification of 'Moral Virtue' would no longer exist:

> Pity *would* be *no more*,
> If we did not make somebody Poor.

It has been said that 'all reification is a forgetting':[56] and here the 'forgotten' interaction that has produced 'Pity' is exposed. With a clumsiness that suggests the difficulty of the realization, the concreteness of the 'Human Abstract' that grows through the poem is asserted to be a false concreteness: it would disappear if 'we' ceased to act in a certain way. If the poetic emphasis, like that of 'A Poison Tree', falls on a destructive process which seems to move further and further beyond human control, this sense remains embedded in the poem like a hidden message. As in 'A Poison Tree', though far less directly, this opening couplet points toward a real world of human relationships, within which action is possible and a different choice might be made: the closing stanza mocks at this 'Tree's distance from it. And thus, far from contradicting the vision presented in 'The Divine Image', 'The Human Abstract' confirms its central premise. Values are not imposed upon man. They are created by him, and their operative force depends on the nature of the relationships in which they are created.

The quatrain with which the notebook draft, 'The human Image', ends is haunting in its vision of passive hopelessness. But it seems poetically displaced from the preceding exploration of the abstract workings of psychosocial processes. This of course is part of the point: the consequences of 'Mystery' will always appear as immutable facts, separate from that which has actually produced them. But in another of·the poems first drafted in the notebook – one whose imagery recalls that of this quatrain – Blake explores exactly this problem in a far more poetically integrated way. The two final stanzas of 'London', with their surrealistic concreteness, have something of the same effect as this final stanza of 'The human Image': there as here the material manifestations of that which in the earlier part of the poem was traced as a strategy of abstraction suddenly appear. But in 'London' the connection between 'the Human Brain' and a mystificatory and exploitative society is at the centre of the poem.

Unlike 'The human Image' or 'The Human Abstract', 'London' identifies its speaker as a lonely wanderer, who passes through the streets of a particular city, and sees it from a lamenting distance:

> I wander thro' each charter'd street,
> Near where the charter'd Thames does flow
> And mark in every face I meet
> Marks of weakness, marks of woe.
>
> In every cry of every Man,
> In every Infants cry of fear,
> In every voice; in every ban,
> The mind-forg'd manacles I hear.

In choosing to present his vision of social disaster thus, Blake was engaging with a familiar literary mode. The assumption of a stance of 'observation', freely passing judgment on that which is before it, is common to much eighteenth-century literature: 'There mark what ills the scholar's life assail.'[57] But nowhere is it more prominent than in that which attempts to describe London, a place of bewildering diversity, changing and growing rapidly, in which a new kind of anonymity and alienation was becoming a remarked-upon fact of life.[58] Indeed, it seems that in the literature of London the implications of this state were beginning to become an explicit preoccupation. Thus, Ben Sedgly in 1751:

No man can take survey of this opulent city, without meeting in his way, many melancholy instances resulting from this consumption of spirituous liquors: poverty, diseases, misery and wickedness, are the daily observations to be made in every part of this great metropolis: whoever passes along the streets, may find numbers of abandoned wretches stretched upon the cold pavement, motionless and insensible, removed only by the charity of passengers from the danger of being crushed by carriages, trampled by horses, or strangled with filth in the common sewers.[59]

'Take survey of', 'meeting in his way', 'observations to be made', 'whoever passes along the streets may find' – the sense throughout is of an anonymous and freely observing stranger, rather than of a member of a society who sees himself as shaped by it and interacting with others within it. Perhaps such a perspective is natural in a documentary work such as Sedgly's. But this sense of the self in the city is central, too, to much of the most powerful imaginative literature of the century, literature which is after all not merely a description of or meditation upon the world, but the recreation of a certain mode of being within it. It is a sense that informs the novels of Defoe: the figures of Roxana and Colonel Jack and Moll Flanders move through the streets from adventure to adventure with a freedom from social constraint which is only possible because of the nature of London life.[60] It is to be found in Gay's *Trivia* and *The Beggar's Opera*; in Boswell's *Journal*; in Johnson's *London*, and even in those of his essays which seem to have nothing to do with London at all:

He that considers how little he dwells upon the condition of others, will learn how little the attention of others is attracted by himself. While we see multitudes passing before us, of whom perhaps not one appears to deserve our notice, or excites our sympathy, we should remember, that we likewise are lost in the same throng, that eye which happens to glance upon us is turned in a moment on him that follows us, and that the utmost which we can reasonably hope or fear is to fill a vacant hour with prattle, and be forgotten.[61]

Here, the tone is one of judicious moralizing. But the imagery is that of the confusing eighteenth-century London street, in which relations with one's fellow beings involve attracting attention, deserving notice, glancing and turning, even *exciting* sympathy: in which the other is the object of observation rather than one with whom one interacts. And the supposedly free individual who sees those who pass before him as a mighty spectacle is himself 'lost in the same throng'.

The eighteenth-century London street was not, then, merely a place where suffering and distress could be seen on a hitherto unprecedented scale: it was also a place where that sense of the other as object – often as feeble and wretched object – which Blake exposes in 'The Human Abstract' ('we ... make somebody Poor') was the dominant mode of relationship. And it is a sense which is an ironic point of reference in 'London'. For this poem begins with a speaker who seems to be a detached observer, who wanders 'thro'' the streets of the city and 'marks' the sights before him. Yet his is not the lively and distinctive London of Defoe or Gay or Johnson: what he records is not variety, but sameness. To him, both streets and river are simply 'charter'd': the different faces which pass all bear the same message, 'Marks of weakness, marks of woe'. And the tight quatrain with its present indicative tense conveys not flexible responsiveness to constantly changing possibilities, but entrapment. What this speaker sees is fatally linked to the way in which he sees it. In the notebook draft, the second word of the third line was 'see': Blake's alteration limits any incipient sense of freedom. The triple beat of 'mark' – an active verb materializing into two plural nouns – registers a new consciousness of this 'I''s implication in the world 'thro'' which he wanders. What he observes is the objectification of his own activity.

'Mark' is not the only change which Blake made in this stanza. In the notebook draft, the first two lines read:

> I wander thro' each dirty street,
> Near where the dirty Thames does flow.   (K170)

The substitution, in the engraved version, of 'charter'd', signals a complex process of poetic thought. For 'charter'd' in 1793 was a word at the centre of political debate: a word whose accepted meaning of 'granted privileges or rights' had been challenged by Paine a year earlier, in a book whose sales had by now reached 200,000:

It is a perversion of terms to say, that a charter gives rights. It operates by a contrary effect, that of taking rights away. Rights are inherently in all the inhabitants; but charters, by annulling those rights in the majority, leave the right by exclusion in the hands of a few ... all charters have no other than an indirect negative operation. They do not give rights to A, but they make a difference in favour of A by taking away the right of B, and consequently are instruments of injustice.[62]

No contemporary of Blake's could have read the two altered opening lines of his poem as an objective description of the trading organization of the city. Their repetition of 'charter'd' forces into prominence the newly, ironically recognized sense that the very language of 'objective' description may be riddled with ideological significance: that beneath the assurance of polite usage may lurk another, 'cheating' meaning.[63] And this sense informs the stanza in a peculiar way. It is as though beneath the polite surface – the observer in London wandering the streets of a city whose 'charter'd' organization he notes, as the guidebooks noted its commercial organization, and whose manifestations of distress and depravity he, like hundreds of other eighteenth-century writers, remarks – there is another set of meanings, which are the *reverse* of those such description could customarily bear. They are not meanings private to Blake: and they are meanings which focus in those sound-linked and repeated words, 'mark' and 'charter'd'.

The ambiguities of 'charter'd' had been explicitly debated: those of 'mark' are perhaps less obvious. Yet Blake, altering the poem in his notebook, has done an extraordinary thing. He has chosen a term commonly found in polite descriptions of London, to indicate the expected attitude of detached interest, and used it in such a way as to evoke a whole cluster of powerful, far from detached and far from polite resonances – resonances which question the value and perhaps even the possibility of such detachment. For 'mark' was not simply used by polite gentlemen to indicate the different sights of London to one another: it was, in the late eighteenth century, a word used on the streets of London by those who were by no means gentlemen, those artisan classes whose newly articulate radical politics were still intertwined with, and sometimes framed in the language of, prophetic millenarianism. Such men did not casually wander through the city marking the sights: with desperate intensity they turned from the Bible to the world around them to read the signs of the coming millenium. The 'marks' which they saw were the 'marks' of God's promise, or – more often – those of damnation, the signs of a rotten society:

And he causeth all, both small and great, rich and poor, free and bond, to receive a mark in their right hand, or in their foreheads:
And that no man might buy or sell, save he that hath the mark of the beast.
(Revelation 13: 16–17)

In this, their 'marking' was akin to that of the prophet or the judge:

And the LORD said unto him, Go through the midst of the city, through the midst of Jerusalem, and set a mark upon the foreheads of the men that sigh and that cry for all the abominations that be done in the midst thereof.

(Ezekiel 9: 4)

(This latter 'marker' is 'a man clothed in linen, with a writer's inkhorn by his side' (verse 3).)[64] And a mark on the face (in part, surely, a reference to the very real marks on the faces of the London crowd)[65] would to them suggest Cain, the 'man of blood' (K176) marked by God, the builder of the first city (referred to in *Poetical Sketches* as 'Cain's city built with murder', K41). Cain's was a city built in 'the Land of Nod', which in the Hebrew was the land of wandering. These Biblical allusions, abstruse though they may seem to the modern reader, would have been felt very immediately by anyone familiar with the language of London streets in the 1790s: felt not as pointing to a particular interpretation – the 'marker' as Ezekiel, or the 'marks' as marks of sin ('weakness') or pity ('woe') – but as signalling a stance towards the city at once very different from that of conventional polite observation, and posing a radical challenge to it.[66]

The feeling of this opening stanza is, then, most unlike that of other eighteenth-century accounts of London – a feeling not of detachment, but of involvement, not of emancipation, but of constriction. And it is a feeling which by the second stanza has become dominant:

> In every cry of every Man,
> In every Infants cry of fear,
> In every voice; in every ban,
> The mind-forg'd manacles I hear.

The illusory freedom of 'wandering' and 'marking', the visible 'marks of weakness, marks of woe' have given way to sounds, sounds which by their nature are less controllable than visual images.[67] The syntactic structure, with main verb and subject postponed until the last two words, is exact in its effect: this speaker is dominated by what he hears, trapped within the world on which he is trying to comment. And the repeated 'every', 'every', 'every', with the monotonously regular rhythm, conveys an impression of sameness even in difference. Almost overwhelmed by that which surrounds him, this thinly present 'I' reduces all to the same miserable message. The world of London debate and dissent, of real controversy and real suffering, of real passing people on the streets, which is in some sense there in the first stanza – at a remove, but felt, in those charged words 'marks' and 'charter'd', and in the images of streets and Thames and of faces meeting and moving on – has here been further abstracted, even, paradoxically, as it threatens to engulf him.

And this sense of entrapment within a world in which no possibility of change can be seen is taken up and confronted in the final line of the stanza. Like 'charter'd', the image of 'mind-forg'd manacles' evokes a contemporary political debate – a debate which concerns precisely this paradox. On the one hand, radical thinkers claimed that crime and suffering ('weakness' and 'woe') were the result of social oppression and official mystification: Godwin in 1793 was to affirm: 'In reality the chains fall off of themselves when the magic of opinion is dissolved.'[68] On the other, conservatives argued that 'human nature' made social control absolutely necessary:

Society cannot exist, unless a controlling power upon will and appetite be placed somewhere; and the less of it there is within, the more there must be without. It is ordained in the eternal constitution of things, that men of intemperate minds cannot be free. Their passions forge their fetters.[69]

On the one hand, the ills of society are traced to the 'objective' manacles of repression, on the other to the 'subjective' failings of human nature. And Blake's use of the image seems an ironic commentary on both sides of the debate. The other-denying mechanisms of repression which are visible and audible all around his speaker are intimately present in the 'mind' which seeks to distance and to judge: the one cannot be said to cause the other, for both are interlocked. The facts which have been presented as alien and unalterable are the manifestations of an activity: that distancing of the other, that inability to realize transforming human *potentia* ('these flowers of London town') which has been implicit in his speaker's stance toward the world no less than in the abstracting (and constricting) legal process of chartering, and the 'bans' which seek licence and prohibit human freedoms. These 'manacles', binding the hands that might help one another, are 'forg'd' *both* for *and* by 'the mind'. There is, significantly, no direction as to whose mind is meant, for this is a condition from which no member of the society, including he who judges it, is exempt. 'Mind-forg'd manacles' expresses both dismay at what the speaker 'hears' and a defeated self-reflexiveness: there can be no position of detachment in this world, and any compassion within it is impotent.

The recognition implicit in this image is analogous to that at the end of 'The Human Abstract': 'There grows one in the Human Brain.' Yet this poem does not, like that, end here. What follows is at once integrally related to and yet startlingly different from what has preceded it:

> How the Chimney-sweepers cry,
> Every blackning Church appalls,
> And the hapless Soldiers sigh
> Runs in blood down Palace walls
>
> But most thro' midnight streets I hear
> How the youthful Harlots curse
> Blasts the new-born Infants tear
> And blights with plagues the Marriage hearse.

Instead of a monotonous, stereotyped picture of passive misery there are vivid images of violent activity: instead of the abstracted 'marking' of a solitary 'I' there is a sharply realized, surrealistic vision of a whole network of social relationships. The syntactic structure in which the 'I' is nominally in control becomes confused: the rhythm changes from iambic regularity to heavy trochees. Blake is alluding to real sights here, as his readers would have recognized: to the smog which covered late eighteenth-century London like a pall, and whose blackening effect on the buildings was frequently noted;[70] to the anti-war slogans that were beginning to be daubed with paint on the walls of public buildings.[71] But these familiar sights here become signs of the inner logic of the society: they constitute a concrete realization of that which has been implicit in the poem from the beginning. The essential mode of relationship within this city – between its institutions and its people – is here portrayed as one of *marking* – blackening, daubing with blood, blighting with plague. The violence of these two stanzas – of the Sweep and Soldier, outside of and marking church and palace, of the harlot, excluded from the society yet infecting it – is the mirror-image of that detached observation, isolated and alienated yet imprinting all with its own damning stamp, dramatized in the opening stanza.

Yet if it is a mirror-image, it is one which is realized in a way in which the image of London in the first two stanzas is not – more definite, more active, more complex. It is not simply that where there were 'faces' there are now actual people, the Chimney Sweeper, the Soldier, the Harlot: the social interconnections which in the first two stanzas were obscured by abstraction have become manifest. The 'marking' of a series of passing impressions has given way to a much more immediate vision of London as a city composed of human beings, not passing and separate, but in relationship. It is a distorted relationship, and felt more directly as such: that reversal of norms which was obliquely registered in the ironic use of 'charter'd' focusses finally in the concrete image of the 'Marriage hearse'. And the previously almost undifferentiated cries are not simply clearer and more distinctive: they have a force of a kind unperceived before. No longer are they the passive signs of a generalized 'weakness' and 'woe': they have taken on a startling – and by the last stanza actively destructive – materiality. The cries have become marks.

The first two stanzas of 'London', then, offer an alienated, observer's account of the city through which, oddly, reversed meanings seem to run: at the third stanza, with startling suddenness, those meanings leap into life. The hidden exclusiveness of 'charter'd' ('charters...leave the right by exclusion in the hands of a few')[72] becomes objectified in the Palace walls deaf to the 'sigh' which marks them, and in the excluding wall which provides no answer to the Chimney Sweeper's cry. And in the final stanza observation turns to revelation, as the 'impolite' Biblical meanings of mark become prominent, with the image of the Harlot and of a plague from which none is spared.[73] The effect is extraordinary. And it brings to mind a third, and not irrelevant, meaning of 'mark'.

'London' seems much closer to Blake's own voice than do many others of the *Songs of Experience*: most obviously, this is because of the way in which it pushes beyond exposure of its speaker's limitations (such as we find in 'Holy Thursday' or 'A Poison Tree') into a more apocalyptic mode. But there is another sense in which it seems to come from Blake, rather than from an anonymous speaker – from 'The Author & Printer W Blake'. For the poem is a relief engraving, made by a process of deliberate and corrosive 'marking'. And the materialization of the Chimney Sweeper's, Soldier's, Harlot's cries recalls, by analogy, this other process in which words become marks – the process of engraving and printing in which Blake was more intimately involved than any other English poet. 'London', like the other Songs, was produced in two stages. The first was the preparation of the stereotype plate. Blake traced his text and design in gum arabic – which is resistant to acid – upon paper: he then applied the paper to the surface of a copper plate. When the plate was exposed to acid, those surfaces not covered with gum arabic were eaten away, and the upraised lines of the design and the words appeared, as in mirror-writing, reversed.[74] This is the 'method' which he described in *The Marriage of Heaven and Hell*: 'printing in the infernal method, by corrosives, which in Hell are salutary and medicinal, melting apparent surfaces away, and displaying the infinite which was hid' (K154). Once this first stage was carried out, the page was then printed from the stereotype and coloured.

The production of protruding stereotype 'marks' within which a reversed meaning was contained and the printing of the real design of which these were but a mirror-image, was thus a familiar process to Blake – and one which he seems to have seen as intrinsically linked to the vision he sought to present.[75] And it is a process which has a curious parallel in the progression of this poem. For the marks which Blake made would appear in relief when corroded by acid, when that which surrounded them was eaten away – just as the 'marking' of the speaker in the first two stanzas traces a single message which becomes more and more prominent as the surrounding world becomes less and less realized. The 'marks' on the plate were the reverse of what was ultimately to appear as the design. And the startling reversal in 'London', from a 'marking' speaker to the visible, actual, violent 'marks' of the two final stanzas – 'marks' which mirror back his own 'marking', not as a reflection but as a realization of the hidden interconnections of a society in which any position of control is illusory – bears an extraordinary resemblance to that moment of reversal with which Blake would have been most familiar: the moment when the relief outline suddenly takes on an existence seemingly independent of the engraver, as the printed result appears. There is even an analogue to the colouring of the page in the colours which appear for the first time in the third stanza, the 'blackning Church' and the blood of the Soldier, the submerged pun of 'appalls'. And the fire which is portrayed halfway down the page recalls the Devil's activity in *The Marriage of Heaven and Hell*: 'with corroding fires he wrote the following sentence now perceived by the minds of men, & read by them on earth' (K150).

To read the poem with this in mind is, I think, to come closer to its essential feeling than it is to see it as a statement either of moral outrage or despair. It is more like the voice of a 'marking' prophet – 'If you go on So, the result is So' (K392); a prophet whose 'marking' is also that of the artist, disclosing the hidden logic of a whole society in a way which transcends rational analysis, creating something which becomes independent of – and capable of questioning – his own activity, as the work of art achieves a revelatory life, beyond anything its creator may consciously have intended.[76] The first half of the poem, with its alienated, abstracting speaker, both dramatizes that mode of relationship which 'makes somebody Poor', and exposes the nature of a society in which it is dominant. In the London depicted here, there is no sense of human potentiality, and no creative change: this world simply *is*. Reciprocal human relationships in which otherness is acknowledged and the needs of all harmonized do not exist: the only relationships – as the recurrent imagery of licensing and prohibition, of buying and selling, of human passivity and misery suggests – are instrumental ones. People have become objects. And the intrinsic import of this is made strikingly manifest in the two final stanzas. 'If you go on So' – in the mode presented in *Songs of Experience* – the linear mode of control and domination, in which there is no realization of the uniqueness of others, no respect for difference or attempt to meet human needs – 'the result is So': a destructive 'blighting' of the whole society. And it is a 'result' which is not projected into the future, but which, the relentless present tense insists, is implicit in what is.

Yet the effect is not one of defeat: these two final stanzas have none of the flattened immobility of 'There souls of men are bought and sold'. Partly, this is because of their 'revolutionary' suggestiveness: those who in the other fragment are passive victims here have a terrible force. There are certainly seditious resonances here, in the familiar subversive figure of the Chimney Sweeper, the possible allusion to anti-war protest in 'Runs in blood down palace walls', even in the dramatic rendering of the voices of the oppressed (in 1795 *Pigott's Political Dictionary* was to define *Groan* simply as 'Sedition'). But Blake's vision is far from simply revolutionary, as a comparison with a modern, anti-colonialist vindication of violence reveals:

when it is their turn to be broken in, when they are taught what shame and hunger and pain are, all that is stirred up in them is a volcanic fury whose force is equal to that of the pressure put upon them. . . first, the only violence is the settler's; but soon they will make it their own; that is to say, the same violence is thrown back upon us as when our own reflection comes forward to meet us when we go towards a mirror.[77]

The violence which erupts in the closing stanzas of 'London' *is* the mirror-image of that denied and suppressed violence implicit in 'charter'd' and 'mark'. Yet if Blake shows this, he also shows that such mirror-imaging provides no escape: for his poem remains locked within the present indicative tense. His images of violence are also images of impotence: the Soldier's sigh 'runs down' the outside of the palace; the Chimney Sweeper and the church remain paralysingly locked together ('to appall' is to dismay into inactivity, rather than to stir into action); the Harlot's curse, effective though it may be, offers no release. The 'revolutionary' import of these images does not, it seems, point toward potential change: and it is not centrally from this that the feeling of excitement in these stanzas comes. Rather, it comes from that surrealistic sharpness of realization, in which meanings hidden from conventional vision are suddenly made manifest: the vividness with which that which in the first two stanzas was distanced and abstracted leaps into life before us, as the work of art leaps into life before the artist.

It is not, however, a realization which is also a transformation, like the growing vision of the children as angels in the Innocent 'Holy Thursday'. The satisfaction here is of a wholly different kind: one which has led one critic to say of the poem that it 'shuts like a box'.[78] If we begin with an isolated observer 'marking' the faces he passes we end with an isolated Harlot and the suggestion of faces blighted with plague: if we begin with a city licensed out to trade we end with love as a financial transaction. That which in the opening stanzas was abstracted by convention is here simply exposed in its human reality. And by the final stanza the speaker merely registers what is around him: the compassion perhaps implicit in his recognition of 'weakness' and 'woe', of the 'haplessness' of the Soldier, has been reduced to passivity by the force of the two doubly emphasized final verbs.[79]

Yet embedded within the stanza is a haunting poetic sense of that which is missing; a sense which Fredric Jameson has declared to be the only way in which 'the concept of freedom' can arise in 'a stagnant time':

an ontological impatience in which the constraining situation itself is for the first time perceived in the very moment in which it is refused ... a sudden perception of an intolerable present which is at the same time, but implicitly and however dimly articulated, the glimpse of another state in the name of which the first is judged.[80]

The closing lines of 'London' contain just such a negative articulation of alternative possibility. For through their images of the babe and of tears, and that forceful final verb 'Blasts', plays a disquietingly counterpointing allusion:

> And pity, like a naked new-born babe,
> Striding the blast, or heaven's cherubin, hors'd
> Upon the sightless couriers of the air,
> Shall blow the horrid deed in every eye,
> That tears shall drown the wind...   (*Macbeth*, Act I, sc. 7)

These lines seem to have fascinated Blake: one of his large colour prints of 1795 was an illustration of them. And that sense of the enormous power of the apparently helpless, of the radical nature of the claim that is made by trust, the transcendent force of 'Pity', which is at their centre, is also central in *Songs of Innocence*: 'Then like a mighty wind they raise to heaven the voice of song', 'Then cherish pity; lest you drive an angel from your door.' Here, at the end of 'London', their evocation underlines, even amidst the images of violence, the absence of any such potency. 'Blasts' has become a verb, cancelling out those drowning tears; this babe has none of the paradoxical 'striding' energy of Shakespeare's – he is 'reducd to misery'. And that 'pity' which in the earlier passage rides out and vanquishes the storm of evil is here nowhere to be found. Unlike the Innocent 'Holy Thursday', this poem does not urge towards action, suggesting the disturbing possibility of a revalued 'Pity': rather, the allusions to *Macbeth* all point towards its paralysing obliteration:

> But most thro' midnight streets I hear
> How the youthful Harlots curse
> Blasts the new-born infants tear
> And blights with plagues the Marriage hearse.

Blake makes it very clear that the disaster portrayed here is not inevitable. It has not been imposed by an unchangeable social order, nor is it the product of 'the ancient curse', the inborn evil of mankind. In 'London' it is shown to be the inevitable result of particular, chosen modes of relating to others, here manifested throughout a whole society. And this realization in one sense does imply its opposite: what has been humanly chosen and created can be humanly reversed. As the 'ancient Proverb' of the 1792 notebook affirms:

> Remove away that black'ning church,
> Remove away that marriage hearse,
> Remove away that – of blood,
> You'll quite remove the ancient curse. (K176)

Yet the difference between the final stanza of 'London' and the achieved vision of *Songs of Innocence* points very sharply to Blake's sense of the limitation of that implicit, negative 'concept of freedom' which might arise out of 'impatience' with and 'refusal' of 'an intolerable present', rather than out of the active realization of potentiality.[81] Against the Pity-less deadlock of 'London' we might place the freely emerging, forward-pointing interplay of 'The Ecchoing Green', that portrait of a society organized in ways characteristic of *Innocence*. The difference is not simply one between a small, known community and a large bewildering city – although the characteristic polite stance of 'marking' the sights of the city provided Blake with a familiar example of that mode of relationship whose logic he wished to explore: it is a more fundamental difference, evident from the very first word of the Song of *Experience*. 'London' begins with an isolated 'I', wandering randomly, and reducing all the phenomena he notes to a common pattern: in 'The Ecchoing Green' the speaking voice is a plural one, which does not attempt to control. There is no 'I' trapped by, yet judging all, but a 'we' which is framed by a living landscape, and makes space to play within it. Where the Experienced speaker registers sameness yet division, the Innocent Song celebrates mutuality in diversity; each of the crescendo of sounds in the opening stanza, each of the activities of the succeeding generations, of dawn and of dusk, is realized separately and clearly, and each harmonizes with the others. But in 'London', this 'ecchoing' interplay of different perspectives is replaced by the unresponsiveness of dividing walls, and the impotent violence of isolated sighs and cries.

And the inherent logic of each of the societies thus produced is revealed in the very different endings of the two poems. 'The Ecchoing Green' as it approaches its close begins to take on the completed shape of a circle: a shape which plays against its other shape of linear progression and its images of cessation and nightfall. There is no such delicate tension in 'London': here, the final stanza is marked with irreversible concreteness. And if it has the excited energy of imaginative definition, it has none of the subtler satisfaction to be found in the Innocent Song: the satisfaction of confirmation in change – a confirmation which forms, against those images of ending, a configuration of continuing possibility, of a 'sport' which will continue unseen. The protagonists there are not, as in 'London', locked in a terrible *stasis*. For the engagement with actuality and its changing potentialities which this poem presents is diametrically opposed to that Experienced detachment and 'marking', that attempt to distance and to control, which is manifested so inescapably not merely in the rigidified, divisive institutions of the society, but in the answering 'marking' of its victims. There, where there is neither creative acceptance of nor interaction with difference, there can be no movement beyond what is. The contrast between these two poems is the essential contrast between the two 'states' which

Songs of Innocence and *Songs of Experience* explore, here writ large as an absolute opposition between two modes of social organization.

Taken together, *Songs of Innocence* and *Songs of Experience* present a view of morality and its place in human affairs that is extraordinary in its difference from that of any other literature of their time. Their radical questioning of 'Ideas of Good & Evil'[82] seems in some ways very close to that of the antinomianism which remained an intimate part of Blake's mental universe to the end of his life.[83] These poems reveal much about the reasons for the continuing potency of that antinomianism in his thinking: for here its implications are realized and explored in terms of the actual society in which he lived. Here, its rejection of the Moral Law is charged with the newly confident ironic energy of Paine-ite demystification: official moral absolutes are challenged by a sharp realization of the social strategies which they justify and perpetuate. Yet Blake's minutely articulated vision of the interconnections between the dominant modes of relationship of a society and the creative or destructive force of the 'virtues' to which it appeals is far more incisive and more subtly exploratory than anything to be found in the writings either of the radicals or of the sectaries. The tree of death and mystery which takes shape within and materializes at the end of 'A Poison Tree' and 'The Human Abstract' might be seen as an ironic version of that 'Mysterious Tree / Of Good & Evil & Mystery' (K759) which Blake was to attack in his most straightforwardly antinomian poem, 'The Everlasting Gospel'. But the way in which these Songs trace the manner of that tree's growth and its relation to human action, its compulsive power and its devastating psychological and social results, has no parallel in antinomian theology. Similarly, the antinomian belief in a coming millennium, the destruction of Babylon, becomes in the *Songs* not a vision of impending divine vengeance, but of a retribution actually immanent within present social relationships. The implicit warnings with which the Innocent 'Holy Thursday' and 'The Chimney Sweeper' end point not towards God's judgment, nor even (as the Paine-ite radicals might) toward the coming revenge of one exploited group upon those who have oppressed them: the disasters they threaten are seen as inescapable in a society whose structures fail to actualize the 'virtues' in which its real creative *potentia* consists. Even the evocative closing image of the Harlot in 'London' seems less the Whore of Babylon of millenarian prophecy than an actual, 'youthful' victim, whose 'curse' brings not revolution but death:

less a harbinger of future doom than the manifest symbol of a society which is even now being destroyed by its own internal logic.

And most importantly, that sense of the divine within the human central to antinomian thinking in all its forms becomes in these poems something more than a theological affirmation of individual human value – and something far more than a demand for the 'rights of man'.[84] For the Songs of *Innocence* trace the manifestations of the 'Divine Image' not in individuals, but in particular, active relationships, relationships which are shown to exist even in the midst of an all–too–familiar world of exploitation and division. In portraying the imaginative love of an anonymous little sweep, the transcendent beauty of the charity-children's ceremony, the world of confidence and security which may be created between mother and child, the 'third joyous kingdom of play',[85] the hope and trust that find their expression and vindication in prayer and its answering, the instinct of sympathy with 'anothers woe', Blake is affirming the fundamental importance of real experiences which the radical protest of his day tended to ignore: experiences which – both collections suggest – must be central to any creative human community, experiences of a mode of relationship quite different from the sterile opposition of privileged and unprivileged, oppressor and oppressed, in terms of which so much of late eighteenth–century English society was structured. Blake does not ignore those dominant exploitative structures or the human deformation and distress they caused: the Songs of *Innocence* are neither sentimental nor escapist. But neither is he guilty of the reverse sentimentalism of despair: one after another the Songs of *Experience* expose the destructive deadlock which results from even well–intentioned ('moral') failure to recognize and actualize that existing *potentia* which the earlier collection celebrated. The demystificatory ironies of these poems may derive some of their energy from that political rejection of official pieties which by 1792 was beginning to be widely articulated in the London which Blake knew: their more radical questioning of any morality, their presentation of the heavens and hells men create for themselves and one another within this world, seems to owe something to the antinomian tradition of which he was the heir. But inheritance is not necessarily a passive thing. And in their precise and sophisticated exploration of the interplay between social being and social consciousness, their articulation of the ways in which a transforming human *potentia* might be realized, Songs of Innocence and Songs of

Experience offer a vision which reaches far beyond that of the antinomian theology or the political radicalism within whose matrix much of Blake's thinking seems to have been formed: a vision finely worked out in the deceptively simple language of song.

6 Morality through Experience: *Lyrical Ballads 1798*

But since a certain inequality of situation is necessary, and the present inequality, apparently more than that necessity requires, I am only desirous that the shade of distinction should rather be relieved than darkened; that in the picture of human life, the poor should not be ignominiously degraded in the background, merely to render the drawing picturesque, but that they should generously be represented on the canvas, with that dignity and importance to which they are really entitled.

(From *The Cabinet*, by a Society of Gentlemen, no. 1, October 1794)

However disconcerting their original readers may have found them, the poems of *Lyrical Ballads* seem much more straightforward in their moral intention than do those of *Songs of Innocence and of Experience*. They contain none of that mocking play with paradox and ambiguity which marks Blake's collection, and none of his ironic awareness of the double-edgedness of the moral terms they use. Indeed, in the Preface to the 1800 edition, Wordsworth claims quite directly that each of 'the Poems in these volumes ... has a worthy purpose'. He does, it is true, go on to distinguish this *purpose* from simple didacticism:

Not that I mean to say, that I always began to write with a distinct purpose formally conceived; but I believe that my habits of meditation have so formed my feelings, as that my descriptions of such objects as strongly excite those feelings, will be found to carry along with them a *purpose*.

But his central assumption remains that 'Poems to which any value can be attached' will ultimately have an unambiguously moral effect: 'the understanding of the being of whom we address ourselves, if he be in a healthful state of association, must necessarily be in some degree enlightened, his taste exalted, and his affections ameliorated'.[1] Such an assumption seems the intimate result of that confidence in a like-minded audience manifested in the plans for *The Philanthropist*, and of an implicit trust – shared with that audience – in the 'ameliorative' power of education.[2] Yet the difference between

Lyrical Ballads and the 'magazine verse' such readers would have expected seems to bespeak a rather more complex attitude towards contemporary moral certainties than this Preface, and the contrast of these poems with Blake's, might at first suggest.

Like children's verse, magazine poetry was a conventionally moralistic genre. The authors of the lyrics and ballads, 'pastorals' and meditative effusions which filled the poetry pages of the magazines were just as eager to instruct and improve their readers, to awaken them to the lot of those less fortunate than themselves, and to set them thinking on more general moral subjects, as were those responsible for the simple didacticism of the children's books. In their sentimental depiction of the plight of the poor and their confident appeal to easy moral platitudes, the vast majority of these poems express the same unquestioning acquiescence in the status quo as do those written for children. But some, at least, explicitly aimed to question it. And it is in relation to such verse as this – verse written by men whose social thinking was in many ways close to Wordsworth's, men who saw their poetry as the vehicle for new and subversive ideas – that we might most fruitfully begin to explore the ways in which *Lyrical Ballads* does question that established 'Moral Virtue' to which Blake's *Songs* seem much more uncompromisingly opposed.

We are peculiarly well placed to do so. For in 1799 Wordsworth's friend Southey published a series of 'English Eclogues', some of which were modelled on poems from *Lyrical Ballads 1798* – an act apparently prompted by his dissatisfaction with the 'strangeness and aukwardness' of the earlier collection.[3] Mary Jacobus has examined the way in which in these verses

poems from *Lyrical Ballads* are returned firmly to the level of the magazine poetry from which they had been raised, stripped of their new thematic depth and narrative sophistication. In other cases, what is idiosyncratic or disturbing ... is replaced by topical humanitarian interest of a quite straightforward kind; the poems become not simply shallower, but more public.[4]

Southey's poems indeed provide a particularly clear example of the conventionalizing process to which original works of art tend to be subjected, of the way in which such works may be re-moulded (either by readers or 'imitators') to conform with established 'public' taste. But it is perhaps even more illuminating to look in the other direction, and examine one of the 1798 *Lyrical Ballads* from the viewpoint afforded by such an imitation. 'Old Man Travelling' was, as we have already seen, one of the least acceptable of the 1798 collection: Wordsworth's own later revisions suggest that even he found it in some way disquieting. And it is one of the poems of which Southey wrote his own, very different, version – 'The Sailor's Mother' – a version which begins thus:

WOMAN: Sir, for the love of God, some small relief
  To a poor woman!
TRAVELLER: Whither are you bound?
  'Tis a late hour to travel o'er these downs,
  No house for miles around us, and the way
  Dreary and wild. The evening wind already
  Makes one's teeth chatter, and the very sun,
  Setting so pale behind those thin white clouds,
  Looks cold. 'Twill be a bitter night!
WOMAN: Ay, sir,
  'Tis cutting keen! I smart at every breath;
  Heaven knows how I shall reach my journey's end,
  For the way is long before me, and my feet,
  God help me! sore with travelling. I would gladly,
  If it pleased God, lie down at once and die.
TRAVELLER: Nay, nay, cheer up! a little food and rest
  Will comfort you; and then your journey's end
  Will make amends for all. You shake your head,
  And weep. Is it some evil business then
  That leads you from your home?
WOMAN: Sir, I am going
  To see my son at Plymouth, sadly hurt
  In the late action, and in the hospital
  Dying, I fear me, now ...[5]

The dialogue continues, touching on several very topical problems – the meaning of patriotism, the sufferings caused by war, and the practice of conscripting offenders as an alternative to prison. By counterpointing the old woman's graphic descriptions of her sufferings with his Traveller's banal 'comfort', Southey achieves a crude dramatic irony which could hardly leave readers familiar with the sight of destitute veterans of the French wars and their families in any doubt as to the poem's moral point:[6]

              Well! well! take comfort,
  He will be taken care of if he lives;
  And should you lose your child, this is a country
  Where the brave sailor never leaves a parent
  To weep for him in want.

But Wordsworth's 'Old Man Travelling' is much more oblique. It is possible to trace an indirect anti-war statement in its juxtaposition of images of natural progression with one of unnatural death. But there is little sociological detail (such as had been prominent in the 'Salisbury Plain' poems),[7] and no obvious appeal either to pacifist feeling or to more general humanitarian sympathies. Instead, the poem begins with a description of an inscrutable and apparently impervious figure – a figure who is gradually transformed by the implied observer into a symbol of enviable 'animal tranquillity'. Instead of Southey's heavy-handed dialogue between poor sufferer and complacent interlocutor there is a much more baffling and really dramatic confrontation, which sharply questions the validity of that opening meditation.[8] For the old man's words disrupt this poem in a way in which Southey's old woman's do not. His feelings about his situation are not, like hers, the conventionalized, sentimentally emphasized feelings of the 'deserving poor': they remain unspoken. He simply offers a bald statement of fact – a statement whose opacity is similar to that of the placard fixed to the blind Beggar in London, which tells 'The story of the Man, and who he was' (*The Prelude*, 1805, Bk. VII, l.614). And the reader expecting, and failing, to find some mediating comment, some authorial direction, is forced into a recognition of the intransigent otherness of one of those whom even compassionate description, even enlightened protest, tended to see as mere objects of polite moral consciousness.

It is true that many of those to whom Wordsworth was closest in these years – even sometimes Southey himself – had a far more exploratory interest in the psychology of the deprived than that displayed in 'The Sailor's Mother'.[9] For educated radicals in the 1790s, a study of such subjects meant a real attempt to move beyond belittling attitudes of concern, and to consider seriously the possible subjective feelings of those who were more likely to be seen simply as 'the poor'. It was an interest which Wordsworth himself shared: in March 1798 while working on the first volume of *Lyrical Ballads*, he sent off to Bristol for a copy of Erasmus Darwin's *Zoonomia*, a lengthy medical treatise whose case-histories of extreme mental states seem to have provided starting-points for several of the poems published in that volume.[10] Yet in 'Old Man Travelling', written during the preceding year, the poetic focus is significantly different. The subject of the poem – the apparent stoicism of the suffering poor – is one which had a continuing imaginative fascination for Wordsworth: it had been extensively explored by the great radical

Dissenter, Joseph Fawcett, in a sermon published in 1795, and probably attended by the poet in 1793:

We are told of an unhappy creature who, during long periods of time, is not only deprived of the pleasures of corporeal activity, but who is also a stranger to ease; who is condemned to pain, as well as to solitude. He, whose sensations are all gay and pleasurable, whose heart, in the fulness of health, laughs and sings along with surrounding nature; and whose leaping pulses have never known what it is to languish; regards such a situation with an eye, that cannot endure to rest, so much as a moment, upon it; and that represents it as utterly insupportable. Yet he, who has long been in it, is not without his solace. Time has lulled his sense of his pain, though it has not been able to lessen its degree, so as to have made patience under it a much easier task, than at first it was to him, than it would be now to you.[11]

However complacent this may appear to the modern reader, the impulse behind Fawcett's sermon – and of the series of which it was part – was radically egalitarian: to affirm the dignity of those who were more frequently seen as almost subhuman.[12] Wordsworth in 1793 would have been attracted to them for precisely this reason. But 'Old Man Travelling' seems to offer an implicit retort to this kind of psychological analysis. Wordsworth makes no attempt to explore the old man's putative feelings: indeed, much of the force of the poem comes from its silent refusal to do so. And that refusal (seemingly against the grain of that contemporary 'progressive' thinking to which Wordsworth himself was attracted) does not merely explain the uneasiness with which its earlier readers received it:[13] it begins to suggest a reason for the poetic 'aukwardness' which marks many of the other poems of the volume.

For in the last six lines of 'Old Man Travelling' it is not only the old man's separateness that is exposed. Here, for the first and only time, the implied meditative speaker from whose perspective the opening vision of 'animal tranquillity and decay' has been offered explicitly enters the verse – enters it in the very encounter which challenges him:

> – *I* asked him whither he was bound, and what
> The object of his journey; *he* replied ...
> [my italics]

His position has become the problem about which the poem pivots: no longer – as for Southey and for Fawcett – a position of meditative certainty, but one of silence before difference, a silence which he does not explain. Instead of offering a single, authoritative analysis, the poem simply juxtaposes two divergent and ultimately antithetical points of view. Yet this implicit questioning of polite assurance has none of the accusatory force, the sense of mutual complicity, to be found in Blake's 'Pity would be no more, / If we did not make somebody Poor.' Unlike Blake's 'we', Wordsworth's 'I' is a privileged speaker whose meditation, though questioned, is in no way related to the old man's situation. It is not, like Blake's 'Pity', seen as actively creating, acquiescing in and perpetuating the social division which has produced it: the cause of the son's death lies outside the poem, and no interaction between the two speakers – beyond that of question and silencing reply – is imagined. This presentation of two discordant voices, each expressing a contrary sense of the world, is very different from that play upon the disparity between 'polite' and 'impolite' meanings to be found in such *Songs of Innocence and of Experience* as 'The Chimney Sweeper' and 'London'. The irreconcilable perspectives which this poem dramatizes are simply opposed: they are not, as in Blake, focussed disconcertingly within the same words. And although it is apparently questioned, that of the reflective polite observer remains primary: even the disquieting speech of the old man is contained within his narrative structure. His silence at the end of the poem is the silence of a bafflement which the reader is called upon to share.

The 1798 version of 'Old Man Travelling' thus in one way confronts, in another evades, the dilemma inherent in any attempt – however thoughtful, however consciously egalitarian – to write from a polite point of view about those who in the late eighteenth century were seen as the lower orders of society. It does foreground a problem which even those educated radicals who tried to find an acceptable way of portraying real social conditions, or to imagine the consciousness of the deprived, tended not to consider: the problem of the position of the polite observer, and the assumed authority of his viewpoint. But Wordsworth's containing narrative frame (within which, in his own later revisions, he completely incorporated the old man's speech, finally excluding it altogether),[14] his failure to explore the relation between the polite assumptions which his poem so strikingly exposes and the world of actual human interaction, the baffled silence of his ending, point towards the difficulty he seems to have found in following through the more radical implications of his own insights. It is a difficulty which is manifested in several poems from the 1798 volume: poems whose 'aukwardness' seems to bespeak less a consistent, coherent challenge to established attitudes than a confusion of imaginative impulse – a confusion which springs from Wordsworth's deeply felt uncertainty as to his own proper relation to his subject-matter.

Indeed, it is significant that one of the most extraordinary poems of these years – one which explores the problem focussed in 'Old Man Travelling' with a nakedness and directness unequalled in any of Wordsworth's other works – is one which he seems to have had some difficulty in composing and finishing, an unnamed fragment which he never published:

> I have seen the Baker's horse
> As he had been accustomed at your door
> Stop with the loaded wain, when o'er his head
> Smack went the whip, and you were left, as if
> You were not born to live, or there had been
> No bread in all the land. Five little ones,
> They at the rumbling of the distant wheels
> Had all come forth, and, ere the grove of birch
> Concealed the wain, into their wretched hut
> They all return'd. While in the road I stood
> Pursuing with involuntary look
> The Wain now seen no longer, to my side
> ———— came, a pitcher in her hand
> Filled from the spring; she saw what way my eyes
> Were turn'd, and in a low and fearful voice
> She said – that wagon does not care for us –
> The words were simple, but her look and voice
> Made up their meaning, and bespoke a mind
> Which being long neglected, and denied
> The common food of hope, was now become
> Sick and extravagant, by strong access
> Of momentary pangs driv'n to that state
> In which all past experience melts away,
> And the rebellious heart to its own will
> Fashions the laws of nature.[15]

These lines were probably written in the spring of 1797, at much the same time as 'Old Man Travelling'. Here, the speaker is identified in the opening word: the poem begins unambiguously from his point of view. But the stark monosyllables of the fourth line break the meditative movement of the verse, and the comma at its centre signals a dramatic shift of perspective: 'Smack went the whip, and you were left...' Suddenly he moves closer to an alignment with those who are 'left', those whose right to existence the smacking of the whip has denied. And in the wake of that shocking 'smack' they begin to appear in the poetry: 'Five little ones / They at the rumbling of the distant wheels / Had all come forth'; ' ——— came, a pitcher in her hand / Filled from the spring'. The world which they inhabit is a place of fearful malevolence. It is apparently indifferent to the simplest claims of humanity – claims whose necessity is unobtrusively suggested by the involuntary stopping of the horse, the children's automatic appearance at its approach, and the contrast between the 'smack' which denies and the 'pitcher' which is naturally 'Filled from the spring'. Its indifference is not even manifested in the direct relation of one man to another, but in unintelligible and dehumanized phenomena, such as the failure of the bread-bearing wagon to stop. And this sense of a perverted and pitiless reality – so immediately and directly presented from the point of view of those who are 'left' – is exactly encapsulated in the woman's 'low and fearful' words 'that wagon does not care for us'.

Yet it is precisely at this point that the polite speaker moves from alignment to meditation and the disturbing force of the woman's perception is denied. For there is a curious shift in the middle of the fragment from the second to the third person, a shift which seems to signify a real unease in the narrator's stance toward his subject-matter.[16] The 'you' of the opening is replaced by a gap in the manuscript – a gap apparently intended to be filled by a name. The woman who speaks is no longer an other to be related to (the present perfect tense of the opening line has, indeed, suggested a continuing relationship) but a 'she' whose words are distanced into narrative. And because they are thus distanced they are not seen as calling for response or (like the old man's much less disturbing statement) silencing the central speaker: they can be placed and diminished. Her point of view – a point of view which the opening lines have made imaginatively compelling – becomes simply a symptom of madness. Privation has made her unable to judge correctly: the sense that it might have provided her with an equally – or possibly more – well-founded vision of the world cannot be admitted. The poem has slid from its initial disturbing insight into a study of politely defined derangement.

And this retreat is reflected in the very language with which Wordsworth tries, sympathetically, to analyse the irrationality of the woman's reaction. For it is language which irresistibly evokes exactly those social facts to which hers is a reasonable response. She is 'neglected', but not merely in her 'mind': the actual Baker's cart is turned away from her door. If she is 'denied / The common food of hope', she is also denied ordinary bread. If her 'state' is one 'In which all past experience melts away', this is no wild aberration, but precisely that which is now demanded of her. Experience has apparently taught her, and her little ones, as it has taught the horse, that the wain *will* stop at her door; that she *will* be accorded the 'common food' of humanity: the 'smack' of the whip now teaches a sterner lesson. Here, concludes the speaker, is a madness in which 'the rebellious heart to its own will / Fashions the laws of nature.' Yet the woman's sense of the wagon's hostility – bizarre as it may seem – is not 'rebelliously' at odds with 'the laws of nature' as Wordsworth presents them here. There is no famine in the land; the wain is loaded. 'Nature', indeed, is bountiful: the pitcher is filled from the spring, the horse stops from habit at her door. The 'laws' which lead to the cracking of the whip are not 'the laws of nature', but human actions – grotesquely, yet from her perspective accurately enough, perceived as a single malevolent impersonal process: 'That wagon does not care for us.' Insistently the poetry registers that which the speaker's attempt to see her 'state' as mere madness would deny.

The attempt to conflate social fact with natural law, at the same moment as that fact is imaginatively perceived as a violation of 'nature', is reminiscent of that meditation upon 'Animal Tranquillity and Decay' which is so sharply questioned by a stark account of the human world in 'Old Man Travelling'. But here, despite – or perhaps because of – the lack of poetic coherence, the significance of that attempt is apparent. For if, unlike the published poem, this fragment offers a powerful imaginative realization of the perspective of those who are 'left', their sense of the incomprehensible, inhuman hostility of that which 'makes them Poor', the speaker too seems unable to move beyond this sense, except by dismissing it as madness. For despite his indignation – 'as if / You were not born to live, or there had been / No bread in all the land' – he, also, sees the woman as 'left', 'neglected', 'denied' and 'driv'n' by a process whose cause is as mysterious and as remote from confrontation in the poetry as the reason for the smacking of the whip, a process which for him seems to have the force of an unquestionable and incomprehensible law. He too is left, 'Pursuing with involuntary look / The Wain now seen no longer': by the woman's side, and yet – as his authoritative 'diagnosis' in the closing lines suggests – by no means sharing her condition.

And it is the imaginative uncertainty manifest in this fragment, as much as any more coherently subversive 'purpose', which disjoints many of the narrative poems of *Lyrical Ballads 1798*. To some extent – as their early reviews suggest – they *were* successful in exposing and questioning the conventionally moralistic assumptions of their progressive late eighteenth-century readers. Southey, for instance, puzzled over 'Goody Blake and Harry Gill'; was it merely a sensationalistic account of a factual incident, or was it meant to teach a lesson? The poem itself seemed to afford him no clue:

> The story of a man who suffers the perpetual pain of cold, because an old woman prayed that he might never be warm, is perhaps a good story for a ballad, because it is a well-known tale: but is the author certain that it is 'well authenticated'? And does not such an assertion promote the popular superstition of witchcraft?[17]

Dr Burney, in *The Monthly Review*, was more naive in his expectation of moral teaching, and more bewildered by the questions left open by the poem:

> Distress from poverty and want is admirably described in the true story of 'Goody Blake and Harry Gill': but are we to imagine that Harry was bewitched by Goody Blake? The hardest heart must be softened into pity for the poor old woman; and yet, if all the poor are to help themselves, and supply their wants from the possessions of their neighbours, what imaginary wants and real anarchy would it not create? Goody Blake should have been relieved of the two millions annually allowed by the state to the poor of this country, not by the plunder of an individual.[18]

Perhaps the contemporary reader who came closest to defining the nature of the difficulty was a reviewer of the 1800 volume, writing in the *British Critic* for February 1801:

> As to the subjects, it must be owned that their worth does not always appear at first sight; but, judging from our own feelings, we must assert, that it generally grows upon the reader by subsequent perusal ... Even where the feeling intended to be called forth is of a rich and noble character, such as we may recur to, and feed upon, it may yet be wrought up so gradually, including so many preparatory circumstances of appropriate manners, of local descriptions, of actual events, etc., that the subtle uniting thread will be lost, without a persevering effort towards attention on the part of the reader.[19]

For to find the 'subtle uniting thread' which will make sense of these poems is by no means easy. To their earliest readers, they were puzzling because they did not seem to fit into any of the categories – of simple sensationalism, of 'sensibility', or of more radical protest –

to which verse on such subjects might be expected to belong. They offer no clear guide as to what the reader is supposed to make of the situations they present: their speakers' exclamations and explanations are often cryptic, and those speakers frequently seem to be questioned within the poem. Yet if, as Wordsworth's own Advertisement to the volume suggests, this is partly a deliberate strategy – an effort to get his readers to 'struggle' with the poems in a more energetic way than that which more conventional verse demanded, and to question the assumptions ('our own pre-established codes of decision') which it characterisically embodied – there are discords and difficulties in the 1798 volume which cannot be explained entirely in this way. To the modern reader, these poems are disconcerting less because they demand 'a persevering effort towards attention' on his part than because of the sometimes embarrassing clarity with which they expose the contradictions implicit in what they attempt.

The poem of which this is most interestingly true is 'Simon Lee'. Like 'Old Man Travelling', this has as its subject one of the victims of an unequal society: like that poem, it refuses to adopt a conventional stance, either of pity or of protest. Indeed, in a series of taunting asides to the reader, it explicitly comments on its own refusal.[20] Like the sub-title of 'Old Man Travelling' ('Animal Tranquillity and Decay: a Sketch') its title ('Simon Lee, the Old Huntsman, with an incident in which he was concerned') seems to promise an easily assimilable portrait of its central character; as in the earlier poem, that implicit promise is undermined by what follows. Even in the first stanza, the possibility of a single authoritative viewpoint is lightly but tellingly questioned:

> In the sweet shire of Cardigan,
> Not far from pleasant Ivor-hall,
> An old man dwells, a little man,
> *I've heard* he once was tall.
> Of years he has upon his back,
> *No doubt*, a burthen weighty;
> *He says* he is three score and ten,
> *But others say* he's eighty.
>
> [my italics]

And as the poems proceeds, this emphasis continues, in a series of echoes of past conversation and present gossip, of the old man's voice itself:

> To say the least, four counties round
> Had heard of Simon Lee ...

He all the country could outrun,
Could leave both man and horse behind ...

Few months of life he has in store,
    As he to you will tell,
For still, the more he works, the more
    His poor old ancles swell.

The sense is of a whole community – a community in which the facts of life are unsentimentally confronted and acknowledged ('Yet meet him where you will, you see / At once that he is poor ... '; 'The weakest in the village') – in which memories and reports join with present perceptions to construct the individual's social identity. The portrait of Simon which emerges is thus very different from anything to be found in more conventional contemporary verse, where such a figure would be presented from a single, polite perspective:

We met an old bare-headed man,
    His locks were few and white,
I ask'd what he did abroad
    In that cold winter's night:

'Twas bitter keen, indeed, he said,
    But at home no fire had he,
And therefore he had come abroad
    To ask for charity.
                        (Southey: 'The Complaints of the Poor')[21]

Simon Lee is a far more complex, less clichéd character than this old man. He is both ludicrous and independent: boastful of and remembered for his past prowess, yet decrepit in ways less lyrically acceptable than 'His locks were few and white.' His life is not one of humble acquiescence, but an unremitting struggle which cannot easily be smoothed into the 'poetical': 'For still, the more he works, the more / His poor old ancles swell.' Southey's poem concludes with a neat quatrain which suggests that 'the poor' are somehow disposed of once the right judgment has been made – any sense of implication or responsibility being deftly transferred to the 'rich':

I turn'd me to the rich man then,
    For silently stood he, –
'You ask me why the poor complain,
    And these have answer'd thee!'

But the narrator of Simon Lee is left with a tangled, inconclusive and continuing set of feelings: feelings aroused by an other who is not generalized into 'the poor', but seen as a unique and irresolvable individual:

> The tears into his eyes were brought,
> And thanks and praises seemed to run
> So fast out of his heart, I thought
> They never would have done.
> – I've heard of hearts unkind, kind deeds
> With coldness still returning.
> Alas! the gratitude of men
> Has oftner left me mourning.

Some of the 'aukwardness' of this poem, then, like that of 'Old Man Travelling', stems from its attempt to suggest the intransigent otherness of one of those who were more likely, in late eighteenth-century poetry, to be simplified into objects of meditation or concern. Here, the attempt is more complex than the abrupt confrontation of the earlier poem; and it leads to an unease in face of that favourite virtue of humble life, 'gratitude', not dissimilar to that expressed by Wordsworth's friend Thelwall in *The Peripatetic* five years earlier:

The story was too circumstantial to be doubted; and Philanthropa, putting a half crown into her hand, hurried away to avoid that profusion of gratitude, which how pleasing soever it may be to the mere spectator, is always painful to the ear of the truly generous benefactor.[22]

Yet like Thelwall's, it is an unease very different from the sardonic, direct attack of *Pigott's Political Dictionary*: '*Grateful* – obsolete. It is at present used for *great fool*.' Where this definition suggests a perspective radically opposed to that of the polite, for Wordsworth and for Thelwall the disquieting implications of 'gratitude' remain a problem within the 'benefactor's consciousness. However challenged they may feel by the situations they present, both end with an implicit affirmation of the primacy of the polite point of view. And this difference points sharply toward another, and more fundamental 'aukwardness' in Wordsworth's portrayal of Simon.

For the effect of that portrayal is very odd: much odder, I think, than those critics who praise the poem for its frustration of expected responses have admitted.[23] It is a portrayal never entirely free of condescension: one in which Simon never quite attains serious stature. Despite the attempt to see him in the round, a figure unassimilable to any single viewpoint, he remains contained within the excessively regular rhythms and exact, often feminine rhymes of an undeviating stanza pattern. There is a curious disjunction between form and subject-matter: between the jaunty, almost jocular effect of the former, and the prosaic misery of the latter:

> He has no son, he has no child,
> His wife, an aged woman,
> Lives with him, near the waterfall,
> Upon the village common.

> And he is lean and he is sick,
> His little body's half awry
> His ancles they are swoln and thick
> His legs are thin and dry.
> When he was young he little knew
> Of husbandry or tillage;
> And now he's forced to work, though weak,
> – The weakest in the village.

And the result is an embarrassing tension between that which is of its nature disquieting and irresolvable and that which completes and resolves; a tension which increases as the poem proceeds and which finds its imaginative fulfilment in the penultimate stanza:

> 'You're overtasked, good Simon Lee,
> Give me your tool' to him I said;
> And at the word right gladly he
> Received my proffer'd aid.
> I struck, and with a single blow
> The tangled root I sever'd,
> At which the poor old man so long
> And vainly had endeavour'd.

The 'blow' which finishes the old man's task makes all of Simon's struggles with it irrelevant: it completes that belittlement of him which has been implicitly present in the tone throughout. If it is a solution, it is one which in its violence seems almost like castration. The effortlessness with which it is delivered makes it an apt and powerful image for the unwitting ease of that paternalistic 'pity' which diminishes that which is to the suffering other impossible – an image which, in its incipient brutality, and in the irrational guilt it seems to inspire, comes closer than anything else in *Lyrical Ballads 1798* to Blake's 'Pity would be no more / If we did not make somebody Poor.'

It is far more ambiguous, however, than Blake: in a way which has enabled at least one sensitive modern critic to write of it from a quite opposite point of view:

At the conclusion of a poem in which the only action has been a slow decay of life, this 'single blow' becomes more than a particular act of charity. It is a powerful and liberating release of protective energy, a gesture of defense, and even revenge, on behalf of a humanity caught in the inexorable processes of natural law.[24]

For it is presented by the speaker as an act of natural charity, the instinctive response of a younger, able-bodied man to the struggles of one who is handicapped by age. Just as the first nine stanzas, with an uncertain egalitarianism, have tried to suggest that Simon, like the 'you' who is constantly addressed and invoked, is not just 'Poor', but 'somebody', with a remembered past and a vivid self-image, so this encounter between the obviously 'gentle' speaker and one who is almost destitute is seen simply as an encounter between two men, in which a common human fate is acknowledged and lamented. On this level, the narrator's 'mourning' is a continuing grief at those 'inexorable processes of natural law' which diminish strength and make such 'gratitude' as Simon's necessary.

Yet to read the poem simply thus is to discount the disturbing force of that final gesture, and to ignore many of the disquieting implications of that which is presented in the poetry. For Simon's life is portrayed with a realistic detail which makes description of the poem's subject-matter as 'the slow decay of life' seem rather less than the whole truth:

> Beside their moss-grown hut of clay,
> Not twenty paces from the door,
> A scrap of land they have, but they
> Are poorest of the poor.
> This scrap of land he from the heath
> Enclosed when he was stronger;
> But what avails the land to them,
> Which they can till no longer?[25]

This is a world very different from that of the speaker, or of the 'gentle reader', with his appetite for edifying tales. The division is registered most intimately in the poem's odd uncertainty of tone; and it finds its ultimate symbolic expression in the quick lopping-off of the root at which the old man labours. In the wake of that sudden 'blow', the narrator's unresolved 'mourning' takes on other, and guiltier, resonances. This is a strange 'tale' for the 'gentle reader', a tale which questions his (and the speaker's) gentleness, even as, in another way, it affirms their gentility.

Yet whatever is recognized (or unconsciously registered) in the muted violence of this face-to-face encounter with the man who has been the subject of the greater part of the poem, the closing lines offer an essentially private reflection:

> I've heard of hearts unkind, kind deeds
> With coldness still returning.
> Alas! the gratitude of men
> Has oftner left me mourning.

The quatrain begins like a proverbial aphorism, echoing that earlier appeal to the reader's fellow-feeling ('I hope you'll *kindly* take it'). But the closing lines turn away from the expected completing moral, away from the simple conclusiveness which has been a feature of the poetry. For the first time in the poem the narrator speaks directly of his feelings – speaks with an intimacy which implicitly addresses itself to that 'gentle reader', who might, through 'silent thought' about this subject, find his 'understanding ... enlightened, his taste exalted, and his affections ameliorated'.[26] Simon, with his embarrassing gushing thanks, has disappeared: the speaker is 'left' alone. And the movement from the 'proverbial wisdom' of the first two of these lines to this private, almost solipsistic confession is an implicit admission that the only possibility for real mutuality of feeling lies not in a world of 'common humanity' which includes both privileged and unprivileged, but between the narrator and his 'gentle reader', a man capable of 'severe thought, and a long continued intercourse with the best models of composition'.[27] Simon is not felt as a persistent and unassimilable presence: what we have is an unfinished (and hopefully 'ameliorative') disturbance in the speaker's feelings, half distanced and half foregrounded by the present perfect continuous tense.

This ending is very different from the conclusions of those of the *Songs of Innocence* which deal with similarly disturbing subject matter. There, the barbed 'morals' point directly into the world of human interaction – 'So if all do their duty, they need not fear harm'; 'Then cherish pity; lest you drive an angel from your door.' Here, there is an introspective 'mourning' – an emotion felt when the other to whom one has related has disappeared. There, Blake tightly controls the several conflicting possibilities of meaning he has evoked: here all the ambiguities of implication aroused in the poem are left confusedly (rather than ironically) in play. 'Mourning' does suggest a more critical attitude towards social inequality than the complacent self-congratulation of conventional 'benevolence': its unresolvedness hints at a lurking guilt, springing irrationally but realistically from the ease with which Simon's efforts have been negated, and pointing toward the disquieting sources of that embarrassment which has been present throughout the poem. Yet alongside this hovers another, incoherently contradictory feeling. For 'mourning' is men's means of coming to terms with that which is accepted as unalterable: if the word registers disquiet, it also suggests resignation. And if there is egalitariansim in 'the gratitude of men' there is also a refusal to recognize those differences between 'men' which have been reflected in the poem's uncertain stance towards its subject-matter, a refusal which tries – against the strain of that uncertainty – to assimilate Simon's plight to a universal human predicament.

The interest of 'Simon Lee' lies in the imaginative fidelity with which it registers the tensions implicit in Wordsworth's enterprise: tensions unremarked or unconfronted by those radical thinkers to whom he was closest. It is the only one of *Lyrical Ballads 1798* in which he shows his easy, egalitarian speaker *acting* in relation to one of the less privileged classes: and the act is imaginatively disturbing in a way unparalleled in any other explicitly 'egalitarian' verse of these years. But the poem finally fails to explore or control that confusion of feeling which its 'incident' arouses. And in its implicit moral 'purpose', that of 'placing my Reader in the way of receiving from ordinary moral sensations another and more salutary impression than we are accustomed to receive from them',[28] it points away from the challenging fact of Simon's existence and into the world of essentially private feeling as surely as the villagers in 'The Old Cumberland Beggar' turn away from the Beggar and from each other in their separate responses. The ending, indeed, seems an admission of isolation:

> Alas! the gratitude of men
> Has oftner *left me* mourning.

Here there is no urgent call to an action in which 'all must' join: the 'tale' which may 'perhaps' be made of the incident must be made separately, by each reader. Moral awareness is implicitly seen as something private. And this makes it the less surprising that in other of the *Lyrical Ballads* of 1798 Wordsworth was able to transpose the insights of 'Old Man Travelling' and 'Simon Lee' into a minor key, and to purge them of their disturbing implications.

Certainly, 'Anecdote for Fathers' has none of the really disconcert-

ing 'aukwardness' of the other two poems. Yet its quietly modulated
stanzas do dramatize – in the less disconcerting, more assimilable
form of an enounter between father and son – that problem which is,
very differently, the subject of each. As its title indicates, it belongs
to a genre which had a great vogue in the magazines: that of the
simple 'anecdote' from which a clear moral lesson might be drawn.
But even here there were – and are – difficulties. As an early reviewer
observed, 'the object of the child's choice, and the inferences, are not
quite obvious': quietly but stubbornly, the poem refuses to fit the
conventional mould. Its 'moral' is not so easily abstracted as its
subtitle seems to claim, and its ending has an inconclusiveness most
unlike the neat summing up appropriate to the 'anecdotal' genre. Yet
initially it seems like the simplest of stories:

> I have a boy of five years old,
> His face is fair and fresh to see;
> His limbs are cast in beauty's mould,
> And dearly he loves me.

So calmly regular is the rhythm that the reader hardly notices that
these lines are not transparently descriptive: they dramatize a far
from disinterested stance toward the world. The sentence of which
the stanza is composed begins with 'I' and circles back to 'me': for
this speaker, the world begins and ends with himself. The child
whose 'lie' is to be the subject of the poem is introduced as his
property: his most important feeling (indeed, the only feeling of his
that is mentioned) is that which relates to 'me'. And as the poem
proceeds, the implications of this unobtrusive egocentricity become
steadily more apparent.

Instead of approaching the world with open receptivity, this
speaker sees all according to his own 'pre-established codes of
decision'.[29] He does not respond to the uniqueness of this morning,
this child, but fits all that is before him into familiar schemata ('His
limbs are cast in beauty's mould'), comparing everything either
explicitly or implicitly to other experiences, past or potential:

> One morn we stroll'd on our *dry* walk,
> Our *quiet* house all full in view,
> And held such intermitted talk
> As *we are wont to do.*

> My thoughts *on former pleasures* ran;
> *I thought of Kilve's delightful shore,*
> My pleasant home, when spring began,
> *A long, long year before.*

A day it was *when I could bear*
To think, and think, and think again;
With so much happiness to spare,
I could not feel a pain.

[my italics]

The verse does not analyse or dwell upon these habits of his: its quiet regularity asks the reader to accept them as inevitable. And it is therefore the more devastating when their real nature is revealed in his conversation with the child, where what has been an idle question becomes an increasingly aggressive attempt to get the boy to 'reason and compare' in the same way as himself.

Edward's obstinate honesty, his literal inability to fit his different experiences into a common mould, dramatically questions the father's closed pattern of responses and rebukes his lack of openness toward the uniqueness of the particular. Like the Idiot Boy's account of his adventures, his 'lie' has the opacity of a description offered in a language foreign to the speaker. And the father's intransigent efforts to 'find him out' expose the coerciveness implicit in the latter's clichéd mode of perception. It is not simply that he cannot see the world freshly: he has no respect for the otherness of this other person. His attitude towards 'his' child is the logical extension of that domineering reduction of the new to his own categories which has been implicit in his sense of the world from the beginning. Wordsworth makes no attempt – apart from that 'lie' – to present the child's perspective: like that of the old man in 'Old Man Travelling' it remains mysterious. But the father's closing reaction – almost a baffled silence, certainly not a conventional 'moral' – invites the reader to share a recognition of the unincorporable difference of that perspective.

On one level, 'Anecdote for Fathers' can be read as an attack on a particular kind of 'progressive' contemporary educational theory, familiar to Wordsworth through his association with Godwin and the Wedgwoods. In a letter to Godwin about an educational project in which Wordsworth was intimately involved, Thomas Wedgwood had written on 31 July 1797: 'From earliest infancy, children should be questioned about recent and remote impressions; or otherwise induced to repeat all their parts. From this would result a habit of the keenest observation & the most retentive memory.'[30] Much, he goes on, will depend on 'the moment seized for instruction, as after moderate meals & every other occasion of animal vivacity'. It is difficult to believe that this story of a 'lie', which is merely a pathetic caricature of adult reasoning, does not in part express Wordsworth's imaginative reaction against this rationalistic project:[31] a project framed by friends who were in many ways like-minded, and whose intentions were benevolent. Certainly, the poem's effect is the more powerful because of the subtlety with which its speaker is presented, not as a tyrant, but as one who in conventional terms is 'sensitive' and cares for his child – and one who is capable of 'learning' from him. The inconclusiveness of the ending suggests a confidence in the existence of at least some similarly disposed readers, who will also be led to realize and question their own assumptions about the proper education of children.

Yet the poem is not merely occasional, a contribution to a contemporary debate: it awakens deeper resonances. For it deals with questions which in other of *Lyrical Ballads 1798* are a source of real embarrassment or 'aukwardness'. That which in 'Old Man Travelling' was seen as an insoluble problem of a divided society here becomes a difficulty with which familial or educational morality must deal. That tendency to reduce otherness to one's own frame of reference, that failure to recognize difference, which the earlier poem exposed, is implicitly recognized in the father's final words: he has 'learnt' from this experience. If the focus on childhood and education allows a less traumatic, more easily integrated realization, it also enables other significances to emerge. The 'enlightened' father whose stance is dramatized in the facile rhythms and trite adjectives of the opening stanzas, who tries so insistently to force that stance upon his child, is a figure for that cultural pressure towards a closed view of experience described in the Advertisement to the volume as 'that most dreadful enemy to our pleasures, our own pre-established codes of decision': the child, in his confusion and his patently arbitrary 'lie', suggests something of the perversion which those 'pre-established codes of decision' impose. And the father's almost bullying importunity ('I said and took him by the arm...', 'I said and held him by the arm...', 'While still I held him by the arm...') registers Wordsworth's sense of the submerged violence of this pressure with a directness which is perhaps only possible because the subject-matter of this poem is less socially problematic than that of others in the volume.

Yet here, as in 'Simon Lee', the challenging confrontation with otherness is collapsed, in the final stanza, into a question of private morality:

Oh dearest, dearest boy! my heart
For better lore would seldom yearn,
Could I but teach the hundredth part
Of what from thee I learn.

There is a curious mixture of humility and unctuousness in these lines – on the one hand, the admission that it is the adult who 'learns' from the child, and that what he 'learns' cannot be 'taught' in his own rationalistic terms; on the other, his complacent conviction that he does 'learn'. This ending conveys far more sense of satisfaction and completion, far less of irresolvable guilt, than does that of 'Simon Lee'. Like that poem, it refuses to offer a clear-cut moral directive to the reader, and the refusal constitutes an implicit criticism of that reductive approach to experience embodied in the characteristic 'anecdote' of the magazines, and exemplified in the father's relentless search for reasons. Yet the change from the narrative past tense of the rest of the poem into the present tense of direct apostrophe here has an effect of framing and distancing, like that of the apostrophizing final stanza of 'Poor Susan'. If the child is one who has not yet succumbed to the pressure of those conventionalizing modes of experience represented by his father, we see only his resistance, only his 'lie' – and even this is presented from the father's perspective. If the last stanza is addressed to him, the address is rhetorical rather than direct: its emphasis falls on the two final words. Although 'learn' is in the present tense, the feeling is less of the continuing challenge of the child's distinctive being than of a now distanced encounter, whose significance for the adult lies in his own moral improvement.

This poem's handling of the adult-child relationship is very different from that of such of the *Songs of Innocence* as 'Infant Joy'. Blake's tightly constructed Song – on a beautifully engraved plate which draws attention to itself as a work of art – presents two quite different voices chiming in echoing responsiveness: it is an image of a mutually satisfying state of creative play. Wordsworth's story – far more discursive, an 'anecdote' rather than an image, and in its casual intimacy imitating 'a man speaking to men' – is told from the adult's point of view: the boy's remains impenetrable. Both poems in their different ways question the deep-rooted contemporary assumption that the correct adult stance toward the child should be one of guidance and 'instruction'. But while in 'Infant Joy' that questioning is implied in the presentation of an alternative vision – a vision of reciprocal self-realization, in which parent and child each call forth answering capacities in the other, in 'Anecdote for Fathers' it is the dramatized subject of the poem. The conventional roles are merely reversed: the adult asserts that he 'learns' from the child, but he is not shown as having his own nurturing strengths. Wordsworth ends with the insight which informs Blake's Song – that what the child needs is love, a recognition of his essential being ('Oh dearest, dearest boy!') – but it remains a private insight, a personal 'admonishment'. [32] The recognition thus hinted at is not actualized, as is the relationship between mother and child in 'Infant Joy'. Here, as in 'Old Man Travelling' and in 'Simon Lee', there is no imaginative sense of what positive interaction with the other – in all his difference and uniqueness – might be like.

The 1798 collection of *Lyrical Ballads*, it is beginning to seem, offers an exploration of the relation between morality and social experience very different from that of *Songs of Innocence and of Experience*. Much more directly than Blake's Songs, these poems engage with the subject-matter of advanced contemporary debate. Like those Songs, they question the unarticulated moral assumptions of the polite reader: most centrally, that paternalistic diminution of the other which insidiously structured late eighteenth-century social thinking, even in its consciously radical manifestations. But unlike the Songs, they do not explore the social implications of those psychic strategies which they question. Figures like the old man of 'Old Man Travelling' and Simon Lee are portrayed as isolated victims of processes displaced from any identifiable agency: the speaker's relation to them remains problematic. The interest is not in what has 'made them Poor', but in the individual psyche of this implicitly questioned speaker, and in his (also implied) capacities for moral awareness and growth, which the reader is invited to share. If they lead to baffled inconclusiveness, they do not, like *Songs of Experience*, end in an immobilizing recognition of the way in which mental and social strategies can confirm and perpetuate each other ('Nor poverty the mind appall', 'The mind-forg'd manacles I hear'): they have a potentially ameliorating 'purpose'. Yet unlike the poems of *Songs of Innocence*, they do not image the possibility of creative, continuing relationship with those whose individual integrity they recognize. Instead, they dramatize moments of confrontation which are also moments of shock: moments in which an implicit morality is arrived at not in 'play', but in admonition.

It might be argued, however, that this is only a partial account of *Lyrical Ballads 1798*. For the volume contains another group of poems, very different from these poems of confrontation, in which Wordsworth does seem to be trying to trace the springs of morality not in 'admonishment' but in more positive experience. It is experience not of man, but of nature. Four of these poems are lyrics – 'It is the first mild day of March', 'Lines written in early spring', 'Expostulation and Reply' and 'The Tables Turned' – lyrics at first sight far closer to the 'effusions' on nature which their readers might have expected than those dealing with the rustic poor are to their conventional contemporary counterparts. Certainly, the notion of turning to nature for moral amelioration was not new: it was prominent in those educated radical circles with which Wordsworth was familiar, as in the more conservative sphere of polite 'sensibility'. Thus, for instance, Thelwall, in *The Peripatetic*:

I often shudder to reflect on the cruel and selfish dispositions which nature seemed at one time to have planted in my bosom. Nor was it 'till frequent opportunities of contemplating, with enamoured eye, the varied beauties of creation, in my eccentric rambles, and indulging the poetical studies to which they conducted, had soothed and meliorated my heart, that the blossoms of sensibility began to unfold themselves, and I awakened to a sympathetic feeling for every sentient tennant [sic] of this many-peopled sphere.[33]

And thus Coleridge, writing to his brother George in March 1798 (and quoting Wordsworth's draft conclusion to 'The Ruined Cottage'):[34]

I love fields & woods & mounta[ins] with almost a visionary fondness – and because I have found benevolence and quietness growing within me as that fondness [has] increased, therefore I should wish to be the means of implanting it in others – & to destroy the bad passions not by combating them, but by keeping them in inaction.

> Not useless do I deem
> Those shadowy Sympathies with things that hold
> An inarticulate Language: for the Man
> Once taught to love such objects, as excite
> No morbid passions, no disquietude,
> No vengeance & no hatred, needs must feel
> The Joy of that pure principle of Love
> So deeply, that, unsatisfied with aught
> Less pure & exquisite, he cannot chuse
> But seek for objects of a kindred Love
> In fellow natures, & a kindred Joy.
> Accordingly, he by degrees perceives
> His feelings of aversion softened down,

A holy tenderness pervade his frame!
His sanity of reason not impair'd,
Say rather that his thoughts now flowing clear
From a clear fountain flowing, he looks round –
He seeks for Good & finds the Good he seeks.

                                        Wordsworth

In these lyrics of nature, written between March and May 1798, Wordsworth seems at first to be expressing a similar confidence that joy in the natural world must lead by natural extension to love for one's fellow human beings. This is the faith that the Victorians seem to have found in his poetry.[35] But on closer examination, these poems seem more complex and more problematic than this. Wordsworth seems to be less interested in drawing moral strength from woods and fields than in exploring a particular mode of experience, which enables a newly creative relationship with that which is beyond the self: experience in which passivity and activity are paradoxically combined:

'The eye it cannot chuse but see,
'We cannot bid the ear be still;
'Our bodies feel, wher'er they be,
'Against, or with our will.

'Nor less I deem that there are powers,
'Which of themselves our minds impress,
'That we can feed this mind of ours,
'In a wise passiveness.
                        ('Expostulation and Reply')

The state described here is the opposite of that intrusive meditation which is questioned in 'Old Man Travelling': one in which the self is realized even as it acknowledges the otherness of that which is before it – a state in some ways very like that of the 'play' imaged in *Songs of Innocence*. Yet this, unlike Blake's Innocence, is a private experience, an individual relation with the natural world: it is not a mode of human interaction. And it is an experience very different from the unease, almost shock, with which the otherness of other men is recognized elsewhere in the volume.

The significance of this difference is perhaps most apparent in 'Lines written in early spring', where Wordsworth tries most directly to connect active receptivity towards the natural world with thoughts of 'what man has made of man'. For the attempted connection introduces a dislocating emphasis on the human observer's separation from nature:

> To her fair works did nature link
> The human soul that through me ran;
> And much it griev'd my heart to think
> What man has made of man.
>
> ('Lines written in early spring')

It is that separation, rather than a Thelwall- or Coleridge-like influx of 'sympathetic feeling' that the poem traces: and it leads to rather more problematic intuitions than that joyful 'holy tenderness' of which Wordsworth had written in the lines quoted by Coleridge. It can hardly be said of this speaker that 'He seeks for Good & finds the Good he seeks.' This poem's awkward fidelity to fact, its oddly jerky breaks and pauses, register a more uneasy sense both of man's relation to nature and of his relation to other men – and of the disjunction between the two.[36] It is a sense which is not explored here: certainly not in a way which takes up the more baffling resonances of relationship with 'man' that such poems as 'Simon Lee' evoke. Instead, this poem tails off rather limply:

> If I these thoughts may not prevent,
> If such be of my creed the plan,
> Have I not reason to lament
> What man has made of man?

It is only the awkwardness of the second line that prevents (and perhaps does not entirely prevent) the stanza sliding into a very familiar trope, a contrast between the innocence of nature and the evils of man in society: the final two lines distance and lyricize that which in other of the 1798 ballads was presented much more directly. Where in 'Old Man Travelling' and 'Simon Lee' the challenging figure of another occupied the foreground and demanded that the speaker himself 'make' something of it, here 'what man has made of man' has receded into a general metaphysical problem. The speaker reflects on a world in which other men relate to each other, rather than one within which he himself lives and must act; one which he can sit apart and 'lament', not one by which he himself is challenged.

In the four nature lyrics of *Lyrical Ballads 1798* Wordsworth seems to be turning to the natural world in order to explore the possibility of a mode of relationship which is not one of unilateral control, which acknowledges and responds to otherness, which grows naturally out of the unwilled areas of the personality, and which might form the basis of more truly moral feeling than any imposed system of morality. But that exploration, separated so entirely as it is from the difficult confrontation with the reality of other men which is the subject of other of the poems, seems more like a withdrawal from the challenging immediacy of problems which were there disturbingly exposed. It is a withdrawal oddly underlined by the fact that in the other three of these lyrics themes which in the earlier 1790s had had much more radical implications are being transposed into the mode of personal pastoralism. In 'It is the first mild day of March' the new Jacobin calendar heralding a new dawning for mankind becomes a domestic one:

> No joyless forms shall regulate
> Our living Calendar:
> We from today, my friend, will date
> The opening of the year.
>
> Love, now an universal birth,
> From heart to heart is stealing,
> From earth to man, from man to earth,
> – It is the hour of feeling.

And in 'Expostulation and Reply' and 'The Tables Turned' arguments which had been at the centre of the passionate political debate following the publication of Burke's *Reflections* are likewise modulated. Where Burke had argued:

We are afraid to put men to live and trade each on his own private stock of reason; because we suspect that this stock in each man is small and that the individuals would do better to avail themselves of the general bank and capital of nations, and of ages.[37]

and Paine had replied:

I am contending for the rights of the *living*, and against their being willed away, and controlled and contracted for, by the manuscript assumed authority of the dead; and Mr Burke is contending for the authority of the dead over the rights and freedom of the living. [38]

Wordsworth offers a light-hearted altercation between 'a friend who was somewhat unreasonably attached to modern books of moral philosophy' and one who favours spontaneous openness to the natural world:

> 'Where are your books? that light bequeath'd
> 'To beings else forlorn and blind!
> 'Up! Up! and drink the spirit breath'd
> 'From dead men to their kind.

'You look round on your mother earth,
'As if she for no purpose bore you;
'As if you were her first-born birth,
'And none had lived before you!'
                    ('Expostulation and Reply')

One impulse from a vernal wood
May teach you more of man;
Of moral evil and of good,
Than all the sages can.

                    . . .

Enough of science and of art;
Close up these barren leaves;
Come forth, and bring with you a heart
That watches and receives.
                    ('The Tables Turned')

These distant echoes of the more radical arguments of the past may be accidental. But the difficulties involved in turning to an individual relationship with nature in order to 'discover what is really important to men'[39] are underlined when it is recalled that one after another those poems in which the challenge of other men is felt most directly undermine the notion that the processes of nature might provide a meaningful analogy for human affairs. In 'Old Man Travelling' the vision of a life 'by nature led / To peace . . .' is cut short by an account of a human world in which there is neither 'animal tranquillity' nor 'decay', but the unpeaceful and untimely destruction of youth. In 'Simon Lee', the attempt to see the old man's struggle as merely a struggle against natural law is questioned by that disturbing gap between privileged speaker and unprivileged subject, and the ambiguous 'blow' with which their encounter ends. And in 'The Thorn', the narrator's dogged quasi-scientific literal-mindedness parodies all attempts to find a human meaning in the facts of nature:

Not five yards from the mountain-path
This thorn you on your left espy;
And to the left, three yards beyond,
You see a little muddy pond
Of water, never dry;
I've measured it from side to side:
'Tis three feet long, and two feet wide.

This 'nature' is intransigent in its otherness. It may be seen optimistically, as all-resolving and beautifying:

And close beside this aged thorn,
There is a fresh and lovely sight,
A beauteous heap, a hill of moss,
Just half a foot in height.
All lovely colours there you see,
All colours that were ever seen,
And mossy network too is there,
As if by hand of lady fair
The work had woven been,
And cups, the darlings of the eye
So deep is their vermilion dye.

But it may equally offer a sense of contorting self-destructiveness –

         the thorn is bound
With heavy tufts of moss, that strive
To drag it to the ground.

– or an image of guilt and sorrow:

Some say, if to the pond you go,
And fix on it a steady view,
The shadow of a babe you trace,
A baby and a baby's face,
And that it looks at you.

The thorn, the pond, the hill of moss remain a group of impenetrable objects, into which meanings may be projected, but meanings which depend absolutely upon the perspective of the individual who confronts them:

'But what's the thorn? and what's the pond?
'And what's the hill of moss to her?
'And what's the creeping breeze that comes
'The little pond to stir?'
I cannot tell.

And the poem ends with a haunting image of unanswered human distress, 'in the silent night', with the stars shining indifferently overhead:

And this I know, full many a time,
When she was on the mountain high,
By day, and in the silent night,
When all the stars shone clear and bright,
Then I have heard her cry,
'Oh misery! oh misery!
'O woe is me! oh misery!'

251

Beside such poems as these, the attempt in the four nature lyrics of
the volume to trace the sources of true moral awareness in one polite
speaker's intercourse with nature seems less than completely con-
vincing.

Yet it is an attempt which is taken up in the final and most
straightforwardly autobiographical of *Lyrical Ballads 1798*, 'Lines
written a few miles above Tintern Abbey', added to the volume after
it had already gone to press. With a new confidence and excitement –
registered in the assured development of the blank verse form – this
poem explores that question which was more naively confronted in
'Lines written in early spring'. What is the connection between those
intuitions arrived at in an individual relationship with the world of
nature and more general problems of morality? And the exploration
is marked by the unresolved ambiguities which the rest of the
volume has revealed.

Unlike that of the lyrics written earlier in 1798, the 'nature'
confronted in 'Tintern Abbey' is one which shows signs of human
occupation. Contemporary accounts describe the valley of the Wye
as a 'scene of desolation':

the poverty and wretchedness of the inhabitants are remarkable. They
occupy little huts raised among the ruins of the monastery; and seem to have
no employment, but begging.[40]

But in Wordsworth's poem such details are distanced enough not to
be disturbing. The opening lines of the poem, like those of 'Lines
written in early spring', focus less upon the scene before him than
upon his observing consciousness:

> Five years have passed; five summers, with the length
> Of five long winters! and again I hear
> These waters, rolling from their mountain-springs
> With a sweet inland murmur.

And the poetry traces not 'poverty and wretchedness', but a
perceptual process: the way in which a 'scene', a framed and
meaningful landscape, is constructed out of the natural wildness
which confronts him:[41]

> Once again
> Do I behold these steep and lofty cliffs,
> Which on a wild secluded *scene impress*
> Thoughts of more deep seclusion; and *connect*
> The *landscape* with the quiet of the sky.
> [my italics]

It is not, as in earlier eighteenth-century landscape poetry, a process in which a 'landscape' is framed by an implicit matching of the actual scene against culturally-determined schemata, but something altogether more intimate. For what enables Wordsworth to see this 'landscape' is, literally, his remembrance of it. He does not shape it in accordance with conventional expectations, as the reiterated 'this', 'this', 'these' 'these' emphasize, he recognizes what he has seen before. And despite the specificity of the place, the operative memories are not those of distinctive landmarks, but the altogether more instinctive memories of a previous experience of looking. In these lines the inarticulate memories that are latent in all perception are being brought to the surface and made conscious.

Wordsworth's interest in this aspect of the perceptual process is indicated by a phrase at the opening of the second section:

> Though absent long,
> These forms of beauty have not been to me,
> As is a landscape to a blind man's eye.

The reference is to the Molyneux problem, that fundamental problem of eighteenth-century perceptual theory:[42]

a congenitally blind person now adult who is suddenly made to see, upon first 'seeing' certain colours, would not think of cats and dogs or any other objects in space although he may know what they are by touch. He would prove quite unable to recognize what they are or to name them. He would get *no meaning* from the spinning mass of colours before his eyes. That is, he would not be able to see.

Contemporary experiments seemed to have proved this hypothesis: the conclusion was that

Seeing is not a simple and direct sensing of physical objects, it is rather a complex conceptual act. It is like making an assertion that something is the case.[43]

And it is this 'assertion that something is the case' and its delighted confirmation in experience that the opening lines of 'Tintern Abbey' dramatize. Without that implicit assertion – one of the most fundamental and instinctive acts of trust – 'these forms of beauty' would not take shape: that which confronts the speaker would be like 'a landscape to a blind man's eye', a meaningless chaos of sense-impressions. But previous experience makes possible that perceptual process of forming recollection which is the subject of these lines. The landscape itself reflects the nature of this activity: for it is one in which apparently unorganized wildness and luxuriant growth in fact bear the unobtrusive marks of human occupation. Similarly Wordsworth, bringing with him the shaping expectations derived from memory, is able to find a humanly meaningful pattern in the almost undifferentiated greenness before him. Orchards and hedgerows, farms and woods would, it seems, merge into one another, did he not distinguish and identify each:

> These plots of cottage-ground, these orchard-tufts,
> Which, at this season, with their unripe fruits,
> Among the woods and copses lose themselves,
> Nor, with their green and simple hue, disturb
> The wild green landscape. Once again I see
> These hedge-rows, hardly hedge-rows, little lines
> Of sportive wood run wild; these pastoral farms
> Green to the very door; and wreathes of smoke
> Sent up, in silence, from among the trees,
> With some uncertain notice. (ll. 11–20).

The process is not one of imposition, but of recognition: one in which that which is subjectively conceived of meets and is answered by – indeed, enables – that which is objectively perceived.

In the earlier nature lyrics of the volume, Wordsworth had begun to explore a state of 'wise passiveness': an uncontrolling receptivity which is also, paradoxically, activity. Here, much more fully, he dramatizes how, in one area of human experience – the simple act of looking at a landscape – such a satisfying mode of relationship with that which is other is possible. And it is this mode of relationship, whose dynamics are so carefully recreated in the opening lines, that becomes in the rest of the poem the pattern for the structuring of more complex later experience:

> Though absent long,
> These forms of beauty have not been to me,
> As is a landscape to a blind man's eye:
> But oft, in lonely rooms, and mid the din
> Of towns and cities, I have owed to them,
> In hours of weariness, sensations sweet,
> Felt in the blood, and felt along the heart,
> And passing even into my purer mind
> With tranquil restoration: – feelings too
> Of unremembered pleasure; such, perhaps,
> As may have had no trivial influence
> On that best portion of a good man's life;

His little, nameless, unremembered acts
Of kindness and of love. Nor less, I trust,
To them I may have owed another gift,
Of aspect more sublime; that blessed mood,
In which the burthen of the mystery,
In which the heavy and the weary weight
Of all this unintelligible world
Is lighten'd: – that serene and blessed mood,
In which the affections gently lead us on,
Until, the breath of this corporeal frame,
And even the motion of our human blood
Almost suspended, we are laid asleep
In body, and become a living soul:
While with an eye made quiet by the power
Of harmony, and the deep power of joy,
We see into the life of things.   (ll. 23–49)

Here, as in 'The Tables Turned', 'sensations sweet' derived from that sense of the natural world available to 'a heart / That watches and receives' are seen as the source of truly moral – and ultimately religious – feeling. But here, the connections which in the earlier poem were simply asserted are more clearly traced in the more sophisticated language of associationist psychology.[44] And as it does this the poetry registers tensions and difficulties which are not to be found in eighteenth-century associationist accounts of the genesis of the moral sense:

And thus we may perceive, that all the pleasures and pains of sensation, imagination, ambition, self-interest, sympathy, and theopathy, so far as they are consistent with one another, with the frame of our natures, and with the course of the world, beget in us a moral sense, and lead us to the love and approbation of virtue, and to the fear, hatred and abhorrence of vice ... It appears also that the moral sense carries us perpetually to the pure love of God, as our highest and ultimate perfection, our end, centre, and only resting-place to which we can ever attain.[45]

What for Hartley was a smooth and inevitable process is for Wordsworth altogether more tentative: 'such, *perhaps*, / As *may* have had no trivial influence'; 'Nor less, *I trust*, / To them I *may* have owed another gift ...'. Such doubts are explicitly acknowledged. But the imaginative difficulty involved in the transition from private 'sensation' to more generally applicable moral and religious feeling – a difficulty which seems to be inherent in the essentially individualistic nature of the associationist model – is reflected less intentionally in the curiously uncertain position of the speaking voice throughout this section. The opening, autobiographical 'I' recedes as the attempt is made to connect his particular remembered experience with the world of interpersonal morality: the locus of moral feeling and action is distanced and 'objectified' into the third person:

> such, perhaps,
> As may have had no trivial influence
> On that best portion of *a good man's* life,
> *His* little, nameless, unremembered acts ...

And although the verse slides back into the autobiographical mode, there is a similar uneasy shift in the final lines of the section. Once again the initial 'I' is abandoned: instead, there is an indefinite first person plural, which attempts to affirm some kind of universal truth for its experience:

> that serene and blessed mood,
> In which the affections gently lead *us* on
>
> . . .
>
> *We* see into the life of things.

By the last section of the poem, the curious blend of underlying doubt and assumed confidence which these shifts of person bespeak has become more disturbingly apparent. Here, what had been a tentatively dramatized chain of associations becomes, on the surface at least, more assertive:

> Knowing that Nature never did betray
> The heart that loved her; 'tis her privilege
> Through all the years of this our life, to lead
> From joy to joy ...   (ll. 123–6)

But the sense of Nature's possible 'betrayal' is there even as it is denied and it is underlined by the echo from 'Old Man Travelling'. 'He is by nature led / To peace ...' that poem had confidently affirmed, only to have its 'chearful faith' severely questioned. Here, it is true, Nature's 'leading' is more subtly presented, not as a process to be passively endured, but as the consequence of that active relationship dramatized in the opening lines:

> for she can so inform
> The mind that is within us, so impress
> With quietness and beauty, and so feed
> With lofty thoughts ...   (ll. 126–9)

The metaphoric force of these verbs is reactivated by experiences presented earlier in the poem. 'Inform' recalls that process in which the features of the natural scene became 'forms of beauty', in which the eye shaped the contours of a landscape which was itself sensed as shaping, and the personality was felt to be 'informed' by them. The second echo of that opening – 'Which on a ·wild secluded scene *impress* / Thoughts of more deep seclusion' – reanimates its sense of the paradoxical force with which apparently passive qualities such as 'quietness' and 'beauty' can act on and in the experiencing mind. And 'feed' recalls the description of the speaker's boyhood –

>   the tall rock,
> The mountain, and the deep and gloomy wood,
> Their colours and their forms, were then to me
> An appetite ...   (ll. 78–81)

– with its similar suggestion of an appetite which is fulfilled by the very things which create it. These are not, then, simply pious platitudes, but affirmations which have their imaginative basis in experiences recreated earlier in the poem. Yet as the passage continues, and these experiences are declared to be the source of a security which 'all / The dreary intercourse of daily life' and its attendant evils cannot disturb, the tone becomes more assertive and more uncertain. For what is being held at bay is insistently present in the poetry:

>   neither evil tongues,
> Rash judgments, nor the sneers of selfish men,
> Nor greetings where no kindness is, not all
> The dreary intercourse of daily life,
> Shall e'er prevail against us.   (ll. 129–33)

Once again the poem has slid into the first person plural: not, as before, the first person plural of would-be confident generalization, but that of an *égoisme-à-deux*.[46] 'Our' integrity is not seen as something to be defined in the interpersonal world, but a privately-held bulwark against it: 'we' occupy a privileged position, separate from and superior to 'evil tongues', 'rash judgments', 'the sneers of selfish men', and 'all / The dreary intercourse of daily life'. This is a sense of self which has been implicit from the opening section, with its distancing of those human presences which might call forth 'kindness' and 'love' into the features of a landscape, its seemingly inevitable movement towards a telling final image:

> Or of some hermit's cave, where by his fire
> The hermit sits alone.

But here it has become the subject of the poetry in a way which reveals the contradictions it entails. For if self is best realized not in interaction with other men, but in isolation from them, if security consists in an unassailable individuality, then the other – unless in some sense (as Dorothy is here) identified with the self – can only be seen as a threat. And such a position is a curious basis for the affirmation of a 'chearful faith that all which we behold / Is full of blessings'. What these lines in fact affirm is a beleaguered subjective individualism: a position which was to find its ultimate expression in such later poems of Wordsworth's as the complacent sonnet-sequence of 1802–4, 'Personal Talk':

> Nor can I not believe but that hereby
> Great gains are mine; for thus I live remote
> From evil-speaking; rancour, never sought,
> Comes to me not; malignant truth, or lie.
> Hence have I genial seasons, hence have I
> Smooth passions, smooth discourse, and joyous thought:
> And thus from day to day my little boat
> Rocks in its harbour, lodging peaceably.

'Tintern Abbey' extends and develops that attempt to transcend the easy moralizing of the magazine verse, to portray an active yet unintrusive relation to that which is other, which was begun in the simpler nature lyrics of *Lyrical Ballads 1798*. The movement from this to an exploration of how 'we' actually arrive at moral feeling must have been entirely natural to one familiar with and in many ways sympathetic to the thinking of such men as Thelwall and Coleridge, as must the framing of that exploration (however tentatively) in the language of associationist psychology. The direction the poem takes is clearly in part determined by the fact that it *is* framed within that language – a language which embodies deeply individualist assumptions.[47] Yet Wordsworth's poem registers the contradictions implicit in its own position in a most revealing way. When it is read in its original context, amongst those 'aukward' *Lyrical Ballads* of 1798, its uncertainties and its unevennesses can be seen as the inevitable result of the confusion of purpose which is manifested in the volume as a whole.

For the poems of *Lyrical Ballads 1798* do not merely attempt to move beyond 'our own pre-established codes of decision', and to find a more honest basis for moral feeling in experiences of a pre-rational kind. In many of them, the recognition of the otherness of other people comes as an unassimilable shock. And the sense of morality which emerges from the volume as a whole is thus more complex and less coherent than the confident closing 'exhortation' of 'Tintern Abbey' might suggest. For it is complicated by the disturbing intuition that moral feeling might not develop un-problematically from a certain kind of positive experience, that it might involve a traumatic questioning of that self whose integrity is the basis of associationist psychology. That which in 'Tintern Abbey' is meditatively distanced –

> For I have learned
> To look on nature, not as in the hour
> Of thoughtless youth, but hearing oftentimes
> The still, sad music of humanity,
> Nor harsh nor grating, though of ample power
> To chasten and subdue ...   (ll. 89–94)

– is in other of the poems 'aukwardly' foregrounded, in the 'harsh' and 'grating' presences of such as the 'Old Man Travelling' and 'Simon Lee'. After such poems, this attempt to conclude the volume seems less than conclusive. For in face of what they present, the relatively peaceful, socially unproblematic experience of looking at a beautiful landscape – an experience of delighted recognition, in which perception and creation seem to be fused – hardly seems an adequate paradigm for all intercourse with that which is external to the self: certainly not for those exchanges in the interpersonal world in which others may prove less amenable than 'These plots of cottage-ground, these orchard tufts'. And Wordsworth's attempt to see this experience both as exercising 'no trivial influence' in that interpersonal world, and also as a kind of psychic retreat from or shield against it, in its very confusion points toward questions which cannot confidently or optimistically be resolved. Yet they are questions which he was to confront in the eighteen months which followed, in an extraordinarily creative way: questions which were to be articulated and explored in the poetry of an entirely different order which was published as *Lyrical Ballads 1800*.

7 Desire and Disillusion: the Goslar Lyrics

> Certainly the greatest disillusion, the greatest discrepancy between
> one's wish and the external facts, is the fact of death.
>
> (Marion Milner, *On Not Being Able to Paint*, London, 1971)

> The experience of the death of others and, subsequently, the
> anticipation of one's own death posit the marginal situation *par
> excellence* for the individual. Needless to elaborate, death also
> posits the most terrifying threat to the taken-for-granted realities
> of everyday life. The integration of death within the paramount
> reality of social existence is, therefore, of the greatest importance
> for any institutional order.
>
> (Peter L. Berger and Thomas Luckmann, *The Social Construction
> of Reality*, Harmondsworth, 1971)

The difference between the two volumes of *Lyrical Ballads* is
extreme. The poems first published in 1800 display few of the
awkwardnesses, the embarrassments and the uncertainties of those
of 1798. Much more markedly than those of the 1798 volume, they
seem the products of an extraordinarily rapid and fertile process of
poetic development: those which were written at Goslar in the
winter of 1798–9 are very different from those written at Grasmere a
year later. Yet compared to the earlier volume, this has a remarkable
poetic coherence. In its assured handling of questions which the
'experiments' of its predecessor were beginning to point towards, it
offers a far more complete articulation of the imaginative bases of a
comprehensive vision of man, of nature, and of human life, than
Wordsworth was to achieve in any other volume published in his
lifetime.

    In some respects, it is true, the first impression is of a retreat from
rather than an engagement with the questions posed by the poems of
1798. Where the first volume depicted awkward, baffling encounters with unassimilable figures – encounters which threw the
position of the polite observer sharply into question – this contains a
series of poems ('The Brothers', 'Michael', Grasmere ballads such as
'The Childless Father' and 'The Two Thieves') which portray a
self-sustaining rural community with its own strengths and

resources, poems in which the embarrassing distance between privileged and unprivileged is not an issue. The generalizing reflections of the earlier nature lyrics and of 'Tintern Abbey' have been replaced by enigmatic, autobiographical hints as to the significance of the presented experience:

> The difference to me.

> And there along that bank when I have pass'd
> At evening, I believe, that near his grave
> A full half-hour together I have stood,
> Mute – for he died when he was ten years old.

> Matthew is in his grave, yet now
> Methinks I see him stand,
> As at the moment, with his bough
> Of wilding in his hand.

Superficially, the effect is of a narrowing in to the personal, the individual, the small circle of friends, the known community: of a turning away from the shocking confrontations, the awkward dislocations, the attempts to offer general statements, of the earlier volume.

Yet these poems are hardly reassuring. The 'nature' depicted in them is most unlike that of 'Tintern Abbey': it is a world indifferent to human purposes and values, a world in which the fact of death has suddenly become prominent. No longer is it a place of retirement.[1] Conflict is not distanced in it, but foregrounded: the muted 'lament' of 'Lines written in early spring' has been replaced by the destructive passion and unresolved guilt of 'Nutting'. And the human world which the volume presents is no less problematic. Instead of lonely confrontation with isolated decaying figures there is, it is true, a vision of community, but it is a vision of community of a peculiarly ambiguous kind.[2] It is not merely that the society presented is one composed of essentially separate individuals: it is one in which human interaction seems to have been replaced by the reading of signs. The Old Cumberland Beggar is less a living man than a 'record which together binds / Past deeds and offices of charity' in individual hearts. Both the later long poems of Grasmere life, 'The Brothers' and 'Michael', take as their starting-point an inanimate object – an unmarked grave, a heap of stones – from which a story can be reconstructed: in both cases, it is the story of a relationship which has ended in hopeless solitude. And in both, the vitality of present communal ties is implicitly questioned by the dramatic structure of the poem. 'The Brothers' pivots on the Priest's ironic non-recognition of the brother whose story he is telling: it ends with an impassive figure whom others cannot 'read', a figure of a kind familiar in Wordsworth's poetry:

> This done, he went on shipboard, and is now
> A Seaman, a grey headed Mariner.

And 'Michael', though addressed with seeming confidence to

> a few natural hearts,
> And with yet fonder feeling, for the sake
> Of youthful Poets, who among these Hills
> Will be my second self when I am gone

tells a story which is about the betrayal of hopes of such continuity through a 'second self'. The 'may' of its ending, pointing to what yet remains, points also to the eventual erosion by natural processes of that humanly created sign which has been the central image of the poem:

> and the remains
> Of the unfinished Sheep-fold may be seen
> Beside the boisterous brook of Green-head Gill.

It seems that these poems are exploring questions about the possibilities of human interaction, and the place of human effort within the non-human universe, in a more disquieting way than Wordsworth's own account of their subject-matter would suggest:

The two poems which I have mentioned ['The Brothers' and 'Michael'] were written with a view to shew that men who do not wear fine cloaths can feel deeply ... The poems are faithful copies from nature; and, I hope, whatever effect they may have upon you, you will at least be able to perceive that they may excite profitable sympathies in many kind and good hearts, and may in some small degree enlarge our feelings of reverence for our species and our knowledge of human nature ... I thought, at a time when these feelings are sapped in so many ways that the two poems might co-operate, however feebly, with the illustrious efforts which you have made to stem this and other evils with which the country is labouring.[3]

For the imaginative structuring, not merely of 'The Brothers' and 'Michael', but of the volume as a whole, is far from improvingly optimistic. There *does* seem to be a pattern of 'secret connections' between the very different poems of which it is composed.[4] There are certain powerful recurring images – images of standing alone by a grave or a memorial ('Hart-Leap Well', 'The Brothers', 'There was a Boy') or simply of being 'left mourning' alone ('The Two April Mornings', the 'Lucy' poems, 'Michael'); images of the ways in which men try to humanize the threateningly indifferent world of nature, and the marks which they seek to make upon it (the transitory hooting of the Boy of Winander, the more permanent 'names' of the Poems on the 'Naming of Places', the tangible monument of 'Hart-Leap Well', the symbolic Sheep-fold of 'Michael'). And there are less focussed but just as significant recurring patterns of feeling. The notion of a traumatic but in some mysterious way 'humanizing' lesson, a lesson arrived at through guilty and solitary experience, is there in many: most obviously, in 'Hart-Leap Well' and in 'Nutting', but more subtly and disturbingly, perhaps, in the 'Lucy' poems. Here, and in several other poems, Wordsworth portrays the loss of a once delighted sense that the world might answer to desire, a loss which seems inevitable. And in some poems at least, he seems to move from this toward an exploration of possible forms of reparation, of the ways in which the absoluteness of that loss might be countered and met.

Yet despite these imaginative correspondences, the volume remains a collection of very disparate pieces. It contains none of the structural parallelisms, the recurrent echoes of words, images and phrases, that bind Blake's *Songs* into an artistic whole. Here, such interconnections are not poetically realized: the poems divide very sharply into different kinds. On the one hand, there are those dealing with intimate private experience, written in Germany during the winter of 1798–9 – 'There was a Boy', 'Nutting', the 'Lucy' poems. On the other, there are those whose subject is communal life, written at Grasmere in 1800 – the poems of Grasmere incident, 'The Brothers', 'Michael'. Yet unlike the divisions which mark the 1798 volume, this seems less the result of a confusion of imaginative impulse than the precise poetic expression of a problem which has become central in Wordsworth's thinking. For as well as these two groups of poems (which are not separate, but intermingled in the arrangement of the volume) there are others – the 'Matthew' poems, the 'Poems on the Naming of Places' – which are explicitly concerned with the relation between subjective experience and that which can be generally shared. It seems that here that division between 'private' and 'public' areas of experience which the 1798 collection tried, and often incongruously failed, to bridge, is itself being poetically examined. And what appears to be emerging is a sense of fundamental opposition between individual subjectivity and what can be publicly known, between the 'I' of intimate, passionate engagement and the 'we' of communal consciousness.

The relationship between subjective feeling and the shared social world, between the formation and development of the individual and the structure of the larger society, had been the subject of much discussion in Wordsworth's own circle in the year preceding his visit to Goslar. Such discussion had centred, logically enough, on the question of education – on how the individual child's capacities were thwarted and hindered by existing modes of socialization, and how they might be fostered by different ones. This was a concern which Wordsworth shared, and had, as we have seen, begun to articulate in *Lyrical Ballads 1798*.[5] And it is the explicit subject of one of Coleridge's contributions to that volume – 'The Nightingale', a poem which begins with an opposition between the stultifying world of 'society' and that of natural beauty, and ends with a resolution to educate a beloved child as 'Nature's playmate'. Wordsworth seems to have seen his own exploration of such questions as a dialogue with that of Coleridge: in 1798–9 he was to frame the first, two-part draft of his autobiographical *The Prelude* with quotations from 'Frost at Midnight' referring to his friend's own childhood experience.[6] But his imaginative sense of the issues involved was by then beginning to focus in a way which exposed significant points of disagreement between them. And nowhere is this more strikingly apparent than in 'There was a Boy' – a fragment written at Goslar and published in the second volume of *Lyrical Ballads*.

'There was a Boy' is very different from 'The Nightingale'. Yet at a pivotal point – ·

> And, when it chanced
> That pauses of deep silence mock'd his skill ...

– it borrows a phrase from Coleridge's poem –

> she knows all their notes,
> That gentle Maid! and oft, a moment's space,
> What time the moon was lost behind a cloud,
> Hath heard a pause of silence...   (ll. 74–7)

– and the echo seems to invite a comparison between them. Certainly, there are parallels between the two poems. In each, there is a central image of the sounds of birds, echoing and answering: in the one, the melodious songs of nightingales calling to one another –

> and far and near
> In wood and thicket over the wide grove
> They answer and provoke each other's songs –
> With skirmish and capricious passagings,
> And murmurs musical and swift jug jug
> And one low piping sound more sweet than all –
> Stirring the air with such an harmony,
> That should you close your eyes, you might almost
> Forget it was not day!   (ll. 56–64)

– in the other, the cry of owls which answer to the imitative hootings of the boy:

> And they would shout
> Across the wat'ry vale and shout again
> Responsive to his call, with quivering peals,
> And long halloos, and screams, and echoes loud
> Redoubled and redoubled, a wild scene
> Of mirth and jocund din.

And central to each is a concern with the relationship between the developing individual and the natural world, with what experience of that world can *teach*. Yet the difference between them is such as to suggest that Wordsworth is not merely developing imaginative insights which he and Coleridge had shared in 1798. His poem seems to be an implicit reply, both to Coleridge and to his own earlier self. After the lengthy meditation of 'The Nightingale', 'There was a Boy' seems starkly truncated. Where Coleridge's poem has an easy 'conversational' intimacy, Wordsworth's opens with an apostrophe which distances the reader –

> There was a Boy, ye knew him well, ye Cliffs
> And Islands of Winander!

– and an uncertainly located speaker, of whom we hear nothing until the second, separated section.[7] The 'pause of silence' in 'The Nightingale' leads to a renewal of the birds' song: the moon emerges from behind a cloud. But here, that pause 'mocks' the boy's skill, and leads to a more disturbing intuition.[8] Coleridge's image of the poet's ideal surrender to nature –

> When he had better far have stretch'd his limbs
> Beside a brook in mossy forest-dell
> By sun or moonlight, to the influxes
> Of shapes and sounds and shifting elements

> Surrendering his whole spirit, of his song
> And of his fame forgetful! so his fame
> Should share in nature's immortality,
> A venerable thing!   (ll. 25–32)

– has been replaced by a different and more involuntary kind of surrender: one of which the boy himself is 'unawares'. And the poem ends not with confident plans for a joyous education as 'Nature's playmate', but beside a grave:

> Mute, for he died when he was ten years old.

This silent confrontation of human mortality is very different from the attempt in 'Tintern Abbey' to see nature as benevolently fostering individual growth and development. To that, and to Coleridge's poem, it offers a bleakly ironic retort. It is not merely the recorded fact of the boy's death which challenges such optimistic associationism, but the whole way in which his activity within an indifferent universe is seen. The world which surrounds him is not the enclosing greenness of 'The Nightingale', but one in which he is dwarfed and exposed:

> ye knew him well, ye Cliffs
> And Islands of Winander! many a time,
> At evening, when the stars had just begun
> To move along the edges of the hills,
> Rising or setting, would he stand alone,
> Beneath the trees, or by the glimmering lake.

He calls to the owls in order to gain some mastery over it – 'That they might answer him' – and the endeavour seems, briefly, successful:

> And they would shout
> Across the wat'ry vale and shout again
> Responsive to his call ...

But the feeling is only momentary. For the shouting of the owls quickly becomes wild and banshee-like, and the echoes – 'redoubled and redoubled' – pass beyond his control:

> with quivering peals,
> And long halloos, and screams, and echoes loud
> Redoubled and redoubled, a wild scene
> Of mirth and jocund din.

This 'scene' is one with which no real interaction is possible: its life is its own. And in the lines which follow the boy is presented not as

active, but as passively expectant, before a nature whose intracta-
bility has changed to 'mocking' silence:

> And, when it chanced
> That pauses of deep silence mock'd his skill,
> Then, sometimes, in that silence, while he hung
> Listening . . .

The suspense which fills the pause after 'chanced' is continued in the
strange verb 'hung': the emerging suggestion is that this child is not
merely unable to control, but literally dependent upon, the world in
which he finds himself. Into this 'silence' comes a quite different
sense of that world and of his place within it from that which he has
imitatively tried to assert:

> a gentle shock of mild surprise
> Has carried far into his heart the voice
> Of mountain torrents, or the visible scene
> Would enter unawares into his mind
> With all its solemn imagery, its rocks,
> Its woods, and that uncertain heaven, receiv'd
> Into the bosom of the steady lake.

The experience, foregrounded by the incongruous present perfect
tense which introduces it, is both movingly beautiful and subtly
disturbing; at once vitally charged and an intimation of mortality.
The 'gentle shock' with which the external, quiet, but quite
intransigent world of nature is 'carried far into his heart' prefigures
the shock of death. And even as the boy's connection with that world
is shown to be involuntary and inescapable, its separation from him
is stressed. The natural scene is sparely but surely evoked – the
stillness of evening, the only motion the changing colour of the
'uncertain' sky; the calmness of the water; the distant sound of
'mountain torrents'; the solidity of rocks and stones. Yet it is a
'scene' rather than a place which he might enter. For the second time
in the poem Wordsworth uses this word: a word which Coleridge
was later to object to as having a

vague sense which has since been too current even in our best writers and
which (unfortunately, I think) is given as its first explanation in Mr
Johnson's Dictionary and therefore would be taken by an incautious reader
as its proper sense. In Shakespeare and Milton the word is never used
without some clear reference, proper or metaphorical, to the theatre.[9]

But that 'vague sense' seems to be a significant part of the meaning.
For this 'scene' has for the boy something of the substantial

insubstantiality of a theatrical manifestation. It is 'visible', not
tangible: a set of 'solemn imagery' on the retina, rather than
something with which real, transforming engagement is possible. In
the two-part *Prelude*, also drafted at Goslar, Wordsworth had used
exactly the same phrase to similar effect:

> And make our infancy a visible scene
> On which the sun is shining ...   (Part I, ll. 463–4)

The description ends with an image of a satisfying union, of a kind
which the child's imitative hootings could not achieve:

> and that uncertain heaven, receiv'd
> Into the bosom of the steady lake.

This world has its own self-sufficiency, which excludes all sense of
his disturbing activities. It is unreachably other, and its rhythms bear
no relation to him at all.

This picture of an isolated child trying to achieve the illusion that
he can control and shape an indifferent universe has an imaginative
power which none of the poems of the 1798 volume achieve. The
benevolent Nature of the earlier volume has gone: instead, Wordsworth portrays something closer to a Newtonian universe of
moving planets and inexorable laws.[10] Coleridge, in 'The Nightingale', had seen education as the benign selection of joyful experience,
the removal of the child from the ambiguous and the threatening (as
Hartley is diverted from his disturbing dream). But this boy is not
protected: his experience is not rationally planned. And what he
implicitly learns is something which 'the Tutors of our Youth'
cannot teach: the difference between what can be 'controuled, tamed
to our bidding' and that within which all human activities must be
contained.[11] The significance of his experience lies precisely in its
ambiguity, its 'gentle' replacement of satisfying illusion by pre-
monitory exclusion. This child, idly playing a childish game, exactly
images that sense of human possibility which Wordsworth was to
explore throughout the second collection of *Lyrical Ballads*. It is a
sense very different from Blake's. For this child's play is not
expressive, but imitative. He does try to create the vital illusion that
the world before him is not – as it seems – entirely alien and remote
from human meanings; he does try to make it 'answer him'. But he
stands alone. His play is not an interplay with an other, or others, in
which each responds to each, and a shared actuality is created: it is
solitary and impotent. He has no nurturing framework, no human

context: he is portrayed simply in relation to the movements of the cosmos ('the stars. . .Rising or setting'), and the 'Cliffs / And Islands of Winander!' The first stress of the first line falls on the past tense – 'There *was* a Boy'. And this sense of solitude and precariousness, within time and space, is emphasized again and again in the line endings:

> would he stand *alone*,
> Beneath the trees . . .

> And, when it *chanced*
> That pauses of deep silence mock'd his skill . . .

> while he *hung*
> Listening. . .

The moment of his 'listening' is syntactically isolated by three appositional phrases: 'Then, sometimes, in that silence. . .' – and there is a similar singling out of a moment, at once particular and recurring, in the closing lines of the poem. It is a sense of arrested continuity within an onward movement which is subliminally analogous to that isolation of the individual boy which is the subject of the poem – and very different from the echoing continuity which is the characteristic sense of significant time in *Songs of Innocence*.

For unlike the mutually shaping interaction of *Innocence*, which points into a changing futurity, the illusion of omnipotent centrality which this child's hootings create is transitory: it ends in silence. Far from providing a basis of joyous security, such as Wordsworth attempted to find in 'Tintern Abbey', his play exposes a fundamental division between himself and that to which he tries to relate. His world is not – like that of *Songs of Innocence* – an actuality which he plays a part in shaping: it is external and other, not humanly created, and not, finally, one with which meaningful interaction is possible. Yet it is the frame within which all human attempts to create meaning are contained: a reality with its own inexorable laws, to which all are subject, and from the perspective of which such attempts seem transitory disturbances.

Within this world, human relationships have a status very different from that which they are depicted as having in *Songs of Innocence*: one which is articulated by the poem's very structure. The description of the boy's solitary experience is succeeded by one of the human community in which he lived: the narrative moves from the past to the present tense. Yet this second, separated section is much briefer and less imaginatively charged than the first. And the community it depicts is one surrounded by nature and dominated by the churchyard: one in which the very place of nurture is over-shadowed by memorials of a mortality in face of which all are ultimately powerless.

> Fair are the woods, and beauteous is the spot,
> The vale where he was born: the Church-yard hangs
> Upon a slope above the village school.

There is no sense here – such as there is, for example, in 'The Ecchoing Green' – that the society is shaped by living human relations, which create their own actuality, and provide an experiential answer to the fact of death. The fundamental difference between the two visions is encapsulated in the poem's closing lines:

> And there along the bank where I have pass'd
> At evening, I believe, that near his grave
> A full half-hour together I have stood,
> Mute – for he died when he was ten years old.

This 'pause of silence' parallels the child's own, earlier, 'listening': and it discloses a similar isolation. The speaker is alone, as was the boy. In place of the chiming interplay of 'Infant Joy', two voices constructing a shared world, there are two arrested silences. Instead of the living image created in play there is the static memory of halted human activity. Although we are told nothing of the speaker's feelings, the sense is that pain rather than 'joy' is the condition of human awareness.

The constellation of feelings which is reaching imaginative definition here is not only very different from anything to be found in *Songs of Innocence*: it is also very different from anything in the 1798 volume of *Lyrical Ballads*. Some of the assumptions remain the same. The abstracted individual of associationist psychology is still the central subject; the relation with nature is still – as in 'Tintern Abbey' – seen as more fundamental than that with other men. But unlike the earlier poems, this finds in these assumptions no basis for optimism. Instead, with extraordinary imaginative fidelity, it registers their tragic implications. Michael Black has written suggestively of the way in which a 'remembered scene' in Wordsworth can encapsulate an irreducibly complex 'world-view':

A 'philosophy' or a world-view is not necessarily a thing one 'thinks' about, moving concepts around like counters; it may become part of the structure of the mind; and all this summoned up as a remembered scene, expressed, with no overt urgency, in terms of brightness and cold (moonlight, marble, prism, sea); with a suppressed contrast between hardness and resistance (marble) and evanescence (ice); and the evocation of an admonitory silent upright figure half-suggesting, half-witholding profound encouragement or warning. These co-presences work better than concepts, because they do more things at once, in a flash, and over the long term.[12]

Here, in this picture of the Boy of Winander, is just such a set of 'co-presences' as those of which Black writes. The isolated figure dwarfed by a world moving according to its own alien laws, yet seeking to create order and meaning within it; the illusory feeling of delighted centrality, followed by a sense of more fundamental passivity; the lonely vigil by a grave; the moment of quiet which is also disquietude – all recur again and again, not only in *Lyrical Ballads 1800*, but elsewhere in Wordsworth's poetry. And this significance is not merely a private, psychological one. They point towards a 'world-view' far more imaginatively coherent than that which *Lyrical Ballads 1798* attempted to convey: a 'world-view' diametrically opposed to that of *Songs of Innocence and of Experience*. The defining human activity, as imaged in this boy's brief life, is not interaction with other men, but a doomed, exciting attempt to create meaning in an indifferent universe. Significant experience is essentially singular. And that common humanity which the 1798 volume tried to affirm has here become a common isolation in face of the inevitable fact of death.

The Boy of Winander's activity barely touches the world he inhabits: it is a moment of imitation which ends in silence. Another of the poems written during the winter of 1798–9, however, explores a much more direct and consummated relation to that world, again through the figure of a solitary child. And here, once again, that exploration questions the optimistic affirmations of the 1798 volume. For the incident presented in 'Nutting' can hardly be assimilated to a 'chearful faith that all which we behold / Is full of blessings'[13] or that the moral sense might grow serenely and painlessly out of delighted experience of nature. The central figure here is not the confident autobiographical 'I' of 'Tintern Abbey', but a past self, about whom the speaker seems uneasy. His 'sallying forth' is described with awkward pomposity:

> a Figure quaint,
> Trick'd out in proud disguise of Beggar's weeds
> Put on for the occasion, by advice

And exhortation of my frugal Dame.
Motley accoutrement! of power to smile
At thorns, and brakes, and brambles, and, in truth
More ragged than need was.   (ll. 7–13)

This child's wishes and feelings have a disturbing potency which the childhood pleasures recollected in the earlier poem do not. There, such pleasures were parenthetically distanced:

(The coarser pleasures of my boyish days,
And their glad animal movements all gone by,)   (ll. 74–5)

– and interaction with nature was seen as harmonious and strengthening. But here there is no such harmony. From the first, the child is presented as obtrusive, an outlandish figure who 'forces' his way into places hitherto 'unvisited':

Among the wood,
And o'er the pathless rocks, I forc'd my way
Until, at length, I came to one dear nook
Unvisited, where not a broken bough
Droop'd with its wither'd leaves, ungracious sign
Of devastation, but the hazels rose
Tall and erect, with milk-white clusters hung,
A virgin scene!   (ll. 15–20)

His response is not one of simple delight, but charged with the tension of unsatisfied desire: the negatives which frame his celebration of this 'virgin scene' all point towards its imagined destruction. Where in 'Tintern Abbey' the details of the landscape were traced and distinguished, here, as the poem proceeds, they recede into the hypothetical and become material for fantasy:

– Perhaps it was a bough beneath whose leaves
The violets of five seasons re-appear
And fade, unseen by any human eye,
Where fairy water-breaks do murmur on
For ever ...   (ll. 29–33)

The child's unselfconscious eagerness steadily gives way to explicit dreams of mastery. The excited interloper of the opening becomes a voluptuary, postponing pleasure in an increasingly elaborated attempt to assert proprietorship:

And with my cheek on one of those green stones
That, flecc'd with moss, beneath the shady trees,
Lay round me scatter'd like a flock of sheep,

> I heard the murmur and the murmuring sound,
> In that sweet mood when pleasure loves to pay
> Tribute to ease, and, of its joy secure
> The heart luxuriates with indifferent things,
> Wasting its kindliness on stocks and stones,
> And on the vacant air. (ll. 34–42)

And the savage attack which follows, in one way sudden and unexpected, is in another merely the acting out of feelings which have been emphasized in the poem from the beginning:

> Then up I rose,
> And dragg'd to earth both branch and bough, with crash
> And merciless ravage ... (ll. 42–4)

Yet the act of destruction seems to lead to a quite new sense of that which has been destroyed:

> and the shady nook
> Of hazels, and the green and mossy bower
> Deform'd and sullied, patiently gave up
> Their quiet being ... (ll. 44–7)

The implicit contrast between the child and the world he has sought to master ('... but the hazels rose'; 'Then up I rose') here comes into focus. This 'patience' is very different from his sensuous postponement of pleasure, this 'being' has an integrity which his libidinous self-posturings do not. And it seems to be this sense of a contrasting and implicitly questioning otherness – an otherness whose separate, unfantasized 'being' is now seen for the first time – that prompts the moral injunction of the ending:

> and unless I now
> Confound my present feelings with the past,
> Even then, when from the bower I turn'd away,
> Exulting, rich beyond the wealth of kings
> I felt a sense of pain when I beheld
> The silent trees and the intruding sky. –
>
> Then, dearest Maiden! move along these shades
> In gentleness of heart with gentle hand
> Touch, – for there is a Spirit in the woods. (ll. 47–55)

But the child's remembered 'pain' seems more complex than its transformation into this gentle moralizing would allow. In its recreation of a lonely traumatic experience, the poem has raised questions about the nature of moral awareness which are far from reassuring. This boy, isolated, yet in his isolation seen as representative,[14] is impelled toward the world not by a desire for the shaping interaction depicted in 'Tintern Abbey', but by voracious appetites – appetites whose satisfaction is very far from satisfying. For as the language of the poem very clearly registers, when they are satisfied the excitement with which desire imbued the world disappears. Instead of the unquiet, electric tension of

> the hazels rose
> Tall and erect, with milk-white clusters hung,
> A virgin scene!

there is flatness and despoliation –

> the shady nook
> Of hazels, and the green and mossy bower
> Deform'd and sullied . . .

– a collection of objects which have none of the luminous potential with which the boy originally invested them. If his 'pain' bespeaks the dawning of guilt, it also conveys a sense of this impoverishment.

The incident presented in this poem is richer and more disquieting in its resonances than anything in the 1798 volume of *Lyrical Ballads*. There, the most violent act directly portrayed is the 'blow' with which old Simon's root is 'sever'd': an act of assistance which, as we have seen, has another, less genial suggestiveness. 'Nutting''s tale of remembered solitary experience might in one way seem a retreat from the socially problematic, embarrassing interpersonal world with which the earlier poem sought to engage. Yet the feeling is less one of evasion than of a new kind of exploration of the imaginative roots of contradictions which the poems of 1798 had exposed. Like the speaker of 'Simon Lee', the boy here is 'left mourning'. But where in the earlier poem the reasons are obscure, uneasily suggested by the jauntiness of the verse, here there is a much subtler poetic articulation of the experiential bases of that 'mourning', an articulation which challenges received morality in an even more disturbing way.

For the questions posed by the child's remembered feelings admit of no easy resolution. His sudden action, isolated and emphasized at the end of a line – 'Then up I rose . . . ' – is an upward movement, the archetypal movement of human hope and endeavour: the culminating expression of all the energy and excitement in the poem.[15] But the act it initiates is an act of destruction. And the poetic sugges-

tion is that the most potent human emotions – those which are most
transforming, most richly imbued with fantasy – are those which
seek to possess and which in the possession destroy their object. The
attempt to satisfy them is self-defeating, for with that satisfaction
comes the loss of the original erotic delight. It is true that this
disillusion is seen as leading to a recognition of the other as
significantly other, 'intruding' (l. 52) in a way which questions
egocentricity, and awakens moral awareness. But the feeling of the
whole presented experience is less one of gain than of loss. The boy's
first tumescent excitement has an imaginative life which his later,
sober realization lacks: the flat conventionality of the closing moral
seems incongruous precisely because it has none of the vitality of his
original 'joy'. The optimistic associationism of 'Tintern Abbey',
with its vision of morality as evolving naturally out of individualistic experience, has been replaced by a sense of morality as the product
of traumatic and painful encounters with that which is other. And
this morality, whose basis is guilt, cannot, it seems, embrace the
most passionate sense of the world or engage the self's deepest
energies.

The 'remembered scene' of 'Nutting', like that of 'There was a
Boy', is one which encapsulates a whole constellation of feelings;
feelings which were to inform Wordsworth's lifelong attempt to
formulate a coherent philosophy of men, of nature and of human life.
The child's attraction to the grove, half presented as a particular
remembered experience and half as paradigmatic, exemplifies a state
which he was to image again and again: a state in which desire
charges the world with beauty and excitement, in which reality is felt
to answer to the self's deepest impulses. In 'Nutting', perhaps more
directly than elsewhere in his poetry, those impulses are seen as
actively destructive. But always he portrays them as essentially
egocentric, blocking awareness of that which is other, to be
remembered with guilt as well as with longing. It is only as they are
checked that truly moral feelings can emerge. And thus, repeatedly,
in the poetry of his greatest years, he presents morality as necessitat-
ing loss, the diminution of original delight:

> And is there one, the wisest and the best
> Of all mankind, who does not sometimes wish
> For *things which cannot be*, who would not give,
> If so he might, to duty and to truth
> The eagerness of infantine desire?
>
> (*The Prelude*, 1798–9 version, Second Part, ll. 20–4)

A power is gone, which nothing can restore:
A deep distress hath *humanized* my soul.
('Elegiac Stanzas Suggested by a Picture of Peele
Castle, in a Storm', ll. 35–6)
[my italics]

It is a view of positive feeling for others very different from that of *Songs of Innocence.*

For central in Wordsworth's poetry is the feeling that the self is fundamentally egocentric, that real recognition of others must come as a traumatic self-questioning, and that desire must be tamed if social 'duty' is to be realized. There is nothing of Blake's assured, poetically articulated sense that there might be a mode of desire that is non-possessive and non-instrumental; that the self might realize itself most fully and delightedly in relation to others; and that the most potent aspirations of men might be actualized in social interaction. It is not that Wordsworth is utterly pessimistic. The isolated individuals whom he depicts are capable of being 'humanized' through pain (as the isolated egocentricity of opposition portrayed in *Songs of Experience* is not); there can be 'strength in what remains behind'. But the imaginative configurations into which his poetry falls are very different from the symmetrical and complementary interplay, the free expression of energy, depicted in *Songs of Innocence.* They are moments of arrested confrontation with figures with whom no interaction seems to be possible – figures such as the old man of 'Old Man Travelling', the Man of 'Point Rash-Judgment', the Blind Beggar and discharged soldier of *The Prelude*. The characteristic movement is toward a private 'admonition': moral awareness is not mutually created, informed with the energy of changing situations, but an individual pulling up short, the suppression of natural impulse.

'There was a Boy' and 'Nutting' both portray the checking of passionate childhood feeling, the one by death, the other by guilt: each in its different way questions the optimistic affirmations of 'Tintern Abbey'. Yet another passage written in 1799, after Wordsworth's return from Goslar, as part of the first draft of *The Prelude*, brings those affirmations to precise poetic definition, and appears to suggest that such feeling might have real creative potency, that there might be a mode of growth through joy. It is a passage of great interest in this context, not merely because it seems at odds with the imaginative import of the published verse, but also because it is Wordsworth's most extended attempt to image an intimate and enriching interaction between two human beings, one which points towards future possibility rather than one which ends in shocked admonishments:

> Bless'd the infant Babe
> (For with my best conjectures I would trace
> The progress of our being) blest the Babe
> Nursed in his Mother's arms, the Babe who sleeps
> Upon his Mother's breast, who when his soul
> Claims manifest kindred with an earthly soul
> Doth gather passion from his Mother's eye!
> Such feelings pass into his torpid life
> Like an awakening breeze, and hence his mind
> Even in the first trial of its powers
> Is prompt and watchful, eager to combine
> In one appearance all the elements
> And parts of the same object, else detached
> And loth to coalesce. Thus day by day
> Subjected to the discipline of love
> His organs and recipient faculties
> Are quickened, are more vigorous, his mind spreads
> Tenacious of the forms which it receives.
> In one beloved presence, nay, and more,
> In that most apprehensive habitude
> And those sensations which have been derived
> From this beloved presence, there exists
> A virtue which irradiates and exalts
> All objects through all intercourse of sense.
> No outcast he, bewildered and depressed:
> Along his infant veins are interfused
> The gravitation and the filial bond
> Of nature that connect him with the world.
> Emphatically such a being lives
> An inmate of this *active* universe;
> From nature largely he receives, nor so
> Is satisfied but largely gives again,
> For feeling has to him imparted strength,
> And powerful in all sentiments of grief,
> Of exultation, fear and joy, his mind,
> Even as the agent of the one great mind,
> Creates, creator and receiver both,
> Working but in alliance with the works
> Which it beholds. – Such verily is the first
> Poetic spirit of our human life,
> By uniform control of after years

In most abated and suppressed, in some
Through every change of growth or of decay
Preeminent till death.
(*The Prelude*, 1798–9, Second Part, ll. 267–310)

That which in 'Tintern Abbey' was assertive yet vague, impassioned yet uncertain, has here achieved poetic realization: the feelings ascribed to 'that blessed mood', 'a sense', 'a presence', 'a motion', 'a spirit', are located in an actual experience – the experience of the baby at the mother's breast. And the nature of those feelings, and their relation to those of later life, are explored with a quite new clarity and assurance. Here, if anywhere, one might expect to find some qualification of that sense of individual isolation, that distrust of the most powerful desires, articulated in such poems as 'There was a Boy' and 'Nutting' – some Wordsworthian equivalent to Blake's 'play'. Certainly, in their emphasis on the importance of the very earliest childhood experience, these lines may be paralleled in this period only by Blake's *Songs*. Yet the contrast could not be more extreme. It is not merely that Wordsworth's is the language of associationist psychology (though his stress on the baby's activity in the process, on love rather than passive association as that which shapes and forms, offers a significant rethinking of some of the most fundamental premises of associationist thought), but that central to his presentation is an acceptance of the individualistic assumptions embedded in that language.[16] Where Blake's 'Infant Joy' presents the relationship between mother and child as one in which each is realized and creatively acknowledged, Wordsworth's sense of what is significant is signalled by his opening phrase. The good experience of the nursing child is seen as the ground of all meaning – 'else detached / And loth to coalesce'. But it is seen only from the child's perspective, as the starting-point for his linear development. The mother's activity is not portrayed: she is simply a passive 'presence' – less another person than a benign environment within which individual development can take place.[17] There is nothing of Blake's sense that this is a relationship in which she too achieves self-realization: the child alone grows and responds actively to the world. Nor is there any sense – such as is articulated in many of *Songs of Innocence* – of the power of helplessness to evoke in others feelings which answer to it: here, the emphasis is on the development of the individual's powers. The picture is of an essentially private subjectivity (albeit one whose growth is made possible by the presence of the mother), gathering sensations into itself rather than entering into relationship with another person:

His organs and recipient faculties
Are quickened, are more vigorous, his mind spreads
Tenacious of the forms which it receives.

those sensations which have been derived
From this beloved presence.

And the organic imagery steadily suggests that these primary
experiences are not social, but natural:

No outcast he, bewildered and depressed:
Along his infant veins are interfused
The gravitation and the filial bond
Of nature that connect him with the world.

The world within which this child finds himself is thus very
different from the mutually created world of 'Infant Joy'. It is a
non-human world, one in which he is potentially an 'outcast', and to
which he is ultimately subject ('Working but in alliance with the
works / Which it beholds'): it is in relation to this world that his·
deepest and most creative feelings are evolved. And because, at this
fundamental level, Wordsworth does not see the individual as a
social being, his sense of how these powerful original feelings might
be related to wider social possibility is very different from Blake's.
Blake never suggests that this particular manifestation of Innocence
– the loving relationship between mother and child – is the necessary
basis of the rest. But the parallelisms between the different *Songs of
Innocence* articulate his conviction that the mutual responsiveness and
answered trust disclosed in interactions such as this might inform a
whole society ('The Ecchoing Green'); might indeed be essential to
the continuing existence of the 'virtues' on which it depends ('The
Divine Image'). One after another, the poems of *Songs of Innocence*
suggest that such interactions point, by their very nature, beyond
themselves, toward more widely shared and potentially universal
experience ('Sweet joy befall thee!', 'And all the hills ecchoed', 'Then
cherish pity; lest you drive an angel from your door', 'And all must
love the human form...'). Blake sees the most vital human energies
as those which are actualized in relation to others: the bleak vision of
Songs of Experience charts the implications of the failure thus to
actualize them. But Wordsworth, as these lines suggest, sees such
energies as belonging to the pre-social individual. And therefore, the
larger society becomes their enemy:

– Such verily is the first
Poetic spirit of our human life,
By uniform control of after years

> In most abated and suppressed, in some
> Through every change of growth or of decay
> Preeminent till death.

The living virtue of the 'Poetic spirit', manifested in the very young child, is almost inevitably lost as the pressures of the culture close in. Only the fortunate can preserve it inviolate.

The pessimistic sense of social possibility that is reaching imaginative definition here is intimately linked to that distrust of 'our own pre-established codes of decision' which Wordsworth had begun to articulate in the Advertisement to *Lyrical Ballads 1798*, and which he was to express more fully in the Preface to the 1800 edition. It is a distrust far more extreme than the criticism of stereotyped poetic diction – that 'large portion of phrases and figures of speech which from father to son have long been regarded as the common inheritance of Poets'[18] – on which much of the argument is focussed. And its difference from Blake's ironic suspicion of the ways in which language may be used to mystify and control here emerges most sharply. For it is a distrust which stems from that sense, so directly expressed in these lines, that the most potent feelings are essentially subjective. From this perspective, language itself, as a shared construct, must be seen as tending to blur and distort the uniqueness and intensity of those feelings. As a twentieth-century writer, whose view is very close to Wordsworth's, puts it:

The fact that language is adult language, the language of an adult civilization, and that the infant is moulded only very gradually from his natural existence into a member of the civilization into which he is born makes the discrepancy between his precivilized, unschematized experience and the categories of civilized, conventional language much greater... The danger of the schemata of language, and especially of the worn currency of conventional language in vogue at the moment when the attempt is made to understand and describe an experience is that the person making this attempt will overlook the discrepancy between experience and language cliché or that he will not be persistent enough in his attempt to eliminate this discrepancy. Once the conventional schema has replaced the experience in his mind, the significant quality of the experience is condemned to oblivion.[19]

Yet to Wordsworth this process is not entirely inevitable. His description of the child's first interaction with the world as a 'poetic spirit', which a fortunate few manage to sustain 'Preeminent till death', registers his conviction that it is through poetry – its deconventionalizing of language, its fidelity to the uniqueness of particular experience – that some of the freshness and potency of that original perception of the world might be maintained, and the constricting schemata of the culture questioned. It is in one way an affirmation of the radical centrality, the cultural subversiveness, of poetry. But it is an affirmation made in face of another, perhaps even stronger, feeling that the essential nature of the most important experience is incommunicable.

It is thus significant that the most powerful poems in the 1800 volume of *Lyrical Ballads* – the three 'Lucy' poems which were printed together near the beginning of the volume – should be the most enigmatically 'private' of all Wordsworth's works. These poems clearly have deep personal resonances: with extraordinary psychological insight they expose the complex of contradictory emotions which constitute what we call grief. Yet to see them merely as expressions of a private psychic crisis is to underestimate the nature of their achievement. For here, as in the other poetry of this extraordinary creative period, the fundamental bases of a whole vision of human possibility are sharply focussed and explored.

The first of the three, 'Strange fits of passion I have known' is in some ways the most baffling. In its wry self-consciousness it seems closer to the more 'experimental' poems of the 1798 volume than to the directly impassioned verse of 'There was a Boy' and 'Nutting'. Yet it is charged with unstated feeling of a peculiarly disturbing kind. The poem purports to be a love poem. But the story it tells is one of a lonely journey toward a goal which is never reached. The 'love' it depicts is not an interaction in which a shared world of confidence is created, but a subjective emotion which exposes rather than transcends individual vulnerabilities. Indeed, as the sequence of 'Lucy' poems proceeds, it becomes clear that Lucy's actual, separate existence only becomes a reality for the speaker after her death. The earliest remaining draft of this poem, it is true, ends with a stanza (unparalleled in the published sequence) which portrays an actual interaction with her;

> I told her this; her laughter light
> Is ringing in my ears;
> And when I think upon that night
> My eyes are dim with tears.[20]

But even this is an incident in the past, sundered from the present by the hint of her subsequent death: the lover ends alone, in tears. And the removal of this stanza from the published version has the effect

VISION AND DISENCHANTMENT

not merely of removing the story's explanatory frame (the final
shock is left sharply foregrounded and unresolved, its 'wayward-
ness' or its prophetic truth uncertain): it also emphasizes the isolation
of the protagonist. His final inconclusive yet fearful exclamation is
addressed to nobody but himself:

> 'O mercy!' to myself I cried,
> 'If Lucy should be dead!'

The 'love' presented in this poem is a peculiar emotion. It does not
lead to satisfying relation with the other: indeed, there is a powerful
sense that it is perhaps destructive of her. For the shock upon which
the narrative turns – the disappearance of that reassuring moon –
depends upon a simple fact: that physical perception *is* by its nature
egocentric, and that the stability of the world as seen from any
individual point of view depends upon that individual's remaining
stationary. On the surface, the lover's reaction is dismissed as 'fond
and wayward'. But the poetic force of that shock, and the suggestions of Lucy's death which surround it, give a very different
impression. In striking contrast to Blake, with his distrust of the
evidence of the senses, Wordworth seems to see the essential
egocentricity of sense-perception as indicative of a real emotional
truth: not merely that love has no creative potency, but that that
which impels the lover toward the beloved object will inevitably
cause it to disappear.[21] The feeling remains subliminal, too irrational
for more than embarrassed confrontation: but it is there, and it was
to be focussed more explicitly (though still hardly stated) in the last
of these three poems.

In 'Strange fits of passion', as in the other poems written at Goslar,
Wordsworth portrays the deepest emotion as locked within the
singleness of subjectivity. But here the traumatic recognition to
which the poem leads is not, as in 'Nutting', a rebuke from which a
subdued morality might grow, but an abrupt ending: a sudden
confrontation of the fact of human mortality. There is no sense –
such as there is in *Songs of Innocence* – that the reciprocal creativity of
love might provide a different kind of experience of that fact, for
here love is solitary and uncreative. It may feel deeply satisfying –
'Kind Nature's gentlest boon!' – but it belongs to the private
individual. And thus, as the poem's central image of perceptual
illusion suggests, it exposes him to utter vulnerability. Here, there is
no 'Ecchoing Green' of mutual recognition, no shared dream which
might answer to the 'dark' and the 'cold'. Instead, there is a lonely

282

traveller moving through a world of indifferent physical objects, inescapably subject to its laws. His seemingly purposeful journeying merely reveals his passivity – 'What once to me befel'. As in 'There was a Boy', human activity is seen as contained within and finally thwarted by a larger cosmic system. But this system is no longer, like those stars 'Rising or setting', in the background of the central figure's consciousness: it presents itself as an immediate shock:

> When down behind the cottage roof
> At once the planet dropp'd.

And this, the pivotal event of the poem, contrasts strikingly with the reassuring presence of that steady moon which had been a central image in Coleridge's poetry during the preceding months:

> 'Still as a Slave before his Lord,
>   'The Ocean hath no blast:
> 'His great bright eye most silently
>   'Up to the moon is cast –
>
> 'If he may know which way to go,
>   'For she guides him smooth or grim,
> 'See, brother, see! how graciously
>   'She looketh down on him.[22]

>   and oft, a moment's space,
> What time the moon was lost behind a cloud,
> Hath heard a pause of silence: till the Moon
> Emerging, hath awaken'd earth and sky
> With one sensation, and those wakeful Birds
> Have all burst forth in choral minstrelsy...[23]

> I hurried with him to our orchard plot,
> And he beholds the moon, and hush'd at once
> Suspends his sobs, and laughs most silently,
> While his fair eyes that swam with undropt tears
> Did glitter in the yellow moon-beam![24]

> And all the City, silent as the moon
> That steeps in quiet light the steady Vanes
> Of her huge temples...[25]

> Or if the secret ministry of frost,
> Shall hang them up in silent icicles,
> Quietly shining to the quiet Moon.[26]

It is a contrast which suggests a real poetic questioning of the assumptions which had shaped Coleridge's verse in 1797 and 1798 – assumptions which Wordsworth himself had sought to share. Here, Coleridge's beneficent universe has become one which directly threatens human purposes. Coleridge's detailed description is replaced by a series of starkly recorded facts: the clopping of the horse, the approach to the cottage, the hypnotic effect of the moon, and its final, jolting disappearance. Experience seems to have been pared down to its most basic elements. And the intimate ease of Coleridge's poems has been replaced by confessional embarrassment. The important feeling is all implied: 'Strange fits of passion I have known...', 'What fond and wayward thoughts will slide / Into a Lover's head.' The effect is to mime in the poem's very strategy the essential isolation which is its subject-matter: to suggest the incommunicability of that powerful, literally sensational, private experience which it presents. The difference from Coleridge's conversational confidence could not be more extreme.

And there is an analogous difference in the muted understatement of the following poem of the sequence. 'She dwelt among th'untrodden ways' is smoother, less awkward, than 'Strange fits of passion': there is certainly no embarrassment here. But, unlike that of the first poem, its subject is a private feeling whose real nature seems to elude communication. Indeed, its difference from public 'knowledge' is emphasized: 'A Maid whom there were none to praise / And very few to love', 'She liv'd unknown, and few could know / When Lucy ceas'd to be', 'The difference to me'. Again, the experience presented is one of love and loss. But here the movement is not one of unconsciousness leading to a traumatic moment of consciousness, of linear narrative cut short: it is one in which the story of Lucy's life and death – now explicitly outlined in the first and last stanzas – is interrupted by a central stanza containing two juxtaposed metaphors. This form is very different from that of the earliest remaining draft of the poem, a longer story ballad which images Lucy's beauty, growth and decline in terms of natural process. For the tighter tripartite structure foregrounds the two central images, so that they operate to quite different effect.

They are images which continue the paradoxical process initiated by the first word of the poem, of singling out its 'unknown' subject and offering a public account of her. Yet what they most poignantly convey is a sense of unbridgeable gap between the speaker's subjective feeling and what he can impart:

> A Violet by a mossy stone
> Half-hidden from the Eye!
> Fair, as a star when only one
> Is shining in the sky!

The two images, of Violet and star, cannot be connected to form even a 'poetic' picture of a girl: they have no point of contact, except that pivotal 'Fair'. It is the first adjective in the poem applied directly to Lucy. And it points less toward her than toward a totally subjective valuing, a valuing whose implicit energy informs the stanza. For despite the fact that they contain no verb, these lines have a power that the quiet narrative description surrounding them does not. The abrupt change of focus, from the small- to the large-scale, from the Violet whose presence is visible only to the minutely discriminating 'Eye', to the star which may be seen by all, from intimacy and fragility to distance and remoteness, calls for a corresponding energy in the reader. Yet it is an energy which has no verbal equivalent. The two images are simply placed side by side. And the effect is not merely to suggest the complexity of that feeling which they seek to express, but also its essential incommunicability.[27] It can be implied, but never articulated.

Like 'Strange fits of passion' this poem seeks to present an inexpressible subjective feeling: here, much more directly than in the preceding poem, the reader feels the transforming energy of that feeling. The reason lies partly in the oddly dynamic effect of those two statically juxtaposed central images, partly in their separation from the narrative begun in the first stanza and ended in the third. For that which by the final stanza is italicized and desperately important, that tense which asserts process and ending, is absent here: there is no verb. The complexity of feeling toward which the stanza points is thus frozen outside time: its permanence is poetically affirmed. It is private, inexpressible. But it is seen as having an unchanging force which the shared, passing knowledge of familiarity and repute referred to in the first stanza does not.

Yet here, as in 'Strange fits of passion', that same feeling which seems to point toward the beloved points inexorably toward the very heart of loss. For the metaphors which in their tenselessness seek to assert endurance and presence bring with them other, opposing feelings. The 'half-hidden' violet is obscure and vulnerable: the star is exposed and inaccessible. These two apparently simple images, framed at the centre of the poem, encapsulate that paradox implicit in the metaphoric process – that even as it aspires to escape the literal it reveals most sharply those fears and uncertainties which ordinary perception would deny. Lucy appears as defenceless and remote: not so much an other with whom interaction might be possible as a unique object, subject to exactly those facts of individual mutability which the 'sweet dreams' of love seemed to transcend. And the love which singles her out and celebrates her uniqueness merely exposes that subjection: it has no creative power.

The final word of the poem is the first explicit admission of the consciousness that informs the whole: 'The difference to me!' Lucy's death makes no 'difference' in the realm of public knowledge, but for this speaker the point of focus of the most intense subjective feeling has gone. In one way, that feeling is forever lost. In the narrative structure of the poem, it is over: the final stanza returns to the language of quiet common sense. But the framed, tenseless images of the central stanza, with their curious static energy, remain. 'The difference to me!' is at once a statement of absolute loss and an affirmation of the primary significance of feeling which is by its very nature inexpressible. The affirmation and the admission of loss seem to be interdependent.

If the central stanza of this poem is pivotally important, there is no such stanza in the third. The bipartite form suggests opposition rather than linear progression: the narrative structure has shrunk to a stark juxtaposition of tenses:

> A slumber did my spirit seal,
>   I had no human fears:
> She seem'd a thing that could not feel
>   The touch of earthly years.
>
> No motion has she now, no force
>   She neither hears nor sees
> Roll'd round in earth's diurnal course
>   With rocks and stones and trees!

By now, it has become clear that the three poems form a sequence, and that the movement from one to the next is as significant as the movement from stanza to stanza. The increasingly truncated shape of each is an exact expression of the developing feeling that the experience being pointed toward is essentially inexpressible. We have moved from confessional embarrassment ('And I will dare to tell / But in the Lover's ear alone') to the understated admission of unshareable emotion ('The difference to me!') to a curious impersonality. And we have moved from a description of 'What once to me befel' to a direct statement of what has befallen Lucy. The story of the first poem, in one way immediately present, was in another distanced by the narrative past tense and the speaker's apologies: the status of the intuition it presented remained uncertain. The second offered definite fact, but in muted form, the girl's death indicated by a flat copula. But in this third poem that which was earlier implied or understated is almost brutally recognized. 'Now' comes to the forefront with shocking force, in verbs whose energy reduces Lucy to an object.

There is, of course, a terrible irony in this progression. For throughout the sequence Lucy is never seen as a changing human being, with thoughts and feelings of her own, who might herself respond to the speaker in changing ways. His opening image of her is a conventional one, presented in the past tense:

> When she I lov'd, was strong and gay
> And like a rose in June ...

And as the sequence continues she becomes, in a curious way, more and more dehumanized by his tranforming vision:

> A Violet by a mossy stone
> Half-hidden from the Eye!

> She seem'd a thing that could not feel
> The touch of earthly years.

It is only in the last stanza of this third poem that she is seen not merely as something loved, but as a person who was once a living agent, with 'motion' and 'force' of her own. Yet this sense of her as a subject rather than an object is felt only as it is negated: 'She neither hears nor sees'. And in the lines which follow she is more fundamentally and absolutely a 'thing' than in either of the two preceding poems.

This final poem focusses a feeling which has been developing throughout the sequence: that guilt which, it has been argued, is an inevitable component of grief for any loved one. It is a guilt which has its basis in the infantile feeling called into play by desire, and made manifest by the loss of its object – the libidinous inability to recognize the separateness of that which is desired ('She seem'd a thing that could not feel / The touch of earthly years') so that its disappearance brings the fear that the very intensity of desire has caused its destruction.[28] Here, the nebulous uneasiness of the first poem, with its haunting feeling that if the speaker had not travelled toward Lucy's house the planet would not have 'dropp'd', has become a much more conscious irony. 'In one of those sweet dreams I slept' is replaced by a direct self-accusation – 'A slumber did my spirit seal'. Lucy has been loved in a way which, while subjectively satisfying, took no heed of her separate reality ('She seem'd a thing . . .'). Now, in an ironic and shocking consummation of that love, she has become a 'thing', with no feelings of her own.

Yet those two stanzas have a power which goes beyond ironic self-accusation. With naked directness they confront that opposition on which each of the two preceding poems has pivoted: the absolute opposition between past illusion and present reality. Against the remembered sense of the world as securely answering to desire is placed an abrupt recognition of facts which seem to bear no relation to desire at all: the safe eternity apprehended in love is replaced by an 'objective' world of time and process. The feeling is exactly that described in another great classic of our literature:

if all else remained, and he were annihilated, the universe would turn to a mighty stranger: I should not seem a part of it.[29]

Here, in the shift from the first stanza to the second, the universe turns to 'a mighty stranger', from a place imbued with and responsive to human feeling ('the *touch* of earthly years') to one alien to and remote from it. The lyrical language of transforming illusion gives way to a different kind of language. For the first time in the sequence, the indifferent universe of the Newtonian science which had been such a central part of Wordsworth's education becomes explicitly present, as the terminology of that science – 'motion', 'force', 'earth's diurnal course' – enters the poetry.[30]

And it is not simply the terminology. For the fact of Lucy's death is now imaged directly, in the form of one of the most central and familiar doctrines of Newtonian physics: that of the impermeability of matter. In the third book of his *Opticks* Newton had argued

that God in the Beginning form'd matter in solid, massy, hard, impenetrable, moveable Particles, of such Sizes and Figures, and with such other Properties, and in such Proportion to Space, as most conducted to the End for which he form'd them . . . And therefore, that Nature may be lasting, the Changes of corporeal Things are to be placed only in the various Separations and new Associations and Motions of these permanent Particles.

It seems to me farther, that these Particles have not only a *Vis inertiae*, accompanied with such passive Laws of Motion as naturally result from that Force, but also that they are moved by certain active Principles, such as is that of Gravity, and that which causes Fermentation, and the Cohesion of Bodies.[31]

Pope, in the *Essay on Man*, was to attempt to versify this doctrine, in lines which reflect a good deal of (unacknowledged) disquiet as to its experiential implications:

> See plastic Nature working to this end,
> The single atoms each to other tend,
> Attract, attracted to, the next in place
> Form'd and impell'd its neighbour to embrace.
> See Matter next, with various life endu'd,
> Press to one centre still, the gen'ral Good.
> See dying vegetables life sustain,
> See life dissolving vegetate again:
> All forms that perish other forms supply,
> (By turns we catch the vital breath, and die)
> Like bubbles on the sea of Matter born,
> They rise, they break, and to that sea return.[32]

But in Wordsworth's confrontation of the end of an individual life there is no attempt to invoke 'the gen'ral Good'. Lucy's death is imaged as a rearrangement of the 'permanent Particles' which composed her body. Suddenly she is seen not from the transforming perspective of subjective love, but from the perspective of that science which purported to disclose a reality uncontaminated by human meanings and purposes, that science whose central methodological premise was precisely its 'objectivity'. And the feeling, exactly encapsulated in the division between the two stanzas, is very different from that of Pope's 'optimistic' commentary. The vision of the final stanza is neither optimistic nor pessimistic: it is simply and absolutely opposed to that of the first.[33] The universe presented here is not a 'great system' whose workings can be analysed: it is a 'mighty stranger', whose distance from human subjectivity is felt directly as a negation:

> No motion has she now, no force,
> She neither hears nor sees.

And the poem is thus not merely a moving statement of irreparable personal loss: it focusses the essential bases of that deeply pessimistic sense of human possibility which informs all the poems of the Goslar period. The subjective feeling of the first stanza is portrayed as a state of self-deceptive illusion, 'sealed' from the 'human fears' of maturity. The sense of invulnerability presented there is devalued in the presentation: seen as blinkered, unrealistic, at a fantasy level even destructive ('She seem'd a thing ... '). Yet it is seen also as having been a state of vital satisfaction, in which the world was felt to be beneficent, a place which answered to desire. And the objective reality of the second stanza bears no relation to human desire at all. On the one hand, there is 'sealed' omnipotent fantasy: on the other, unalterable fact. The suggestion is not simply that 'now' is forever opposed to what was, but that there is an absolute division between human feeling and the objective world, between illusion and reality.

For Wordworth envisages no alternative to that first, suspect, subjective 'slumber' except disillusionment. There is no sense that 'spirit' might be actualized in relation to the other, that human desire might inform and transform the world: simply a bleak transition to a vision of isolation and helplessness before those facts of time and death which thwart individual purpose. Those facts are not seen as the whole truth about the world as experienced. They come as a shock and are felt as a negation precisely because they are not, because the sense of absolute trust and security within a universe focussed around one 'beloved presence' has been so powerfully realized. Yet that sense is seen as infantile and impotent, 'sealed' within a single consciousness rather than mutually created, unable to make any 'difference' beyond the ultimate knowledge of loss. The transforming illusion it provides is portrayed merely as a failure to have the proper 'human fears'. There is no feeling that delight in the other might enhance rather than block awareness of her separate reality, or that desire might be expressed and answered in such a way as to create a shared and satisfying human world, different both from private subjectivity and objective fact. The recognition of Lucy's otherness is simply a recognition of mortality, of her subjection to a system remote from human meanings: it comes only when relation-ship with her is impossible.

And here we are approaching the heart of Wordsworth's differ-ence from Blake. For Blake does not present feelings of trust and security as infantile illusions which must be shattered in order for maturity to be achieved: nor does he suggest that they are simply private feelings. Desire, he suggests throughout *Songs of Innocence*, *can* be creatively answered. The child – the baby in 'Infant Joy', even little Tom Dacre in 'The Chimney Sweeper' – is not isolated: there is another who cares for and responds to him, in a process of mutual realization. Instead of the Boy of Winander, whose hootings are 'sometimes' met with silence, who learns, finally, that he cannot bend the world to his own desires, there are the playing children of

'Nurse's Song', whose Nurse responds and whose world 'ecchoes' joyfully to them. Instead of the bleak confrontations of *Lyrical Ballads*, 'distress' is answered by the 'Mercy Pity Peace and Love' to which it appeals. And the mutual trust created in such experiences is seen as the very fabric of human society, without which it would perish. Throughout, the focus is on the living actuality which can be created in human relationships. But the image which emerges most powerfully in the Goslar lyrics is very different. It is that of an isolated individual – in Blake's terms, an Abstract – confronting a non-human universe, in which the ultimate fact is that of death. Human desire is seen as disturbing, sometimes explicitly as destructive: a subjective feeling which creates its own subjective world of illusion, to be 'corrected' by the recognition of reality.[34] There is no answering other with which it can engage, in the creation of a shared world, for the loved object is confronted in its otherness only as it is lost. Subjectivity and objectivity are simply opposed, and the facts of the Newtonian universe finally dominate.[35]

The 'Lucy' poems lead to a stark dead end. Years later, in the first of his *Essays upon Epitaphs*, Wordsworth was to write with deep feeling of the paralysing effect which the sense of the human predicament presented there could have on all social relations, unless 'counterbalanced' by a belief in immortality:

for my own part, it is to me inconceivable, that the sympathies of love towards each other, which grow with our growth, could ever attain any new strength, or even preserve the old, after we had received from the outward senses the impression of death, and were in the habit of having that impression daily renewed and its accompanying feeling brought home to ourselves, and to those we love; if the same were not counteracted by those communications with our internal Being, which are anterior to all these experiences, and with which revelation coincides, and has through that coincidence alone (for otherwise it could not possess it) a power to affect us. I confess, with me the conviction is absolute, that, if the impression and sense of death were not thus counterbalanced, such a hollowness would pervade the whole system of things, such a want of correspondence and consistency, a disproportion so astounding between means and ends, that there could be no repose, no joy. Were we to grow up unfostered by this genial warmth, a frost would chill the spirit, so penetrating and powerful, that there could be no motions of the life of love; and infinitely less could we have any wish to be remembered after we had passed away from a world in which each man had moved about like a shadow.[36]

No such 'counterbalancing' belief is presented in *Lyrical Ballads 1800*. Yet another group of poems written at Goslar and published in that volume suggests that the questions which seem to lie behind this *Essay upon Epitaphs* were already beginning to trouble Wordsworth. The 'Matthew' poems, like those about Lucy, focus on human mortality. But they are not confessional accounts of lonely subjective experience. Their very form (the first an account of a public 'epitaph', the second and third reported dialogues) suggests a concern very different from that of the Lucy poems: a concern with the consolations which men attempt to offer one another in face of a seemingly indifferent universe, with the nature of the human relationships that can be made despite a sense of fundamental isolation, and with 'what remains behind' in a world in which individual death is the ultimate reality.

The subject of the first is one of those monuments which men 'rear' against time and change, by which they seek to perpetuate that which is gone:

> This tablet, that thus humbly rears
> In such diversity of hue
> Its history of two hundred years.

The interest, however, is not in that generalized 'history', but in a particular individual:

> – When through this little wreck of fame,
> Cypher and syllable, thine eye
> Has travell'd down to Matthew's name,
> Pause with no common sympathy.

Unlike Lucy, he is commemorated by a 'name'. And instead of simply confronting his absence, the speaker attempts to recall him as he lived:

> The sighs which Matthew heav'd were sighs
> Of one tir'd out with fun and madness;
> The tears which came to Matthew's eyes
> Were tears of light, the oil of gladness ...
> Yet sometimes when the secret cup
> Of still and serious thought went round
> It seem'd as if he drank it up,
> He felt with spirit so profound.

But the description is oddly generalized and external. As Wordsworth was later to argue, in the first of his *Essays upon Epitaphs*:

every man has a character of his own, to the eye that has skill to perceive it. The real cause of the acknowledged want of discrimination in sepulchral memorials is this: That to analyse the characters of others, especially of those whom we love, is not a common or natural employment of men at any time. We are not anxious unerringly to understand the constitution of the minds of those who have soothed, who have cheered, who have supported us: with whom we have been long and daily pleased or delighted. The affections are their own justification. The light of love in our hearts is a satisfactory evidence that there is a body of worth in the minds of our friends or kindred, whence that light has proceeded. We shrink from the thought of placing their merits and defects to be weighed against each other in the nice balance of pure intellect; nor do we find much temptation to detect the shades by which a good quality or virtue is discriminated in them from an excellence known by the same general name as it exists in the mind of another.[37]

There is an absolute distance between description and presence, between the necessarily general account that must be offered of a vanished human being and the unique individuality known to love. Here, even loving recollections cannot convey the essence of the living Matthew. The closing stanza turns away from the reader to apostrophize the opaque and 'silent' figure who has been the poem's subject, in a tacit admission of the difference between the actual past relationship with him and the abstraction of such memories as can be preserved and 'remain':

> – Thou soul of God's best earthly mould,
> Thou happy soul, and can it be
> That these two words of glittering gold
> Are all that must remain of thee?

Yet despite the implicit pessimism of this conclusion, it has none of the poignancy of that 'difference' which is the subject of the 'Lucy' poems. Matthew has become generalized into an embodiment of enduring human qualities, in a phrase which suggests not only acceptance of his mortality – 'Thou soul of God's best earthly mould' – but also the absence of that intensity of feeling, that remembered transfiguring illusion – 'She seem'd a thing that could not feel / The touch of earthly years' – that made such acceptance impossible there. The painful intuitions of the other Goslar lyrics have been removed to a meditative distance. It is in the two following poems of the group – poems in which the consideration of a monument is replaced by a description of a remembered interchange – that Wordsworth explores their implications with a directness that permits of no such distancing. Both 'The Two April Mornings' and 'The Fountain' turn upon an admission of irrevocable loss. But both, as their titles suggest, entertain the possibility of some form of renewal; and in both cases it is a renewal of a more living kind than that represented by gilt letters on a memorial. The first begins with an image of natural recurrence:

> Yon cloud with that long purple cleft
> Brings fresh into my mind
> A day like this which I have left
> Full thirty years behind.
>
> And on that slope of springing corn
> The self-same crimson hue
> Fell from the sky that April morn,
> The same which now I view!

Yet this is a sameness which is also difference. The two mornings are distinguished even as they are likened: the memory of the past haunts but in no way merges with the present. And this sense of a seeming identity which is not identity is the subject of the story which follows – a story of love for a dead child, and of another child who appeared by her grave:

> And, turning from her grave, I met
> Beside the church-yard Yew
> A blooming Girl, whose hair was wet
> With points of morning dew.
>
> A basket on her head she bare,
> Her brow was smooth and white,
> To see a Child so very fair,
> It was a pure delight!
>
> No fountain from its rocky cave
> E'er tripp'd with foot so free,
> She seem'd as happy as a wave
> That dances on the sea.

The effect, enhanced by the form, is in some ways akin to that of the 'revenant' ballads, with their tales of supernatural returns.[38] The images of the final stanza recall those of Florizel's speech to Perdita – the lost who was found – in *The Winter's Tale*:

> When you do dance, I wish you
> A wave o' th' sea, that you might ever do
> Nothing but that; move still, still so,
> And own no other function.
>
> (Act IV, sc. iv, ll. 140–3)

Indeed, Matthew's memory encapsulates the paradox of Florizel's 'move still': the Girl he saw is at once moving and forever framed, a perfect image. Yet the feeling evoked by this echo – the irrational feeling that this girl might indeed replace she who has gone – is seen as a temptation to be resisted. For the Shakespearian suggestions are of contrast, rather than of confirmation. Where Florizel's speech is directly, presently addressed to an actual girl, Matthew's describes a vision that is past. Where *The Winter's Tale* celebrates a change that is fruition, a fulfilment which restores the lost, this poem points not forward but backward, toward a nebulous, never-realized time –

> she would have been
> A very nightingale.

– and toward a loss that is irrevocable. And where Shakespeare's final scene presents the moving image of a likeness that comes to be seen as identity, here likeness is not identity, and even the wish that it were is refused:

> There came from me a sigh of pain
> Which I could ill confine;
> I look'd at her and look'd again;
> – And did not wish her mine.

The refusal – whose difficulty is marked by the doubly punctuated pause before it – comes as the poem's anti-climactic climax. That sense of natural recurrence and renewal which is central to *The Winter's Tale* is here rejected as an image of what is possible in human relationships: there can be no replacement, even in 'wish', of the original object of love. The 'two April mornings' which give the poem its title may appear almost the same, the one living again in the other: but they are not. And this Girl is not the dead Emma: to 'wish' that she were would be to deny the uniqueness of that love which is felt most intensely in the sharpness of grief:

> Six feet in earth my Emma lay,
> And yet I lov'd her more,
> For so it seem'd, than till that day
> I e'er had lov'd before.

It is a refusal which is presented less as a rejection of new happiness than as an acceptance of the cost of loving a particular, perishable individual, an affirmation of the integrity of that love.

In this, this poem is reminiscent of the 'Lucy' poems. Matthew's last words are ' – And did not wish her mine': there, too, the speaking voice breaks off as the absoluteness of loss is recognized. But here, the entertainment of the possibility of replacement, and the reported dialogue point beyond that recognition toward the world of continuing human relations. And the imaginative con-figuration that emerges is a striking and suggestive one. The poem does not end with Matthew's voice: he is seen, from a different, later perspective, in a final stanza which provides a muted parallel to that describing his love for the dead Emma:

> Matthew is in his grave, yet now
> Methinks I see him stand,
> As at that moment, with his bough
> Of wilding in his hand.

Just as the child whose loss he so starkly confronted ('Six feet in earth my Emma lay') retained her particularity in his memory, so a sharp particular image of him remains for the speaker. The recognition that these figures are gone, beyond the reach of distorting desire, gives them a piercing clarity. No present subjective longing, such as that which transfigured Lucy, is allowed to blur their otherness: they are placed in the past, removed from the possibility of *any* interaction. And this structure has its thematic counterpart in Matthew's resistance to any 'wish' concerning the actual Girl who appeared to him: her image, similarly, is preserved fresh and inviolate for thirty years. The poem is informed by distrust of those 'wishes' that would deny mortality. For the suggestion is that it is only by resisting them, by maintaining a perspective of disillusion-ment, that the separateness, the unique individuality of both self and other can be maintained.[39]

Yet, as the 'Lucy' poems show, the most powerful and satisfying human feeling is that which does seek to deny mortality in this way: that which 'dreams' a world which answers to desire. In those poems, such feeling is seen as essentially egocentric, blurring – in some way perhaps even destroying – the loved object's separate being: it leads only to guilty disillusionment and loss. Here, as that disillusionment is accepted and the other is seen with sharpness and clarity, the possibility of any present intensity of feeling disappears. The figures who appear distinctly are seen, rather than desired: and they are seen as figures in the past. Although the poem reports a dialogue between two sympathetic friends, there is little sense of dramatic interaction. The transitions between the stanzas are jerky and thought-provoking, pointing in their blankness toward that which cannot be articulated or shared. And the linear narrative which the poem seemed initially to promise is curiously disconti-nuous and regressive in its effect: each stanza, in its syntactic and rhyming completeness, encapsulates and points backward to a particular, halted moment in the past, as the last stanza points backward and frames the whole.

The pattern of the poetry is a distinctive one, and one very different from that which emerges when Blake engages with questions of time and change, of loss and renewal. The world of 'The Ecchoing Green' is one in which feelings are shared and acknowledged: it is spoken in the confident first person plural. But here – and even more centrally in the poem which follows – Wordsworth emphasizes the distance between the two protagonists: the narrator is singular, and left alone at the end. Instead of a process of completed and answering activity, of present mutual fulfilment, there is a series of arrested images from the past. Where in 'The Ecchoing Green' the stress was on the recurrence of typical modes of experience ('Such, such were the joys'), on a mutual recognition and acceptance of the processes of life, here it is on the uniqueness of the particular human being at a particular vanished moment, on the perishable and private autobiographical memory – a memory which stretches backward rather than forwards. The final, static image of the poem, placed and distanced by 'Matthew is in his grave', is finished and complete: it does not, like the ending of Blake's poem, point forward into an area of continuing possibility.

The third of the Matthew poems takes up the same concerns in a different way. Its title, 'The Fountain', evokes the earlier poem's image of tempting recurrence. And its sub-title, 'A Conversation', like the other Coleridgean echoes in this 1800 volume, once again signals an implicit engagement with the presuppositions which had shaped the verse of both poets in 1798. For here there is no confident rendering of the subtle movements of an intimately speaking voice, such as one finds in Coleridge's conversation poems, or in 'Tintern Abbey': here, as in the previous poem, the slightly disconcerting transitions from stanza to stanza draw attention to what cannot be said, to the unbridgeable distance between the two speakers. The suggestion, once again, is that the most significant dimension of experience is incommunicable. From the very beginning, indeed, the difference between these two 'Friends' is emphasized:

> A pair of Friends, though I was young,
> And Matthew seventy–two.

The young man lightly assumes that there can be an easy harmony between human and natural worlds:

> Now, Matthew, let us try to match
> This water's pleasant tune
> With some old Border-song, or catch
> That suits a summer's noon.

Matthew is silent in face of this suggestion. And the speech which he eventually makes in reply carries the authority of experience. Here, as in the preceding poem, the images are of recurrence and renewal – images which sharpen rather than answer to a sense of individual isolation and transience:

> 'Down to the vale this water steers,
> How merrily it goes!
> 'Twill murmur on a thousand years,
> And flow as now it flows.
>
> And here, on this delightful day,
> I cannot chuse but think
> How oft, a vigorous Man, I lay
> Beside this Fountain's brink.
>
> My eyes are dim with childish tears,
> My heart is idly stirr'd,
> For the same sound is in my ears,
> Which in those days I heard.

The concern is far from simply with lost youth. For the gnomically enigmatic stanzas which follow are at once an exact dramatization of an old man's half-private reverie, and a sophisticated poetic device drawing attention to that area of inexpressible subjective experience toward which the two preceding poems have pointed:

> Thus fares it still in our decay:
> And yet the wiser mind
> Mourns less for what age takes away
> Than what it leaves behind.
>
> The blackbird in the summer trees,
> The lark upon the hill,
> Let loose their carols when they please,
> Are quiet when they will.
>
> With Nature never do *they* wage
> A foolish strife; they see
> A happy youth, and their old age
> Is beautiful and free.

But we are press'd by heavy laws,
And often, glad no more,
We wear a face of joy, because
We have been glad of yore.

If there is one who need bemoan
His kindred laid in earth,
The household hearts that were his own,
It is the man of mirth.

My days, my Friend, are almost gone,
My life has been approv'd,
And many love me, but by none
Am I enough belov'd.'

Part of Matthew's argument is a simple one. Human beings cannot share the untroubled, accepting spontaneity of nature because of their desire to resist time and change. But he does not image that desire as it was imaged in the 'Lucy' poems, as a remembered transfiguring illusion of permanence and security. Instead, removed from the sharpness of immediate loss, he sees it as that which impels men to construct a continuing social reality in face of mutability – a reality which is not 'what age takes away', but 'what it leaves behind'. And 'what it leaves behind' cannot restore or compensate for what has been lost: it is itself a source of pain. For the social personality – that public self which is recognized by others and conforms to socially accepted expectations – is here felt as a denial of the true self, a 'face' which masks rather than expresses real emotion. This division is not, like that between the memorial name and the living man in the first poem, reflected upon from a distance. As Matthew's haltingly authoritative words suggest, it is intimately felt as a split within the individual himself: between that 'I' which was realized in the first, lost intensity of love ('the household hearts that were his own') and the public 'me', who 'wears a face of joy' because it has come to be expected of him, that 'me' which can be 'approv'd' and 'lov'd' by 'many'. The essential isolation that is thus affirmed is confirmed by the young man's sympathetic inability to understand it:

'Now both himself and me he wrongs,
The man who thus complains!
I live and sing my idle songs
Upon these happy plains.

299

> And, Matthew, for thy Children dead
> I'll be a son to thee!'
> At this he grasp'd his hands, and said,
> 'Alas! that cannot be.'

Like the pause before the visionary Girl in the preceding poem, Matthew's grasping of his hands registers and resists the temptation to assuage the pain of loss by accepting some form of present reparation. And his banal truism affirms both the uniqueness of the original love, and the integrity of the self which has been defined in it. He does not grasp the young man's hands: he grasps his own, in a closing-off from any further attempt at intimacy. His refusal to accept that loss is not absolute, that recurrence is possible within human experience, is presented as the only freedom within an inescapable subjection to time and change: a freedom registered in the halts and pauses and slight surprises of his speech, very different from the neatness of those 'witty rhymes' and 'pleasant tunes' into which his youthfully simplistic companion has tried to persuade him:

> Now, Matthew, let us try to match
> This water's pleasant tune
> With some old Border-song, or catch
> That suits a summer's noon.
>
> Or of the Church-clock and the chimes
> Sing here beneath the shade,
> That half-mad thing of witty rhymes
> Which you last April made!

And there is thus a poignant irony in the final stanza:

> And, ere we came to Leonard's Rock,
> He sang those witty rhymes
> About the crazy old church-clock
> And the bewilder'd chimes.

Matthew has once again become a 'grey-hair'd Man of glee', that public self who conforms to public expectation by fitting experience into a cheeringly repeatable mould. The casually mentioned name, 'Leonard's Rock', seems here without significance: but, as the later Grasmere poem, 'The Brothers', placed earlier in the volume, tells, behind it lies a complex and painful story. And there is something of a similar feeling about Matthew. He has reverted to his 'face of joy', which masks far deeper and unexpressed emotions. As in the previous poem, we are offered a final, external image of him; here

THE GOSLAR LYRICS

mocking at the time which he cannot transcend in rhymes which are 'half-mad'. And the distance between this image and that private self toward which he can only point remains unbridged.

The sense of human possibility that emerges from these two poems is very different from anything to be found in Blake's *Songs* – different, in its acceptance of individual isolation, from that creative interaction envisaged in *Songs of Innocence*; different, too, in its implicit valuing of that acceptance, from that exposure of sterile egocentricity which *Songs of Experience* present. The feeling is not one of a necessary connection – for good or for ill – between human beings, but of fundamental separateness. Here, as in 'The Ecchoing Green', the subject is a dialogue between old and young. But here the image is not of the one answering to and 'ecchoing' the other, of a whole community organized by 'play': it is of two individuals whose conversation reveals rather than bridges the distance between them – a distance which is registered not by confirmation and recognition, but by silence and bafflement. If the younger man learns from these exchanges, what he learns is unarticulated. Matthew, speaking from his heart, remains separate and inscrutable.

And if each poem entertains that possibility of cyclic recurrence which is presented in 'The Ecchoing Green', it is here a possibility which is rejected for human beings. Like that poem, these explore the ways in which men accept the passing of time and face the loss of certain kinds of experience. But here such acceptance is a tragic acceptance of the finality of individual loss, not an acceptance made meaningful by a response to others' succeeding experience. Each individual pursues a unique and unrepeatable trajectory through time, alone. The most powerful feeling is private, and relates to that which is past, rather than informing and transforming the present: Indeed, the rejection of any new intensity of feeling – 'And did not wish her mine', 'Alas! that cannot be' – seems an affirmation of personal integrity. Where in Blake's song the fact that experience is 'ecchoed' and need is answered is of central significance, here such 'ecchoing' and answering is seen as a temptation to be resisted, because it involves a blurring and conventionalizing of that which is unique and private. The 'witty rhymes' which *can* be shared are trivial compared to the feelings thus negatively affirmed. And the private is separated from, and seen as far more powerfully engaging than, the public dimension of experience.

Yet the 'private' itself is presented in these poems less as an area of intimate interpersonal relations than as a 'sealed' subjectivity.

301

Feeling is, indeed, a kind of property of the individual rather than a relation to that which is other: a sense imaged very exactly in Matthew's grasping of his own hands. The vital feelings are for the dead, the more vital because they *are* dead. And the characteristic pattern which emerges – a pattern realized differently, shockingly, in the 'Lucy' poems – is of the transformation of the subject into an object; of the hearing, seeing, remembering individual (Emma, the 'blooming Girl', Matthew) into something externally seen, an image in others' consciousness, distanced and receding. That fundamental hopelessness about the possibility of creative interaction with the object of 'love', which was articulated in 'Nutting' and in the 'Lucy' poems has here become a larger hopelessness about the capacity of human beings to construct a shared world of feeling which might engage their deepest energies, and answer to or provide some other than tragic experience of individual death and destruction. In these poems, the only common feeling envisaged is a shared acceptance of a common human condition, that fate which each individual has to accept – 'we are press'd by heavy laws'. There is no sense that a different actuality might be made by creative human interaction. And thus, despite their implicit valuing of the integrity of the perishing individual, these poems point toward an imaginative sense of social possibility that contrasts strikingly in its pessimism with Blake's.

8   Names and Signs: the Poems of Grasmere

> A life has come to an end. For that life or towards it no more
> initiatives are possible. There is only the stillness of death. Perhaps
> the stillness suggests peace, but at first its fixity is terrible. And the
> fixity acts retrospectively. None of the life which is over can now
> be changed. The bereaved goes back to live again his part in that
> life. If he could relive it as he originally lived it, he would be able to
> experience the still open possibilities of the life now ended. But
> when the bereaved return to the past, they can never entirely forget
> what has prompted their return: they go back to the past to foretell
> a death... It is then as though the elements of the past line the
> circumference of the circle, and the future elements withdraw,
> losing all immediacy. I have nothing to live for now.
>
> (John Berger and Jean Mohr, *A Seventh Man*,
> Harmondsworth, 1975)

After his extraordinarily creative period at Goslar, Wordsworth
seems to have written little for several months. And when he began
to write again, in October 1799, it was poetry of a very different
kind, reflecting a very different situation.[1] No longer was he living in
isolation in a foreign country: he had returned to an England in
which he felt a new sense of being at home. The poetry of this period
which he published in *Lyrical Ballads 1800* – the 'Poems on the
Naming of Places', 'The Brothers', 'Michael', the shorter lyrics of
Grasmere life – seems the very direct expression of this, for one after
another these poems explore the ties of memory and affection that
sustain first a group of friends, and then a whole community. At
first, they appear quite unrelated to those earlier Goslar lyrics which
had so bleakly delineated the essentially private nature of the most
significant experience, the impossibility of a creative interaction
which would engage the deepest energies of the self with those of
others, and the necessity for the loss of 'infantine desire' in
'humanized' maturity. Yet the feelings brought to such sharp
definition there have not disappeared: they inform and shape this
new vision of human community and of what is possible within it.

The five 'Poems on the Naming of Places' appear, indeed, direct
attempts to reply to that question which the Goslar lyrics left blankly

unanswered: how might the 'rocks and stones and trees' of an indifferent universe be endowed with human meaning? Each recounts an experience which has led to the naming of a particular local place, either by the poet or by the poet and a group of friends. As their subject-matter would imply, these are much more easily conversational poems than those written at Goslar. But in each case the experience portrayed is more disturbing than might at first appear, and presents problems which the 'naming' cannot resolve. And in each case, they are problems which other of the lyrical ballads have exposed.

The first of the group, 'It was an April Morning' opens with images which recall those of the lyrics of spring 1798:

> It was an April Morning: fresh and clear
> The Rivulet, delighting in its strength,
> Ran with a young man's speed, and yet the voice
> Of waters which the winter had supplied
> Was' soften'd down into a vernal tone.
> The spirit of enjoyment and desire,
> And hopes and wishes, from all living things
> Went circling ...   (ll. 1–8)

Here, as in those lyrics, there is real uncertainty in the attempt to affirm a 'link' between the natural world and human emotion. The confident metaphors of the opening give way to a more and more insistent sense of division:

> The budding groves appear'd *as if* in haste
> To spur the steps of June; *as if* their shades
> Of various green were hindrances that stood
> Between them and their object ...   (ll. 9–12)

> The stream, so ardent in its course before,
> Sent forth such sallies of glad sound, that all
> Which I till then had heard, *appear'd* the voice
> Of common pleasure.   (ll. 22–5, my italics)

This uneasiness is less prominent than that which dislocates 'Lines written in early spring', but it expresses a similar feeling. And it leads here to an oblique intuition of mortality:

> beast and bird, the lamb
> The Shepherd's dog, the linnet and the thrush
> Vied with this waterfall, and made a song
> Which, while I listen'd, seem'd like a wild growth

> Or like some natural produce of the air
> That could not cease to be.   (ll.25–30)

The parenthesis, 'while I listen'd', and the negated suggestion of the final clause hint at the transience of the scene: a hint which prepares for the foreshadowing of the speaker's death and Emma's in the closing lines. It is very lightly done. But it is significant that it is in the wake of this that the act of naming – the announced subject of the poem – is presented.

For it seems to be a growing sense of the otherness of this place, its separation from anything that the speaker can create or control, which leads to the desire to name it. And naming thus appears as an act of proprietorship, the only kind of proprietorship possible:

> I gaz'd and gaz'd, and to myself I said,
> 'Our thoughts at least are ours; and this wild nook,
> My EMMA, I will dedicate to thee.   (ll. 37–9)

The act is private, an assertion of the 'single self'.[2] Although it commemorates a beloved person, it does not, like the naming of Blake's 'Infant Joy', emerge from a process of creative interaction. 'EMMA', indeed, has not appeared in the poem until now. The 'thoughts' which this name signifies remain unarticulated: and the existence projected for it is one of increasing distance from the experience to which it points:

> And, of the Shepherds who have seen me there,
> To whom I sometimes in our idle talk
> Have told this fancy, two or three, perhaps,
> Years after we are gone and in our graves,
> When they have cause to speak of this wild place,
> May call it by the name of EMMA'S DELL.   (ll. 42–7)

In 'Infant Joy' actuality *is* the continuing shared world constructed by human 'naming'. But here the 'real' world, the foreign world of nature, is separate from and unmarked by those 'thoughts' which the 'name' seeks, opaquely, to memorialize; and there is no confidence in that 'name''s continuance. Others 'may' use it: it will be known to 'two or three, perhaps'. The feeling is one of uncertainty, of a gradual petering out.

In the second of the 'Poems on the Naming of Places,' the disquieting suggestions which are here merely touched upon have become more prominent. We first hear of the name which is its subject from the admonitory Vicar: to him, it is an intrusion on the landscape, a meaningless hieroglyph which demands explanation:

> He with grave looks demanded, for what cause,
> Reviving obsolete Idolatry,
> I like a Runic Priest, in characters
> Of formidable size, had chisel'd out
> Some uncouth name upon the native rock,
> Above the Rotha, by the forest side.   (ll. 26–31)

The story the poem tells is (like those of 'The Two April Mornings'
and 'The Fountain') one in which the most amicable human
intercourse is marked by incomprehension and distance:

> your heart
> Is slow toward the sympathies of them
> Who look upon the hills with tenderness,
> And make dear friendships with the streams and groves.
>   (ll. 5–8)

> our cordial Friend
> Who in the hey-day of astonishment
> Smil'd in my face ...   (ll. 66–8)

Even the beloved friend to whom it is addressed has not been able, at
that crucial moment, to share the speaker's feelings:

> And when we came in front of that tall rock
> Which looks towards the East, I there stopp'd short,
> And trac'd the lofty barrier with my eye
> From base to summit; such delight I found
> To note in shrub and tree, in stone and flower,
> That intermixture of delicious hues,
> Along so vast a surface, all at once,
> In one impression, by connecting force
> Of their own beauty, imag'd in the heart.
> – When I had gaz'd perhaps two minutes' space,
> Joanna, looking in my eyes, beheld
> That ravishment of mine, and laugh'd aloud.   (ll. 42–53)

However sympathetic, Joanna's laugh registers a felt division
between the two. And the answer she receives is not from the man
she confronts but from the world which surrounds her. Like that
which comes to the Boy of Winander it is an answer which suddenly
reveals the inhuman foreignness of that world:

> The rock, like something starting from a sleep,
> Took up the Lady's voice, and laugh'd again:

> That ancient Woman seated on Helm-crag
> Was ready with her cavern; Hammar-Scar,
> And the tall Steep of Silver-How sent forth
> A noise of laughter; southern Loughrigg heard,
> And Fairfield answer'd with a mountain tone:
> Helvellyn far into the clear blue sky
> Carried the Lady's voice, – old Skiddaw blew
> His speaking trumpet; – back out of the clouds
> Of Glaramara southward came the voice;
> And Kirkstone toss'd it from his misty head.   (ll. 54–65)

The catalogue of familiar names cannot domesticate what is happening: like the earlier poem's 'echoes loud / Redoubled and redoubled', these pass beyond human control. The living voice becomes an 'it', to be tossed from crag to crag, and the feeling is reminiscent of that change from active being to inanimate passivity which was the subject of so many of the Goslar poems. This half-attractive echoing is very different from 'Roll'd round in earth's diurnal course': but the sinister suggestion is there, and it is to this that Joanna seems to respond:

> And, while we both were listening, to my side
> The fair Joanna drew, as if she wish'd
> To shelter from some object of her fear.   (ll. 74–6)

For the first time in the story, uncomprehending confrontation is replaced by a common 'listening' and a drawing together. And it is this remembered moment which seems to have inspired the speaker's solitary naming of the place where it occurred:

> – And hence, long afterwards, when eighteen moons
> Were wasted, as I chanc'd to walk alone
> Beneath this rock, at sun-rise, on a calm
> And silent morning, I sate down, and there,
> In memory of affections old and true,
> I chisel'd out in those rude characters
> Joanna's name upon the living stone.
> And I, and all who dwell by my fire-side
> Have call'd the lovely rock, Joanna's Rock.   (ll. 77–85)

The unease is contained within a domestic framework, the unnerving experience softened to the 'memory of affections old and true'. But it is less a celebration of the living strength of those affections than an attempt to find some way of dealing with that frightening sense of a reality beyond human control which Joanna's laugh unleashed. A lasting name is carved into the rock from which those echoes sprang, a name which has an undisturbing fixity that the living voice did not. But the gesture – made, Priest-like (l. 28), memorializing, in silence and alone – is like that of cutting a tombstone. And the immobility of this name is that of an 'uncouth' (l. 30) hieroglyph, meaningless to those who do not know the story behind it, needing to be interpreted by the speaker who chiselled it there.

The non-human world that is presented in this poem is a good deal more disquieting than its speaker – one of those 'Who look upon the hills with tenderness, / And make dear friendships with the streams and groves' – seems able to admit. It may appear delightful, 'imag'd in the heart' (l. 50), but the human beings who inhabit it have no real control over it; nothing can alter its ultimately threatening otherness. Although it seeks to celebrate the domestic affections, the poem portrays human relationships as areas of difficulty and unintelligibility. The only moment of real closeness is one in which the protagonists draw together against a common 'fear'. The name which would commemorate that moment is an alien intrusion, an eyesore, incomprehensible to all but a few. For a little while it can be explained, as the speaker explains it for the Vicar. But the poem, significantly, does not record his response to this story: it ends not with a continuing conversation, but with a sign whose meaning was fixed in the past, standing like an epitaph: Joanna's Rock. That which was once alive, with all the disturbing ambiguity of life, is here literally petrified.

Despite its affectionate conversational form this poem conveys a deeply pessimistic sense of what can be achieved in and perpetuated by human relationships within a universe indifferent to human purposes. And a similar pessimism shapes the following poem, superficially a poem of love and 'communion':

> There is an Eminence, – of these our hills
> The last that parleys with the setting sun.
> We can behold it from our Orchard-seat,
> And, when at evening we pursue our walk
> Along the public way, this Cliff, so high
> Above us, and so distant in its height,
> Is visible, and often seems to send
> Its own deep quiet to restore our hearts.
> The meteors make of it a favourite haunt:
> The star of Jove, so beautiful and large

THE POEMS OF GRASMERE

In the mid heav'ns, is never half so fair
As when he shines above it. 'Tis in truth
The loneliest place we have among the clouds.
And She who dwells with me, whom I have lov'd
With such communion, that no place on earth
Can ever be a solitude to me,
Hath said, this lonesome Peak shall bear my Name.

Here, the central contrast is between that human intimacy which the two preceding poems sought to affirm, and an inaccessible, voiceless solitude. The first words are a statement of stark, unmediated fact – 'There is an Eminence' – set apart by the punctuation, and dominating what follows. And although the remainder of the opening sentence attempts to domesticate and personify – the bald and singular 'Eminence' becomes merely one of 'these *our* hills', its isolation sentimentalized into a conversation with the sun – the tension remains, and animates the poem. 'We' walk 'Along the public way'; but the Cliff is high and distant, and offers an opaque surface, 'visible' to the senses, yet – like the 'scene' which confronted the Boy of Winander – remote from human meaning. It '*seems* to send / Its own deep quiet to restore our hearts': but the imagery which portrays it is that of unconnectedness and inaccessibility, imagery which makes the attempt to assert some kind of possession seem mildly but absolutely incongruous:

The loneliest place *we have* among the clouds.

And the naming the poem describes thus seems as much an acknowledgement of separation as a celebration of concord. Here it is 'She' who names: and the suggestion of likeness between the speaker and the 'Eminence' she names for him quietly conveys a quite other feeling than that of 'communion'. Even in this closest of relationships he is seen to be distant, inaccessible: the 'solitude' which he says can never be his is nevertheless seen by her. The feeling, a feeling of the difference between a subjectively affirmed 'love' –

Whom *I* have lov'd
With such communion, that no place on earth
Can ever be a solitude *to me* ...

– and that which is 'visible' even to the most intimate other, is less definite, and more poignant, than irony. Once again the poem ends not with a sense of continuing relationship, but in the opaque fixity of a name.

309

This sense of an unbridgeable gulf between human beings is explored very differently in the fourth and most interesting poem of the sequence. Here, the earlier suggestions of distance and incomprehension between people, of a nature that is fundamentally alien and a naming that can neither encapsulate nor perpetuate the experience to which it points, are more disturbingly present. And here, there is a new kind of questioning of the domestic ideal that has hitherto been affirmed. The poem begins with an image of 'privacy':

> A narrow girdle of rough stones and crags,
> A rude and natural causeway, interpos'd
> Between the water and a winding slope
> Of copse and thicket, leaves the eastern shore
> Of Grasmere safe in its own privacy.   (ll. 1–5)

But the causeway is rough, a point of division; and there is a felt incongruity in the description of the friends' activity which follows:

> And there, myself and two beloved Friends,
> One calm September morning, ere the mist
> Had altogether yielded to the sun,
> Saunter'd on this retir'd and difficult way.
> – Ill suits the road with one in haste, but we
> Play'd with our time; and, as we stroll'd along,
> It was our occupation to observe
> Such objects as the waves had toss'd ashore.   (ll. 6–13)

This 'way' along which they saunter is to others a place of difficulty: that light reflection highlights a whole area of unease. For like that of the child in 'Nutting', theirs is an expedition marked by a certain lordliness of feeling: they 'play' with their time, that irredeemable commodity, in a way reminiscent of his gloating 'play' with the flowers. Like his, their attitude towards the world which confronts them is one of dalliance: not, as in the earlier poem, informed by fantasies of possession and despoliation, but nevertheless trivializing, the projection of 'vacancy':

> And in our vacant mood,
> Not seldom did we stop to watch some tuft
> Of dandelion seed or thistle's beard,
> Which, seeming lifeless half, and half impell'd
> By some internal feeling, skimm'd along
> Close to the surface of the lake that lay
> Asleep in a dead calm, ran closely on
> Along the dead calm lake, now here, now there,

> In all its sportive wanderings all the while
> Making report of an invisible breeze
> That was its wings, its chariot, and its horse,
> Its very playmate, and its moving soul.   (ll. 16–27)

The lines, with their echo of 'The Eolian Harp', evoke that doctrine of the 'one life' in nature which had once so fascinated Wordsworth and Coleridge.[3] But here, such speculation, the privilege of the polite, is presented as the idle 'occupation' of an empty hour. And as the poem proceeds the projective intrusiveness of their stance becomes more apparent:

> – And often, trifling with a privilege
> Alike indulg'd to all, we paus'd, one now,
> And now the other, to point out, perchance
> To pluck, some flower or water-weed, too fair
> Either to be divided from the place
> On which it grew, or to be left alone
> To its own beauty. Many such there are,
> Fair ferns and flowers, and chiefly that tall plant
> So stately, of the Queen Osmunda nam'd,
> Plant lovelier in its own retir'd abode
> On Grasmere's beach, than Naid by the side
> Of Grecian brook, or Lady of the Mere
> Sole-sitting by the shores of old Romance.   (ll. 28–40)

As in 'Nutting', fantasy becomes more prominent than reality. And although the fantasy is less explicitly destructive, the feeling, here as there, is one of a privileged and potentially aggressive assumption of superiority to that which they confront. 'Too fair . . . to be left alone / To its own beauty': the distortion of the scene before them into a romantic literary landscape and the act of plucking are clearly but unobtrusively linked.

And the implications of this are made shockingly apparent in the incident which follows. The fanciful observation of the scene before them turns to an equally fanciful observation of the human presences within it:

> – So fared we that sweet morning: from the fields
> Meanwhile, a noise was heard, the busy mirth
> Of Reapers, Men and Women, Boys and Girls.   (ll. 41–3)

The language is that of eighteenth-century pastoral: it is from this perspective, 'Feeding unthinking fancies', that they first see the Man who stands before them:

>   when suddenly,
> Through a thin veil of glittering haze, we saw
> Before us on a point of jutting land
> The tall and upright figure of a Man
> Attir'd in peasant's garb, who stood alone
> Angling beside the margin of the lake.   (ll. 47–52)

Like the landscape, he provokes 'ready comments': comments which, as the lines suggest – 'with one and the same voice / We all cried out' – invoke a set of polite attitudes as stereotyped and intrusive as those which were applied to the natural scene:

>   he must be indeed
> An idle man, who thus could lose a day
> Of the mid harvest, when the labourer's hire
> Is ample, and some little might be stor'd
> Wherewith to chear him in the winter time.   (ll. 56–60)

This man is not one of the industrious and therefore deserving poor.[4] Yet the accusation of idleness rings oddly from this carefully delineated position of idle privilege: a 'privilege' *not* 'Alike indulg'd to all'. And in the lines which follow it is traumatically questioned:

> Thus talking of that Peasant we approach'd
> Close to the spot where with his rod and line
> He stood alone; whereat he turn'd his head
> To greet us – and we saw a man worn down
> By sickness, gaunt and lean, with sunken cheeks
> And wasted limbs, his legs so long and lean
> That for my single self I look'd at them,
> Forgetful of the body they sustain'd. –
> Too weak to labour in the harvest field,
> The man was using his best skill to gain
> A pittance from the dead unfeeling lake
> That knew not of his wants.   (ll. 61–72)

  Even as they approach him the man is held at a distance by the demonstrative 'that'. They merely come 'close': he still stands 'alone'. But the pause after that word marks the dramatic reversal of the poem. Suddenly, their sense of him as a figure in the landscape, an object of speculation, gives way to something entirely different. He is another man, who turns to greet them. His greeting is not recorded: 'we', the reader and the trio who approach him, are still observers. But what we see is quite unlike that earlier view, obscured by mist and clichéd preconceptions. It is an image too direct and particular to be mediated even by pity, the image of a man whose relation to the world is very different from theirs. He stands alone, rather than sauntering companionably: he is not lightly engaged in capricious play, but 'using his best skill' in a struggle for survival. And the natural world to him is not a place into which he can project picturesque meanings, but one of utter 'unfeeling' indifference.

In some ways, this moment is reminiscent of the awkward encounters between privileged and unprivileged presented in the 1798 volume. But the figure of the Man emerging through the mist has a disturbing power which those of the 'Old Man Travelling' and Simon Lee did not. This upright lonely shape is not simply an unfortunate sufferer, but an image which haunts the observer in an unassimilable way. As in a dream, one feature becomes grotesquely, hypnotically prominent, so that he can neither be dealt with as a person nor forgotten as a spectacle:

> his legs so long and lean
> That for my single self I look'd at them,
> Forgetful of the body they sustain'd.

The figure he presents is one which was to appear again and again in the poetry of Wordsworth's greatest years. It is there most impressively in *The Prelude* of 1805: in the description of the discharged soldier in Book IV –

> He was of stature tall,
> A foot above man's common measure tall,
> Stiff in his form, and upright, lank and lean;
> A man more meagre, as it seem'd to me,
> Was never seen abroad by night or day.   (ll. 405–9)

– of the drowned man rising 'bolt upright' with 'ghastly face' from the lake in Book V; of the Blind Beggar with 'upright face' in Book VII:

> And on the shape of the unmoving man,
> His fixed face and sightless eyes, I look'd
> As if admonish'd from another world.   (ll. 620–2)

This recurring image of an arrested upright man has, as Michael Black has pointed out, a peculiarly compelling effect:

The admonishment is not a verbal moral; it is the world outside turning itself once more into a dream-configuration, with its symbols long familiar but still not understood, nor ever likely to be.[5]

And here, in 'Point Rash-Judgment', with its dramatic revelation of social division, this familiar 'dream-configuration' emerges.[6] It seems that the incident recorded here was one which awakened feelings of an irresolvably disturbing kind.

They are feelings which certainly do not seem to be resolved, or even summed up, by the name with which the poem ends: the 'uncouth' moral epithet, 'Point Rash-Judgment'. As in 'Nutting', projective fantasy has been cut short by a traumatic recognition of otherness: like 'Nutting', this poem attempts to turn that recognition into a moral lesson. But this lesson is even more obviously inadequate than that of 'Nutting', for the Man's plight could hardly be alleviated simply by wiser judgment on the part of those who approach him. The difference between their situation and his remains. Indeed, by the end of the poem, he has disappeared. Instead of his disquieting presence, there is a 'memorial name'. And the closing lines dramatize its bestowal in a peculiarly revealing way.

They begin with an explicit turning away from the reader:

> I will not say
> What thoughts immediately were ours, nor how
> The happy idleness of that sweet morn,
> With all its lovely images, was chang'd
> To serious musing and to self-reproach.   (ll. 72–6, my italics)

And this authorial refusal to communicate the 'thoughts' to which the confusing experience has given rise has its counterpart in the process which the poetry depicts. The aggressiveness implicit in the friends' 'unthinking' stance is turned inward: their 'ready comments' rebound upon themselves, in a movement which not only excludes relationship with the Man before them but also with one another. No longer do they speak 'with one and the same voice' (l. 55): they have been shocked out of the common response of cliché. But the images which follow are not those of a more fruitful kind of interaction: they are images of inwardness and self-restraint:

> Nor did we fail to see *within ourselves*
> What need there is to be *reserv'd in speech*
> And *temper all our thoughts* with charity.   (ll. 77–9, my italics)

The exclaiming 'we' becomes a group of separate individuals, each feeling a similar but essentially private guilt:

> My Friend, Myself, and She who then receiv'd
> The same admonishment . . .   (ll. 81–2)

Their original unity-in-superficiality has been shattered by an experience which, though its cause is in each case the 'same', belongs properly to the 'single self' (l. 57).

The experience which leads to the naming of the place seems, then, to be one of a turning away from engagement. It is a retreat into private subjectivity which has been implicit in the poem ever since the first, dramatic confrontation with the Man, for in an important sense that confrontation was not dramatic at all. *His* words were not recorded: *his* sense of those he turned to greet remained unexplored. He appeared simply as a disturbing image, seen first through the mist, and then clearly; first, intrusively, as 'idle', and then, realistically, as destitute. The trio who approached him question themselves because of this silent figure: but they do not conceive of him as an other with whom they might interact. They introspect, and he disappears from the poem. As in 'The Old Cumberland Beggar', Wordsworth presents a set of distinct but similar reactions to one who is less a fellow human being than an opaque symbol: here, as there – 'To each recalling his peculiar boons' – the result is an increased sense of individual separateness. But here, the privileged perspective is itself questioned: the feeling is not one of 'self-congratulation', but of self-reproach. And there is no longer even an ambiguous attempt to portray the dynamics of a real community. There is only a common agreement on the name with which the poem ends: a name which memorializes not the original shocked confrontation with the Man, not even a positive rule of conduct derived from it, but the inward-turning act of self-castigation which followed.

This fourth of the 'Poems on the Naming of Places' points, like the promontory which is named in it, out of the world of social interaction: towards privacy rather than relationship, self-restraint rather than expressiveness. It ends with a 'memorial' to past experience rather than a sense of future possibility. The effect is of a dead end. And if in this it is like the 'Lucy' poems, it is like them also in the basic imaginative configuration which it traces. For the clearing of the mist as the friends approach the Man, their abrupt change from a perspective of 'unthinking' carelessness to one of impotent shocked awareness, is paralleled by that movement from transforming illusion to guilty disillusion which emerged again and again in the poems of the Goslar period. Here the intensity of those earlier lyrics is muted by the domestic setting and the attempt to present the experience in a more easily conversational mode:

'illusion' is not a state of intense desire but the careless playfulness of a privileged group. It is challenged not by the fact of death, but by their encounter with one less privileged. But that encounter, with its familiar imaginative shape, foregrounds the wider social implications of that deep pessimism about human relations which the Goslar lyrics expressed.

Here, as in those lyrics, illusion and reality are absolutely opposed: 'illusion' is associated with guilt, with intrusiveness, with a failure to recognize the otherness of the other. The most spontaneous feelings – here, the 'unthinking fancies' of those who can afford to 'play' with their time – are seen as fundamentally appropriative, instinct with aggression: however frivolous they may seem, this is what at basis they *mean*. Such feelings cannot be creatively actualized: hence, confrontation with difference – a real acknowledgement of that which is other – leads not to interplay, but to paralysis and guilt. The ideal to which the poem 'points' is one of self-control, the denial rather than the actualization of impulse: it finds its ultimate expression in a warning. And, as the poem very clearly reveals, thus contorted back upon itself, feeling cannot engage with the world in such a way as to change it.

Without some experience of creative interaction between desire and the external world, between illusion and reality, there can be no feeling of correspondence between that which is objectively perceived and that which is subjectively conceived of, and hence no effectual sense of actuality.[7] In *Songs of Innocence*, Blake imaged such experience as fundamental to the creative being of a whole society. Here, in this entirely different account of a domestic incident, Wordsworth seems to be articulating the essential hopelessness about social possibility which results from its absence. Where in *Songs of Innocence* there is recognition of and interaction with difference, a fulfilment which points challengingly forward, here there is opposition, confrontation, disillusionment and dead-end. No alternative, non-appropriative impulse, no non-destructive way of actualizing feeling in a shared social world is envisaged: the most that can be hoped for is effective inhibition.

It might, of course, be argued that the particular perspective which the poem dramatizes – that of polite gentlemen sauntering at ease around a countryside where others were close to starvation – permits nothing other than awareness of guilt:[8] and that this poem hardly expresses Wordsworth's most comprehensive views as to what is possible within society. Yet it *is* curiously significant. It is not merely that the imaginative structure of the experience it portrays is strikingly similar to that of the powerful lyrics of the Goslar period, not that its central image of the upright admonitory figure is a characteristic and recurring one in Wordsworth's poetry. For it is, also, the only poem in the 1800 volume of *Lyrical Ballads* in which Wordsworth explicitly engages with that social difference which lay at the heart of his enterprise, the difference between the men of whom he chose to write and the privileged position he shared with his audience. And when one compares it with that Song of *Innocence* in which Blake most directly confronted the same problem (for *Songs of Innocence* no less than *Lyrical Ballads* is a collection of poems written for a polite audience) the guilty distrust of impulse and the retreat into private resolution presented here can be seen to have very far-reaching implications.

Like this poem, Blake's 'Holy Thursday' depicts an occasion of polite play – an attempt to see an ambiguous, even disturbing social reality as harmonious and reassuring. But in that poem, such 'play', however suspect some of its motives, is portrayed as potentially transforming. The presented experience is one in which quotidian reality is gradually informed with transfiguring illusion: it points not away from but towards a shared actuality. The 'obtuse angle' which Blake adopts towards his subject-matter enables the realization of a hitherto unsuspected experiential possibility even within this equivocal 'play': a possibility which is neither escapist nor sentimental, but constitutes its own bitingly immediate questioning of that world in which 'the Subtil make the innocent, Poor'.[9] But the 'play' which Wordsworth presents in 'Point Rash-Judgment' is an idle, self-assertive activity: it obscures rather than transforms reality. And the reality which it obscures is the world of work, of a hopeless struggle against an indifferent nature. The transition from the one to the other is abrupt and shocking: there is no sense that there might be any connection between them. The result is inward-turning, para-lysed self-reproach in face of what seems to be unalterable fact. 'Holy Thursday' ends by urging all toward the active realization of possibility: the warning which is part of its ending leaves no room for passivity. But 'Point Rash-Judgment' commemorates a private admonishment, and it points, as it warns, away from direct engagement. The 'charity' it invokes is not a cherishing of impulse ('Then cherish pity . . . ') but a checking of spontaneity ('And temper all our thoughts with charity'): its end is not action, but the lifeless fixity of a name.

In his later poetry, it is true, Wordsworth was to attempt to explore the sources of positive social feeling in a way which seems very different from this. Yet it is striking that his most extended such attempt, Book VIII of *The Prelude*, entitled 'Love of Nature Leading to Love of Mankind', returns to this problematic area between illusion and reality, and explicitly portrays it as the place within which concepts of human possibility are formed. Here, once again, appears the figure of a man seen through the mist – a figure very different from the starving Peasant of 'Point Rash-Judgment':

> Seeking the raven's nest, and suddenly
> Surpriz'd with vapours, or on rainy days
> When I have angled up the lonely brooks
> Mine eyes have glanced upon him, few steps off,
> In size a giant, walking through the fog,
> His sheep like Greenland bears; at other times
> When round some shady promontory turning,
> His Form hath flash'd upon me, glorified
> By the deep radiance of the setting sun;
> Or him have I descried in distant sky,
> A solitary object and sublime,
> Above all height, like an aerial Cross,
> As it is stationed on some spiry rock
> Of the Chartreuse, for worship. Thus was man
> Ennobled outwardly before mine eyes,
> And thus my heart at first was introduc'd
> To an unconscious love and reverence
> Of human nature; hence the human form
> To me was like an index of delight,
> Of grace and honour, power and worthiness.
>
> (ll. 397–416)

Here, the veil of illusion is seen as enabling a basic hopefulness which without it would be impossible:

> were it otherwise
> And we found evil fast as we find good
> In our first years, or think that it is found,
> How could the innocent heart bear up and live?
>
> (ll. 443–6)

But beneath the apparent optimism lies the same constellation of feelings which the earlier poem had so sharply exposed. The first, illusory sense of the Shepherds is carefully distinguished from the reality:

> Meanwhile, this creature – spiritual almost
> As those of books, but more exalted far,
> Far more of an imaginative form –
> Was not a Corin of the groves, who lives
> For his own fancies, or to dance by the hour
> In coronal, with Phyllis in the midst,
> But, for the purposes of kind, a man
> With the most common – husband, father – learn'd,
> Could teach, admonish, suffered with the rest
> From vice and folly, wretchedness and fear.
> Of this I little saw, car'd less for it,
> But something must have felt.   (ll. 417–28)

The experience of seeing them 'ennobled' and transformed is not a present possibility. Moreover, and crucially, it is a subjective experience: a necessary but past stage in the development of an individual sensibility. These Shepherds are not, like the protagonists of *Songs of Innocence*, 'glorified' by human interaction. As in 'Nutting', where the grove is perceived in its intensest beauty at the moment before it is touched, their transfiguration depends, precisely, upon their being 'remov'd' from its scope:

> But blessed be the God
> Of Nature and of man that this was so,
> That men did at the first present themselves
> Before my untaught eyes thus purified,
> Removed, and at a distance that was fit.   (ll. 436–40)

The feeling is that no good – certainly no good basis for future trust – can come out of actual relationships: a feeling of pessimism not only about human nature (men must be purified to be loved) but about social possibility. The best sense of others that can be achieved is achieved from a distance. It is not the vivid, immediate particularity apprehended by love ('There's little Tom Dacre . . . '), but something analogous to a *sign*:

> hence the human form
> To me was like an index of delight.

'Point Rash-Judgment', with its shock of disillusionment and its private admonition, seems to focus a structure of feeling central to Wordsworth's poetry: a structure of feeling perhaps more pessimistic than he could later explicitly admit. It is not surprising that the next, and last, of the 'Poems on the Naming of Places' should signal a retreat from the disquieting confrontation imaged there. The place it names is not an accusing, pointing promontory, but a place of refuge, free of human presences:

> Our walk was far among the ancient trees:
> There was no road, nor any woodman's path,
> But the thick umbrage, checking the wild growth
> Of weed and sapling, on the soft green turf
> Beneath the branches of itself had made
> A track which brought us to a slip of lawn,
> And a small bed of water in the woods.
> All round this pool both flocks and herds might drink
> On its firm margin, even as from a well
> Or some stone-bason which the Herdsman's hand
> Had shap'd for their refreshment, nor did sun
> Or wind from any quarter ever come
> But as a blessing to this calm recess,
> This glade of water and this one green field.
> The spot was made by Nature for herself:
> The travellers know it not, and 'twill remain
> Unknown to them ...   (ll. 1–17)

That which in the earlier poems was disturbingly other is here reassuringly so. This natural scene has neither the threatening foreignness of that of 'To Joanna' nor the 'dead unfeeling' indifference of that of 'Point Rash-Judgment': it is a self-enclosed, self-sustaining world whose distance from troubling human concerns enables it to be seen as an image of peace and security. And the echo from John of Gaunt's celebration of England in *Richard II* –

> This fortress built by Nature for herself
> Against infection and the hand of war.
>   (Act ii, sr. i, ll. 43–4)

– points suggestively forward to the last of the 'Lucy' poems, written perhaps a year later, but not published until 1807. There, the sharpness of loss is muted by a portrayal of continuing attachment to a mutually beloved place: the 'rocks and stones and trees' of 'A slumber did my spirit seal' are softened into nostalgic, pastoral, and explicitly patriotic images:

> I travell'd among unknown men,
>   In lands beyond the sea;
> Nor, England did I know till then
>   What love I bore to thee.

'Tis past – that melancholy dream!
  Nor will I quit thy shore
A second time; for still I seem
  To love thee more and more.

Among thy mountains did I feel
  The gladness of desire
And she I cherish'd turn'd her wheel
  Beside an English fire.

Thy mornings show'd, thy nights conceal'd,
  The bowers where Lucy play'd;
And thine is too the last green field
  Which Lucy's eyes survey'd.[10]

This is not the non-human world of the Goslar lyrics, whose inexorable processes claimed Lucy as a 'thing'. It is a humanized 'England', with a reassuring permanence which allows it to be the object of a present and growing intensity of feeling – feeling satisfying in a way not envisaged in interpersonal relationships. The sense is of an evasion and a blurring of the painful isolation which those earlier poems confronted. And there is a similar sense in this last of the 'Poems on the Naming of Places'. That nature which the earlier poems of the sequence presented as alien and unreachable has become the familiar, enduring object of a much easier 'love' than is possible between human beings:

And if a man should plant his cottage near,
Should sleep beneath the shelter of its trees,
And blend its waters with his daily meal,
He would so love it ...   (ll. 18–21)

The mortality which the other poems hinted at has been distanced into the hypothetical, to be softened and met by the image of a beloved surviving place:

He would so love it that in his death hour
Its image would survive among his thoughts.   (ll. 21–2)

The five 'Poems on the Naming of Places' do not, like the three 'Lucy' poems published sequentially in this volume, form a significant progression. They are less tightly structured, their preoccupations less sharply defined. Yet the feelings which emerge in them are exactly those which were exposed in the Goslar lyrics – feelings of the impotence or destructiveness of human desire, of the fundamental isolation and separateness of human beings, of the indifference of nature and the prominence of mortality. Where in the Goslar lyrics such feelings were seen as private and incommunicable, here there is an attempt to memorialize them in a series of 'names' which others may use, 'names' which are affixed to a common landscape. But the Advertisement which is prefaced to the five poems reveals something of the pessimism with which that attempt is informed:

By Persons resident in the country and attached to rural objects, many places will be found unnamed or of unknown names, where little Incidents will have occurred, or feelings been experienced, which will have given to such places a private and peculiar interest. From a wish to give some sort of record to such Incidents or renew the gratification of such Feelings, Names have been given to Places by the Author and some of his Friends, and the following Poems written in consequence.

The 'interest' is a 'private and peculiar one', to which only 'some sort of record' can be given. And, as the poems which follow suggest, each of these 'Names' needs to be explained by an account of the experience which led to it: it is a mere 'uncouth' sign of that which was once more fully present. They are thus suggestively different from those 'names' which are pivotal in *Songs of Innocence*. They are fixed and reified – in one case, actually chiselled in rock – rather than changingly operative within human relationships. They point toward that which is past and, fundamentally, unshareable, rather than toward an open-ended and other-directed future. The disclaimers and qualifications with which each act of naming is presented, no less than the intimate conversational tone, indicate that such meaning as they do convey is available only to the sympathetic few: not to the 'all' or the 'you' so uncompromisingly addressed in Blake's Songs. And instead of being mutually created, in a process of interaction, so that different perspectives interpenetrate within them, they are monologic, with a single, ultimately disappearing, meaning.

Something of the significance of these differences can be seen in a passage from *Home at Grasmere*, which Wordsworth seems to have written several years after the publication of *Lyrical Ballads 1800*. Here he argues, apparently much more positively, for the recreative power of the shared memorials which men make of their experience: the image is of a whole valley humanized by the remembered associations of a past and present community:

No, we are not alone; we do not stand,
My Emma, here misplaced and desolate ...
We shall not scatter through the plains and rocks,
Of this fair Vale and o'er its spacious heights
Unprofitable kindliness, bestowed
On Objects unaccustomed to the gifts
Of feeling, that were cheerless and forlorn
But few weeks past, and would be so again
If we were not. We do not tend a lamp
Whose lustre we alone participate ...
Mortal though bright, a dying, dying flame.
Look where we will, some human heart has been
Before us with its offering; not a tree
Sprinkles these little pastures, but the same
Hath furnished matter for a thought, perchance
To some one is as a familiar Friend.
Joy spreads and sorrow spreads; and this whole Vale,
Home of untutored Shepherds as it is,
Swarms with sensation, as with gleams of sunshine,
Shadows or breezes, scents or sounds.
                              (*Home at Grasmere*, MS. B., ll. 646–67)[11]

Such associations are seen, very directly, as providing an answer to that feeling of individual isolation, 'misplaced and desolate' in an indifferent universe, which had been the subject of the Goslar poems. But the poetry, through its repeated denials, clearly registers the suppressed presence of that feeling: of the fear that objects might indeed be 'cheerless and forlorn' 'If we were not', that any sense of the world as humanly meaningful is self-projected illusion, 'dependent upon us alone, / Mortal though bright, a dying, dying flame.' And the sense of community which emerges from this memorializing of individual experience through a shared landscape is as ambiguous as – and revealingly reminiscent of – that to be found in 'The Old Cumberland Beggar':[12]

                         Nor deem
These feelings – though subservient more than ours
To every day's demand for daily bread,
And borrowing more their spirit and their shape
From self-respecting interests – deem them not
Unworthy therefore and unhallowed. No,
They lift the animal being, do themselves
By nature's kind and ever present aid
Refine the selfishness from which they spring,

323

Redeem by love the individual sense
Of anxiousness with which they are combined.
(*Home at Grasmere*, MS. B., ll. 667–77)[13]

The picture is not one of the mutual creation of a shared world, but of separate individuals, basically 'selfish', yet 'refined' and 'redeemed' by a common activity of association, an activity in which they relate not to one another – here, not even to an old scarcely human man – but to 'nature'.

The feelings exposed in this later poem inform the vision of community presented in the two longest poems of *Lyrical Ballads 1800*. Both 'The Brothers' and 'Michael' portray the human implications of a real contemporary social process – the disintegration of such self-sustaining rural communities as those of West Cumberland. Wordsworth, as the letter he sent with a gift of the volume to Charles James Fox suggests, was keenly aware both of this process and of its causes:

the spreading of manufactures through every part of the country ... the heavy taxes upon postage ... workhouses, Houses of Industry, and the invention of Soup-Shops ... the encreasing disproportion between the price of labour and that of the necessaries of life ...[14]

It is an awareness which indicates his distance from what John Berger has called 'the Romantic idealization of Nature':

The inhabitant of the modern metropolis tends to believe that it is always somehow possible to scrape a bare living off the land – unless it is a desert: or a dust bowl. The belief is part of the Romantic idealization of Nature, encouraged by the fact that the city lives off a surplus transported from the countryside and amassed in the city where it suggests the wealth of a cornucopia. The belief is far – in every sense – from the truth. Nature has to be bribed to yield enough. Peasants everywhere know this. Rural poverty means that there is nothing to bribe with. It is not a question of working harder. The further working of the land is withdrawn as a possibility ... Every day [the peasant] hears about the metropolis. The name of the city changes. It is all cities, overlaying one another and becoming a city that exists nowhere but which continually transmits promises ... it is openness that the metropolis represents for him. Within that openness is opportunity. The opportunity to earn a living; to have enough money to act.[15]

Wordsworth's sense of this now global phenomenon is strikingly registered in these two poems. The story of each hinges on the departure of a central character, who must leave the community to repair the family fortunes: in each, a dehumanized world of distant financial transactions brings about the collapse of the family. Yet despite Wordsworth's specific recommendation of the poems to Fox, neither contains anything like the direct political appeal to be found in 'The Old Cumberland Beggar': there is no suggestion that even if these 'unletter'd villagers' cannot prevent the forces which threaten their way of life, the 'Statesmen' who formulate social policy might. Instead, in each case, the poetic structure is backward-looking and elegiac. And the problem of the relation between the polite narrator and the rustics whose story is told – that problem so disconcertingly confronted in 'Point Rash-Judgment' – is not considered at all.

Yet the feeling is less of a turning away from than of a focussing upon the imaginative tensions that the 'Poems on the Naming of Places' reveal. As in those poems, in each of these a central image is that of a sign – in 'The Brothers' a stoneless grave, in 'Michael' a 'straggling heap of unhewn stones': a sign whose meaning is explained by the narration of the story which lies behind it. And here, as there, but much more prominently, there is a sense of the failure of the actual human relationships which are presented. The Priest does not recognize the man to whom he speaks: Luke never returns from the city to redeem his father's hopes. Such failures are symptomatic of that disintegration of community which Wordsworth was concerned to expose. But the power of the presentation is not merely that of realism. For each of these poems charts the implications of that deep-rooted constellation of feelings about man and nature and human life, about individual and social possibility, which has been emerging, sometimes sharply, sometimes confusedly, in Wordsworth's other poetry of these years.

Indeed, 'The Brothers' directly echoes one of the Goslar lyrics:

> He had found
> Another grave, near which a full half hour
> He had remain'd ...
> (ll. 82–4)

But here, the moment is contained within an explanatory narrative framework. Leonard, the central character, has returned to the valley which was his home after an absence of many years: this, he suspects, is his brother's grave. Here, the baffled silence of 'There was a Boy' is broken by another's voice: that of the Priest, with his tales of communal affection and memory. And Leonard's anxious reading of the enigmatic face of the landscape –

Towards the church-yard he had turn'd aside,
That, as he knew in what particular spot
His family were laid, he thence might learn
If still his Brother liv'd, or to the file
Another grave was added. – He had found
Another grave, near which a full half hour
He had remain'd, but, as he gaz'd, there grew
Such a confusion in his memory,
That he began to doubt, and he had hopes
That he had seen this heap of turf before,
That it was not another grave, but one
He had forgotten. He had lost his path,
As up the vale he came that afternoon,
Through fields which once had been well known to him.
And Oh! what joy the recollection now
Sent to his heart! he lifted up his eyes,
And looking round he thought that he perceiv'd
Strange alteration wrought on every side
Among the woods and fields, and that the rocks,
And the eternal hills, themselves were chang'd.   (ll. 78–97)

– is succeeded by the Priest's quite different sense of a world animated and made meaningful by shared associations, of a community in which

We have no need of names and epitaphs,
We talk about the dead by our firesides.   (ll. 179–80)

The starkness of the Goslar lyrics is countered, then, by an affirmation of the enduring continuity of human affections. But the poem begins, ironically, with irascibility and 'rash-judgment':

These Tourists, Heaven preserve us! needs must live
A profitable life: some glance along,
Rapid and gay, as if the earth were air,
And they were butterflies to wheel about
Long as their summer lasted; some, as wise,
Upon the forehead of a jutting crag
Sit perch'd with book and pencil on their knee,
And look and scribble, scribble on and look,
Until a man might travel twelve stout miles,
Or reap an acre of his neighbour's corn.

But, for that moping son of Idleness
Why can he tarry *yonder*? – In our church-yard
Is neither epitaph nor monument ...   (ll. 1–14)

And the quiet suspense of the conversation which follows depends upon the Priest's non-recognition of Leonard: a non-recognition which provides a constant, disquieting counterpoint to his confident picture of communal memory and concern. Leonard's poignantly ironic remark –

> Your dalesmen, then, do in each other's thoughts
> Possess a kind of second life ...   (ll. 185–6)

– exactly expresses the feeling which informs the whole. For the story the Priest goes on to tell is one of a 'second life' which was merely 'a kind of' life – that 'second life' which the dalesman offered the child James after his brother's departure, and which ended, seemingly inevitably, with his death. In losing his original home he is shown to have suffered a loss which the community could not repair: the 'twenty homes' which he was given could not replace the lost original one:

> He was the child of all the dale – he liv'd
> Three months with one, and six months with another:
> And wanted neither food, nor clothes, nor love,
> And many, many happy days were his.
> But, whether blithe or sad, 'tis my belief
> His absent Brother still was at his heart.
> And, when he liv'd beneath our roof, we found
> (A practice till this time unknown to him)
> That often, rising from his bed at night,
> He in his sleep would walk about, and sleeping
> He sought his Brother Leonard   (ll. 353–63)

The story of his eventual death provides a powerful image of the inadequacy of such communal bonds to sustain a basic hopefulness. Similarly, Leonard's retreat from the 'home' to which he had returned is impelled by his realization that the kind of recognition or even love which he might now find there could not answer to those 'cherish'd hopes' (l. 436) with which he came. Like Matthew, he turns away from such consolation: the poem ends with an image of his inscrutable figure, forever now inexpressive of his inner being. He has become a stranger on the earth:

> This done, he went on shipboard, and is now
> A Seaman, a grey headed Mariner.

'Michael', too, depicts an absolute loss, which the sympathy of the community is powerless to redeem. But here, the portrayal is not simply elegiac: it is complicated by a more persistent emphasis on human hope and endeavour. The central image is not that of a grave, but of a Sheep-fold, the product of hopeful, life-sustaining toil. It is an image very different from any of the other images of human labour in the two collections of *Lyrical Ballads*: not, like those of 'Simon Lee' and 'Point Rash-Judgment', one of futile struggle against nature, but one of a building that was inspired by love: an image not of chopping down, but of lifting up. And here, more than in any other poem of the volume, the possibility of a creative potency in human affections, of some sort of redemption from the inexorable processes of time and change, is hauntingly entertained:

> from the Boy there came
> Feelings and emanations, things which were
> Light to the sun and music to the wind;
> And that the Old Man's heart seemed born again.
> Thus in his Father's sight the Boy grew up:
> And now when he had reached his eighteenth year,
> He was his comfort and his daily hope.   (ll. 210–16)

Yet the story the poem tells is one of hopes thwarted, of labour unfinished, of love which exposes to almost unendurable pain. Luke does not return from the city; Michael cannot complete the building of the Sheep-fold; the trust of which it was the symbol is broken. And there is a strong poetic suggestion that such failure is inevitable. For this tale of affection and aspiration is introduced by images of solitude and ruin:

> such
> As journey thither find themselves alone
> With a few sheep, with rocks and stones, and kites
> That overhead are sailing in the sky.
>
> It is in truth an utter solitude,
> Nor should I have made mention of this Dell
> But for one object which you might pass by,
> Might see and notice not. Beside the brook
> There is a straggling heap of unhewn stones!   (ll. 9–17)

The child who brings 'hope with it, and forward-looking thoughts' is seen as necessarily doomed to disappoint:

> Or that a child, more than all other gifts,
> Brings hope with it, and forward-looking thoughts,
> And stirrings of inquietude, when they
> By tendency of nature *needs must fail*.   (ll. 154–7, my italics)

After a long scene of farewell and mutual promises, that human act on which the story turns – Luke's defection in the city – is presented in the rapid space of five lines, lines in which he is seen less as an agent than as the victim of a process beyond his control:

> Meantime Luke began
> To slacken in his duty, and at length
> He in the dissolute city gave himself
> To evil courses: ignominy and shame
> Fell on him, so that he was driven at last
> To seek a hiding-place beyond the sea.   (ll. 451–6)

Even the love which is symbolized in the Sheep-fold has no 'strength' beyond that of 'comfort': it provides a way of bearing the inevitable, not of changing it:

> There is a comfort in the strength of love;
> 'Twill make a thing endurable, which else
> Would break the heart ...   (ll. 457–9)

The feeling is one which Wordsworth was to express directly, again through the image of a child, in *The Prelude* of 1805:

> But I behold
> The lovely boy as I beheld him then,
> Among the wretched and the falsely gay,
> Like one of those who walk'd with hair unsinged
> Amid the fiery furnace. He hath since
> Appear'd to me ofttimes as if embalmed
> By Nature – through some special privilege
> Stopp'd at the growth he had – destined to live,
> To be, to have been, come and go, a child
> And nothing more, no partner in the years
> That bear us forward to distress and guilt,
> Pain and abasement; beauty in such excess
> Adorned him in that miserable place.
> (Book VII, ll. 394–406)

Here, as in 'Michael', where Luke's departure from his home leads inexorably to his ruin, a feeling about the city is covertly generalized to include all human possibility: 'the years / That bear *us* forward to distress and guilt ... '. This is the necessary end of maturity: human life is seen less as action and choice than as an unwilled progression to this end. The best 'privilege' is neither to grow nor to change: to be, as this child seems, 'embalmed by Nature'. And similarly, in 'Michael', hope itself is less a hope for new and unknown possibilities than for something very close to stasis:

– Even to the utmost have I been to thee
A kind and a good Father: and herein
I but repay a gift which I myself
Receiv'd at others hands, for, though now old
Beyond the common life of man, I still
Remember them who lov'd me in my youth.
Both of them sleep together: here they liv'd
As all their Forefathers had done, and when
At length their time was come, they were not loth
To give their bodies to the family mold.
I wish'd that thou should'st live the life they liv'd.

(ll. 371–81)

This essentially conservative hope finds its expression in an 'emblem' which is a memorial to the past: an 'anchor' and a 'shield' against a world in which 'fear' and 'temptation' are most prominent:

When thou art gone away, should evil men
Be thy companions, let this Sheep-fold be
Thy anchor and thy shield; amid all fear
And all temptation, let it be to thee
An emblem of the life thy Fathers liv'd.   (ll. 416–20)

It is an inert material object rather than an active energy. And in the end the trust for which it stands is powerless against those dimly realized and impersonally presented forces which threaten it.

Yet the Sheep-fold which Michael began to build remains. Here, as in the other poems of 1800, Wordsworth's interest is not merely in loss, in the ultimate impotence of human affections and aspirations, but in 'what remains behind': and here 'what remains behind' is a laboriously created sign of exactly those affections and aspirations. Like the 'names' of the 'Poems on the Naming of Places', this 'straggling heap of unhewn stones' can be given significance by a reconstruction of the story which attaches to it:

And to that place a story appertains,
Which, though it be ungarnish'd with events,
Is not unfit, I deem, for the fire-side,
Or for the summer shade.   (ll. 18–21)

It is part of a whole world of communal report and memory which the dalesmen have made for themselves:

When Michael telling o'er his years began
To deem that he was old, *in Shepherd's phrase*,
With one foot in the grave.   (ll. 90–2)

> I may truly say,
> That they were *as a proverb* in the vale
> For endless industry. (ll. 95–7)

> I of this Lamp
> Speak thus minutely: for there are no few
> Whose memories will bear witness to my tale.
> The Light was famous in its neighbourhood,
> And was *a public Symbol* of the life,
> The thrifty Pair had liv'd. For, as it chanc'd
> Their cottage on a plot of rising ground
> Stood single, with large prospect North and South,
> High into Easedale, up to Dunmal-Raise.
> And Westward to the village near the Lake.
> And from this constant light so regular
> And so far seen, the House itself by all
> Who dwelt within the limits of the vale,
> Both old and young, was *nam'd* The Evening Star. (ll. 133–46)

> Thence in our rustic dialect was call'd
> The CLIPPING TREE, a *name* which yet it bears. (ll. 178–9)

> And Isabel sate silent, for her mind
> Was busy, *looking back into past times,*
> There's Richard Batemen, thought she to herself,
> He was a parish-boy ... (ll. 266–9)

> and *'tis believ'd by all*
> That many and many a day he thither went,
> And never lifted up a single stone. (ll. 473–5)

> [my italics]

Yet the community thus evoked is less one of present interaction than of 'proverbs' and 'phrases', 'names' and 'symbols', which are the records of past experience. And even the easy, conversational opening awakens doubt as to the potential future audience for this 'Tale':

> although it be a history
> Homely and rude, I will relate the same
> For the delight of a few natural hearts,
> And with yet fonder feeling, for the sake
> Of youthful Poets, who among these Hills
> Will be my second self when I am gone. (ll. 34–9)

The story it introduces is one in which the hope of a 'second self' is disappointed, in which 'forward-looking thoughts' all fail. What survives is backward-looking: a sign whose meaning, like that of those others which the community share, depends on the continuing presence of those who can interpret it, a sign whose impotence to shape the future is the subject of the 'history' which follows. And it is a sign which, unlike the names of the 'Poems on the Naming of Places', or even the grave of 'The Brothers', presents a compelling image of present disintegration: 'There is a straggling heap of *unhewn* stones!'

Much more movingly than those names or that grave, the Sheep-fold stands as a symbol of the human effort to preserve and memorialize hopes and affections in significant form. Unlike those other memorials, it is a product of long and hopeful toil, toil which eventually falters as hope disappears. Here, as in the other poems of 1800, the human relations that are commemorated fail: but here that failure is seen more sharply and directly – not as incomprehension or departure, but as the breaking of a trust. And here there is a much more poignant and disquieting sense, not merely of the precariousness and ineffectiveness of the sign that is created, but also of the distance between this 'emblem' which others may see and the 'real and substantial action and suffering'[16] for which it stands. For here, as in the 'Matthew' poems, Wordsworth stresses the gulf between individual subjectivity and that self which can be known by others:

> Next morning, as had been resolv'd, the Boy
> Began his journey, and *when he had reach'd*
> *The public Way, he put on a bold face.*   (ll. 434–6; my italics)

It is across this gulf that Michael's sufferings are seen. The lines which come closest to describing his feelings about Luke's defection are curiously revealing:

> There is a comfort in the strength of love;
> 'Twill make a thing endurable, which else
> Would break the heart.   (ll. 457–9)

Instead of an account of particular emotion (is the 'love' here referred to Michael's love for the lost Luke, or his earlier love for the landscape in which he works – or that 'pity' with which his neighbours regard him?), the reader is offered a general reflection, a reflection less reassuring than it surface meaning might suggest. ''Twill make a thing endurable' conveys not so much the sense of suffering softened and made bearable as of suffering hardened into a permanent mould: made into a 'thing', which others may see, a 'thing' very different from those actual feelings which 'break the heart'. Immediately after these lines the poem distances itself from Michael:

> Old Michael found it so.
> I have conversed with more than one who well
> Remember the Old Man, and what he was
> Years after he had heard this heavy news.   (ll. 459–62)

The attempt to record his feelings gives way to a more external description, which draws its authority from the shared memories of the community:

> His bodily frame had been from youth to age
> Of an unusual strength. Among the rocks
> He went, and still look'd up upon the sun,
> And listen'd to the wind; and as before
> Perform'd all kinds of labour for his Sheep,
> And for the land his small inheritance.
> And to that hollow Dell from time to time
> Did he repair, to build the Fold of which
> His flock had need. 'Tis not forgotten yet
> The pity which was then in every heart
> For the Old Man – and 'tis believ'd by all
> That many and many a day he thither went,
> And never lifted up a single stone.   (ll. 463–75)

Yet the feeling is not one of community, but of impenetrable isolation. Michael is no longer a subject, but the object of others' consciousness: like Matthew, like Leonard, the 'grey headed Mariner', he has changed from a loving, feeling, speaking individual into an enigmatic figure whose inner life can never be known.

Michael's remembered actions become public indications of feelings which remain unexpressed and unanswered. And the distance thus marked is imaged, very exactly, in that distance which the poem emphasizes, between actual human emotion and the sign which is its memorial. It is a distance which widens as the ability to reconstruct the meaning of that sign is lost over time. The last paragraph of the poem is a catalogue of disappearances. One after another those things which focussed the communal memory have changed or gone: the traces which 'may' still be seen are tenuous:

Three years, or little more, did Isabel,
Survive her Husband, : at her death the estate
Was sold, and went into a Stranger's hand.
The Cottage which was nam'd The Evening Star
Is gone, the ploughshare has been through the ground
On which it stood; great changes have been wrought
In all the neighbourhood, yet the Oak is left
That grew beside their Door; and the remains
Of the unfinished Sheep-fold may be seen
Beside the boisterous brook of Green-head Gill.   (ll. 482–91)

The series of passive verbs suggests a process removed from any identifiable human agency, a process which can neither be controlled nor resisted. It is a process of gradual collapse, not merely of the community – as the Stranger replaces those who were 'known', as the signs which bore shared meanings disappear – but of all human struggle in face of encroaching unmeaningness. The poem ends with 'rocks and stones and trees': not the anonymous 'rocks and stones and trees' of the Goslar lyric, but those which bear the marks of ineffective human effort – the 'remains' of an *unfinished* Sheep-fold', which are simply 'a straggling heap of *unhewn* stones', a particular tree which once grew beside a now-vanished 'Door'. The signs of human presence have not quite gone. Still, these remains 'may be seen' by the discerning eye: the brook still bears its name. The bleakness of that earlier lyric is countered by an ambiguous affirmation of continuing human meaning. But such meaning depends less on present or future creativity than on the ability to descry these fast-disappearing symbols of the past. And the human history to which they point is one of tragic defeat.

Wordsworth's own view of this poem, and of its companion poem 'The Brothers' was more optimistic than this. He seems to have seen them less as portraying doomed hopes and futile struggle than as offering a picture of an actually existing, though threatened, community – one which might provide a model of positive social possibility. Yet his description of their subject-matter is revealing:

I have attempted to draw a picture of the domestic affections as I know they exist amongst a class of men who are now almost confined to the North of England. They are small independent *proprietors* of land here called statesmen, men of respectable education who daily labour on their own little properties ... Their little tract of land serves as a kind of permanent rallying point for their domestic feelings, as a tablet upon which they are written which makes them objects of memory in a thousand instances when they would otherwise be forgotten. It is a fountain fitted to the heart of social man, from which supplies of affection, as pure as his heart was intended for, are daily drawn.[17]

Just as in the 'Poems on the Naming of Places', features of the inanimate landscape are appropriated and named, so that they become 'a kind of permanent rallying point for ... domestic feelings', so here the system of peasant proprietorship is seen as a means of preserving and maintaining such feelings throughout a whole society. And here, as there, there is a striking lack of confidence in the enduring or creative power of these 'affections'. It is not merely that Wordsworth suggests that without such a 'rallying point' as is represented by the ownership of land 'in a thousand instances... they would otherwise be forgotten'. Even their survival is ambiguously seen. They may live on merely as 'objects of memory' or – in a curious shift of metaphor – as 'supplies': preserved deposits from the past, rather than that which animates continuing human relationships.

The feelings expressed here inform both poems. They *do* seek to celebrate 'the domestic affections': in both, the lasting intensity of familial love is movingly depicted. Yet such love is seen as having no creative power, as leading merely to isolation and loss. It does not connect the individual to the wider society, but actually cuts him off from it. James cannot find a second 'home' after Leonard's departure, and finally dies: to Leonard,

> This vale, where he had been so happy, seem'd
> A place in which he could not bear to live.   (ll. 439–40)

Michael, though seen by all, is alone at the Sheep-fold. In each case, that which the community is able to offer merely emphasizes the distance between what is subjectively felt and that which others can 'know'. Yet it is this external knowledge – rather than an interaction which might engage the deepest feelings – which is seen as binding the community together:

> We talk about the dead by our fire-sides.
> ('The Brothers', l. 180)

The process is conservative rather than creative: a means of keeping alive that which would otherwise be lost. To the unknowing stranger, the landscape, which 'like a book preserves the memory' of past experience for the dalesmen, has no such human meaning;[18] the unmarked grave is a mere 'heap of turf'; the Sheep-fold a 'straggling heap of unhewn stones'. Leonard and Michael are simply a 'grey headed Mariner', and an old man going about his daily work. The community is defined by its common understanding of what would otherwise be unintelligible: by that mutual knowledge of past human actions which gives a shared significance to inanimate objects, by that remembrance of individual life histories which enables such opaque figures as those of these central characters to be seen as moving indications of the strength of 'domestic affections'.

And hence the only real community which Wordsworth envisages is that of the small group to whom such knowledge is possible. Social bonds cannot be sustained in the city, for the city is an anonymous confluence of mutual strangers. In 'Michael', this feeling is summed up simply in an adjective – 'the dissolute city' (l. 453): in the London book of *The Prelude* of 1805 he was to explore it more directly:

> how men lived
> Even next-door neighbours, as we say, yet still
> Strangers, and knowing not each other's names.
> (Book VII, ll. 119–21)

Without such knowledge, the social world is a place of lifeless signs, of surfaces whose meaning cannot be revealed: 'Face after face – the string of dazzling wares' (l. 173); 'Shop after shop, with symbols, blazoned names' (l. 174); 'fronts of houses, like a title-page / With letters huge inscribed from top to toe' (ll. 177–8); 'Advertisements of giant size, from high / Press forward in all colours on the sight' (ll. 210–1); 'every character of form and face' (l. 238); 'all the strife of singularity – / Lies to the ear, and lies to every sense – / Of these and of the living shapes they wear / There is no end' (ll. 574–7); until, particularly:

> How often in the overflowing streets
> Have I gone forwards with the crowd, and said
> Unto myself, 'The face of every one
> That passes by me is a mystery.'
> Thus have I looked, nor ceased to look, oppressed
> By thoughts of what, and whither, when and how,
> Until the shapes before my eyes became
> A second-sight procession, such as glides
> Over still mountains, or appears in dreams,
> And all the ballast of familiar life –
> The present, and the past, hope, fear, all stays,
> All laws of acting, thinking, speaking man –

Went from me, neither knowing me, nor known.
And once, far travelled in such mood, beyond
The reach of common indications, lost
Amid the moving pageant, 'twas my chance
Abruptly to be smitten with the view
Of a blind beggar, who, with upright face,
Stood propped against a wall, upon his chest
Wearing a written paper, to explain
The story of the man, and who he was.   (ll. 595–615)

The beggar is a 'spectacle' (l. 616) to be regarded rather than a man
to be engaged with: the confrontation leads, as in 'Point Rash-
Judgment', simply to a private moral 'admonishment'. His 'written
paper' is an image of that which can be 'known' of others, a 'story'
quite different from the actual, unknown, 'acting, thinking, speaking man'.

But the feeling is not simply one about the city as opposed to the
country: it is a feeling about the very nature of social bonds. If
Wordsworth's depiction of the signs of the city offers a disturbing
sense of the distance between what is actually felt and suffered and its
public 'indications', that sense can be traced, just as surely, in these
earlier poems of Grasmere. The beggar's untold 'story' has its
equivalent in the stories of Leonard and of Michael: his 'unmoving'
shape, visible and isolated, is paralleled by their known yet
impassive figures. In both country and city the social process is
portrayed less as one in which men relate to one another than as one
of the reading of signs – in the city, isolated bafflement before a
bewildering conglomeration of hieroglyphs; in the country, mutual
decipherment of those whose history is known. It is a process in
which men themselves become signs to others. 'Real and substantial'
feeling is subjective and unactualizable: others are not partners in
interaction but objects of consciousness.

These poems of Grasmere very sharply focus the difference
between Wordsworth's vision of human possibility and that of
Blake. Both present the deepest affections as essential to any
continuing hope. But where Blake portrays those affections as they
are realized and answered in reciprocal human relationships,
Wordsworth sees them always as essentially subjective, and from a
perspective of loss. The world of *Songs of Innocence* is an 'ecchoing'
interpersonal one, but these poems depict isolated individuals,
known to others only by their histories. Like such *Songs of Innocence*
as 'The Divine Image' and 'The Ecchoing Green', they explore the

ways in which the values of a community might – or might not – be transmitted from generation to generation. But where Blake's *Songs* present experiences which actualize and perpetuate a 'divine image' of immanent human possibility, here the inheritance is a material one: land, which serves as a shared 'record' of vanished 'affections'. For Blake, the creative life of the community depends on a continuing process of interaction, in which trust is answered and otherness recognized, a process which is not confined to a small known group, but potentially includes all of humanity, and points forward into an open-ended future. But for Wordsworth, communal feeling is commemorative, restricted to those who can 'know' one another, and essentially backward-looking: the central image is not the dynamic creativity of play, but the reified sign of past presence. Indeed, 'The Brothers' and 'Michael' directly question that affirmation which is the subject of such poems as the Innocent 'Nurse's Song' and 'The Ecchoing Green' – that those who come after may replace and reanimate the 'joys and desires' of those who went before. In Wordsworth's imaginative universe there can be no 'second self', no living replacement of that which has gone. Human life is singular and ends finally in ruin. And thus, while 'The Divine Image' closes with an urgent injunction to 'all', an injunction which points to a space of human freedom –

> And all must love the human form,
> In heathen, turk or jew.
> Where Mercy Love and Pity dwell
> There God is dwelling too.

– 'Michael', the final poem of *Lyrical Ballads 1800*, closes with a passive verb which addresses nobody in particular, and with an image of unfinished labour and encroaching nature – the relics of a past meaningful only to the disappearing few:

> and the remains
> Of the unfinished Sheep-fold may be seen
> Beside the boisterous brook of Green-head Gill.

Conclusion

Blake's *Songs of Innocence and of Experience* and Wordsworth's *Lyrical Ballads* cannot, without great over-simplification, be assimilated to a common 'Romanticism'. There are, of course, significant similarities between the two collections. Each was published within a commercially successful minor literary genre: each challenges the expectations shaped by that genre, and thus, implicitly, some of the most fundamental and pervasive assumptions of the dominant culture of late eighteenth-century England. Each explores areas of experience – childhood, the lives of the unprivileged, the imagination – which that culture had devalued or ignored, and stresses their central importance to any vision of human possibility. And each makes a deeply serious claim for poetry as a dynamic and recreative mode of knowledge:

> Every child may joy to hear.[1]

> Hear the voice of the Bard!
> Who Present, Past, & Future sees...[2]

> Aristotle, I have been told, has said, that Poetry is the most philosophical of all writing: it is so: its object is truth, not individual and local, but general and operative; not standing upon external testimony, but carried alive into the heart by passion; truth which is its own testimony, which gives competence and confidence to the tribunal to which it appeals, and receives them from the same tribunal.[3]

In all these ways, both Blake and Wordsworth can be seen as affirming fundamental human values – the importance of the primary affections, the power of the imagination – against the deformations of an exploiting social system: as the first voices in what has been called 'the long Romantic critique of industrial capitalism'.[4] Yet the differences I have been tracing between the two collections are so striking and so absolute as to suggest that such a general account of their subject-matter smoothes out what is most distinctive and challenging about each, that which might question and reshape our thinking about fundamental human values, about social possibility, and about the ways in which men and women might or might not make their own destinies. Resistance to dominant social forms and affirmation of alternative ways of feeling may, it seems, be of very different kinds and lead in very different directions.

The poems of *Lyrical Ballads* offer not so much answers to the questions which confront those who try to think creatively about human possibility today as a revealing articulation of a particular way of confronting them. In many ways, Wordsworth, the Cambridge-educated radical, deeply disillusioned with the course he had seen the French Revolution taking, guiltily aware of the manifest inequalities within his society, wishing at once to transcend its complacently paternalistic attitudes and to affirm a 'common humanity' with those from whom he was separated by privilege, may be seen as a prototype of a certain kind of modern left-wing intellectual. *Lyrical Ballads 1798*, with its awkwardnesses and uncertainties of tone, its sometimes contradictory stances, more directly than any other of his published works reveals the difficulties he faced in finding a position from which to write at all. These are difficulties which, as we have seen, the 1800 edition in one way appears to evade: it contains almost nothing, apart from 'Point Rash-Judgment', to match that embarrassed confrontation of social division which disrupts the earlier volume. Yet this apparent evasion seems to have enabled an unparalleled poetic exploration of the logic of that isolated individualism which is implicit in the poems of 1798. Poem after poem in *Lyrical Ballads 1800* suggests that the most significant experience is essentially private and non-communicable. None of the poems portray satisfying relations between people: though there is some attempt to celebrate the domestic affections, those which dramatize interaction emphasize distance and division. Isolation and separateness are seen as the human condition. The deepest passions are never, here, creatively realized: indeed, the intimation is that by their very nature they are destructive. The constellation of feelings, set out thus, is perhaps familiar:[5] the interconnections between them and the experiential force of them are not.

Yet to read these poems from the perspective provided by *Songs of Innocence and of Experience* is to see that the vision they present is based on a number of dichotomies which have no place in Blake's imaginative universe. So interlocking are these that it is difficult to say which is primary: each seems to presuppose the others. In *Lyrical Ballads*, subjective feeling and objective reality are permanently opposed: desire is 'corrected'[6] by recognition of that which is before

CONCLUSION

it, rather than realized in interaction with it. Individual subjectivity confronts a world which is unchangeably other, both in its human and non-human aspects. Where in *Songs of Innocence* 'the eagerness of infantine desire'[7] is actualized and answered in a way which creates new and changing possibilities, in *Lyrical Ballads* it must give way to a maturity which involves recognition of an immutable reality. Other men are not partners in interaction: rather, they are objects of knowledge. Similarly, the world of nature is the objective world of the Newtonian universe: a world alien to human purposes, and very different from the animated nature of *Songs of Innocence*. The ultimate biological fact is the fact of individual death: not, as in *Songs of Innocence*, the creative cycle of sexuality, reproduction and nurture. The public self is at a distance from the private: there is a similar distance between the sign and that which it signifies. There is certainly nothing like Blake's sense that expression and communication might be one: that the shaping and objectifying and answering of feeling might create a shared world within which 'names' might be plastic and operative rather than reified and abstracted.

And these oppositions are focussed in that opposition between the personal and the social which may be traced in both volumes of *Lyrical Ballads*. It is an opposition which is in one way an affirmation: an insistence on the fundamental importance of that edge of unique individual experience unshaped by the (to Wordsworth, inevitably deadening) conventions of the culture. But it is an opposition which leads not towards a sense that 'all' must play their part in the creation of a potentially limitless human world ('The Divine Image'), but towards a valuing of the small known community: a community composed of individuals familiar with one another's private histories, rather than of those whose identity is shaped in continuing interaction. The larger society seems to be a threat to such community, a place in which real human sympathies cannot survive. Such a feeling – as the London book of *The Prelude* was later, more extensively, to suggest – has close affinities with the polite eighteenth-century fear of the 'mob': it is one which contrasts strikingly with that vision presented by Blake in the Innocent 'Holy Thursday': 'The hum of multitudes was there, but multitudes of lambs.' And it is a feeling which points away from any kind of creative future as surely as Blake's poem points toward it. For the basis of the society depicted in *Lyrical Ballads* is not, as in *Songs of Innocence*, a forward-pointing vital interplay: it is a common recognition of signs which point backward to a now-vanished past –

341

not that which men create, but that which they know. The pattern is not one of change and possibility, but of seemingly necessary decay. One after another, these poems end blankly on images of loss and diminution: finally, on a heap of stones.

Many of the conceptions I have been tracing in *Lyrical Ballads* – the abstraction of the isolated individual, the tragic materialism, the suspicion of human impulse, the opposition between reality and desire – are familiar enough to us today. The sharpness and clarity with which their implications are realized and followed through to their sterile dead end throw the presuppositions of much contemporary thinking into critical relief. Taken together, the poems form a vision which, for all its attempt to affirm the integrity of all men, is deeply pessimistic as to human possibility. It is a vision which bleakly questions any attempt to find in Wordsworth the inspiration for a contemporary political *praxis*.

For, as *Lyrical Ballads* clearly demonstrates, without some sense of how human beings might relate creatively to one another, any aspiration toward a society in which the needs and desires of all might be acknowledged can end only in defeat. What such a sense might be, where it might come from, how it might relate to the dominant modes of perception and relationship of an alienating society – these are questions crucial to any radical perspective today.[8] And they are therefore questions with which several of the most interesting of contemporary thinkers about possibilities for creative social change in Britian have sought to engage. Thus Raymond Williams:

we live in a world in which the dominant mode of production and social relationships teaches, impresses, offers to make normal and even rigid, modes of detached, separated, external perception and action: modes of using and consuming rather than accepting and enjoying people and things. The structure of feeling of the [childhood] memoirs is then significant and indispensable as a response to this specific social deformation ... It is not so much the old village or the old backstreet that is significant. It is the perception and affirmation of a world in which one is not necessarily a stranger and an agent, but can be a member, a discoverer, in a shared source of life. Taken alone, of course, this is never enough. Indeed, its displacement to fantasies about old villages and old backstreets can diminish even its immediate significance. To make an adult, working world of that kind would involve sharp critical consciousness and long active agency. Yet we can see here, in a central example, the true aetiology of some of the powerful images of country and city, when unalienated experience is the rural past and realistic experience is the urban future ... For we have really to look, in country and city alike, at the real social processes of alienation, separation, externality, abstraction. And we have to do this not only critically, in the necessary history of rural and urban capitalism, but substantially, by affirming the experiences which in many millions of lives are discovered and rediscovered, very often under pressure: experiences of directness, connection, mutuality, sharing, which alone can define, in the end, what the real deformation may be.

(*The Country and the City*, London, 1971, p. 298)

If you base your work, as I do, on the indissoluble unity of individual and social experience, then you do have a problem explaining in non-metaphysical terms those acts and responses which are not, so to say, prepared by social circumstances or relations as we can ordinarily assess them. My present position, which I develop in *Marxism and Literature*, is that however dominant a social system may be, the very meaning of its domination involves a limitation or selection of the activities it covers, so that by definition it cannot exhaust all social experience, which therefore always potentially contains space for alternative acts and alternative intentions which are not yet articulated as a social institution or even project.

(*Politics and Letters*, London, 1979, p. 252)

Thus, Edward Thompson, writing of William Morris:

His intention was to embody in the forms of fantasy alternative values sketched in an alternative way of life... And in such an adventure two things happen: our habitual values (the 'commonsense' of bourgeois society) are thrown into disarray. And we enter into Utopia's proper and new-found space: *the education of desire*. This is not the same as 'a moral education' towards a given end: it is, rather, to open a way to aspiration, to 'teach desire to desire, to desire better, to desire more, and above all to desire in a different way'.

(Postscript; 1976, to *William Morris*, pp. 790–1)

Thus Sheila Rowbotham:

How then do people come to see the possibility of socialism? How do we conceive and imagine a completely different society, involving not only change in the external structures but an inner transformation of our consciousness and our feelings? How do we begin to connect our own experience to other people's? ... We need to make the creation of prefigurative forms an explicit part of our movement against capitalism. I do not mean that we try to hold an imaginary future in the present, straining against the boundaries of the possible until we collapse in exhaustion and despair. This would be utopian. Instead such forms would seek both to consolidate existing practice and release the imagination of what could be. The effort to go beyond what we know now has to be part of our experience of what we might know, rather than a denial of the validity of our own

343

experience in face of a transcendent party. This means a conscious legitimation within the theory and practice of socialism of all those aspects of our experience which are so easily denied because they go against the grain of how we learn to feel and think in capitalism. All those feelings of love and creativity, imagination and wisdom which are negated, jostled and bruised within the relationships which dominate in capitalism are nonetheless there, our gifts to the new life.

(*Beyond the Fragments*, London, 1979, pp. 119, 147)

Each of these accounts is suggestive. Yet each is (perhaps necessarily) abstract. And beside these attempts to formulate what 'alternative acts and alternative intentions' might be like, where they might be manifested and how they might relate to the 'dominant ... social system', the assurance and complexity with which Blake handles similar questions in *Songs of Innocence and of Experience* stands out sharply. The vision presented in these poems seems to be one with which our contemporary social thinking has hardly begun to reckon. In its 'Minute Particularity' it shows – far more powerfully than any definition – how such a sense of alternative possibility might be rooted in some of our actual experiences, yet threatened most immediately by much that we ourselves do. And in its poetic precision it suggests ways in which our thinking about such possibility might be refined and clarified.

Usually, it is the Songs of *Experience*, with their powerful dramatization of the ways in which patterns of domination and exploitation may be internalized as 'mind-forg'd manacles' and come to seem immutable, which are seen as Blake's most powerful criticism of his society. I have in this book been offering a different view: that it is in the Songs of *Innocence*, with their 'contrary' depiction of realized human *potentia*, that we find the essential – and really challenging – bases of his vision. These Songs do not present an inexplicable goodness miraculously untainted by the deformations of the society in which it occurs, an abstract, a-historical *humanitas*. Rather, they portray actual manifestations of a mode of human relationship rarely considered by social theorists, either in Blake's day or in ours, and implicitly affirm its centrality. And in doing so they radically question our commonly accepted sense not only of how society might be structured, but of what its essential structuring principle *is*.

One after another these poems image a 'play' devoid of intrusion or violation, a 'play' in which possibilities uncontaminated by the dominant forms of the society emerge as a radical challenge to it. The

344

focus is less on a particular group or particular situations (though many of these poems concern those who might be seen as the victims of society) than on a particular mode of interaction: one which Blake traces both in interpersonal relationships ('Infant Joy', 'Nurse's Song') and in larger social structurings ('The Ecchoing Green', 'The Divine Image'). It is a mode of interaction characterized by openness and responsiveness to rather than distortion and domination of the other, by the expression of vulnerability and need, and an answering vindication of the trust implicit in the expression; a mode of interaction in which both self and other achieve their fullest realization and create a mutually satisfying actuality. It is not so much a co-operative creativity toward a shared end, as that very different kind of creativity which results from the real interplay of difference, and evolves its own changing ends. To call it 'unalienated experience' is to abstract that which is much more concretely presented and to generalize that which is more particularly deline-ated. Yet *Songs of Innocence*, with its informing imaginative concep-tion of a mode of relationship which enables the self-realization and the mutuality of all, gives the most powerful portrayal in our literature of what such experience is like.

And the startling thing is that it is not portrayed as an utopia, a vision of what might be or even of what once was: it is portrayed as what *is*. In marked contrast to the 'state' presented in the Songs of Experience, with their limited and criticized speakers, their hypo-thetical arguments, this 'organiz'd Innocence' is portrayed directly and indicatively, almost always in the form of a dialogue between voices which are never criticized. It is shown unambiguously, within actually existing human relationships. And it is seen not merely as desirable, but as essential to continuing human interaction.

Today such a claim – when it is made – is usually confined to the early mother–child relationship, a relationship in which the need for mutual trust in and recognition of the other is peculiarly evident. Thus Winnicott:

in the baby's *experience* of life, actually in relation to the mother or mother-figure, there usually develops a degree of confidence in the mother's reliability ... the mother's ... love does not only mean meeting dependency needs, but it comes to mean affording the opportunity for this baby ... to move from dependence to autonomy.

A baby can be *fed* without love, but lovelessness or impersonal *manage-ment* cannot succeed in producing a new autonomous human child. Here where there is trust and reliability is a potential space, one that can become an infinite area of separation, which the baby, child, adolescent, adult may creatively fill with playing, which in time becomes the enjoyment of the cultural heritage.

The special feature of this place where play and cultural experience have a position is that *it depends for its existence on living experiences*, not on inherited tendencies.[9]

But Blake's sense of the importance of this kind of creative love extends a good deal further than this. In 'Infant Joy' – that poem whose title links it most directly to the 'Introduction' to *Songs of Innocence* – he does seem to be exploring the way in which the interaction between mother and child can create a world very different from that projected by the untrusting, fearful awareness of vulnerability to be found in *Songs of Experience*: a world of trust in which each is satisfied and from which the child can go independently forward. But the Songs of *Innocence* are not concerned with the individual child's development. Even in this poem about the naming of a particular child, individual identity is shown to emerge in interaction: it is on that interaction, rather than on the child alone, that the poetry concentrates. And the tiny world presented here is paralleled in the collection by the larger community of 'The Ecchoing Green' and the universal affirmations of 'The Divine Image': a series of structurally similar imagings of creatively enabling trust. To Blake, it seems, such trust is not something which is manifested only in the mother–child relationship: he sees it as potentially informing the 'play' of a whole community. And he shows how it animates – indeed, is essential to the continuing existence of – those 'virtues' to which 'all' appeal.[10]

Yet if the Songs of *Innocence* affirm that trust exists, if they focus upon the ways in which it may be traced even through the deformations of an exploiting social system, there is nothing complacent about the vision they present. It does not imply blindness to those deformations: rather, it is the essential experiential source of the sense that they are so. And it is thus a vision which leads to a sharply critical awareness of the ways in which the values to which men appeal may be deformed and distorted as well as realized: one which exposes rather than blurs conflict within the society. 'Holy Thursday' ends with an image of violence; 'Peace' disappears from the final stanza of 'The Divine Image'; the chimney sweeper offers less reassurance than threat. One after another these Songs emphasize the absolute necessity for the active realization of those virtues on which they pivot: 'And all must love the human form ...'; 'Then cherish pity, lest you drive an angel from your door';

CONCLUSION

'So if all do their duty, they need not fear harm.' It is an absolute necessity because – as these poems obliquely but unmistakably suggest, as *Songs of Experience* makes more sharply clear – the only alternative to such active creation of the conditions for trust is an active destruction of the shared human world. In 'A Poison Tree' transitive and reciprocal human relationship is denied: the desire to manipulate the other becomes displaced and reified in the alien and coveted object, and ends in isolation and death. On a different scale, 'London' portrays a whole society of isolated individuals, a society whose institutions are reified divisions rather than symbolic expressions of social bonds, a society in which that 'Pity' which is creative love is totally absent. And it is shown to be a society whose essential processes are actively destructive, which is not held together by that buying and selling and contracting on which it depends, but is actually being 'blasted' and 'blighted' apart. Seen in this light, the import of 'The Divine Image', of the urgent stinging 'morals' of 'Holy Thursday' and 'The Chimney Sweeper' is clear. Those virtues to which 'all' appeal and on which the very existence of the society depends will disappear unless they are maintained: 'you' may actually be driving the angel from 'your door'.

Yet these double-edged 'morals' reverberate with a dual hope and warning quite different from the protest and complaint to be found in *Songs of Experience*. For where the Experienced speakers define and condemn a world which contains no possibility of creative change, these point toward the space of human freedom. Partly, as we have seen, their message is one of threat. But partly, they offer a startling affirmation. The Innocent mode of relationship is a present potentiality: its messenger, the 'angel', is actually at 'your door'. It may, as the Songs of *Experience* show, be unapparent when 'reality' is seen through the framework of impoverished expectations. But it is there, even within a competitive, dehumanizing and unequal world: manifest in those experiences in which weakness is nurtured, dependency is answered, need is met, and the well-being of others is actively sought. It is, Blake suggests, the very basis of any shared human world: at once that which creatively transforms the society and that which must be maintained if it is to exist at all. For there cannot be society without trust, and trust is formed in the experience of its being answered. That vigorous love, that imaginative 'Pity', that wondering recognition of others which these poems present are not peripheral, but essential. And they may not be passively invoked: they must be actively and continually created.

347

Notes

Introduction

1 Richard Herne Shepherd, in the Preface to his edition of *Songs of Innocence and of Experience* (London, 1868): 'the general resemblance in tone and style, the similarities of subject and metre between the Songs of Innocence and of Experience published in 1798–94 and the Earlier Poems of Wordsworth, published in 1798, 1800 and 1807, such pieces as Goody Blake and Harry Gill, Poor Susan, The Two Thieves, Rural Architecture, Alice Fell, and all that class of poems which drew down on Wordsworth the ridicule of Jeffrey and other self-constituted critics of the period. There is precisely the same exquisite tenderness and noble simplicity in Blake. Some dozen of his Songs of Innocence might assuredly have been printed in the Lyrical Ballads and have passed for Wordsworth's, and on the whole the attentive student who follows out this hint, with the two books before him, will discover coincidences of thought and expression which are very remarkable. Wordsworth did not, however, see the poems of Blake till a later period, when he spoke of them with a generous admiration, which he did not often accord to the writings of his contemporaries' (pp. viii–ix).

2 Recorded in Crabb Robinson's diary for 10 March 1811, and quoted by G. E. Bentley Jr, *William Blake: The Critical Heritage* (London, 1975), p. 54.

3 Recorded in Crabb Robinson's diary for 20 May 1838, and quoted by Bentley, *William Blake*, p. 47.

4 Anon., 'Art. 2. *A Father's Memoirs of His Child*. By Benjamin Heath Malkin...', *Literary Journal*, 2nd series, II (July 1806), pp. 34–5. Quoted in Bentley, *William Blake*, p. 45.

5 Christopher Lake Moody, 'Art. 37. *A Father's Memoirs*...', *The Monthly Review*, n.s., LI (October 1806), p. 217. Quoted in Bentley, *William Blake*, p. 45.

6 *British Critic*, XIV (October 1799), pp. 364–5.

7 *The Monthly Review*, XXIX (June 1799), p. 202.

8 William Hazlitt, 'Mr Wordsworth', *The Spirit of the Age* (London, 1825), p. 233.

9 See Lodwick Hartley, *William Cowper; the continuing revaluation* (Chapel Hill, N.C., 1960) for an account of Cowper's contemporary reputation.

10 'Truth', ll. 317–36. Cowper, *Poetical Works*, ed. H. S. Milford (Oxford, 1967), pp. 37–8. Hazlitt quotes and praises the lines in 'On Thomson and Cowper', *Lectures on the English Poets* (London, 1818), pp. 185–6.

11 See the notes to the poem in *Lyrical Ballads*, Brett and Jones, p. 294 and in Wordsworth's *Poetical Works*, ed. E. de Selincourt and Helen Darbishire

(5 vols., Oxford, 1940–9), vol. IV, p. 448, which suggests that modern editors share this view.

12 Wordsworth uses this word in the Advertisement to the 1798 volume in trying to define the difficulties he expects his readers to have with the poems.

13 For a discussion of this aspect of the poem, see Geoffrey Hartman, 'The Poet's Politics', *Beyond Formalism* (New Haven, 1970), pp. 252–4.

1. Poetic 'Simplicity': Blake's *Songs* and Eighteenth-Century Children's Verse

1 Other links (with hymn and pastoral) are suggested by Martha England, in M. England and J. Sparrow, *Hymns Unbidden: Donne, Herbert, Blake, Emily Dickinson and the Hymnographers* (New York, 1966), p. 47.

2 Which was also published in collections, superficially not unlike *Lyrical Ballads*. See John E. Jordan, *Why the Lyrical Ballads?* (California, 1976).

3 J. H. Plumb, 'The New World of Children in Eighteenth-Century England', *Past & Present* 67 (May 1975). F. H. Darton, *Children's Books in England* (Cambridge, 1932) describes the rise of children's publishing. Zachary Leader, *Reading Blake's Songs* (London, 1981) gives a good account of such books and of the educational theories surrounding them.

4 Plumb, 'The New World of Children', p. 70.

5 For a fuller account of Newbery's publishing activities see Charles Welsh, *A Bookseller of the Last Century* (London, 1885) and S. Roscoe, *John Newbery and his successors, 1740–1814* (Wormley, 1973).

6 Leader, *Reading Blake's Songs*, pp. 1–4.

7 This at a time when the average weekly wage for a labourer in the south of England was from ten shillings to twelve shillings per week, all of which went on food, fuel and other essentials. Elizabeth W. Gilboy, *Wages in Eighteenth-Century England* (Cambridge, Mass., 1934) ch. 1, esp. pp. 58–9; and pp. 260–1.

8 Plumb, 'The New World of Children', p. 81.

9 William Ronksley, *The Child's Week's-Work: or, a Little Book, so nicely suited to the Genius and Capacity of a little Child, both for Matter and Method, that it will infallibly Allure and Lead him on into a Way of Reading with all the Ease and Expedition that can be desired* (London, 1712).

10 John Bunyan, *A Book for Boys and Girls* (London, 1686), pp. 40–1.

11 'The Snail', in Bunyan, *A Book for Boys and Girls*, p. 63. 'Gare' is an obsolete verb meaning to look out, take care.

12 For a discussion of this see Gordon Rattray Taylor, *The Angel-Makers* (London, 1958); I. Pinchbeck and M. Hewitt, *Children in English Society* (2 vols., London, 1958).

13 Mrs Barbauld, *Hymns in Prose*, 6th edn (London, 1794).

14 *Letters of Charles and Mary Lamb 1796–1820*, ed. E. V. Lucas (London, 1912), pp. 260–1. For Coleridge's views on this subject and its importance, see his third autobiographical letter to Thomas Poole, written in 1797: 'my

father was fond of me, and used to take me on his knee, and hold long conversations with me. I remember, that at eight years old I walked with him one winter evening from a farmer's house, a mile from Ottery – and he told me the names of the stars – and how Jupiter was a thousand times larger than our world – and that the other twinkling stars were Suns that had other worlds rolling round them – and when I came home, he showed me how they rolled round – . I heard him with a profound delight and admiration; but without the least mixture of wonder or incredulity. For from my early reading of Faery Tales, and Genii etc. etc. – my mind had been habituated *to the Vast* – and I never regarded *my senses* in any way as the criteria of my belief. I regulated all my creeds by my conceptions not by my *sight* – even at that age. Should children be permitted to read Romances, and Relations of Giants and Magicians, and Genii? – I know all that has been said against it; but I have formed my faith in the affirmative. – I know no other way of giving the mind a love of "the Great", and "the Whole". – Those who have been led to the same truths step by step thro' the constant testimony of their senses, seem to me to want a sense which I possess. – They contemplate nothing but parts – and all *parts* are necessarily little – and the Universe to them is but a mass of *little things* – It is true, that the mind *may* become credulous and prone to superstition by the former method – but are not the Experimentalists credulous even to madness in believing any absurdity, rather than believe the grandest truths, if they have not the testimony of their own senses in their favour? – I have known many who have been *rationally* educated, as it is styled. They were marked by a microscopic acuteness; but when they looked at great things, all became blank and saw nothing – and denied (very illogically) that any thing could be seen; and uniformly put the negation of a power for the possession of a power – and called the want of imagination Judgment, and the never being moved to Rapture Philosophy! –' (*Collected Letters of Samuel Taylor Coleridge*, ed. Earl Leslie Griggs (2 vols., Oxford, 1956), letter 210).

For a similar modern view, see Bruno Bettelheim, *The Uses of Enchantment: the Meaning and Importance of Fairy Tales* (London, 1976).

15 See Peter Burke, 'Oblique Approaches to the History of Popular Culture' in *Approaches to Popular Culture*, ed. C. W. E. Bigsby (London, 1976), pp. 73–4.

16 Iona and Peter Opie, *The Lore and Language of Schoolchildren* (Oxford, 1959).

17 On the illustration of early children's books, see Joyce Irene Whalley, *Cobwebs to Catch Flies* (London, 1974).

18 See Leonard de Vries, *Flowers of Delight* (London, 1965), p. 274.

19 For an account of such books, see Whalley, *Cobwebs*, ch. 1.

20 John Huddlestone Wynne, *Choice Emblems, Natural, Historical, Fabulous, Moral, and Divine. For the Improvement and Pastime of Youth* (London, 1772). Later re-titled *Riley's Emblems*, it went into nine editions by 1799 (Roscoe, *John Newbery*, pp. 275–6).

21 See V. de Sola Pinto, 'Isaac Watts and William Blake', *Review of English*

Studies, 20 (1944); Alicia Ostriker, *Vision and Verse in William Blake* (Madison, Wis., 1965), pp. 210–14; John Holloway, *Blake: the Lyric Poetry* (London, 1968), pp. 30–54.

22 Holloway, *Blake: the Lyric Poetry*

23 David Erdman, *Blake: Prophet Against Empire*, revised edition (Princeton, 1969), pp. 123–30; Nick Shrimpton, 'Hell's Hymnbook: Blake's *Songs of Innocence and of Experience* and their models' in *Literature of the Romantic Period 1750–1850*, ed. R. T. Davies and B. G. Beatty (Liverpool, 1976).

24 Holloway, *Blake: the Lyric Poetry*, pp. 40–1.

25 See the review of Trusler's book published in the *Analytical Review*, vol. VIII (1790), p. 103: 'this volume, far from being calculated to fix moral and religious principles on a firm basis, appears, to us, to be a mass of vulgar prejudices and affected sentiments ... we really think that the worldly maxims, which have been spun out in the volume before us, have a greater tendency to narrow than enlarge the understanding, to teach suspicion rather than inspire benevolence.'

This hostile reviewer takes for granted that the aim of a child's book should be to 'fix moral and religious principles on a firm basis', 'to enlarge the understanding', 'to inspire benevolence' – all aims which Blake was to find far from unproblematic.

26 Letter to Dr Trusler, 23 August 1799 (K793).

27 See Leader, *Reading Blake's Songs*, p. 184. She is shown, significantly, combing the boy's hair. Cf. Emanuel Swedenborg, *Arcana Coelestia*, par. 2125: 'There were seen children who were combed by their mothers so cruelly that the blood ran all around, which represented that such is the education of infants at this day.'

28 Nick Shrimpton, 'Hell's Hymnbook', pp. 23–6.

29 Alexander Gilchrist, *Life of William Blake*, 2nd edn (London, 1880), vol. I, p. 73; Allan Cunningham, 'William Blake', *Lives of the Most Eminent British Painters, Sculptors, and Architects*, revised 2nd edn, vol. II (London, 1830), par. 55.

30 'Gentle Jesus, Meek and Mild' first appeared in the collection *Hymns and Sacred Poems*, issued by John and Charles Wesley in 1742, and was subsequently published in the section 'Hymns for the Youngest' in Charles Wesley's *Hymns for Children*, 1763.

31 For an excellent discussion of Charles Wesley's precision of language, see Donald Davie, *Purity of Diction in English Verse* (London, 1952), ch. 5.

32 The phrase, of course, is T. S. Eliot's, from his essay on Blake: 'William Blake', *The Sacred Wood* (London, 1920).

33 See E. P. Thompson, *The Making of the English Working Class* (Harmondsworth, 1968); Morton D. Paley, 'William Blake, The Prince of the Hebrews, and the Woman Clothed with the Sun', in *William Blake: Essays in Honour of Sir Geoffrey Keynes*, ed. Morton D. Paley and Michael Phillips (Oxford, 1973); J. F. C. Harrison, *The Second Coming: Popular Millenarianism 1780–1830* (London, 1979), esp. ch. 4, which traces links between Brothers, the Swedenborgians and Paine-ite radicals.

34 See A. L. Morton, *The Everlasting Gospel* (London, 1958).

35 *Arcana Coelestia*, par. 1876.

36 *Dialogues on the Nature, Design and Evidence of the Theological Writings of the Hon. Emmanuel Swedenborg with a Brief Account of Some of his Philosophical Works* (London, printed for a Society of Gentlemen, 1788), p. 39.

37 For example, Thomas Paine, *Age of Reason* (London, 1794), Part I, p. 53: 'the flights and metaphors of the Jewish poets, and phrases and expressions now rendered obscure by our not being acquainted with the local circumstances to which they applied at the time they were used, have been erected into prophecies, and made to bend to explanations at the will and whimsical conceits of sectaries, expounders and commentators. Every thing unintelligible was prophetical, and every thing insignificant was typical. A blunder would have served for a prophesy; and a dish-clout for a type.'

38 William Hamilton Reid, *The Rise and Dissolution of the Infidel Societies in this Metropolis* (London, 1800; new impression, 1971, ed. Victor E. Neuberg), pp. 69–70.

39 Harrison, *The Second Coming*, pp. 75–85.

40 *The Rights of Priests* (1795?), p. 7. See ch. 3 for a fuller discussion of these publications.

41 *The Three Principles of the Divine Essence: The Works of Jacob Behmen, The Teutonic Theosopher*, ed. George Ward and Thomas Langcake (London, 1764–81), vol. I: 'Therefore let this be told you, ye Jews, Turks, and other Nations; you need not lack for any other, there is no other Time at hand, but the time of the Lily' (ch. 25, par. 95). 'The Lily will not be found in Strife or Wars, but in a friendly humble loving Spirit' (ch. 27, par. 32).

Cf. also Boehme's *Of Regeneration* (Bath edn, 1775), par. 166: 'Therefore I say, that whatsoever fighteth and contendeth about the letter, is all Babel. The letters of the word proceed from, and stand all in, one root, which is the spirit of God; as the various flowers stand all in the earth and grow by one another. They fight not with each other about their differences of colour, smell, and taste, but suffer the earth, the sun, the rain, the wind, the heat and cold, to do with them as they please; and yet every one of them groweth in his own peculiar essence and property.'

42 *The Three Principles of the Divine Essence*, ch. 17, par. 36.

43 Children in the new Church, though they 'signified innocence', were still to be instructed rather than heard. See Robert Hindmarsh, *Rise and Progress of the New Jerusalem Church* (London, 1861), p. 109: 'The first object, to which the attention of the members present [at the Second General Conference of the New Church, 5–7 April 1790] was called, was the preparation of a Catechism for the instruction of Children, according to the principles of the New Church.'

44 *Signatura Rerum, The Works of Jacob Behmen*, vol. IV, ch. I, paras. 1, 14, 15.

45 Cf. his parody of Swedenborgian wisdom in *The Marriage of Heaven and Hell*.

2. Poetic 'Simplicity': *Lyrical Ballads* and Magazine Verse

1 Robert Mayo, 'The Contemporaneity of the *Lyrical Ballads*', *PMLA*, 69 (1954).

2 See John E. Jordan, *Why the Lyrical Ballads?* (Berkeley, 1976), esp. pp. 115–27. On pp. 187–9 Jordan gives a list of about fifty such volumes published in 1798.

3 Mayo, 'Contemporaneity', p. 488.

4 See pp. 50–3.

5 See Jordan, *Why the Lyrical Ballads?*, pp. 67–8. The *Monthly Magazine* was the journal to which Coleridge recommended readers of *The Watchman* when he finally ceased publication: 'the New MONTHLY MAGAZINE; a Work, which has almost monopolized the talents of the Country, and with which I should have continued a course of literary rivalship with as much success, as might be supposed to attend a *young Recruit* who should oppose himself to a Phalanx of disciplined Warriors. Long may it continue to deserve the support of the Patriot and the Philanthropist, and while it teaches RATIONAL LIBERTY, prepare it's readers for the enjoyment of it, strengthening the intellect by SCIENCE, and softening our affections by the GRACES!' (*The Watchman*, X, 13 May 1796), quoted in *The Collected Works of Samuel Taylor Coleridge*, vol. 2, ed. Lewis Patton, pp. 374–5).

6 Like *Songs of Innocence*, the 1798 edition of *Lyrical Ballads* cost five shillings. See ch. 1, n. 7.

7 On the ballad revival in the magazines (and on the significant difference between *Lyrical Ballads* and the ballad imitations) see Mary Jacobus, *Tradition and Experiment in Wordsworth's Lyrical Ballads (1798)* (Oxford, 1976), ch. 9.

8 From *The Flapper*, 30 (14 May 1796), reprinted in *Eighteenth-Century Critical Essays*, ed. Scott Elledge (Cornell, 1961), vol. II, pp. 1105–8.

9 For a fuller discussion of these magazines see Mayo, 'Contemporaneity', and Derek Roper, *Reviewing before the Edinburgh 1788–1802* (London, 1978).

10 See Leslie F. Chard, II, *Dissenting Republican: Wordsworth's Early Life and Thought in their Political Context* (The Hague, 1972), esp. pp. 157–65, for a discussion of Wordsworth's intellectual affinities and actual links with this group.

11 George Dyer, *Memoirs of the Life and Writings of Robert Robinson* (London, 1796), p. ix.

12 Lucy Aikin, *Memoir of John Aikin*, quoted in Chard, *Dissenting Republican*, p. 160.

13 *Monthly Magazine* (February 1796), Preface.

14 Joseph Fawcett, 'The Contrast', *Poems* (London, 1798), pp. 129–36.

15 Cf. the significant linking of 'simplicity' and 'correctness' (traced by Jordan, *Why the Lyrical Ballads?*, chs. 3 and 4) in contemporary criticism of such verse: 'Although the reviewer gives lip service to the emotional side of

the critical spectrum, what the journal really stresses is correctness and propriety. Pratt, for instance, 'always writes to the heart; and hence his productions have acquired their popularity' – but the characteristics of his muse are 'suavity, simplicity, elegance, and tenderness' (July 1807), and the Poetical Sketches of T. Gent 'merit the praise of correctness, simplicity, and sometimes elegance' (August 1807)' (Jordan, p. 82).

16 Ibid., pp. 113–15; Mayo, 'Contemporaneity', pp. 517–21.

17 Mayo, 'Contemporaneity', p. 491.

18 See Jordan, *Why the Lyrical Ballads?* ch. 4, for a full account of this.

19 1798 Advertisement, Brett and Jones, p. 7.

20 'Inscription for a Coppice', *Town & Country Magazine*, XXVI (1794), p. 130. Mary Moorman, *William Wordsworth: the Early Years* (Oxford, 1957), p. 289, quotes from Joseph Gill's Racedown diary for 1796: 'F.P [John Frederick Pinney] had … my Town and Country Magazines for Mr. Wordsworths etc. amusement.'

21 The nearest – though very different – contemporary analogue is Blake's 'Mad Song' from *Poetical Sketches* (1784), a relatively unknown lyric which likewise shows Shakespearean influence.

22 Letter to John Wilson, in *The Letters of William and Dorothy Wordsworth; the Early Years: 1787–1805* ed. Ernest de Selincourt, 2nd edn revised by Chester L. Shaver (Oxford, 1967), p. 357. The derivation of 'idiot' is from the Greek *idiotes*, a private and separate person. Mary Jacobus, *Tradition and Experiment*, pp. 250ff., has an interesting discussion of 'The Idiot Boy' as a 'burlesque of the supernatural ballad'.

23 Thomas Parnell, *Poems on Several Occasions* (London, 1722), pp. 21–2.

24 For a fuller discussion of 'Jacobin' verse, see Mayo, 'Contemporaneity', pp. 495–506; Jordan, *Why the Lyrical Ballads?*, pp. 133–154.

25 See *Letters: the Early Years*, p. 126.

26 Letter to Mathews, 23 May 1794, *Letters: the Early Years*, p. 119.

27 E.g. the article by William Taylor of Norwich in March 1796 on Bürger's poetry; 'Is Verse Essential to Poetry?' (July 1796); 'The Phenomena of the Wye, during the Winter of 1797–8', by John Thelwall, a series of essays beginning in May 1798; 'On the Probable Future Amelioration of the Human Race' (January 1799).

28 It published a feminist essay, 'Are Literary and Scientific Pursuits suited to the Female Character?' in April 1796, and a warmly approbatory obituary of Mary Wollstonecraft in September 1797.

29 Which carried the notice of the publication of *Lyrical Ballads*.

30 This, of course, would have been less likely to be true of the women than of the men. On the education of the latter, see Anthony Lincoln, *Some Political and Social Ideas of the English Dissenters* (Cambridge, 1938); Ben Ross Schneider, *Wordsworth's Cambridge Education* (Cambridge, 1957).

31 See Schneider, *Wordsworth's Cambridge Education*, p. 211, for an account of the anti-revolutionary impact of Godwin's *Political Justice* on such groups.

32 Joseph Fawcett, *Sermons delivered at the Sunday-evening Lecture, for the Winter Season, at the Old Jewry* (2 vols., London, 1795), II, p. 108.

33 For a fuller discussion of this see Leo Lowenthal and Marjorie Fiske, 'The Debate over Art & Popular Culture in Eighteenth-century England', in *Common Frontiers of the Social Sciences*, ed. Mira Komarovsky (Illinois, 1957); Leo Lowenthal, *Literature, Popular Culture and Society* (Palo Alto, 1961), J. H. Plumb, *The Commercialization of Leisure* (Reading, 1973) and *In the Light of History* (London, 1972); Paul Fritz and David Williams, *The Triumph of Culture: Eighteenth-century Perspectives* (Toronto, 1972).

34 *Biographia Literaria*, ed. George Watson (London, 1975), p. 277.

35 E. H. Gombrich, *Art and Illusion* (London, 1960); Anton Ehrenzweig, *The Hidden Order of Art* (London, 1967).

36 See M. G. Jones, *The Charity School Movement: A Study of Eighteenth-Century Puritanism in Action* (Cambridge, 1938).

37 See, for example, the prayer quoted below on p. 124.

38 See Robert J. Bator, 'Eighteenth-Century England versus the Fairy Tale', *Washington State University Research Studies*, 39 (March 1971).

39 See, for example, Trusler's *Proverbs Exemplified* (1790), quoted on p. 15.

40 See the Preface to M. J. Naylor, *The Inantity [sic] and Mischief of Vulgar Superstitions; Four Sermons preached at All-Saints' Church, Huntingdon* (Cambridge, 1795): 'I am aware that by many, Witchcraft, the principal object of the subsequent discussions, will be despised and ridiculed as exploded legendary nonsense, unworthy even of being ranked with those *pretty* stories which divert the nursery, and amuse the infant mind. Perhaps a more extensive acquaintance with the prejudices and superstitions of the lower orders of the community, might induce them to look upon it as not entirely undeserving of some serious regard ... lamentable experience but too clearly proves, how extremely deep these notions are still engraven upon the minds of thousands, notwithstanding the great advances in learning and knowledge, which have been made within the two last centuries. The belief of these extravagancies was indeed gradually yielding to the powerful progress of science, but of late it has again been nourished and revivified, in no inconsiderable degree, by the many extraordinary relations, which the late venerable MR WESLEY inserted in his Arminian Magazine' (pp. iii–v).

41 See R. W. Malcolmson, *Popular Recreations in English Society, 1700–1850* (Cambridge, 1973).

3. The Real Language of Men

1 V. N. Volosinov, *Marxism and the Philosophy of Language* (New York, 1973), p. 93.

2 For a discussion of the disputes on this subject which took place in the Swedenborgian Church in the early 1790s see John Howard, 'An Audience for *The Marriage of Heaven and Hell*', *Blake Studies*, III, (Fall 1970). On the

Dissenters see Anthony Lincoln, *Some Political and Social Ideas of the English Dissenters* (Cambridge, 1938); Ben Ross Schneider, *Wordsworth's Cambridge Education* (Cambridge, 1957); Leslie F. Chard, II, *Dissenting Republican: Wordsworth's Early Life and Thought in their Political Context* (The Hague, 1972).

3 For example, the 'Church and King mob' which destroyed Priestley's laboratory and books in Birmingham in 1791, and also made an attempt on the Swedenborgian church nearby. (Robert Hindmarsh, *Rise and Progress of the New Jerusalem Church* (London, 1861), p. 131n.)

4 From the Preface to his edition of the poems of Thomas Gray, quoted in *Life of Gilbert Wakefield*, vol. II (London, 1804), p. 311.

5 See Lincoln, *Ideas of the English Dissenters*, pp. 62–5.

6 For a discussion of the debate about popular education in the eighteenth century, see Victor E. Neuburg, *Popular Education in Eighteenth Century England* (London, 1971) ch. 1.

7 Thomas Hartley, Preface to Emanuel Swedenborg's *Heaven and Hell* (London, 1789), p. xviii.

8 John Howard, 'An Audience', p. 31, discusses this dispute briefly, suggesting that it partly springs from the conservative Hindmarsh's association of Priestley with dangerous democratic principles. There is a fuller discussion of the many points of theological disagreement in the reviews of these *Letters* (and of the Swedenborgian Joseph Proud's *Candid and Impartial Reply to the Rev. Dr. Priestley's Letters*) which appeared in the *Analytical Review*, XI (1791), pp. 517–22; XIV (1792), pp. 190–3.

9 Joseph Priestley, *Letters to Members of the New Jerusalem Church* (Birmingham, 1791), pp. 56–7, 59.

10 Robert Hindmarsh, *Letters to Dr. Priestley* (London, 1792), p. 282.

11 Ibid. pp. 284–5.

12 This debate has a long history, in opposition to sectaries (and especially Quakers) during the seventeenth century. See Michael Austin Halls, 'Andrew Marvell and Transitions in Seventeenth-Century Prose', unpublished Ph.D. thesis, University of Cambridge, 1979.

13 K752.

14 See C. T. Odhner, *Hindmarsh* (Philadelphia, 1895); Howard, 'An Audience'.

15 Plato, *Phaedrus*, 275, in *Works*, trans. Thomas Taylor (5 vols, London, 1804), vol. III, p. 368.

16 Note by Thomas Taylor: 'true being, the proper object of intellect'.

17 Plato, *Epistle VII*, in *Works*, vol. V, p. 615.

18 Cf. Paine's remark, during the controversy following the publication of *Common Sense*: 'I scarcely ever quote; the reason is, I always think' (quoted in *Rights of Man*, ed. Henry Collins (Harmondsworth, 1969), p. 12).

Cf. also Richard Brothers, *A Revealed Knowledge of the Prophecies and Times*, Book II (London, 1794), p. 69: 'No man ought to advance the writings or opinion of another to assist his own, when what he says is

NOTES TO PP. 61-6

proved to be in opposition to the words of Christ, neither ought he to go back to the Law, which was for the Jews alone in their own country, to look for a precedent to favour his delusive method of reasoning, when the thing he wants to justify is quite contrary to the blessed Gospel of Peace and Salvation.'

19 Plato, *Phaedrus*, 276-7, in *Works*, vol. III, pp. 367-8.

20 George Mills Harper, *The Neoplatonism of William Blake* (Chapel Hill, 1961), pp. 46-9. For Blake's view on 'obscurity' in 1790 see his annotations to Swedenborg's *The Wisdom of Angels Concerning the Divine Providence*. To Swedenborg's contention that 'all the grandest and purest Truths of Heaven must needs seem obscure and perplexing to the Natural Man at first View', he retorts, 'Lies & Priestcraft. Truth is Nature.' Swedenborg continues, 'until his intellectual Eye becomes accustomed to the Light, and can thereby behold it with Satisfaction'. This is scored by Blake, and he comments '– that is: till he agrees to the Priests' interest' (K131).

21 Jacob Boehme, *The Mysterium Magnum, The Works of Jacob Behmen*, eds George Ward and Thomas Langcake (London, 1764-81), vol. III, ch. 35, par. 61.

22 Jacob Boehme, *The Three Principles of the Divine Essence, The Works*, vol. I, ch. 26, par 18.

23 Jacob Boehme, *Signatura Rerum, The Works*, vol. IV, ch. 10, par, 69.

24 See E. P. Thompson, *The Making of the English Working Class* (Harmondsworth, 1968), pp. 781-837.

25 Perhaps a reference to the Latinate English of the Scottish Enlightenment.

26 The term 'radical culture' is Thompson's (see note 24). One might, in this connection, compare Blake's use of proverbs with Cobbett's. Both are attracted to these repositories of the wisdom of an oral culture. But where in Cobbett the proverbial expression is simply a natural part of a plain-spoken, particular, colloquial style, Blake's use of the form is much more sophisticated. In the 'Proverbs of Hell' he plays upon the fact that the proverb is a form which encapsulates and calls upon the listener to identify with a concrete narrative situation, a very different form from the abstracted generalization which is natural to a literate mode of communication. In presenting a series of proverbs not as part of an argument whose tenor is clear, but simply as a series, he is calling upon his readers to identify with one such situation after another – and to recognize that the 'lesson' which they might abstract from any one may contradict that of the next. The intention is to expose such abstraction of always-true values as problematic, a deformation of the ambiguities and contradictions of concrete actuality.

27 Cf. Thomas Astle, *The Origin and Progress of Writing* (London, 1784), p. 208: 'When the ancients wrote on softer materials than wood or metal, other instruments were used for writing with, of which reeds and canes seem to have been the first.'

28 Cf. Taylor, *Phaedrus*, 276: 'He will not, therefore, with anxious and hasty

diligence, write them in black water.' A modern editor translates this: 'Then it won't be with serious intent that he "writes them in water" or that black fluid we call ink' and notes that the italicized phrase is a proverbial phrase for useless labour. (*Plato's Phaedrus*, trans. with Introduction and Commentary by R. Hackforth (Cambridge, 1952), p. 159). Taylor's translation of *Phaedrus* was not published until 1792, but it is certainly possible that Blake attended Taylor's lectures in 1784 and 1785 and may have heard this passage – which would certainly have interested him deeply – quoted or discussed (Harper, *Neoplatonism of William Blake*, pp. 21-3, 37-45).

29 In other of the Songs, and elsewhere in Blake's writings, the movement from visual to aural images – the reverse of that presented here – is a movement *towards* immediacy. See my discussions of 'Holy Thursday' (*Innocence*), pp. 123-4, and 'London', p. 212. Cf. also Thomas R. Frosch, *The Awakening of Albion* (Ithaca, N.Y, 1974), pp. 105ff.

30 Thomas Paine, *Rights of Man*, pp. 63-4.

31 Cf. Ernst Cassirer, *Language and Myth* (New York, 1946), p. 98: 'If language is to grow into a vehicle of thought, an expression of concepts and judgments, this evolution can be achieved only at the price of forgoing the wealth and fullness of immediate experience. In the end, what is left of the concrete sense and feeling content it once possessed is little more than a bare skeleton. But there is one intellectual realm in which the word not only preserves its original creative power, but is ever renewing it; in which it undergoes a sort of constant palingenesis, at once a sensuous and a spiritual reincarnation. This regeneration is achieved as language becomes an avenue of artistic expression. Here it recovers the fullness of life; but it is no longer a life mythically bound and fettered, but an aesthetically liberated life.'

32 Cf. David Punter, 'Blake, Marxism and Dialectic', *Literature and History*, 6 (Autumn 1977), p. 235: 'Urizen is both a writer and a reader, much of his time being devoted to poring over his tomes: but Blake makes it very clear that Urizen's learning is useless, because it is unconnected with life. While Urizen reads, chaos spreads around him: he is not able to use his knowledge, for to him knowledge is severed from reality.'

33 Jack Goody and Ian Watt, 'The Consequences of Literacy' in *Literacy in Traditional Societies*, ed. Jack Goody (Cambridge, 1968), p. 53.

34 Cf. the sense of words as rigid, curbing, stiff and fixed – but oddly seductive – in *Jerusalem*, Plate 55, 34-35:

> But first they said: (& their Words stood in Chariots in array
> Curbing their Tygers with golden bits & bridles of silver
> and ivory).

Cf. also Alicia Ostriker's suggestive observation: 'As an engraver, he was accustomed to a medium which resisted the craftsman's hand, not one which yielded pliantly to it' (*Vision and Verse in William Blake* (Madison, Wis., 1965), pp. 208-9).

35 One might also note his interest in those written forms which seem closest to the forms of an oral culture – the almanac ('Auguries of

Innocence'), proverbs, popular prophecies, the rhymes of folklore. John Adlard, *The Sports of Cruelty* (London, 1972) discusses Blake's use of 'fairies, folk-songs, charms and other country matters', but there remains much interesting work to be done in this area.

36 For a fine discussion of this interplay in Blake's work generally see W. J. T. Mitchell, 'Blake's Composite Art', *Blake's Visionary Forms Dramatic*, ed. David V. Erdman and John E. Grant (Princeton, 1970).

37 Preface to *Lyrical Ballads* (1802 edition), Brett and Jones, p. 258.

38 Ibid., p. 257.

39 Brett and Jones, p. 315.

40 Ibid., p. 316.

41 See above pp. 43–4

42 Preface, 1802 addition, Brett and Jones, p. 256.

43 1800 Preface, Brett and Jones, p. 268.

44 I.e. 'Inscription for the Spot where the HERMITAGE stood on St. Herbert's Island, Derwent-Water', 'Inscription for the House (an Outhouse) on the Island at Grasmere', 'Lines Written with a Slate-pencil upon a Stone, the largest of a heap lying near a deserted Quarry, upon one of the Islands at Rydale'.

45 For an interesting discussion of Wordsworth's use of this tense see Julian Boyd and Zelda Boyd, 'The Perfect of Experience', *Studies in Romanticism*, 16 (Winter 1977).

46 Advertisement to the 1798 volume, Brett and Jones, p. 7.

47 Brett and Jones, pp. 246–7.

48 See *Biographia Literaria*, ed. George Watson (London, 1975), p. 199. 'I object, in the very first instance, to an equivocation in the use of the word 'real'. Every man's language varies according to the extent of his knowledge, the activity of his faculties and the depth or quickness of his feelings. Every man's language has, first, its individualities; secondly, the common properties of the class to which he belongs; and thirdly, words and phrases of universal use. The language of Hooker, Bacon, Bishop Taylor and Burke differs from the common language of the learned class only by the superior number and novelty of the thoughts and relations which they had to convey. The language of Algernon Sidney differs not at all from that which every well educated gentleman would wish to write, and (with due allowances for the undeliberateness and less connected train of thinking natural and proper to conversation) such as he would wish to talk. Neither one or the other differ half as much from the general language of cultivated society as the language of Mr. Wordsworth's homeliest composition differs from that of a common peasant. For 'real' therefore we must substitute *ordinary*, or *lingua communis*. And this, we have proved, is no more to be found in the phraseology of low and rustic life than in that of any other class. Omit the peculiarities of each, and the result of course must be common to all.'

49 James H. Averill, *Wordsworth and the Poetry of Human Suffering* (Ithaca and London, 1980), p. 127, says of ll. 79–87 of the poem that 'The analogy

between the old, nearly blind man and a parish registry of charitable deeds tends to turn the Beggar into a piece of writing, as if words only could bring our days and ways each to each.'

He goes on (pp. 128–9) to trace Wordsworth's sense of the Beggar's social function to 'Lucretian and stoic theories of tragic response': 'The leading English source of this view is Addison's *Spectator* 418: "When we read of Torments, Wounds, Deaths, and the like dismal Accidents, our Pleasure does not flow so properly from the Grief which such melancholy Descriptions give us, as from the secret Comparison which we make between ourselves and the Person who suffers".'

50 Preface, 1802 addition, Brett and Jones, p. 250.

51 Jacob Viner, 'Man's Economic Status', *Man Versus Society in Eighteenth-Century Britain*, ed. James L. Clifford (Cambridge, 1968), p. 29.

52 1800 Preface, Brett and Jones, p. 250.

53 Preface, 1802 addition, p. 261.

54 *Essay upon Epitaphs* I, p. 57. The phrase 'the general language of humanity' comes in the sentence immediately before this.

55 Preface, Brett and Jones, p. 251.

56 On the meaning of this word in the late eighteenth and early nineteenth centuries see Susie I. Tucker, *Enthusiasm* (Cambridge, 1972), esp. pp. 52–6. Cf. also the address 'To the Public' at the opening of *Jerusalem*: 'The Enthusiasm of the following Poem, the Author hopes no Reader will think presumptuousness or arrogance when he is reminded that the Ancients entrusted their love to their Writing, to the full as Enthustiastically as I have who Acknowledge mine for my Saviour and Lord; for they were wholly absorb'd in their Gods' (K620–1).

57 Ben Ross Schneider, *Wordsworth's Cambridge Education*, p. 155.

58 Ibid., pp. 40–7.

59 Cf. Wordsworth's letter to Charles James Fox, 14 January 1801, *The Letters of William and Dorothy Wordsworth: The Early Years 1787–1805* (ed. Ernest de Selincourt, rev. C. L. Shaver (2nd edn, Oxford, 1967), pp. 314–15. Cf. also Coleridge, *Biographia Literaria*, pp. 190–1.

V. G. Kiernan, 'Wordsworth and the People', *Marxists on Literature*, ed. David Craig (Penguin, 1975), p. 179, remarks: 'Unlike the pauperized masses of the south a great many of [the Lakeland peasantry] were still small independent farmers, rather hugging the chains of sentiment that bound them to a poor soil than hating their condition, and thus seeming to prove that for the spirit of man poverty – which Wordsworth was accepting for himself too – was not the worst, or an unbearable, evil.'

60 E. P. Thompson, 'The Crime of Anonymity', *Albion's Fatal Tree* (see n. 71 below). For an example of such a letter, see below, pp. 161–2.

61 *Rights of Man*, p. 98.

62 *The Philanthropist*, 30 (19 October 1795).

63 Cf. Volosinov, *Marxism*, pp. 74ff.

64 Henry Collins, Introduction to *Rights of Man*, p. 11: 'Quakerism had

another if less predictable influence on Paine's life. His father's objection to Latin, with its Popish associations, ensured that Thomas was not taught the language at Thetford Grammar School. But Latin, in the society of eighteenth-century England, was the normal passport into the world of letters, and this fact, too, was to leave its mark on Paine throughout his life. His later reading, though wide, was patchy and his cast of mind was never academic. His ignorance, not only of Latin but of every other foreign language, ruled out the possibility of his becoming a scholar even had he shown the inclination.'

65 *The Happy Reign of George the Last. An Address to the Little Tradesmen, and the Labouring Poor of England*, by A Republican (n.d.); this quotation is on the title-page.

66 *An Account of Some Peculiar Manners and Customs of the People of Bull-Land, or the Island of Contradictions*, faithfully detailed by Old Hubert (London, n.d.), p. 2.

67 *A Sketch by Old Hubert* (London, n.d.), p. 11.

68 *A Political Dictionary, by the late Charles Pigott, Esq.* (London, Daniel Eaton, 1795). Eaton also published composite 'dictionaries', giving extracts not only from Pigott but also from other radical writers such as Gerrald and Barlow, and bearing titles such as *A Warning to Tyrants, The Voice of the People, The Excellence of the British Constitution*, in cheap serial form.

69 *A Political Dictionary for the Guinea-Less Pigs, or a Glossary of Emphatical Words Made use of by that Jewel of a Man, Deep Will* [i.e. Pitt] (n.d.), price 3d.

70 While at the same time beginning, in Part II, no. IV (1794), more than twenty years before Hone, to publish parodies of prayers and the Creed.

71 Cf. E. P. Thompson, 'Patrician society, plebeian culture', *Journal of Social History* (Summer 1974); 'Eighteenth-century English society: class struggle without class?', *Social History*, 3 (May 1978); John Brewer, *Party Ideology and Popular Politics at the Accession of George III* (Cambridge, 1976); Douglas Hay, Peter Linebaugh, John G. Rule, E. P. Thompson, and Cal Winslow, *Albion's Fatal Tree: Crime and Society in Eighteenth-Century England* (London, 1975).

72 See Richard D. Altick, *The English Common Reader* (Chicago and London, 1959), pp. 69–72.

73 One finds a similar, unironic, self-consciousness in some of the more radical religious writings of the period: e.g. *The True Narrative and Journal of John Wright, Carpenter* (London, 1794), the spiritual autobiography of one of two working men who travelled to join the famous Society of Illuminati in Avignon in 1789, and who became followers of Richard Brothers: 'although it is very certain beyond all doubt, that the divine influence always testified to the truth and soundness of the law of GOD in all ages, and always gives the true meaning of it; but the *devil* and his agents also make use of the sayings of the man of GOD, and the meaning that they give of them in all them that yield to it, they overturn the counsel and will of God … if we do not speak from *Heaven!* we must speak from *Hell*, and if we do not know how to discern betwixt them, how shall we know how to speak at all aright' (pp. 45, 46).

NOTES TO PP. 91–4

Melvin J. Lasky, 'The English Ideology', *Encounter*, XXXIX (December 1972), discussing this period, notes that it is a 'striking fact that in heightened moments of historic action the actors themselves become very aware of words and their special consequences' (p. 32). He goes on to argue that this hyperconsciousness was inhibiting to English radicalism: 'A revolutionary, thus handicapped, is hopelessly tongue-tied. The English radical, proud of his linguistics, his maturity, and his commonsensical sobriety, found himself being consistently cut off from those extravagant resources of spontaneity and youthful, if sometimes infantile, energy. "Exert your faculties, Sir; think but a little," Holcroft affirms, "and you will find, that, when we thus amuse ourselves with words, we act like children ... " Once deprived of the weapons of phraseology, the English radical found himself helpless before the withering contempt of his equally word-wary opponents ... At bottom, the failure of the revolutionary ideology to cross the Channel safely was associated with the inability of the English public mind to make welcome (in a prescient phrase used in a Parliamentary debate in 1790) "the strange mixture of metaphysics with politics, which we are witnessing in the neighbouring country"' (p. 32).

I would argue that the really revolutionary thrust of the English radicals lay precisely in their suspicion of the tainted rhetoric of abstraction, their awareness of the necessity to expose the ideological differences blurred by that rhetoric. The failure of the revolutionary ideology is 'associated' not with this suspicion, but with the over-simplifying desire to affirm a common language, a common humanity.

74 See below, pp. 165–70.

75 *Estimate of the Value of National Opulence to the Mass of the People. From the Peripatetic, Politics for the People*, Part I, no. VI (London, 1793), pp. 74–5.

76 John Thelwall, *The Peripatetic: or Sketches of the Heart, of Nature and Society; in a Series of Politico-Sentimental Journals in Verse and Prose* (London, 1793), p. 101.

77 Joseph Priestley, *An Answer to Mr Paine's Age of Reason* (London, 1795), p. 45.

78 Letter to Daniel Stuart, 7 April 1817, *The Letters of William and Dorothy Wordsworth: The Middle Years 1806–1820*, ed. Ernest de Selincourt, revised by Mary Moorman and A. G. Hill, 2nd edn (2 vols, Oxford, 1969–70).

79 These phrases are taken from later in the same letter, where Wordsworth deplores the fact that 'Everything has been put up to market and sold for the highest price it would bring. Farmers used formerly to be attached to their Landlords, and labourers to their Farmers who employed them ... A country squire, or substantial yeoman, used formerly to resort to the same shops which his father had frequented before him, and nothing but a serious injury real or supposed would have appeared to him a justification for breaking up a connexion which was attended with substantial amity and interchanges of hospitality from generation to generation. All this moral cement is dissolved, habits and prejudices are broken and rooted up; nothing

being substituted in their place but a quickened self-interest... The ministry will do well if they keep things quiet for the present, but if our present constitution in church and state is to last, it must rest as heretofore upon a moral basis; and they who govern the country must be something superior to mere financiers and political economists' (ibid., pp. 375–6).

80 Letter to Charles James Fox, 14 January 1801, *Letters: The Early Years*, p. 315.

81 The likeness between these two poems was first noted by Alexander Gilchrist, *Life of William Blake* (enlarged edn, London, 1880), p. 74.

82 In the former case, songs of social protest such as those written by Cowper about the negro slave trade, in the latter, the nostalgic 'ballads' of the magazines.

83 Jonas Hanway, *A Sentimental History of Chimney Sweeps* (London, 1785): 'How the masters obtain these children, would be mysterious, were it not known that numbers of the least virtuous, or most necessitous among the labouring poor, part with their children at any rate... Orphans, who are in a vagabond state, or the illegitimate children of the poorest kind of people, are said to be sold; that is, their service for seven years is disposed of for twenty or thirty shillings; being a smaller price than the value of a *terrier*: but it is presumed that the children of poor parents, who cannot find bread for a numerous family, make up by much the greater part of the number of the *climbing boys*' (p. 24); 'If the boy is under a master who has constant, regular employment, as soon as his *morning's work* is done, he is generally sent to seek for further business, or, as they term it, *to call the streets*' (p. 26); 'We may figure to ourselves, the boy called from the bag of soot on which he slept, oftentimes walking a mile or two to his work' (p. 27).

84 Although as Alicia Ostriker notes in *Vision and Verse in William Blake* (Madison, Wis., 1965), p. 72: 'Blake also, I think uniquely among English poets except Browning, sometimes slips extra stresses in among his anapests, generating quite novel rhythms. He does this a few times, in the first "Chimney Sweeper", where he lets the speaker's enthusiasm overflow into extra accents for an effect of wide-eyed eagerness:

> That thousands of sweepers, Dick, Joe, Ned & Jack
>
> And by came an Angel who had a bright key
>
> Then down a green plain leaping, laughing they run'.

85 *The Chimney Sweeper's Friend and Climbing Boy's Album*, ed. James Montgomery (London, 1824), p. 175.

86 Humphrey Tristram Potter, *A New Dictionary of the Cant and Flash Languages* (rev. edn, 1800). The phrase is also noted in Grose, *A Classical Dictionary of the Vulgar Tongue* (2nd edn, 1788).

87 Robert Southey, *Letters from England: by don Manuel Alverez Espriella* (2nd edn, London, 1806), vol. I, pp. 143–4.

88 Hanway, op. cit., *A Sentimental History*, p. 7, pp. 77–9.

89 Cf. Hanway, pp. 38–9: 'Much has occasionally been said on the subject of *instructing* the lower classes of the people, as if the superior in condition might exult over the inferior, by keeping him in ignorance of what is common to all of us as accountable creatures. Christianity allows for no such distinction among men: it is not necessary to the great plan of *subordination*, and it counteracts the divine principle of *charity*, and obedience on principle. *Instruction* is the foundation of social connexions; the origin of obedience to human as well as divine laws, and the foundation of every thing that is humane, manly, rational, and religious ... We owe it to God and our country, to inform our inferiors what our religion requires of them'.

90 M. Dorothy George, *London Life in the Eighteenth Century* (Harmondsworth, 1966), p. 242.

91 Ibid., quoted on p. 252.

92 Enid Porter, *The Folklore of East Anglia* (London, 1974), p. 26, cites a case in Suffolk as late as 1969.

93 Emanuel Swedenborg, *Concerning the Earths in our Solar System* (London, 1787), section 79. Kathleen Raine, *Blake and Tradition* (London, 1969), vol. I, pp. 25–6 discusses the closeness of the imagery in this passage to that of Blake's poem.

94 John Brewer, *Party Ideology*, p. 184.

95 This is what distinguishes it most sharply from the much more direct protest of 'The Chimney Sweeper' from *Songs of Experience*, with *its* reference to the May Day procession of the sweeps and its straightforward attack on polite morality:

> And because I am happy, & dance & sing,
> They think they have done me no injury:
> And are gone to praise God & his Priest & King
> Who make up a heaven of our misery.

Here, that which was the substance of the positive vision in the earlier poem is regulated to a subordinate clause, and the child is alone in his dancing, 'a victim on the altar of misery' (Hanway, *A Sentimental History*, p. 90), rather than one of many, a potentially subversive force. And all that he says is a complaining reply to his politely compassionate interlocutor: he is seen as an *object* of that compassion from the beginning, 'a little black thing'.

96 The bleak plight of country-born servant girls in late eighteenth-century England is discussed in George, *London Life*, pp. 119–20.

97 Vol. I, section XIX, p. 220. 'Poor Susan' was probably written in 1797 (Mark L. Reed, *Wordsworth, The Chronology of the Early Years, 1770–1799* (Harvard, 1967), p. 323). Wordsworth persuaded Joseph Cottle to borrow *Zoonomia* for him in June 1797, and returned it in May 1798 (Brett and Jones, p. 282).

98 Cf. Blake in his annotations to Wordsworth's *Poems*: 'Imagination has nothing to do with Memory' (K783).

99 Cf. Ernst G. Schachtel, *Metamorphosis* (London, 1963), p. 320: 'Childhood amnesia covers those aspects and experiences of the early personality

which are incompatible with the culture. If they were remembered, man would demand that society affirm and accept the total personality with all its potentialities. In a society based on partial suppression of the personality such a demand, even the mere existence of a really free personality, would constitute a threat to the society. Hence it becomes necessary for the society that the remembrance of a time in which the potentialities of a fuller, freer, and more spontaneous life were strongly present and alive be extinguished. In memory's service of this purpose one may distinguish two processes which overlap and shade into one another. One process leaves the culturally unacceptable or unusable experiences and the memory thereof to starvation by the expedient of providing no linguistic, conceptual, and memory schemata for them and by channeling later experience into the experience schemata of the culture. As the person, in the process of education, gradually comes to live more and more exclusively within the framework of the culturally and conventionally provided experience schemata, there is less and less to remind him of the possibility of trans-schematic experience. As his memory schemata develop in accordance with the schematized experience, they become unfit to preserve and recall trans-schematic experience.'

100 *The Prelude* (1798–9), Part II, ll. 20–4:

> And is there one, the wisest and the best
> Of all mankind, who does not sometimes wish
> For *things which cannot be*, who would not give,
> *If so he might*, to duty and to truth
> The eagerness of infantine desire?   [my italics]

101 'Ode: Intimations of Immortality from Recollections of Early Childhood', l. 77.

4. Vision and Morality: *Songs of Innocence*

1 See esp. David Erdman, *Blake: Prophet Against Empire*, revised edn (Princeton, 1969), pp. 125ff.
2 Priscilla Wakefield, *Perambulations in London, and its Environs . . . in Letters. Designed for Young Persons* (London, 1809), p. 417.
3 See David Edward Owen, *English Philanthropy 1660–1960* (Cambridge, Mass., 1965), pp. 11–13.
4 See L.C. Knights, *Drama and Society in the Age of Jonson* (Harmondsworth, 1962), pp. 95ff. on the actual decay of 'housekeeping' in the seventeenth century.
5 For a discussion of such complaints see *Notes & Queries*, 3rd ser. (20 December 1862), pp. 481–3.
6 See Sidney and Beatrice Webb, *English Local Government*, vol. III, *The Manor and the Borough*, pp. 646–8. Cf. also their description of London Aldermen: 'From 1689 to 1835 the Aldermen were, even at their election, almost invariably elderly men whose energies had been dulled by hard work

and the keenness of their struggle to amass wealth, and whose opinions were tempered by the material prosperity which they had won ... they showed themselves – in the main – to be well-conducted, stupid folk; too wealthy to be personally corrupt; too kindly disposed not to be foolishly indulgent to particular individuals; too smugly unimaginative not to be carelessly cruel to vagrant and pauper, debtor and criminal' (pp. 657–8, 668).

7 For examples of such songs, see *Notes & Queries*, 3rd ser. (20 December 1862), pp. 481–3.

8 For a discussion of these contradictions, see Raymond Williams, *The Country and the City* (London, 1973), pp. 30–4.

9 *Round About Our Coal Fire, or Christmas Entertainments* (1740), pp. 1–2, 5–6. Cf. also Smollett, *Humphrey Clinker* (Oxford, 1966), p. 164: 'This gentleman is declared opponent of the ministry in parliament; and having an opulent fortune, piques himself upon living in the country, and maintaining *old English hospitality*. By the bye, this is a phrase very much used by the English themselves, both in words and writing; but I never heard it out of the island, except by way of irony or sarcasm. What the hospitality of our fore-fathers has been,I should be glad to see recorded, rather in the memoirs of strangers who have visited our country, and were the proper objects and judge of such hospitality, than in the discourse and lucubrations of the modern English, who seem to describe it from theory and conjecture.'

10 *A Political Dictionary, by the Late Charles Pigott, Esq.* (London, 1795), p. 5. Cf. also *Pearls Cast before Swine by Edmund Burke, scraped together by Old Hubert* (London, n.d.), p. 2: 'When men imagine that their food is only a cover for poison, and when they neither love nor trust the hand that serves it, it is not the name of the *roast beef of old England*, that will perswade them to sit down to the table that is spread for them.'

11 Possibly there is some background allusion to the traditional plebeian 'mock mayor' ceremony, in which the social hierarchy was burlesqued by electing a great drinker as 'mayor'. Cf. Robert Malcolmson, *Popular Recreations in English Society 1700–1850* (Cambridge, 1973), pp. 81–2.

12 Wakefield, *Perambulations*, pp. 181–2. The plate as engraved for *Songs of Innocence*, with its stiff lines of marching figures and its crowded be-tendrilled lettering, seems to emphasize – even more sharply than the 'hobbledehoy' rhythm – another aspect of the scene, pointed out twenty years later by a correspondent to the *Monthly Magazine*: 'As I was there pretty early, and before many of the children had taken their places, the first observation I made was that, notwithstanding the immense theatre erected and provision made, there was yet hardly sufficient room to accomodate the whole of the different schools; many of the children finding a difficulty in seating themselves, and, when settled, were much crowded. Owing to this probably it was, that some few were occasionally had down to the school-mistresses below, to be plied with smelling-bottles to be kept from fainting.' (*Monthly Magazine*, 23 (1 July 1807), pp. 554–6).

13 George Rudé, *Hanoverian London 1714–1808* (London, 1971), pp. 139–40.
14 Stanley Gardner, *Blake* (London, 1968), pp. 19–21.
15 Opening prayer from *Poor Girls' Primer* (Sheffield girls' charity school, 1789). Quoted by M. G. Jones, *The Charity School Movement* (Cambridge, 1938), p. 75.
For an interesting comparison with Blake's transformed sense of the children, see *A Sermon preached in the Parish-Church of Christ-Church, London, on Thursday May the 19th, 1774: Being the Time of the Yearly Meeting of the Children Educated in the Charity Schools, in and about the Cities of London and Westminster*, by Rev. Robert Pool Finch, D.D. (London, 1774), pp. 31–2: 'Animated therefore by a spirit of holy emulation, let us with an invincible fortitude resolve, that, in an age too much marked by indifference, and scepticism, and irreligion, nothing shall separate us from the love of GOD which is in CHRIST JESUS our LORD; through whom we look forward to a better world than this with an unbounded prospect of everlasting joy, when the kingdom of grace shall be consummated in the kingdom of glory; when the praises of the infant tongue shall be improved into seraphic transport; when the most perfect harmony shall inspire and unite all its subjects; when Hallelujah, the LORD GOD Omnipotent reigneth, shall be incessantly proclaimed.'
16 Jones, *Charity School Movement*, p. 61.
17 Owen, *English Philanthropy*, p. 3.
18 From Blake's annotations to Lavater's *Aphorisms on Man*, made in 1788.
19 From *The Times*, 6 June 1788; quoted by Erdman, *Blake, Prophet*, p. 122.
20 Jones, *Charity School Movement*, pp. 59–61.
21 Mrs Trimmer, *The Family Magazine*, (June 1788), p. 427.
22 *A Sermon preached in the Parish-Church of Christ-Church, London, on Thursday May the 19th, 1774: Being the Time of the Yearly Meeting of the Children Educated in the Charity Schools, in and about the Cities of London and Westminster*, by Rev. Robert Pool Finch, D.D. (London, 1774), p. 22.
23 *A Sermon Preached ... on Thursday May the 3rd, 1776*, by Rev. Richard Kaye, D.D. (London, 1776), p. 6.
24 *The Times*, 6 June 1788.
25 *Sermon Preached by Canon Gastrell of Christchurch at the Annual Meeting of the Charity Schools ... June 5, 1705*.
26 It is, significantly, sung at one of those moments when mutual unhappiness is tacitly admitted: 'They play'd at forfeits, & try'd every method to get good humour' (K59).
27 Jonathan Shipley, *A Sermon Preached at the Yearly Meeting of the Children Educated in the Charity-Schools in the Cities of London and Westminster* (London, 1777). Quoted and discussed by Jacob Viner, 'Man's Economic Status', in *Man Versus Society in Eighteenth-Century Britain*, ed. James L. Clifford (Cambridge, 1968), pp. 34–5.

NOTES TO PP. 126-7

28 In the draft, they were originally explicitly likened to angels, *not* seen *as* angels:

> When the whole multitude of innocents their voices raise
> Like angels on the throne of heav'n, raising the voice of praise.

(K59)

The revised (and eventually published) version is much more powerfully suggestive.

For a similar sense of an 'angelic' dimension immanent within the most ordinary facts of everyday life see *The True Narrative and Journal of John Wright, Carpenter* (London, 1794), written by one who moved in circles very familiar to Blake, and describing his journey to visit 'the Spiritual Society' of Illuminati in Avignon in 1789: 'we saw within about sixty yards of the place a *man as we thought* sitting under a tree, the sight of whom, rather surprised the brethren, he was apparently eating bread, the brethren asked him who he was, he said a *traveller* that had come out of ITALY to see his relations at *Avignon* who were all poor, so he was going back. The brethren gave him some money and left him, but one of the brethren having some thoughts, that he was something *more than* MAN, enquired at the *word* of the LORD, and the answer was, that it was the ARCHANGEL RAPHAEL' (p. 19).

This spiritual 'reading' of everyday occurrences was perhaps more common than a reading of the polite literature of the late eighteenth century would lead one to suppose: it is certainly prominent in the very popular writings of Richard Brothers (of whom Wright became a follower) and, later, of Joanna Southcott, no less than in the more developed doctrines of the Swedenborgians.

Cf. also *The True Narrative and Journal of John Wright*, p. 57: 'Innocence and simplicity transform man into an angel of light.'

29 Some at least of the 'Holy Thursday' processions seem to have been held on Ascension Day, that feast of the church which celebrates man rising as God.

30 See, for example, Robert W. Malcolmson, *Popular Recreations in English Society 1700–1850* (Cambridge, 1973); Douglas Hay, Peter Linebaugh, John G. Rule, E. P. Thompson and Cal Winslow, *Albion's Fatal Tree* (London, 1975); John Brewer, *Party Ideology and Popular Politics at the Accession of George III* (Cambridge, 1976).

Cf. also Rev. Newton Ogle, D.D., *A Sermon preached in the Parish-Church of Christ-Church, London, On the Thursday May the 4th, 1775: Being the Time of the Yearly Meeting of the Children Educated in the Charity-Schools, in and about the Cities of London and Westminster* (London, 1775), pp. 18–19: 'We all know the force of necessity, when thus joined with corrupt manners: they mutually tend to encourage each other: and at this instant we see their united force, especially in this great metropolis, increased to such a height as to bear down like a tide upon us, and baffle even the efforts of civil power itself. The short and usual remedy in this case, is that of terror and legal punishment: but this is by no means adequate to an evil which may grow faster than the remedy can be applied; and which at best can never reach the moral cause of it. The truly humane and christian part, is to go to the bottom of the mischief, and, as far as is in our power, to prevent those bad habits which are the cause of it. The education of the children of the poor seems to bid fairer for this than any other scheme yet devised, unless we could effect that harder task the reformation of the rich.'

31 E.g. *1 Henry IV*, Act III, scene 3, ll. 170–1:
> Go make ready breakfast, love thy husband, look to thy servants, cherish thy guests.

32 Cf. Blake's identification of love with the 'Poetic Genius', in his 1788 annotations to Swedenborg's *Wisdom of Angels Concerning Divine Love and Divine Wisdom* (K89ff.).

33 Cf. Erik Erikson, 'Play and Actuality', in *Play and Development*, ed. Maria W. Piers (New York, 1972), p. 165: 'For if reality is the structure of facts consensually agreed upon in a given stage of knowledge, actuality is the leeway created by new forms of interplay. Without actuality, reality becomes a prison of stereotypy, while actuality must always retest reality to remain truly playful.'

34 There have been many attempts to define 'play'. One of the earliest is in Friedrich Schiller, *On the Aesthetic Education of Man*, first published in 1795. A basic modern account is J. Huizinga, *Homo Ludens: A Study of the Play-Element in Culture* (London, 1949). An altogether more interesting account, from a psychoanalytic point of view, is D. W. Winnicott, *Playing and Reality* (Harmondsworth, 1974). Attempts to formulate a sociological theory of play include Anthony Giddens, 'Notes on the Concepts of Play and Leisure', *The Sociological Review*, 12 (March 1964), pp. 73–90; Richard Burke, '"Work" and "Play"', *Ethics*, 82, 1 (1971), pp. 33–47; and, most interestingly, Francis Hearn, 'Toward a Critical Theory of Play', *Telos*, 30 (1976–77). See also Gregory Bateson, 'A Theory of Play and Fantasy', in *Steps to an Ecology of Mind* (St Albans, 1973).

35 Cf. the recurring motif of 'framing' and enclosing in the illustrations to the volume.

36 Cf. Huizinga, *Homo Ludens* , pp. 13–14: 'in child-life performances of this kind are full of imagination. The child is *making an image* of something different, something more beautiful, or more sublime, or more dangerous than what he usually *is* . . . The child is quite literally "beside himself" with delight, transported beyond himself to such an extent that he almost believes he actually is such and such a thing, without, however, wholly losing consciousness of "ordinary reality". His representation is not so much a sham-reality as a realization in appearance: "imagination" in the original sense of the word.'

37 See above p. 30 and ch. 1, n. 44.

38 For an attack on the notion that language is *necessarily* appropriative and imperialistic see Anthony Wilden, *System and Structure* (London, 1971) pp. 473–4, 472, 262, 263: 'according to the Lacanian theory, because the

dominant ideology is one of the reification and the entification of human beings as objects of Imaginary exchange, the dominant category of LINGUISTIC signification – that of the human function which becomes an "identity", a Name – drives the subject, already reified in the Real, to alienate himself in the Word.... But so long as, in a real world of oppressive relations, the question of subjectivity is necessarily posed for the INDIVIDUAL – rather than for the collective – then the subject's quest for identity will remain a quest for the justification of his alienation: a quest for a name in an Imaginary discourse, an empty word ... Lacan's statement that "there is no dialogue" betrays a particular definition of the Symbolic (language) which is peculiar to our culture ... Obviously, the mere fact that language has to be learned from others, engenders this command relationship between the child and "authority". This is Lacan's point in describing the Other as the "locus of the Word" ... It seems very obvious that only in a culture with deeply programmed ELITIST metarules does the correlation of "Other" and "authority" with particular forms of knowledge, behaviour, and status, hold good ... "Authority" and "mastery" are only equivalent to "parent" and "professor" (or whatever) in a culture which employs Imaginary digitilization to turn dynamic differences into static oppositions.'

Cf. his whole ch. 17, 'The Ideology of Opposition and Identity'. This is precisely what Blake shows in opposing his 'Two Contrary States'. That of *Songs of Experience* is not inevitable: the 'Contrary State' presented in *Songs of Innocence* – in which identity is arrived at not in opposition but in relationship – is a realized possibility.

39 Cf. Erik Erikson, *Insight and Responsibility* (New York, 1964), pp. 116–17: 'there is something in the anatomy even of mature hope which suggests that it is the most childlike of all ego-qualities, and the most dependent for its verification on the charity of fate; thus religious sentiment induces adults to restore their hopefulness in periodic petitionary prayer, assuming a measure of childlikeness towards unseen, omnipotent powers ... Hope is verified by a combination of experiences in the individual's "prehistoric" era, the time before speech and verbal memory. Both psychoanalysis and genetic psychology consider central in that period of growth the secure apperception of an "object". The psychologists mean by this the ability to perceive the *enduring quality* of the *thing world* while psychoanalysts speak loosely of a first love-object, i.e. the experience of the care-taking person as a *coherent being*, who reciprocates one's physical and emotional needs in expectable ways and therefore deserves to be endowed with trust, and whose face is recognized as it recognizes. These two kinds of object are the first knowledge, the first verification, and thus the basis of hope.'

40 I am calling 'the care-taking person' here the mother for convenience: there is nothing in the poem to indicate that it is a mother.

41 As Coleridge noted, commenting on this poem in a letter to C. A. Tulk, 12 February 1818.

42 Erik Erikson, *Insight*, p. 231. For a psychoanalytic account of the relationship between such experience and imagination, see Fred Plaut, 'Reflections about Not Being Able to Imagine', *Journal Anal. Psychol.* 11 (1966): 'The capacity to form images and to use these constructively by recombination into new patterns is – unlike dreams or fantasies – dependent on the individual's ability to trust.'

43 Winnicott, *Playing and Reality*, p. 75.

44 Friedrich Schiller, *On the Aesthetic Education of Man*, ed. and trans. Elizabeth M. Wilkinson and L. A. Willoughby (Oxford, 1967), p. 107.

45 Cf. Hearn, 'Theory of Play', p. 146: 'The centrality of the category of labor to the Marxian dialectic has fostered in large measure the neglect of play and the denunciation of any serious effort to appreciate the potentially liberating qualities of the non-instrumental.'

46 Adrienne Rich, *Of Woman Born: Motherhood as Experience and Institution* (London, 1977), p. 52.

47 Peter Berger, *A Rumour of Angels* (London, 1971), pp. 72–4.

48 Cf. Malcolmson, *Popular Recreations*, esp. pp. 89ff.

49 Robert Slaney, *An Essay on the Beneficial Direction of Rural Expenditure* (London, 1824), quoted in Malcolmson, pp. 107–8.

50 Isaac Watts, 'Against Idleness and Mischief', from *Divine Songs Attempted in Easy Language for the Use of Children* (1715).

51 see above, p. 134.

52 Cf. J. L. Austin, 'Performative Utterances', *Philosophical Papers* (Oxford, 1961) pp. 220–39. Cf. also Thomas R. Frosch, *The Awakening of Albion* (Ithaca and London, 1974), pp. 106–7, for a discussion of Blake's poetically articulated sense of the way in which 'spoken words [can] become as directly instrumental as tools or physical actions'.

53 For a suggestive discussion of this transformation in music, see Susanne K. Langer, 'The Image of Time', *Feeling and Form* (London, 1953), ch. 7.

54 *Collected Letters of Samuel Taylor Coleridge*, ed. Earl Leslie Griggs, IV, p. 545.

55 The phrase is from Blake's annotations to Lavater (K77). Cf. the 1791–3 notebook poem, 'Eternity', where the sense of 'eternity' is similarly linked to a non-egocentric acceptance of flux:

> He who binds to himself a joy
> Does the winged life destroy;
> But he who kisses the joy as it flies
> Lives in eternity's sun rise.

56 Berger, *Rumour of Angels*, pp. 94–5.

57 *Arcana Coelestia*, 862.

58 Cf. Schiller, *Aesthetic Education*, p. 109 (on the 'Juno Ludovisi'): 'The whole figure reposes and dwells in itself, a creation completely self-contained, and, as if existing beyond space, neither yielding nor resisting; here is no force to contend with force, no frailty where temporality might break in. Irresistibly moved and drawn by those former qualities, kept at a

distance by these latter, we find ourselves at one and the same time in a state of utter repose and supreme agitation, and there results that wondrous stirring of the heart for which mind has no concept nor speech any name'.

59 Marion Milner, *On Not Being Able to Paint*, 3rd edn (London, 1971), p. 29. 'Illusion' is here being used, it should be stressed, without the pejorative sense it often bears – 'mere' illusion.

60 Schiller, *Aesthetic Education*, p. 215.

61 Cf. Blake's impatience with Rousseau: 'Rousseau thought Men Good by Nature: he found them Evil & found no friend. Friendship cannot exist without Forgiveness of Sins continually' (K682). 'Friendship' – relating to others in the real world (rather than formulating theories about them) – involves 'Forgiveness of Sins continually' rather than idealization.

62 Malcolmson, *Popular Recreations* pp. 107–17.

63 Stanley Gardner, *Blake* (London, 1968), pp. 74–5.

64 Cf. *A Descriptive Catalogue* (K576): 'A Spirit and a Vision are not, as the modern philosophy supposes, a cloudy vapour, or a nothing: they are organized and minutely articulated beyond all that the mortal and perishing nature can produce. He who does not imagine in stronger and better lineaments, and in stronger and better light than his perishing, mortal eye can see, does not imagine at all.'

65 Cf. Sigurd Burckhardt, 'The Poet as Fool and Priest', *ELH*, 23 (1965) pp. 284–5: 'if the poet allows his words no more than their functional identity in the body of the "living language", he surrenders his sovereignty as an artist; he creates nothing, says nothing that is true beyond the partial and distorted truths this language has seen fit to grant us. He must tear the words out of their living matrix, so that they may not merely mean, but be ... an even more primitive way than punning to strip words of their meanings is repetition ... A word we have been accustomed to look through as mere auxiliary and expletive ... becomes something in its own right, a dimension of existence, by repetition.'

66 The connection between these two poems was first noted by Henry G. Hewlett, in 'Imperfect genius: William Blake', *Contemporary Review*, XXVIII (1876) pp. 756–84.

67 Cf. Winnicott, *Playing and Reality*, pp. 13–14: 'From birth, therefore, the human being is concerned with the problem of the relationship between what is objectively perceived and what is subjectively conceived of, and in the solution of this problem there is no health for the human being who has not been started off well enough by the mother ... at some theoretical point early in the development of every human individual an infant in a certain setting provided by the mother is capable of conceiving of something that would meet the growing need that arises out of instinctual tension. The infant cannot be said to know at first what is to be created. At this point in time the mother presents herself ... The mother's adaptation to the infant's needs, when good enough, gives the infant the *illusion* that there is an external reality that corresponds to the infant's own capacity to create.'

68 Although the Swedenborgians, who would have approved the poem's affirmation of the divine within the human, would not have found the reference to the Jews innocuous.

69 *Moral Essays: Epistle III*, Epistle to Allen, Lord Bathurst (written 1730–2, published 1733), ll. 21–4.

70 E. P. Thompson, 'Patrician Society, Plebeian Culture', *Journal of Social History*, 7 (Summer 1974), pp. 382–405. For a discussion of such riots, see his 'The Moral Economy of the English Crowd in the Eighteenth Century', *Past & Present*, 50 (February 1971), pp. 76–136.

71 For a discussion of the nature of riots in London in the later eighteenth century see Rudé, *Hanoverian London*, pp. 202ff.

72 *The Happy Reign of George the Last. An Address to the Little Tradesmen and the Labouring Poor of England* (n.d.), p. 3.

73 *The Rights of Priests* (Citizen Lee, n.d.), p. 2.

74 Cf. Blake's notebook of 1791–3:

> Soft deceit & idleness,
> These are beauties sweetest dress.   (K182)

Cf. also a later, more ironic sense of the mystificatory nature of the appeal for social 'peace': 'Yet Hell is the most peaceable, and justice therein the best administered of any other kingdom I ever heard of! No wars! no riots! no tumults or insurrections! no traitorous correspondence! no sedition, or attempt to alienate the affections of Lucifer's subjects from his person! no attempt to vilify and bring into contempt the constitution of the empire! But, on the contrary, the virtues most prevalent, are unity, peace, and concord, throughout the whole of Lucifer's dominions. In hell, the public tranquillity is never disturbed in no state or apartment. There you will hear of no such odious names as Paine or Priestley, to alarm and terrify you by their attempts to subvert the government of the country' (*The Rights of the Devil; or Consolation for the Democrats*. 1st edn, Sheffield (n.d.); 2nd edn, London, Citizen Lee (n.d.), p. 14).

75 Leon Radzinowicz, *A History of English Criminal Law* (London, 1948), vol. I, pp. 4–5: 'Broadly speaking, in the course of the hundred and sixty years from the Restoration to the death of George III, the number of capital offences had increased by about one hundred and ninety.'

76 John Brown, *An Estimate of the Manners and Principles of the Times* (London, 1757), p. 21.

77 Douglas Hay, 'Property, Authority, and the Criminal Law', *Albion's Fatal Tree*, pp. 40, 48–9.

78 Thomas Day, *The Children's Miscellany* (London, 1780).

79 Christopher Smart, *Hymns for the Amusement of Children* (London, 1775). This example is particularly interesting in that it comes from the pen of one who in the year following this was himself imprisoned and appealing for 'relief' in letters to friends; and who in his 'mad' (i.e. uncommercial) verse 'prophesied' against the society that 'made somebody Poor'. See *Jubilate Agno*, Fragment C, ll. 65, 72, 73:

For I prophecy that there will be more mercy for criminals.

For I prophecy that they will not dare to imprison a brother or sister for debt.

For I prophecy that hospitality and temperance will revive.

This double awareness perhaps accounts for the revealing stiltedness (very different from the mellifluities of contemporary sentimentalism) of his 'Relief I will communicate'.

80 There seem to have been disputes in the New Church between May 1789 and April 1790 over a translation of Swedenborg's *Chaste Delights of Conjugial Love*, and the whole question of free love (Erdman, *Blake: Prophet* p. 176n.).

81 Quoted in E. P. Thompson, 'The Crime of Anonymity', in Hay *et al.*, *Albion's Fatal Tree*, p. 311–12. Cf. his whole discussion of 'this minatory anonymous "voice of the poor" 'on scores of issues, throughout the eighteenth century and well into the nineteenth, the only protest that can be known' (p. 272).

82 Cf. Lescek Kolakowski, *Marxism and Beyond* (London, 1971), pp. 170–1: '*Let us not underestimate the positive role of hypocrisy.* A social system based on lawlessness, constraint, and misery does not, all appearances to the contrary, become more effective in the long run by hiding behind a front of humanistic phraseology. At a given moment, this facade turns against the social system, because it was always alien and was imposed only by force of historical circumstances ... This facade sometimes begins to live a life of its own, and when it contradicts a system, it produces and nourishes the seeds of the destruction of the system. When an excessive attachment to tradition prevents the system from throwing off his deceptive attire, it may become a Deianira's shirt.'

83 Erikson, *Insight and Responsibility*, p. 113: 'The weakness of the newborn ... is truly relative. While far removed from any measure of mastery over the physical world, newborn man is endowed with an appearance and with responses which appeal to the tending adults' tenderness and make them wish to attend to his needs; which arouse concern in those who are concerned with his well-being; and which, in making adults care, stimulate their active care-taking.'

5. The Morality of Experience: *Songs of Experience*

1 The dates of the notebook drafts of *Songs of Experience* are not certain. David Erdman, in his edition of *The Notebook of William Blake* (Oxford, 1973) suggests 1791–2.

2 Swedenborg, *The True Christian Religion*, 701.

3 David Erdman, *Blake: Prophet Against Empire*, rev. edn (New York, 1969), p. 176n.

4 For a fuller discussion of popular responses to Burke's phrase, see James T. Boulton, *The Language of Politics in the Age of Wilkes and Burke* (London, 1963), pp. 259–60.

5 Most of these cheap publications, with the exception of those published in periodical parts, are undated. The majority seem to have been printed between 1793 and 1795. See R. K. Webb, *The British Working Class Reader 1790–1848* (repr. New York, 1971), pp. 36–41.

6 Specifically, disputes about the establishment of an ordained priesthood. See C. T. Odhner, *Hindmarsh* (Philadelphia, 1895).

7 *New Jerusalem Magazine* (1790), p. 95.

8 For a discussion of the presuppositions of the charity sermons, see Jacob Viner, 'Man's Economic Status' in *Man Versus Society in Eighteenth-Century Britain*, ed. James L. Clifford (Cambridge, 1968), pp. 32–3 and p. 158n.

9 See G. E. Bentley, Jr, *Blake Books* (Oxford, 1977), p. 381 for an account of the publication of the double volume. The evidence he adduces seems to indicate reluctance on Blake's part to publish *Songs of Experience* (though not *Songs of Innocence*) alone.

10 Erdman, *Blake: Prophet*, p. 122.

11 For a discussion of this transitive use of 'appal', in Frend and in Blake, see E. P. Thompson, 'London' in *Interpreting Blake*, ed. Michael Phillips (Cambridge, 1978) pp. 16–17n.

12 Cf. Fredric Jameson, *Marxism and Form* (Princeton, 1971), p. 90: 'What if the fact of our judgment stood as a judgment on us, rather than on the Utopian speculation that we are unable to take seriously? What if our judgment were itself a measure and a symptom of our own incapacity to support such thinking, of our own repression of the principle of futurity, smothered under the realism of the reality principle and the massive weight of what is? What if it were this very psychologism, the cynical reductionism, of the reality principle itself that turned out to be not reality, but just another symptom?'

13 Cf. the rational utopias of Thomas Spence and Thomas Paine, and their visions of instant accomplishment: 'When I first began to study, I found every art and science a perfect whole. Nothing was anarchy but language and politics. But both of these I reduced to order, the one by a new alphabet the other by a new constitution' (Thomas Spence, *Important Trial* quoted in O. Rudkin, *Thomas Spence and his Connections* (London, 1927), p. 59).

'As reforms, or revolutions, call them what you please, extend themselves among nations, those nations will form connexions and conventions, and when a few are thus confederated, the progress will be rapid, till despotism and corrupt government be totally expelled, at least out of two quarters of the world, Europe and America' (Thomas Paine, *Rights of Man*, ed. Henry Collins (London, 1969), p. 292).

14 *Rights of Priests* (n.d.), p. 4.

15 One of the most interesting attempts to question the prevailing social orders from a plebeian perspective seems, in fact, to have been uninfluenced by these radical writings. This is *A Brief Account of the Manner of the Lord's Gracious Dealings with Me*, by William Bryan (London, 1795): a spiritual autobiography by the man who accompanied John Wright on his pilgrimage to Avignon (see above, ch. 4, n. 28). Bryan was a spiritual 'seeker' of a

kind very reminiscent of Blake. For several years he had associated with the Quakers and at the time of writing his autobiography was a follower of Richard Brothers: he and Wright were known to the Swedenborgians, who took an interest in the Avignon circle (Robert Hindmarsh, *Rise and Progress of the New Jerusalem Church* (London, 1861), pp. 47–9).

Bryan worked first as a copper-plate printer and engraver until 'no man would employ me, saying, as I had once been mad, and left my business [to go to Avignon] I might take another fit of insanity, and do so again' (p. 29). He then worked as a druggist. Bryan's account is of interest because his vision of social injustice can be seen emerging out of his own experience, as an apothecary treating first the poor, and then soldiers returning from Ireland: he judges the status quo not from the point of view of rational radicalism, but from that of radical Christianity: 'I was made to see that the mystery of iniquity had worked as deeply in the line of physic as any other. If I was at any time sent for I must give only the medicine which I knew would be likely in the most speedy and effectual manner to bring about my patient, and no more than was necessary: I could not croud in draught after draught to enlarge my bill ... I am confident that the true knowledge is not witheld from any man by the Lord, but man rejecting him rejects the true light, whereby the true knowledge is communicated to the understanding; and instead of looking into, and endeavouring to reject in themselves, what-soever that light discovers unto them is not of God, but of the devil and themselves, by which the light in their understandings would increase ... then the bent of all the faculties of the mind are turned to seek only how they can most effectually gather together gold and silver, that they may obtain authority over others, and procure for themselves and families those things which feeding their lusts cannot satisfy, and setting their hearts upon them, are led to oppress and distress the poor, to whom many times their illness is a sufficient, very heavy and sore affliction, without the doctor's fee or the apothecaries bill, which, if not paid, must be put into the hands of an attorney, whose business, more false and more oppressive than the rest, to complete his calamity, whether the man is well or ill, whether he has it or has it not, he must either pay or go to a prison.

Every tradesman is obliged, more or less, to enter with his mind into the same system of iniquity, or he cannot live. The divine, so called, the priests too, of almost all denominations *divine for money*, and *prophesy for hire*; and the words of the prophet, "*My sheep have strayed on the tops of all the mountains, saith the Lord – their teachers have caused them to err*," are fulfilled this day; therefore what follows must also soon come to pass, "*I myself will search them out, and gather them, saith the Lord*;" therefore all you who set your hearts against oppression, and whose spirits abhor iniquity, who are ready to sacrifice *your all*, yea even *life itself*, for righteousness sake, and that goodness and truth may be established on the earth, lift up your heads, look for your deliverer; for the promises of Jehovah, to put down all oppression, with them that do oppress, and who commit evil in the land, is about to be fulfilled in this day ... when man will not oppress man, but *Love* alone shall reign; when no man shall say to his neighbour, know the Lord, but all shall know him, from the least to the greatest; when righteousness shall cover the earth, as the waters cover the *sea*, when the nations of the earth shall not more be governed by the sensual, selfish, evil will of man, in the principle of destruction and war, which is the principle of hell and the infernals. But the Lord himself, the Lord shall be kind over all the earth, and he shall be the only Lord, for the foolish, vain, and proud titles that men have taken up in blasphemy against him, and called the most worthless, and professedly evil by, will be no more' (pp. 29–30, 31–2).

16 Cf. Blake's ironic conflation of 'experience' and 'experiment' in *All Religions are One* (1788), quoted above p. 150, and n. 28 below.

17 See twentieth-century critical discussion of the poem. Those who see Blake as endorsing the Clod's view include Mark Schorer, *William Blake: the Politics of Vision* (New York, 1946), pp. 205–6 and John Beer, *Blake's Humanism* (Manchester, 1968), p. 72. Those who favour the Pebble include Jean Hagstrum, 'William Blake's "The Clod & the Pebble"' in *Restoration and Eighteenth-Century Literature: Essays in Honor of Alan Dugald McKillop*, ed. Carroll Camden (Chicago, 1963), pp. 381–8; and (with some reservations) Thomas Edwards, *Imagination and Power* (London, 1971), pp. 155–6.

18 Swedenborg, *The True Christian Religion*, 400: 14.

19 Another, obsolete, meaning offered by the *OED*, and perhaps ironically in play here, is 'Mild, gentle'.

20 Cf. Blake's mirror-writing at the opening of the second book of *Milton*: 'A Negation is not a Contrary' (K518).

On negatives in poetry see Susanne Langer, *Feeling and Form* (London, 1953), pp. 242–3 and Sigurd Burckhardt, 'The Poet as Fool and Priest', *ELH*, 23 (1965), pp. 288–9.

21 See note 9 above.

22 For a different kind of exploration of a 'love' which involves repression rather than realization of self, see 'My Pretty Rose-tree' from *Songs of Experience*, with the draft of which Blake's notebook begins:

> A flower was offer'd to me
> Such a flower as may never bore;
> But I said, 'I've a pretty rose tree,'
> And I passed the sweet flower o'er.
>
> Then I went to my pretty rose tree
> ~~In the silent of the night~~
> To tend it by day & night
> But my rose ~~was turned from me~~
> ~~was fill'd~~ turn'd away with Jealousy
> And her thorns were my only delight.

Here, in a poem which seems closer to a simple description of a personal crisis than any of the other Songs, Blake exposes the logic of that appropriation, refusal and sterile deadlock which the other drafts were to explore in different terms. The speaker's rejection of the flower is paralleled by the rose's 'turning away' from him: these two who would maintain an exclusive claim upon one another end in separation. For that individualistic self-control which is implicit in the refusal of desired relationship ('But I said ... ') is here shown to be fatally linked to the notion that the other can be possessed ('I've a pretty rose tree') and 'tended' rather than related to in its otherness. That 'love' which would manifest itself in self-restraint, in a rejection of the gifts of life, is exposed, in the reiterated 'I', 'I', 'my' of the poem, to depend upon a manipulative and isolating self-assertion, which makes satisfaction either of self or of other impossible. The final word of the poem points toward 'The Clod & the Pebble', where the insight arrived at in this poetic diagnosis of an interpersonal dilemma has been transposed into an engagement not with the details but with the presuppositions of contemporary debate.

23 Cf. Martin Buber, *I and Thou*, trans. Walter Kaufmann (Edinburgh, 1970): 'The ego does not participate in any actuality nor does he gain any. He sets himself apart from everything else and tries to possess as much as possible by means of experience and use ... He knows himself as a subject, but this subject can appropriate as much as it wants to, it will never gain any substance: it remains like a point, functional, that which experiences, that which uses, nothing more ... all of its eager "individuality" cannot help it to gain any substance' (p. 114).

' – When man does not test the *a priori* of relation in the world, working out and actualizing the innate You in what he encounters, it turns inside. Then it unfolds through the unnatural, impossible object, the I – which is to say that it unfolds where there is no room for it to unfold. Thus the confrontation within the self comes into being, and this cannot be relation, presence, the current of reciprocity, but only self-contradiction' (p. 119).

24 For a more particular contemporary reference, see Gordon Rattray Taylor, *The Angel Makers* (London, 1973), pp. 326–7, for an account of the late eighteenth-century controversy over swaddling.

25 Hazard Adams, *William Blake: A Reading of the Shorter Poems* (Seattle, 1963), p. 288. Cf. also Jean Hagstrum, 'The Fly', *William Blake: Essays for S. Foster Damon*, ed. Alvin H. Rosenfeld (Providence, 1969), who sees the final stanza as 'a simple assurance of salvation' (p. 381).

26 See Paul Fussell, *The Rhetorical World of Augustan Humanism* (Oxford, 1965), ch. 10, for a discussion of insect imagery in eighteenth-century literature, and of the way in which it focussed very fundamental issues: 'To the Augustans, the newly accessible world of bugs, although interesting in a quaint way, is useful primarily as evidence of the "fallen" and unredeemable squalor of that part of the creation which is sub-human. But to the Moderns, bolstered by the entomological enthusiasms of the Royal Society, the world of insects suggests an optimistic, often Deistic conviction of divine benignity' (p. 241).

27 The notebook draft (K182–3) shows how carefully Blake deleted the adjectives which might indicate his speaker's attitude.

28 In the *Shorter Oxford English Dictionary* the last usages of 'experience' to mean 'experiment' are given as 1763 and 1780. In this parody of a scientific syllogism, Blake seems to be playing on an actual, recently disappeared (or perhaps disappearing) double sense of the word.

29 Cf. E. A. Burtt, *The Metaphysical Foundations of Modern Physical Science; A Historical and Critical Essay* (London, 1925), p. 236: 'the general picture of the universe and of man's place in it which went forth under [Newton's] name was essentially that which had been constructed and powerfully worked out by the great mathematical metaphysicians who had preceded him, and that in its most ambiguous and least construable form. The tremendous problems thrust upon us by that picture he, no more than they, appreciated, for in the main he also adopted their way, especially More's, of evading those problems by the appeal to God. But it was of the greatest consequence for succeeding thought that now the great Newton's authority was squarely behind that view of the cosmos which saw in man a puny, irrelevant spectator (so far as a being wholly imprisoned in a dark room can be called such) of the vast metaphysical system whose regular motions according to mechanical principles constituted the world of nature.'

See also, C. C. Gillispie, *The Edge of Objectivity* (Princeton, 1960), p. 146: '[Newtonian science] moves from descriptions and measurements to abstract generalizations. Strictly speaking, therefore, Newtonian science could never get outside itself, and might be said to be a tautology, or at least to accomplish nothing of human interest or value. The trouble was not in the evidence. No one complained of the mathematics. But taken as an explanation of the universe, the system failed – or rather, it was no explanation at all, since no cause could be assigned and no mechanism imagined for its central principle, the principle of attraction.'

For a discussion of the growing awareness of this in the later eighteenth century see Ben Ross Schneider, *Wordsworth's Cambridge Education* (Cambridge, 1957), *passim*, and esp. pp. 126ff.

30 Swedenborg, *The True Christian Religion*, 568.

31 This version is that printed in *The Oxford Dictionary of Nursery Rhymes*, ed. Iona and Peter Opie (Oxford, 1951), pp. 286–7. They report versions of it in 'several proverb collections', including one of 1659, and in *Gammer Gurton's Garland* (1784). John Adlard, *The Sports of Cruelty* (London, 1972) discusses Blake's familiarity with traditional rhymes.

32 Cf. William Godwin, *Enquiry Concerning Political Justice*, ed. Isaac Kramnick (London, 1976), p. 601: 'Every moralist can tell us that morality eminently consists in "the government of the tongue". But this branch of morality has long been inverted. Instead of studying what we shall tell, we are taught to consider what we shall conceal. Instead of an active virtue, "going about doing good", we are instructed to believe that the chief end of man is to do no mischief. Instead of fortitude, we are care-

fully imbued with maxims of artifice and cunning, misnamed prudence.

Let us contrast the character of those men with whom we are accustomed to converse, with the character of men such as they ought to be, and will be. On the one side, we perceive a perpetual caution that shrinks from the observing eye, that conceals, with a thousand folds, the genuine emotions of the heart ... Such characters as ours are the mere shadows of men, with a specious outside perhaps, but destitute of substance and soul. When shall we arrive at the land of realities, where men shall be known for what they are, by energy of thought, and intrepidity of action!'

33 Cf. Wilden, *System and Structure*, p. 70: 'it is the social and socializing function of human desire to structure our desires on what the Other desires (or desires us to desire), the desired 'object' serving as a simple mediator between desiring subjects'.

Cf. also *Jerusalem*, Plate 66, ll. 53–6:

> By Invisible Hatreds adjoin'd, they seem remote and separate
> From each other, and yet are a Mighty Polypus in the Deep!
> As the Mistletoe grows on the Oak, so Albion's Tree on
> Eternity. Lo!
> He who will not commingle in Love must be adjoin'd by
> Hate. (K703)

34 Cf. *Jerusalem*, Plate 43, ll. 59–60:

> 'Instead of Albion's lovely mountains & the curtains of Jerusalem,
> 'I see a Cave, a Rock, a Tree deadly and poisonous, unimaginative.'
> (K673)

35 For a discussion of these accounts see Geoffrey Grigson, *The Romantics* (Cleveland, Ohio, 1962), pp. 340–1.

36 *New Magazine of Knowledge Concerning Heaven and Hell* (1790), p. 36.

37 Genesis 3: 3: 'But of the fruit of the tree which is in the midst of the garden, God hath said, Ye shall not eat of it, neither shall ye touch it, lest ye die.'

38 Noted by Kathleen Raine in *Blake and Tradition* (Princeton, 1968), vol. II, p. 39.

39 Philip J. Gallagher, 'The Word Made Flesh: Blake's "A Poison Tree" and the Book of Genesis', *Studies in Romanticism*, 16 (Spring 1977), pp. 237–49.

40 Swedenborg, *The True Christian Religion*, 324. Cf. *Vala, or The Four Zoas*, Night 2, l. 388 (K290): 'I have planted a false oath in the earth; it has brought forth a poison tree.'

41 Swedenborg, *The True Christian Religion*, 520.

42 Cf. Blake's annotations to Watson (K393): 'I cannot conceive the Divinity of the books in the Bible to consist either in who they were written by, or at what time, or in the historical evidence which may be all false in the eyes of one man & true in the eyes of another, but in the Sentiments & Examples, which, whether true or Parabolic, are Equally useful as Examples given to us of the perverseness of some & its consequent evil & the honesty of others & its consequent good. This sense of the Bible is equally true to all & equally plain to all.'

43 Cf. his annotations to Swedenborg's *Wisdom of Angels Concerning Divine Providence* (K131–3), apparently written about 1790, where the central issue is Swedenborg's predestinarianism.

44 Gregory Bateson, *Steps to an Ecology of Mind* (St Albans, 1973), p. 177: 'metaphor is an indispensible tool of thought and expression – a characteristic of all human communication, even of that of the scientist. The conceptual models of cybernetics and the energy theories of psychoanalysis are, after all, only labelled metaphors. The peculiarity of the schizophrenic is not that he uses metaphors, but that he uses *unlabelled* metaphors. He has special difficulty in handling signals of that class whose members assign Logical Types to other signals.'

45 Karl Marx, *Economic and Political Manuscripts*, in *Karl Marx: Early Writings*, trans. and ed. T. B. Bottomore (London, 1963), p. 125.

46 Karl Marx, *Capital* (Moscow and London, 1959), I, p. 72.

47 Cf. the doctrine much emphasized by antinomian sects, that private property was not merely the result of the Fall of man, but *was* the Fall:that the abolition of private property would 'remove the ancient curse' (K176). For a clear discussion of this, see Christoper Hill, *Milton and the English Revolution* (London, 1977), p. 346.

48 E.g., perhaps most famously – or notoriously – Soame Jenyns, *A Free Inquiry into the Nature and Origin of Evil* (London, 1757).

49 Donald Davie, *Articulate Energy* (London, 1955), p. 82, finds that 'the movement of the mind through the first couplet is checked on the rhyme, retracts, and goes through the same motions all over again', and that we have in this stanza 'two sentences parallel in syntax, rhythm, and meaning'. Yet the syntactical (surely not rhythmic?) parallelism merely serves to blur a significant development, and 'slides us into narrative' rather sooner than Davie argues.

50 From now on I shall be quoting from the text of the engraved version.

51 Davie, *Articulate Energy*, p. 81.

52 E.g. Gregory Bateson, quoted at the head of this chapter; Frederick Perls, Ralph F. Hefferline, Paul Goodman, *Gestalt Therapy* (London, 1973), pp. 488ff.; E. P. Thompson, *Protest and Survive* (London, 1980), p. 28.

53 For a clear account of the internal and external dynamics of this master–slave complicity see Erich Fromm, *Fear of Freedom* (London, 1942), pp. 83–4.

54 M. Dorothy George, *London Life in the Eighteenth Century* (Harmondsworth, 1966), pp. 119–20.

55 George Rudé, *Hanoverian London 1714–1808* (London, 1971), pp. 250, 253.

56 Theodor Adorno in a letter to Walter Benjamin, quoted by Martin Jay in *The Dialectical Imagination* (London, 1973), p. 267.

57 Johnson, 'The Vanity of Human Wishes', l. 159. The opening lines of this poem are perhaps the dramatization *par excellence* of this stance:

Let observation with extensive view,
Survey mankind, from China to Peru;
Remark each anxious toil, each eager strife,
And watch the busy scenes of crouded life.

58 See Rudé, *Hanoverian London*, ch. 1; Raymond Williams, *The Country and the City* (London, 1973), pp. 142–52; Max Byrd, *London Transformed: Images of the City in the Eighteenth Century* (New Haven and London, 1978).

59 Ben Sedgly, *Observations on Mr. Fielding's Enquiry* (London, 1751), pp. 22–3, quoted in Byrd, *London Transformed*, p. 23.

60 See Byrd, *London Transformed*, esp. pp. 26–8, for an excellent discussion of this. Cf. also Richard Sennett, *The Fall of Public Man* (Cambridge, 1977), pp. 28–122, on the more general issue of 'role-playing' within the eighteenth-century city.

61 Samuel Johnson, *The Rambler* 159.

62 Paine, *Rights of Man*, ed. Henry Collins (London, 1969), pp. 242–3. On the sale of the volume, see Henry Collins' Introduction to this edition, p. 36, and Richard Altick, *The English Common Reader*, p. 70.

For a fuller discussion of the debate over 'charters', see Erdman, *Blake: Prophet*, pp. 276–7 and E. P. Thompson, 'London', in *Interpreting Blake*, ed. Michael Phillips, pp. 6–10. An interesting footnote is provided by Burke himself, who seems to have drawn attention to this ambiguity in the word as early as 1784: 'The charters, which we call by distinction *great*, are public instruments of this nature; I mean the charters of King John and King Henry the Third. The things secured by these instruments may, without any deceitful ambiguity, be very fitly called the *chartered rights of men*.

These Charters have made the very name of a Charter dear to the heart of every Englishman. But, Sir, there may be, and there *are* Charters, not only different in nature, but formed on principles the *very reverse* of those of the great Charter. Of this kind is the Charter of the East-India Company. *Magna Charta* is a Charter to restrain power, and to destroy monopoly: the East India Charter is a Charter to establish monopoly, and to create power. Political power and commercial monopoly are *not* the rights of men; and the rights to them derived from Charters, it is fallacious and sophisticated to call "the Chartered Rights of men". These Chartered Rights ... do at least suspend the natural rights of mankind at large; and in their very frame and constitution are liable to fall into a direct violation of them.' (Taken from 'a short Abstract from Mr. Burke's celebrated speech upon the East India Bill, in which the line of distinction between the different sorts of Charters is drawn with great truth and great precision', *Chartered Rights* (1784)).

63 Cf. Blake's notebook entry of these years:
Why should I care for the men of thames,
Or the cheating waves of charter'd streams? (K166)

64 These 'marks' are marks of salvation. Harold Bloom, *Poetry and*

Repression (New Haven, 1976) argues that this is 'the precursor-text' of the poem. This seems rather literal-minded, and at odds with the pervasive sense that the 'marks', like the marks of the Beast, might be marks of damnation. Michael Ferber, '"London" and its Politics', *ELH*, 48 (1981), pp. 310–38, prefers (similarly rather literally) to trace them to Revelation: but argues that it is 'best to dwell little on either of them, lest you wander entirely out of the poem (p. 320)'. I would point less to a specific allusion – a key to the 'message' of the poem – than to a whole cluster of Biblical resonances, whose importance consists in their evocation of a quite different – and much more engaged – contemporary usage of 'mark' than that of polite convention.

65 Sennett, *The Fall of Public Man*, p. 70. The notion of reading character from the face would have been familiar to Blake from Lavater's *Essays on Physiognomy*, for the first volume of which (1789) he had engraved three plates.

66 For further discussion of the suggestiveness of 'mark' see E. P. Thompson, 'London', pp. 10–14; Heather Glen, 'The Poet in Society: Blake and Wordsworth on London', *Literature and History*, 3 (Spring, 1976); Stan Smith, 'Some Responses to Heather Glen's "The Poet in Society"', *Literature and History*, 4 (Autumn, 1976).

67 This point is well made by Thompson, 'London', pp. 18–19.

68 Godwin, *Enquiry Concerning Political Justice*, p. 149. See Thompson, 'London; p. 15, and Ferber, '"London" and its Politics', pp. 321ff., on Blake's change in the draft from 'german' (signifying, as Ferber notes, 'a kind of German yoke theory aimed at the House of Hanover') to 'mind-forg'd': a change which – like his use of 'charter'd' – does not simply place him on the radical side of a contemporary debate, but offers a rather more complex perspective on it.

69 Edmund Burke, *Letter to a Member of the National Assembly* (1791), *Writings and Speeches* (London, Beaconsfield edn, n.d.), vol, IV, pp. 51–2.

70 E.g. Priscilla Wakefield, *Perambulations in London* (1809), p. 146. Ferber, '"London" and its Politics', p. 325, discusses the different possible meanings of 'appals' and concludes: 'I think it makes the line more coherent to entertain the paradox of the church paling at the chimney sweeper's cry while blackening on its own, than to imagine the cry doubling that blackening by casting a pall.'

Cf. a suggestive Swedenborgian image for that Moral Virtue which is uninformed by a sense of spiritual potentiality, in *The True Christian Religion*, 503: 'We have also separated charity from all relation to what is spiritual, and have made it a merely moral virtue; and so we have done likewise with the decalogue... On this supposition... would not the church be like the black face of a chimney-sweeper, the only white spots about which are in his eyes?'

71 John Brewer, *Party Ideology and Popular Politics at the Accession of George III* (Cambridge, 1976), p. 153.

72 Paine, quoted above, p. 210; see also note 62 above.

73 See Thompson, 'London', p. 23, for a discussion of the image of the Harlot in English radical Dissent in the eighteenth century.

74 David Bindman, *Blake as an artist* (Oxford, 1977), p. 43, offers a clear account of this process.

75 See Robert N. Essick, 'Blake and the Traditions of Reproductive Engraving', *Blake Studies*, 5 (Autumn, 1972).

76 For suggestive discussions of the work of art as a discovery see 'Joanna Field' (Marion Milner), *On Not Being Able to Paint* (London, 1950) and Anton Ehrenzweig, *The Hidden Order of Art* (London, 1967).

77 Jean-Paul Sartre, Preface to Frantz Fanon, *The Wretched of the Earth* (Harmondsworth, 1967), p. 15.

78 Thompson, 'London', p. 23.

79 Both words are strongly sound-linked: each stands at the beginning of a line.

80 Fredric Jameson, *Marxism and Form*, pp. 84–5.

81 Jameson, *Marxism and Form*, quoted above, p. 218.

82 A phrase scrawled by Blake on the fourth page of the notebook in which the poems of *Songs of Experience* were drafted (K889, n. 161).

83 Blake's sectarian background has never been satisfactorily explored. A. L. Morton, *The Everlasting Gospel* (London, 1958) points to similarities between his ideas and those of the antinomian sects: certainly, his intimacy with those ideas is evident throughout his lifetime's work. But – as I argue – his relation to that tradition was not a passive one. And his attitude towards actual membership of a sectarian group is indicated not merely by his revulsion from the New Church, but also in his annotations to Lavater (1788), where he underlines aphorism 339 ('he who adheres to a sect has something of its cant', K74) and comments on aphorism 416 ('He, who to obtain much will suffer little or nothing, can never be called great; and none ever little, who, to obtain one great object, will suffer much'): 'The man who does this is a Sectary: therefore not great' (K77).

84 See Hill, *Milton*, pp. 302ff.

85 Schiller, quoted above, p. 144.

6. Morality through Experience: *Lyrical Ballads 1798*

1 1800 Preface, Brett and Jones, pp. 246–7.

2 See above, pp. 50–1.

3 The phrase is Wordsworth's, from his Advertisement to the volume, Brett and Jones, p. 7. Southey's views were expressed in a review in *The Critical Review*, xxiv (October 1798).

4 Mary Jacobus, 'Southey's Debt to *Lyrical Ballads* (1798)', *RES*, new ser., xxii (1971), pp. 20–36.

5 Robert Southey, *Ballads, Metrical Tales and other poems* (London, 1854) p. 118.

6 Cf. John Thelwall, *The Peripatetic; or Sketches of the Heart, of Nature and Society; in a series of Politico-Sentimental Journals in Verse and Prose* (London, 1793), vol. III, pp. 141–6: 'at a time when poor fellows are wheedled into the naval service by such pompous pretences of provisions for their wives and families, it is important to shew what kind of relief is afforded to the wants of those who seem most entitled to our compassion ...

The poor husband was a weaver, but that as he had been to sea in the former part of his life, he had been pressed at the breaking out of the war, and had left her no other means to support her two infants and provide for the season of pain and perplexity that was approaching, but the labour of her own hands. "... In this distress I applied to the overseers of the parish; but they only gave me a *shilling*, and bade me call again a fortnight, and I should have *another*". Such was the tale of the poor creature whom these *British Slave merchants*, these *wholesale dealers in their brethren's blood*, had left to rot in the cold embraces of Want and Misery, that the stay and comfort of her life, the father and protector of her infants, might lavish his limbs and life for them in a struggle, in which (to say the least of it) neither he nor his family, had the slightest interest or concern: and, alas! how many thousands are there at this time languishing for the same cause, in situations of equal misery. The story was too circumstantial to be doubted.'

7 See Stephen Gill, '"Adventures on Salisbury Plain" and Wordsworth's Poetry of Protest 1795–97', *Studies in Romanticism* XI (1972), pp. 48–65, and Mary Jacobus, *Tradition and Experiment in Wordsworth's Lyrical Ballads (1798)* (Oxford, 1976), pp. 148ff.

8 See above, pp. 6–7.

9 For a discussion of this, see Jonathan Wordsworth, *The Music of Humanity* (New York, 1969), pp. 62–5.

10 See above, p. 104. For a fuller discussion of Wordsworth's use of *Zoonomia*, and interest in extreme psychological states, see James H. Averill, *Wordsworth and the Poetry of Human Suffering*, pp. 152–68.

11 Joseph Fawcett, 'On the comparative Sum of Happiness and Misery in Human Life', *Sermons*, vol. II, pp. 89–90.

12 See above, p. 53.

13 And its contemporary ones. Cf. John Jones, *The Egotistical Sublime* (London, 1954), p. 63, who argues that the concluding lines 'do violence to the nature of the old man' and Mary Jacobus, *Tradition and Experiment*, pp. 180–1, who finds it 'incongruous ... that ... he should emerge from his animal tranquillity to tell a human story'.

14 Brett and Jones, p. 295.

15 *Poetical Works*, ed. E. de Selincourt and Helen Darbishire (5 vols., Oxford, 1940–9), vol. 1, pp. 315–16. Jonathan Wordsworth, *The Music of Humanity*, pp. 5–6 suggests that these lines were probably written 'in the period immediately following the completion of *The Borderers* in spring 1797'.

16 Cf. the longer poem on which Wordsworth now began to work, 'The

Ruined Cottage', where a complex narrative structure is used to distance the urgency of the story.

17 *Critical Review*, XXIV (October 1798).

18 *Monthly Review*, XXIX (June 1799).

19 *British Critic*, XVII (February 1801).

20 See above, p. 44.

21 Southey, *Minor Poems* (London, 1854), pp. 166–7.

22 Part of the story of the sailor's widow, quoted above, n. 6.

23 Paul D. Sheats, *The Making of Wordsworth's Poetry 1785–1798* (Cambridge, Mass., 1973), pp. 188–93; Andrew L. Griffin, 'Wordsworth and the Problem of Imaginative Story: the Case of "Simon Lee"', *PMLA*, 92 (1977), pp. 392–409.

24 Sheats. *Making of Wordsworth's Poetry*, p. 192.

25 See Kenneth Maclean, *Agrarian Age: a Background for Wordsworth* (New Haven, 1950), pp. 20–1 for a discussion of the particular detail of these lines.

26 1800 Preface, Brett and Jones, p. 247.

27 1798 Advertisement, Brett and Jones, p. 8.

28 1800 Preface, Brett and Jones, p. 248.

29 1798 Advertisement, Brett and Jones, p. 7.

30 David Erdman, 'Coleridge, Wordsworth and the Wedgwood Fund', *Bulletin of the New York Public Library*, 60 (September and October, 1956).

31 Cf. the project of another of this circle, Thomas Beddoes (in a letter quoted in *Memoirs of the Life of Thomas Beddoes M.D.* by John Edmonds Stock, M.D. (London, 1811) p. 129): 'to establish a manufacture of RATIONAL TOYS. I believe parents are become sufficiently attentive to education, to give such a scheme support; and fortunately it cannot alarm any prejudice ... The particulars of the design are too numerous to be given here. It comprehends engravings and a good deal of letter-press. I have in view not merely information in mechanics, chemistry, and technology, but the improvement of the senses, by presenting in a certain order and upon principle, objects of touch along with objects of sight. In this important business, we have hitherto trusted to chance. But there is every reason to suppose that INTELLIGENT ART will produce a much quicker and greater effect. Should instruction addressed to sense, be made in any country the principle of education; should the best method of cultivating the senses be studied, and should proper exercises be devised for reproducing ideas (originally well defined,) sometimes with rapidity, at others in diversified trains, the consequence is to me obvious. The inhabitants of that country would speedily become ... far superior to the rest of mankind in intellect and efficiency.'

32 A favourite word of Wordsworth's, often used of his encounters with baffling otherness: cf. 'Resolution and Independence', stanza XVI:

> Or like a man from some far region sent,
> To give me human strength, by apt admonishment.

and *The Prelude* (1805), Book VII, ll. 620–2:

And on the shape of the unmoving man,
His fixed face, and sightless eyes, I look'd
As if admonish'd from another world.

33 Thelwall, *The Peripatetic*, vol. I, p. 101.

34 *Collected Letters*, ed. Earl Leslie Griggs (2 vols., Oxford 1956), pp. 397–8.

35 See Humphrey House, 'Wordsworth's Fame' (BBC Third Programme, 1947), repr. *English Critical Essays, Second Series*, ed. Derek Hudson (London, 1958).

36 See above, p. 40–2.

37 Edmund Burke, *Reflections on the Revolution in France*, ed. Conor Cruise O'Brien (London, 1968), p. 183.

38 *Rights of Man*, ed. Henry Collins (London, 1969) p. 64.

39 1800 Preface, Brett and Jones, p. 246.

40 Extract from Gilpin's *Observations on the River Wye*, quoted in Charles Heath, *Descriptive Account of Tintern Abbey* (Monmouth, 1793). This is a recurring theme in the accounts extracted by Heath.

41 For a discussion of the word 'scene' in the context of such eighteenth-century approaches to landscape, see John Barrell, *The Idea of Landscape and the Sense of Place 1730–1840: An Approach to the Poetry of John Clare* (Cambridge, 1972), p. 24.

42 Ernst Cassirer, *The Philosophy of the Enlightenment*, trans. F. C. A. Koelln and J. P. Pettegrove (Princeton, 1951), pp. 108–20 and Colin M. Turbayne, *The Myth of Metaphor* (rev. edn, Columbia, S.C., 1970), pp. 106–12, offer accounts of this problem and its importance.

43 Turbayne, *The Myth of Metaphor*, pp. 108–9.

44 On Wordsworth's debt to associationist psychology, see ch. 7, n. 16.

45 David Hartley, *Observations on Man* (2 vols, London, 1749), vol. I, p. 497.

46 See Richard J. Onorato, *The Character of the Poet: Wordsworth in The Prelude* (Princeton, 1971), p. 82, for an interesting close discussion of the lines addressed to Dorothy, in which, he suggests, Dorothy is not seen as particular and other but is confused with Wordsworth's former self.

47 For a discussion of this feature of associationist psychology, see Leslie Stephen, *History of English Thought in the Eighteenth Century* (London, 1876), pp. 69–70 and Basil Willey, *The Eighteenth-Century Background* (Harmondsworth, 1962), p. 139.

7. Desire and Disillusion: the Goslar Lyrics

1 For a discussion of this conception of nature amongst the Wordsworth circle in the late 1790s, see Kelvin Everest, *Coleridge's Secret Ministry: The Context of the Conversation Poems* (Hassocks, Sussex, 1979).

2 See my discussion of 'The Old Cumberland Beggar' (written in 1797 but first published in this volume), above, p. 84.

3 Letter to Charles James Fox, 14 January 1801, in *Letters: the Early Years*, ed. E. de Selincourt, rev. C. L. Shaver (2nd edn Oxford, 1967).

4 The phrase is Francis Wrangham's, from his review, '*Lyrical Ballads* in Two Volumes by William Wordsworth' in *The British Critic* (February 1801).

5 Not merely in 'Anecdote for Fathers', but also, more obliquely, in 'Tintern Abbey' and those shorter nature lyrics which attempt to explore the ways in which sensibility is shaped and formed.

6 Part 1, ll. 7–8:

> O Derwent, travelling over the green plains
> Near my 'sweet birth-place'.

Part 11, ll. 496–7:

> Thou, my Friend, wast reared
> In the great city 'mid far other scenes.

7 In an early draft of the poem, which does not include the second section, the boy is referred to first in the third, and then in the first person. (Reproduced in *The Prelude 1798–9*, ed. Stephen Parrish (Ithaca, New York, 1977) pp. 86–7.)

8 Cf. Coleridge, 'The Nightingale', ll. 67–8:

> Their bright, bright eyes, their eyes both bright and full,
> Glistning ...

with 'There was a Boy', ll. 18–19:

> Then, sometimes, in that silence, while he hung
> Listening ...

The two sound-linked words, 'Glistning' and 'Listening', each at the beginning of a line, pinpoint the difference between the two poems. The first is a clear particular observation of nature, the second a state of human subjectivity, a passive expectancy to which the expected answer does not come.

9 *Biographia Literaria*, ed. George Watson (London 1973), vol. 11, ch. xx, p. 233, n.1.

10 See Geoffrey Durrant, *Wordsworth and the Great System* (Cambridge, 1970), pp. 24–5.

11 These phrases are taken from the passage which immediately precedes the inclusion of 'There was a Boy' in the 1805 version of *The Prelude* (Book v, ll. 370–88). Coleridge is not, of course one of those whom Wordsworth is attacking here: his targets are the rational educationalists satirized in 'Anecdote for Fathers'.

12 Michael Black, 'On Reading: Some Lines of Wordsworth', *The Critical Review*, 19 (1977), pp. 86–7. Such 'co-presences' might, I think, be extended to include not merely images, but also such other poetic features as rhythmic cadences and grammatical structures.

13 'Tintern Abbey', ll. 134–5.

14 Throughout, the boy's feelings have been presented not as peculiar to himself, but as common human experience:

NOTES TO PP. 274–83

> such suppression of the heart
> As joy delights in . . .
>
> A temper known to those who, after long
> And weary expectation, have been blest
> With sudden happiness beyond all hope.
>
> In that sweet mood when pleasure loves to pay
> Tribute to ease, and, of its joy secure
> The heart luxuriates with indifferent things.

15 Cf. Christopher Ricks, 'The Twentieth-Century Wordsworth', in Reuben A. Brower ed., *Twentieth-Century Literature in Retrospect* (Cambridge, Mass., 1971), pp. 357–8 on the importance of the word 'up' in Wordsworth's poetry.

16 On Wordsworth's intrinsic associationism see Arthur Beatty, *William Wordsworth: his Doctrine and Art in their Historical Relations* (Madison, Wisc., 1922). Basil Willey, 'David Hartley and Nature's Education' in *The Eighteenth Century Background* (Harmondsworth, 1962); Colin Clarke, 'Nature's Education of Man', *Philosophy*, XXIII (1948); Robert Langbaum, 'The Evolution of Soul in Wordsworth's Poetry', *PMLA*, LXXXII (May 1967), pp. 265–72.

17 In the later, 1850, version she is more active, but her activity consists of little more than sentimental tenderness. For a discussion of the difference between the two versions, see F. R. Leavis, *Revaluation* (London, 1936), pp. 156–60; Donald Davie, *Articulate Energy* (London, 1955), pp. 112–5.

Cf. Adrienne Rich, *Of Woman Born: Motherhood as Experience and Institution* (London, 1976), pp. 35–6: 'Most of the literature of infant care and psychology has assumed that the process toward individuation is essentially the *child's* drama, played out against and with a parent or parents who are, for better or worse, givens.'

18 1800 Preface, Brett and Jones, p. 251.

19 Ernst G. Schachtel, *Metamorphosis* (London, 1963), pp. 295–6.

20 Sent in a letter to Coleridge, 14 or 21 December 1798, *Letters: the Early Years*, p. 414.

21 E.g. Simon Stuart, *New Phoenix Wings: Reparation in Literature* (London, 1979), pp. 117–18: 'The thought is "wayward" less because it is far-fetched – for both the first draft of the present poem and the other Lucy poems make it clear that Lucy actually died – than because irrational anxieties contain wishes. And when unconscious wishes are as it were omnipotently fulfilled, as this one seemed to be, the consequent desolation is intensified by the sense of guilt at being oneself responsible for the death.'

22 'The Rime of the Ancyent Marinere', *Lyrical Ballads 1798*, ll. 419–26.

23 'The Nightingale', *Lyrical Ballads 1798*, ll. 75–80.

24 'The Nightingale', ll. 101–5.

25 MS Fragment, ? September 1798, *Poems*, ed. John Beer (London, 1974), p. 224.

26 'Frost at Midnight', ll. 72–4.

27 For an illuminating discussion of this, see Hugh Kenner, *The Art of Poetry* (New York, 1966), pp. 37ff.

28 E.g. Marion Milner, *On Not Being Able to Paint* (London, 1971), p. 66: 'what one loves most, because one needs it most, is necessarily separate from oneself; and yet the primitive urge of loving is to make what one loves part of oneself. So that in loving it one has, in one's primitive wish, destroyed it as something separate and outside and having an identity of its own.'

29 Emily Brontë, *Wuthering Heights*, ch. 9.

30 For a discussion of Wordsworth's familiarity with and use of this terminology, see Ben Ross Schneider, Jr, *Wordsworth's Cambridge Education* (Cambridge, 1957), and Geoffrey Durrant, *Wordsworth and the Great System*.

31 Sir Isaac Newton, *Opticks*, based on 4th edn, 1730 (New York, 1952), p. 400.

32 *An Essay on Man*, Epistle III, ll. 9–20.

33 Cf. A. P. Rossiter, 'Ambivalence', in *Angel With Horns: Fifteen Lectures on Shakespeare* (London, 1961).

34 Cf. *The Prelude* (1805), Book XI, ll. 374–5:
    Yet in the deepest passion, I bow'd low
    To God, who thus corrected my desires.

35 This is not to say that these poems merely accept the Newtonian world-view: their realization of the transforming power (however ultimately impotent) of human desire prevents any such simple reading. In an implicit answer to the 'contracted self' presupposed by Newtonian science Wordsworth seems to be suggesting that it is not through '"objective' knowledge, but through experiences such as these – experiences of intense, omnipotent-seeming subjective love, and inevitable loss – that an understanding of one's place within the non-human world is arrived at.

36 *Essay upon Epitaphs*, I, pp. 51–2.

37 *Essay upon Epitaphs*, I, pp. 56–7.

38 Allan Bold, *The Ballad* (London, 1979) defines 'revenant ballads' thus: 'concerned with a person who returns from the grave not as a disembodied ghost but as a substantial figure . . . Revenants return for many reasons: for love, for revenge, for peace of mind.' There are many such ballads; well-known examples are 'James Harris' ('The Daemon Lover', Child 243), 'The Wife of Usher's Well' (Child 79a).

39 And also, possibly, the fear of further loss avoided: though Matthew's quiet stoicism would seem to qualify such a reading.

8. Names and Signs: the Poems of Grasmere

1 Mark Reed, *Wordsworth: the Chronology of the Early Years 1770–1799* (Cambridge, Mass., 1967), pp. 266–85. The important unpublished poetry of this period was, of course, the Second Part of the two-part *Prelude* (including 'Bless'd the infant Babe . . . ').

2 'Point Rash-Judgment', ll. 67.

3 Cf. 'The Eolian Harp', ll. 44–8:

> And what if all of animated nature
> Be but organic Harps diversly fram'd,
> That tremble into thought, as o'er them sweeps
> Plastic and vast, one intellectual Breeze,
> At once the Soul of each, and God of all?

For a discussion of Wordsworth's interest in this subject, see H. W. Piper, *The Active Universe: Pantheism and the Concept of Imagination in the English Romantic Poets* (London, 1962), pp. 79ff.

4 See John Barrell, *The Dark Side of the Landscape: the Rural Poor in English Painting 1730–1840* (Cambridge, 1980), for a discussion of the connection between industry and virtue in polite images of the poor in the late eighteenth century.

5 Michael Black, 'On Reading', *The Critical Review*, 19 (1977), p. 84.

6 Not, however, for the first time in his poetry. He had already drafted the passage describing the drowned man in the first Part of the two-part version of *The Prelude* (1798–9), ll. 274–80.

7 See, especially, D. W. Winnicott, *Playing and Reality* (London, 1974).

8 Dorothy Wordsworth's *Journals* of this period contain numerous accounts of rural poverty and destitution.

9 Blake, annotations to Watson (1798), K384.

10 Sent in a letter to Mary Hutchinson, 29 April 1801, *Letters: the Early Years* (Oxford, 1967), p. 333.

11 *Home at Grasmere*, ed. Beth Darlington (Ithaca and Hassocks, Sussex, 1977), p. 78.

12 See above, pp. 82–4.

13 *Home at Grasmere*, ed. Beth Darlington, p. 78.

14 Letter to Charles James Fox, 14 January 1801, *Letters: the Early Years*.

15 John Berger and Jean Mohr, *A Seventh Man* (Harmondsworth, 1975), pp. 24, 23.

16 From the 1802 addition to the Preface to *Lyrical Ballads*, Brett and Jones, p. 256.

17 Letter to Charles James Fox, *Letters: the Early Years*.

18 'Michael', l. 70.

Conclusion

1 'Introduction' to *Songs of Innocence*.

2 'Introduction' to *Songs of Experience*.

3 From the 1802 addition to the Preface to *Lyrical Ballads*, Brett and Jones, p. 257.

4 E. P. Thompson, *William Morris: Romantic to Revolutionary* (London, 1977), p. 785.

5 Cf. Charles Taylor, *Hegel and Modern Society* (Cambridge, 1979), p. 161:

'The demand for absolute freedom raises the dilemma of self-dependence in its acutest form. And the renewed saliency of irrational and destructive cravings makes us question the very idea of autonomy, and undermines the idea of an unambiguous attribution of desire, or alternatively of our unambiguous identification with the nature in us which desires. The course of modern history has made the perspective of Schopenhauer, as presented to us by Freud and others, very familiar and plausible.'

6 *The Prelude* (1798–9), First Part, l. 360, quoted in ch. 7, n. 34.

7l *The Prelude* (1798–9), Second Part, l. 24, quoted in ch. 3, n. 100.

8 Taylor, *Hegel* pp. 154–5: 'The idea of overcoming the injustice and expressive deadness of our world at one stroke by recovering control and radically reshaping it according to a freely chosen design exercises a profound attraction well beyond the boundaries of official Marxism. We find it almost everywhere among the protest and libertarian movements of our day... To the extent that these aspirations to radical freedom are influenced by Marx, they descend also from Hegel. But what is much more important, they encounter the same dilemma which emerged from our discussion of Marxism. They face the same emptiness, the same temptation to the forceful imposition of their solution on an unyielding world, the same inability to define a human situation once the present imperfect one is swept away...

But this whole tradition, whether Marxist, anarchist, situationist or whatever, offers no idea at all of what the society of freedom should look like beyond the empty formulae: that it should be endlessly creative; have no divisions, whether between men or within them, or between levels of existence (play is one with work, love is one with politics, art is one with life); involve no coercion, no representation etc. All that is done in these negative characterizations is to think away the entire human situation. Small wonder then that this freedom has no content.'

In *Songs of Innocence*, however, Blake, uninfluenced by Hegel but sharply aware of the particularities of the world in which he lived, imaged not a contentless future society of freedom, not a 'negative' which 'thinks away the entire human situation', but an 'organiz'd Innocence' which he saw actually existing around him, in experiences which offered a powerful alternative to the official structures of the 'imperfect' society within which they took place.

9 D. W. Winnicott, *Playing and Reality* (Harmondsworth, 1974), p. 127.

10 For a suggestive contemporary indication of the ways in which an acknowledgment of the importance of such experiences might be essential to a programme for political change (within a very different kind of society), see Rudolf Bahro, 'Perspectives for General Emancipation', in *The Alternative in Eastern Europe*, trans. David Fernbach (Norfolk, 1978), pp. 291, 293–4: 'Public opinion must discriminate against all those customary practices of socialization that produce anxiety in the child, disturb a trusting orientation to the social and the natural environment, poison initiative with

feelings of guilt, devalue achievements, break the child's will and turn its energies back on itself, where they form the basic model for mistrust, spitefulness, aggression and substitute behaviour of all kinds ...

Why are there some children who master the demands of school as if in play – however irrational these may be? Because in their development from the earliest years on, everything that promotes pleasure in life, confidence in the environment, involvement in communication, has decisively out-weighed the experiences of unhappiness. Because they were cared for by physically intact parents and were not deprived of any joys ...

Society could do very much to increase the probability of a happy childhood, an excellent socialization in every sense, within a few genera-tions.'

Index

INDEX

Cowper, William, 3, 4–7 *passim*, 34–5, 348 n.9
Cunningham, Allan, 23

Darton, F. H., 349 n.3
Darwin, Erasmus, 81, 104, 193, 364 n.97
Davie, Donald, 203, 351 n.31, 381 n.49, 389 n.17
Day, Thomas, 159
Defoe, Daniel, 209, 210
Dissenting radicals, 35–6, 51–3, 57–60, 353 n.10, 354 n.30, 354 n.31
Durrant, Geoffrey, 388 n.10, 390 n.30
Dyer, George, 35–6, 53

Eaton, Daniel, 89, 168, 361 n.68
Edwards, Thomas, 377 n.17
Ehrenzweig, Anton, 55, 384 n.76
England, Martha, 349 n.1
Erdman, David, 171, 351 n.23, 365 n.1, 374 n.1, 382 n.62, 386 n.30
Erikson, Erik, 131, 369 n.33, 370 n.39, 374 n.83
Essick, Robert N., 384 n.75
European Magazine, 34
Everest, Kelvin, 387 n.1

Family Magazine, 121
Fawcett, Joseph, 35, 36, 37, 53, 228
Ferber, Michael, 382 n.64, 383 n.70
Fiske, Marjorie, 355 n.33
Flapper, The, 34–5
Foxton, Thomas, 12, 14
Frend, William, 60, 173, 375 n.11
Fritz, Paul, 355 n.33
Fromm, Erich, 381 n.53
Frosch, Thomas R., 371 n.52
Fussell, Paul, 378 n.26

Gallagher, Philip J., 380 n.39
Gardner, Stanley, 146
Gay, John, 209, 210
Gentleman's Magazine, 35, 52, 193
George, M. Dorothy, 99, 364 n.90, 364 n.96
Giddens, Anthony, 369 n.34
Gilboy, Elizabeth W., 349 n.7
Gilchrist, Alexander, 23, 363 n.81
Gill, Joseph, 354 n.20
Gill, Stephen, 385 n.7
Gillispie, C. C., 379 n.29
Gilpin, John, 252

Godwin, William, 213, 242, 354 n.31, 379 n.32
Goldsmith, Oliver, 40–1
Gombrich, E. H., 55
Goody, Jack, 70
Griffin, Andrew L., 386 n.23
Grigson, Geoffrey, 380 n.35

Hagstrum, Jean, 377 n.17, 378 n.25
Halls, Michael Austin, 356 n.12
Hanway, Jonas, 98, 363 n.83, 364 n.89
Harper, George Mills, 357 n.20
Harrison, J. F. C., 351 n.33
Hartley, David, 255
Hartley, Thomas, 58, 67
Hartman, Geoffrey, 349 n.13
Hay, Douglas, 158–9
Hazlitt, William, 1, 2, 3, 348 n.10
Hearn, Francis, 369 n.34, 371 n.45
Hewitt, M., 349 n.12
Hewlett, Henry G., 372 n.66
Hill, Christopher, 381 n.47
Hindmarsh, Robert, 58–9, 352 n.43
Holcroft, Thomas, 10
Holloway, John, 15, 350 n.21
Hone, William, 63
House, Humphrey, 387 n.35
Howard, John, 355 n.2, 356 n.8
Huizinga, J., 369 n.34

'Inscription for a Coppice' (anon.), 38–42

Jacobus, Mary, 225, 353 n.7, 354 n.22, 385 n.7, 385 n.13
Jameson, Fredric, 218, 375 n.12
Jenyns, Soame, 381 n.48
Johnson, Joseph, 9, 35, 93
Johnson, Samuel, 62, 208, 209, 210, 381 n.57
Jones, John, 385 n.13
Jones, M. G., 355 n.36
Jordan, John, 349 n.2, 353 n.15

Kiernan, V. G., 360 n.59
Knights, L. C., 365 n.4
Knox, Alexander, 34–5
Kolakowski, Lescek, 374 n.82

Lamb, Charles, 13, 14
Landor, Walter Savage, 1
Langbaum, Robert, 389 n.16
Langer, Susanne, 371 n.53, 377 n.20

INDEX

INDEX